Retail Marketing

Retail Marketing

Sean Ennis

London   Boston   Burr Ridge, IL   Dubuque, IA   Madison, WI   New York   San Francisco
St. Louis   Bangkok   Bogotá   Caracas   Kuala Lumpur   Lisbon   Madrid   Mexico City
Milan   Montreal   New Delhi   Santiago   Seoul   Singapore   Sydney   Taipei   Toronto

Retail Marketing
Sean Ennis
ISBN-13 9780077157654
ISBN-10 0077157656

Published by McGraw-Hill Education
Shoppenhangers Road
Maidenhead
Berkshire
SL6 2QL
Telephone: 44 (0) 1628 502 500
Fax: 44 (0) 1628 770 224
Website: www.mheducation.co.uk

British Library Cataloguing in Publication Data
A catalogue record for this book is available from the British Library

Library of Congress Cataloguing in Publication Data
The Library of Congress data for this book has been applied for from the Library of Congress

Content Acquisitions Manager: Leiah Norcott
Product Developer: Alice Aldous
Content Product Manager: Ben Wilcox
Marketing Manager: Geeta Kumar

Text Design by Hard Lines
Cover design by Adam Renvoize
Printed and bound in Spain by Grafo, Basauri

ISBN-13 9780077157654
ISBN-10 0077157656

Dedication

To my wife Liz
To the memory of Jarlath McHugh
To my great Aussie friends: Frank and Judy Clarke

Brief Table of Contents

Detailed Table of Contents

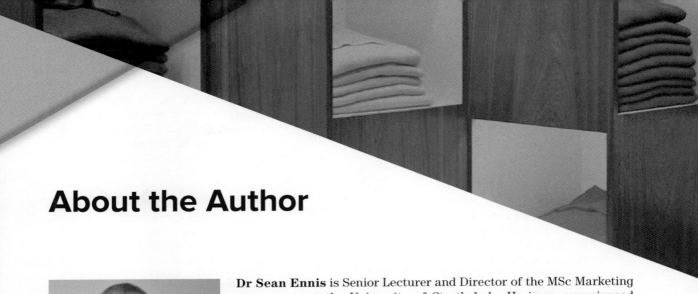

About the Author

Dr Sean Ennis is Senior Lecturer and Director of the MSc Marketing programme at the University of Strathclyde. He is an experienced retail practitioner, consultant and lecturer with over 20 years' experience in academia, during which he has taught retailing at both undergraduate and postgraduate levels. His extensive teaching experience has covered many overseas locations including Hong Kong, Singapore, Malaysia, Dubai, Oman, Bahrain, Abu Dhabi, Mumbai, Delhi, Shanghai, Athens and Switzerland.

Preface

In 2002, when Peter J. McGoldrick published the second edition of his book *Retail Marketing* (McGraw-Hill Education), he noted in his preface that 'many parts of the world have now seen a dramatic metamorphosis within the retailing industry, as retailers have ceased to play the subordinate role in the marketing of consumer goods'. He argued that this change has forced retailers to develop 'a more rigorous and systematic approach to retail marketing'.

When developing the material for this book 13 years on from McGoldrick's seminal text, I was struck by the prescience of the above quote. In this intervening period it can be argued that the retail sector has undergone a transformation across all aspects of the business and marketing process.

The transformation of the Internet and the consequent opportunities for retailers to develop robust online retail channels has led to a rethink about retail strategy. This has had 'knock-on' effects on many fundamental elements of the retail marketing mix. Retailers are querying the rationale for opening up more physical store outlets, for instance. As increasing numbers of shoppers worldwide make greater use of online channels, retailers have had to respond by developing an omni-channel approach in order to connect with shoppers across the different touchpoints in the buying process. In the coming years it is reasonable to assume that retailers will further rationalize their physical operations and formats to address the shifting attitudes and buying patterns of their respective target markets.

Since the turn of the century, when McGoldrick wrote the second edition of his book, we have seen major developments in the areas of social media platforms and usage. The plethora of social media sites such as Facebook, Twitter and Instagram has fundamentally changed the way in which consumers communicate with each other. They are no longer the 'passive' individuals that existing marketing texts seem to portray. They share views, experiences, perceptions and behaviours online and also engage proactively with retailers through such modes of communications. Retailers in response have had to become more transparent both in their dealings with shoppers and in terms of assessing the implications of the various comments posted by shoppers about their retail operations.

Advances in mobile technology and marketing have also created opportunities and threats for retailers. Location-based apps allow retailers to track shoppers and proactively connect with them with messages and recommendations about new products and merchandise, based on the shopper's previous buying transactions and preferences.

The issues of social responsibility, corporate citizenship and sustainability have always been in existence. It can be argued, however, that in the last decade greater attention and scrutiny has taken place on the performance of retailers in these areas. For instance, unethical sourcing policies by retailers have appeared prominently in the media. In response, retailers have to develop a robust and meaningful strategy in this area.

This book in many ways updates material covered by McGoldrick's text and addresses the transformative changes that have taken place since its publication in 2002.

My approach to this book

The book is designed with undergraduate and postgraduate students in mind. It also has relevance for people working in the different areas of retail marketing and management. I have tried to capture a healthy balance between theory and practice. I have taught this subject for over 25 years and have always found with both groups of students that relevant case examples of good and poor practice succeed in enlivening the subject matter and more importantly make the subsequent discussion and analysis relevant to them.

However, such a practical and 'real-life' approach has to be counterbalanced by consideration of the relevant research that has taken place in the various dimensions of retail marketing. Over the last ten years or so, the amount of scholarly research has grown exponentially: dedicated academic retailing journals such as the *Journal of Retailing* and the *International Journal of Retail & Distribution Management* are a testament to the depth of research being generated across the different business schools. I hope that I have achieved this correct balance.

When teaching the subject of retail marketing, I have found that many textbooks fall down because they tend to take an unduly narrow focus. For instance, a particular book may only focus on the North American retail environment and ignore developments in other areas of the world. I have tried to address this by including a range of discussion cases drawn from a wider geographic environment. I would like to encourage readers and lecturers to put forward further examples and cases for our online support area that accompanies this text. I particularly welcome contributions from regions such as Africa where retailing is evolving at a quick pace.

Significant aspects of this book

I have tried to write a book that largely updates and replaces the extremely valuable book that was written by McGoldrick in 2002. This is reflected in the structuring and sequencing of the chapters where I have addressed the elements of the retail marketing mix that he covered. However, I feel that this book contributes something more than a simple update. I would highlight the following areas:

- I have written a chapter (3) on the role of retailing in the context of the supply chain. I have done so because it is my experience that many students fail to see the importance of the relationships between retailers and other members of the supply chain. Quite simply, no retailer can succeed in delivering a coherent and relevant value proposition unless it operates within a co-operative and co-ordinated supply chain. Put simply, retailers do not operate in isolation. Chapter 4 further explores the relationships between retailers and suppliers.

- In Chapter 11 I examine the issue of sustainability and its implications for retailers. This is a topic that has not previously received the same level of attention in retailing books and hopefully this chapter redresses this imbalance.

- In Chapter 10 (Retail Marketing Communications) I include substantive sections on the roles that social media platforms and mobile marketing communications play in shaping overall retail communications strategy. This recognizes the shift in approach by retailers in the context of connecting, conversing and listening to their respective target markets.

- In the chapter on managing the selling environment, we look at how technological advances such as augmented reality and digital platforms enable retailers to provide a broader range of services to shoppers.

- Across a number of chapters (1, 2 and 8) we assess the concept of omni-channels and the implications for retailers as they develop new ways of engaging with shoppers across the various touchpoints in the buying process. This incorporates discussion on online retail channels.

- In the final chapter (13) we assess the overall impacts of the transformative developments for retailers and consider future trends as we project ahead over the next few years. This chapter acts as a useful synthesis of preceding analysis and discussion in the earlier chapters.

Structure of the book

The book is structured around three parts. Case studies, vignettes and discussion questions are presented throughout the chapters to enhance the reading experience, provide practical examples and encourage further exploration of the topics. The detailed content of each chapter is identified in Chapter 1. I identify a couple of significant highlights from each chapter here.

Part 1: The customer

Chapter 1: Retail marketing: an introduction

- Introducing the key elements of retail marketing and its value to customers and retailers

Chapter 2: Understanding the retail consumer

- The changing shopper
- Online shopping motives
- Blending positioning attributes with shopper benefits

Part 2: Supply chain issues

Chapter 3: Retailing and its role in the supply chain

- Trends and developments in supply chain management
- Retail supply chains
- Obstacles to designing and implementing demand chain management

Chapter 4: Managing retailer–supplier relationships within the supply chain

- Trends and developments in stakeholder relationships
- How valid is the view that a shift in power has taken place?
- Areas of collaboration and co-ordination

Part 3: Retail marketing strategy

Chapter 5: Managing the selling environment

- The retail selling environment
- Retail as theatre
- Experiential marketing
- In-store marketing communications at point of purchase

Chapter 6: Retail brand strategy

- Building the brand
- Corporate branding in the retail sector
- Benefits and challenges arising from store brand development
- Retail store loyalty

Chapter 7: Managing customer service

- Customer experience management
- Setting appropriate service levels
- Managing customer service online
- Constraints to effective customer service design and implementation

Chapter 8: Retail location strategy

- Location from a micro and macro perspective
- Planning policy in the retail sector
- Regeneration of city centres
- Trends and developments in managing shopping malls and centres

Chapter 9: Designing and implementing retail pricing strategy

- Common misconceptions about pricing

- The challenge of pricing in the retail context
- How can retail price strategy design and formulation be improved?
- Trends and developments

Chapter 10: Designing and implementing effective marketing communications strategies

- Components of retail integrated marketing communications
- The relevance and contribution of the social media platforms
- The effectiveness of traditional communications media
- Online retail channels as a marketing communications tool

Chapter 11: Retailing and sustainability

- Sustainability and retailing: the key issues for marketing
- Retailers and sustainability within the supply chain
- Retailer sustainability strategies: the evidence
- The voice of the shopper

Part 4: Retail internationalization

Chapter 12: Retailing and internationalization strategy: development and implementation

- Selection criteria for evaluating international markets
- Retail internationalization entry options
- Challenges involved in transferring a retail format
- International retail divestment

Chapter 13: Retailing: the impacts of social and technological change

- Technology and information
- The store of the future
- How receptive are consumers to these developments?
- Implications for retailing and the supply chain

In summary, the retail sector has and continues to generate change, transformation and velocity in terms of introducing new business models and marketing initiatives. Many retailers have to 'run in order to keep still'. There is no evidence to suggest that this is likely to change any time soon.

In this book I have attempted to document and analyse these major developments and placed them in context with regard to empirical research across different topic areas. I have enjoyed writing this book and I hope that you gain something from reading it and reflecting on the concepts, theories and case studies in the book.

Good luck with your studies and to your future career: hopefully in the retail area!

Sean Ennis
March 2015

Acknowledgements

Our thanks go to the following reviewers for their comments at various stages in the text's development:

Jesper Aastrup, Copenhagen Business School
Neil Brooks, Oxford Brookes University
Marius Bresler, University of Johannesburg
Chris Dunn, Coventry University
Fiona Ellis-Chadwick, Loughborough University
Albertina Jere, Cape Peninsula University of Technology
Ulf Johansson, Lund University
Kannika Leelapanyalert, Birkbeck, University of London
Jake Monk, Canterbury Christ Church University
Sarah Montano, University of Birmingham
John Ward, Staffordshire University
Judy Taft, Nottingham Trent University

We would also like to thank the following individuals for participating in interviews for this textbook and its accompanying online resources:

Russell Donaldson
Sam McLean
Kevin McNally
Alessandro Petrelli
Antony Ranger

Photo acknowledgements

Figure 5.6 © Alistair Laming / Alamy
Figure 5.7 © Alex Segre / Alamy

Guided Tour

Chapter contents

The topics covered in each chapter are mapped out at the start, for ease of access and to help you structure your teaching and learning.

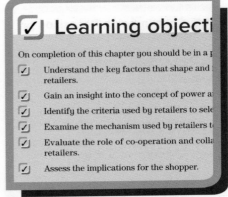

☑ Learning objecti

On completion of this chapter you should be in a p

☑   Understand the key factors that shape and retailers.

☑   Gain an insight into the concept of power a

☑   Identify the criteria used by retailers to sele

☑   Examine the mechanism used by retailers t

☑   Evaluate the role of co-operation and colla retailers.

☑   Assess the implications for the shopper.

Learning objectives

Expected learning outcomes are summarised at the beginning of each chapter. Bear these in mind as you work through the chapter to help guide your learning.

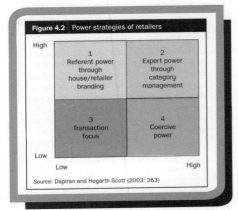

Figure 4.2   Power strategies of retailers

Source: Dapiran and Hogarth-Scott (2003: 263)

Figures and Tables

Each chapter provides a number of figures and tables to help you to visualise key marketing concepts and theories.

ies for retailers to drive improvement
information can be included in digital
clearly because the information is not
downside of this is that it may irritate
gy that is used in sports stadia with

f the concept of augmented reality in
d helpful for shoppers. This concept
in-store and exterior activities. Scan
ll effects of AR in action.

with each other in a more meaningful
lize how items of clothing can look on
he process. Retailers can run various
hile there, encourage them to engage

QR codes

Dowload a free QR code reader to your phone or tablet and scan the QR codes to be taken directly to videos and online resources.

tor to the economy

f sustained recession. As of early 2015,
tterns across different countries vary.
th (Euromonitor International, 2015b).
idence of growth in the area of mobile
high level of price-conscious shoppers,

local retailers such as Otto are shifting
etailers were relatively slow to shift to
this direction.
. Combined with low interest rates and
performance. This redressed the poor
to a greater degree of caution and an

@ Technology

Throughout the text you will see the @ icon signposting digital topics which are further explored in Chapter 13.

4.5 Case in point: Recession pit

The relationship between retailers and suppliers
Wal-Mart's massive clout to press suppliers for co
own store brands, analysts said. For those that
stores such as Saks Inc. gave during the holiday s
be shouldered by their suppliers in the form of wh
   'In this downturn a lot of suppliers got presse
the suppliers thought would happen,' said David
at Rochdale Investment Management, which own
any exposure to apparel suppliers. 'With some of
suppliers to bear the brunt of it.'
   The apparel industry has been among the wo
nature. Industry-wide apparel sales in the first H
NPD Group said Wednesday.
   Suppliers such as Polo Ralph Lauren Corp. ha
between retailers and vendors not only because i

Case in Point boxes

Case studies are drawn from a broad range of companies from around the globe and challenge you to think critically in evaluating real life marketing scenarios.

Vignettes

Shorter case studies prompt you to think about how key concepts can be applied in practice; they are a quick snap-shot view into the world of retail and are great for class discussion.

Vignette: Topshop

Topshop, the UK fashion retailer, attracted
show at London Fashion Week on Sunday, w
the broadcast. The show, streamed live on
with friends using the social network. View
messages about the Topshop show, called
retailer trended globally on the latter socia
including a printed panel dress, sold out w
USA, where it has just opened boutiques in

Source: http://www.digitalstrategyconsulting.com
best_virals_of_2012

Activity

IKEA uses software to analyse traffic patter
a layout that forces shoppers to follow a p
difficult for them to exit sections that they
are placed in such a way that they are diffi
planned route. Almost like robots. The disp
their merchandise; for example, kitchen se
experience and it can be argued that this c
be further argued that IKEA addresses th
enjoy the experience of shopping for house
up with the inconvenience of having to follc
pay for products as well as potential delays
concern to customers and IKEA has attract

Activities

At various points throughout the text, the author challenges you to explore topics concepts further and to practice the skills and concepts taught.

Practitioner interviews

The author has conducted a series of interviews with retail professionals from a variety of companies. These are presented in relevant chapters and provide an insight into the retail industry, allowing you to reflect on how what you have learned in the chapter affects day-to-day job roles in retail.

The practitioner view
Managing retailer–supplier rela

Kevin McNally, National Account M

Kevin McNally manages a number of products
few years has worked closely with the main gr
   We asked Kevin for his views on a number o
suppliers in a highly competitive retail sector.

How would you describe the typical re

Kevin notes that the typical relationship, from I
to build very collaborative long-term, win-win
building a joint business plan that will drive sa
   'P&G's approach is one of building joint val
with retailers over 2–3-year planning cycles a

Chapter outcomes

- The issue of sustainability has i
- The term 'sustainability' is an un
  mental protection, corporate soc
- Retailers have to be cognizant o
  sively on profit as the only reas
  stakeholders such as society in g
  and stores.
- The triple bottom line concept is
  retailers.
- Increasingly, retailers are recoc

Chapter outcomes

The main points of the chapter are summarized to allow you to check that you have retained all the key concepts.

End-of-chapter Discussion questions

These are designed to prompt critical opinions and debates surrounding key elements of each chapter.

Discussion questions

1 Examine the extent to which you
   forms such as TV and print adverti
2 Assess the dangers associated wit
   munications strategy.
3 Evaluate the view that retailers a
   platforms as part of their marketin
4 Identify the main steps involved in
5 Many commentators argue that the
   online channels to promote and sel
   with this view.
6 Why should a supplier become inve

Case study: Lush

Lush is a soap and toiletries comp
sition: making products by and u
of animals when testing products
soaps.

Lush recognizes the importan
sales. You smell the company befo
and soap assails your olfactory ser

The shelving within the store d
signage and information about the

End-of-chapter Case studies

Longer, analytical case studies at the end of relevant
certain chapters which can prompt class discussion or in-
depth study.

Testbank

50+ automatically gradable questions for each chapter;
choose how many questions to deploy to your class and
filter by difficulty level, topic, learning objective
and Bloom's category.

Author blog

Visit www.ennisretailmarketing.com for regular
commentary and extra Retail Marketing resources.

Online Learning Centre

www.mheducation.co.uk/textbooks/Ennis

Students: Helping you to Connect, Learn and Succeed

We understand that studying for your module is not just about reading this textbook. It's also about researching online, revising key terms, preparing for assignments, and passing the exam. The website above provides you with a number of FREE resources to help you succeed on your module, including a regularly updated author blog which will provide you with up-to-date discussion of topical Retail Marketing issues, links to articles and videos and additional case study material.

www.ennisretailmarketing.com

Lecturer support: Helping you to help your students

The Online Learning Centre also offers lecturers adopting this book a range of resources designed to offer:

- **Faster course preparation**- time-saving support for your module
- **High-calibre content to support your students**- resources written by your academic peers, who understand your need for rigorous and reliable content
- **Flexibility**- edit, adapt or repurpose; test in EZ Test or your department's Course Management System. The choice is yours.

The materials created specifically for lecturers adopting this textbook include:

- Lecturer's manual to support your module preparation, with case notes, guide answers, teaching tips and more
- PowerPoint presentations to use in lecture presentations
- Image library of artwork from the textbook
- Testbank of automatically gradable questions for each chapter.

To request your password to access these resources, contact your McGraw-Hill Education representative or visit **www.mheducation.co.uk/textbooks/Ennis**

<u>Let us help make our content your solution</u>

At McGraw-Hill Education our aim is to help lecturers to find the most suitable content for their needs delivered to their students in the most appropriate way. Our **custom publishing solutions** offer the ideal combination of content delivered in the way which best suits lecturer and students.

Our custom publishing programme offers lecturers the opportunity to select just the chapters or sections of material they wish to deliver to their students from a database called CREATE™ at

http://create.mheducation.com/uk/

CREATE™ contains over two million pages of content from:
- textbooks
- professional books
- case books – Harvard Articles, Insead, Ivey, Darden, Thunderbird and BusinessWeek
- Taking Sides – debate materials

Across the following imprints:
- McGraw-Hill Education
- Open University Press
- Harvard Business Publishing
- US and European material

There is also the option to include additional material authored by lecturers in the custom product – this does not necessarily have to be in English.

We will take care of everything from start to finish in the process of developing and delivering a custom product to ensure that lecturers and students receive exactly the material needed in the most suitable way.

With a custom publishing solution, students enjoy the best selection of material deemed to be the most suitable for learning everything they need for their courses – something of real value to support their learning. Teachers are able to use exactly the material they want, in the way they want, to support their teaching on the course.

Please contact your local McGraw-Hill Education representative with any questions or alternatively contact Warren Eels **e: warren.eels@mheducation.com**

1

The customer

Part contents

Retail marketing: an introduction

☑ Learning objectives

On completing this chapter you should be in a position to achieve the following objectives:

- ☑ Understand what is meant by retailing and the scope of a retailer's activities.
- ☑ Assess the contribution of the retail sector to society in general and the economy in particular.
- ☑ Understand the contribution of the retail sector to overall economic performance globally.

▶

◀   ☑   Consider retailing as a career for graduates.

☑   Examine the main trends and developments in retailing.

☑   Detail the structure and layout of this text.

1.1 Introduction

Welcome to our examination of retail marketing!

Arguably the retail sector is the most exciting area to study on any undergraduate or postgraduate marketing curriculum. Over the last decade or so, the landscape of retailing, and in particular how suppliers, retailers and shoppers interact, has fundamentally changed. The following chapters indicate that this has happened for a number of reasons. Primarily, these changes have been driven by advances in digital technology. This has led to the ever-increasing use of apps by retailers to connect and converse with their target markets via tablets, iPhones, Androids and smartphones. Shoppers have become more proactive and assertive in terms of how they engage with retailers. This is evidenced by the wide adoption of such devices.

The developments in social media platforms have opened up a different way of communicating between shoppers and retailers. The former have much greater access to information on issues such as pricing, special promotional offers and new product launches than ever before. Moreover, shoppers share their experiences and knowledge with other like-minded individuals through a range of platforms such as Facebook, Twitter and Instagram. Some shoppers post blogs. Retailers, in turn, create their own social media platforms where they can connect, listen and converse with their respective target markets. This is in contrast to more traditional marketing communications tools, such as TV, radio and print advertising, which are largely 'one-way' communications (retailer to shopper). Mobile and digital communications tools allow for a 'two-way' communication process. Increasingly, we hear retailers claiming that they can hold 'conversations' with their target market.

This book explains that there has been an exponential growth in online shopping over the last decade. This has raised questions as to whether this form of shopping will replace or reduce the importance of physical stores or outlets.

In this first chapter we define what is meant by retailing and identify its position within the context of the overall supply chain. We assess the contribution of the retail sector to the overall economy in a number of selected countries and in a global context. We assess the role that retailing plays in society and the opportunities that exist for graduates who wish to seek a career in this area.

We then look at some of the key trends in retailing and subsequently investigate them more fully in the following chapters. We also consider the different retail formats employed by retailers and discuss them in the context of how such formats evolve and change over time.

1.2 Retailing defined

Retailers exist because it is not possible in many cases for manufacturers of products to sell direct to the ultimate (end) customer. While there are exceptions to this (pure online retailers who sell direct; for example, Amazon), for many, the sheer scale of operations allied to the vast range of products and the geographic coverage required mean that an intermediary has to step in and resell the products to

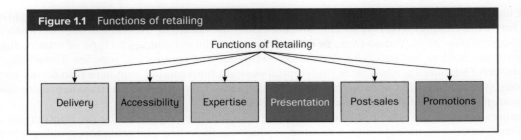

Figure 1.1   Functions of retailing

the end user. Retailers perform a number of critical functions for the manufacturers and these are high-lighted in Fig. 1.1.

They can be summarized as follows:

- Develop a physical or virtual presence so that shoppers can make a visit and examine the merchandise.
- Provide expertise in the form of salespeople who advise shoppers and, where relevant, make demonstrations as to how the items work (for example, electrical retailing).
- Present the merchandise in an attractive store environment.
- Deal with any issues that subsequently arise over issues such as customer complaints, warranties, replacement of items and returns.
- Work closely with manufacturers to develop promotions, special offers and co-operate with new product launches.
- Through their store and online operations, enable manufacturers to access shoppers across wide geographic locations.

Retailing covers a vast swathe of activity across the product spectrum. Quite simply any item (physical product or service) that requires reselling usually involves a retailer who performs some or all of the functions listed above.

Retailing has been defined as 'the set of business activities that adds value to the products and services sold to consumers for their personal or family use' (Levy and Weitz, 2004: 6). This view introduces the notion of value and the importance of enhancing the value proposition for the final consumer (that is, the shopper). If an organization does not in some way add value to the product/service proposition, it is unlikely to survive for very long in a competitive business environment.

Coughlin et al. (2006: 425) put forward the view that retailing 'consists of the activities involved in selling goods and services to ultimate consumers for personal consumption'. This definition explicitly recognizes the key role of selling as part of the retailer's fundamental role and area of responsibility. In essence, a retailer resells products and services developed by manufacturers and suppliers.

Finally, we look at the observations of Rosenbloom (2013: 24) who notes that 'retailers consist of business firms engaged primarily in selling merchandise for personal or household consumption and rendering services incidental to the sale of goods'. This introduces another dimension to the role of the retailer; that of providing services that are deemed to be essential or relevant to the delivery of the value proposition. This is important because in Chapter 7 on customer service, we discuss that shoppers increasingly are demanding higher standards of service in the context of their engagements with retailers (either physically or virtually).

Dant and Brown (2008) urge some caution with regard to defining what is meant by retailing. At first glance, it is easy to assume that the retailer's activities and responsibilities are directed at the consumers (business to consumer: B2C). However, a closer examination reveals that a significant proportion (arguably the critical elements) of its engagements are with other members of the supply chain: most notably the suppliers and manufacturers. This introduces a business-to-business (B2B) dimension. This is an important observation because in many cases retailers play a critical role in enhancing the brand image of the supplier's merchandise and in many instances work closely with them to develop new products for the marketplace.

In Chapter 2 we look more closely at the role of retailing with the context of the overall supply chain. We go further in Chapter 3 by considering and assessing the nature of the relationships between retailers and one of their main stakeholders in the supply chain: the suppliers. The type of relationship will vary between retailers and suppliers, depending on the size and category of supplier. The stronger and more powerful suppliers are in a more preferential position than smaller suppliers who do not have the necessary resources to offer substantive promotional plans. This aspect of retail management takes us very clearly into the business-to-business (B2B) domain.

Retailers perform the essential role of reselling merchandise (supported by the appropriate range of services) to the end user through a number of channels including physical stores, online channels, mobile and digital channels. The 'end-user' in this definition refers explicitly to the consumer or shopper.

Many of the retail sectors are characterized by a highly competitive and pressurized environment. As a consequence retailers tend to be at the forefront in terms of employing marketing as a mechanism to develop and deliver a relevant value proposition to their target markets. This imperative is captured in the title of this book: retail marketing.

We consider how retailing has evolved from an unstructured and unsophisticated approach to one of sophistication and complexity. We consider the concept of the value proposition and how retailers play a fundamental role in managing value across the supply chain as they attempt to address existing and potential needs of shoppers. This is central to the role played by marketers in any organization and the retail sector is no exception. The challenge for retail marketers is to create, manage and deliver the retail value proposition to the final customer. Without a strong supply chain it will be difficult to achieve this objective. In particular, we examine the shift away from retailers acting as institutions that simply move merchandise on to the shopper to being powerful influencers and shapers of what consumers buy.

The chapter also examines trends and developments within the retail sector and in particular focuses on the changing roles and responsibilities of retailers.

1.3 Retailing and its role in society

The retail sector is one of the most important contributors to the overall wellbeing of society in general and the economy in particular. In many ways it provides a strong indication of the relative health of the economy. When a country's economy is performing well, it means that more people are in gainful employment, are earning money and crucially are in a strong position to spend it. Conversely in a recessionary period, the reverse happens: unemployment rises, income levels drop and there are fewer propensities to spend money on items that are not deemed to be essential to everyday living.

When we refer to the retail sector, this includes all items sold in shops and online, with the latter growing significantly over the last decade or so. In the UK, the wholesale and retail sector contributed roughly 16 per cent of economic output in 2012. It also makes up 16 per cent of overall employment in the UK.

A recent report (Rhodes, 2014: 3) noted that:

> **"**In April 2014, consumers in the UK spent around £27 billion. For every £1 spent in the retail sector (online and in shops, but excluding petrol stations), 47p was spent in food stores and 46p was spent in non-food stores. The remainder was spent in other types of retailers, such as market stores or mail order catalogues.**"**

This sector has over 428,000 businesses that represent around 10 per cent of all business enterprises in the UK. In terms of contribution to the economy, however, it is estimated that it accounts for over 35 per cent of total turnover. This underlines the significance of the retail sector within the overall economy.

In the European context the retail sector contributes over 13 per cent of the workforce across the twenty-eight countries: the second largest contributor after the manufacturing sector (Oxford Institute of Retail Management, 2014). While large retailers tend to dominate in certain regions such as northwest Europe (UK, Germany, France, Benelux), southern and eastern Europe are dominated by small and medium-sized retail enterprises. Over 25 per cent of employees in the retail sector in Europe work on a part-time basis. This is reflected in the number of students and older individuals who are either seeking to re-enter employment after raising a family or those who only wish to work on a part-time basis.

The multiplier effect is also relevant in the context of the retail sector. This is an attempt to measure the effect of spending in one sector on other sectors. In the retail sector such an effect can be seen in the ways in which retailers deal with suppliers (procurement and negotiation) and also in terms of stimulating demand for products and services. We can see this also in the case of employment. The Oxford Institute of Retail Management (2014: 33) states that:

> **"***In the US, the National Retail Federation calculated that whilst the retail sector directly employs 28.1 million Americans; overall, it supports a total of 41.6 million workers in both retail and other sectors representing 24.1% of total U.S. employment or almost one in every four jobs in the nation.***"**

Retailing makes a significant contribution in other ways besides economic and employment issues. Retailers are at the forefront in reshaping the structures and layout of cities, towns and local communities. This is evidenced by the emergence of large retail parks, shopping malls and out-of-town store locations. This can work in a positive and a negative sense. Some towns and cities have suffered because of the emergence of out-of-town locations. Large retailers, because of their dominance, have forced many small independent retailers to close their operations. As a result some shopping streets and prime city locations are left neglected. On a more positive note, certain cities have been rejuvenated by high street developments and these have led to an increase in shoppers visiting such locations.

The retail sector also tends to be a pioneer in the area of information technology (IT) as retailers seek to drive greater efficiencies in their operations. Retailers also have a major influence on our lifestyles and how we socialise with people. Many shopping malls and centres are positioned as 'entertainment facilities' where people can meet, interact, socialize and extend their visit beyond the simple act of shopping. This is evidenced by the appearance of restaurants, cinemas, sports centres and so on. For many people in many countries, shopping is cited as being the most popular leisure activity.

1.4 The contribution of the retail sector to the economy

Since about 2008, economies globally have suffered from a period of sustained recession. As of early 2015, there are signs that economies are beginning to revive. Growth patterns across different countries vary.

In Germany, the retail sector continues to show healthy growth (Euromonitor International, 2015b). This has been largely driven by online retailing. There is also evidence of growth in the area of mobile Internet retailing. The German retail sector is characterized by a high level of price-conscious shoppers, in contrast to other European markets.

Amazon.de is a clear leader in the online retailing area. Other local retailers such as Otto are shifting the focus of their business strategy to online retailing. Grocery retailers were relatively slow to shift to this area, although in 2014 Edeka, Lidl and Rewe were moving in this direction.

In Sweden, consumers experienced rising disposable incomes. Combined with low interest rates and low inflation, this allowed most sectors of retail to deliver a solid performance. This redressed the poor performance of earlier years due to the recession. This has led to a greater degree of caution and an aversion to risk on the part of shoppers.

As is the case in many European countries, a small number of grocery retailers dominate proceedings. Axfood, Coop, BergendahisGruppen, Lidl, ICA and Netto account for the clear majority of sales. ICA, with sales of over SEK 1,000 billion, is larger than the other five players combined (Euromonitor, 2015c).

The French retail sector also exhibited slow growth, again caused by the stagnation that occurred over the previous four or five years. Again Internet retailing dominated the landscape. Retailers in the grocery and non-grocery sectors increasingly recognize the need for multi-channel platforms. Companies such as Primark and Marks & Spencer entered the French market in 2014 and they engendered a more competitive environment in the clothing sector (Euromonitor, 2015a).

Retailing in the South African market generated 10 per cent growth in 2013 (Euromonitor, 2014b). This is a market that is polarized in terms of income levels, which resulted in retailers competing aggressively on price and through sustained marketing campaigns.

Due to higher inflation levels (caused by rising fuel and electricity prices), shoppers cut back on spending on non-grocery items. The growing middle-class sector conversely continued their spending on items, particularly in the DIY and home improvement sectors.

Shoprite Holdings continued its dominant position. The arrival of Wal-Mart (through its acquisition of a domestic retailer called Massmart) generated strong competition also. The increasing number of Internet users should ensure that this part of the retail sector continues to grow.

Finally, we look briefly at the Australian sector. Retailing grew by 2 per cent in value terms in 2013 (Euromonitor, 2014a). Australian shoppers were also exhibiting a degree of caution in their spending patterns. The mining sector, a key catalyst in driving the economy forward, had begun to slow and this exacerbated the degree of uncertainty surrounding the overall economy.

The two top retail brands were Coles (Westfarmers) and Woolworths. Both operations accounted for around 39 per cent of overall retail sales. As in other markets, Internet retailing exhibited a strong degree of growth.

1.5 Retailing as a career

Before we embark on a detailed study of retailing it is worth considering the potential opportunities that arise for a career in this field.

Retailing contributes significantly to the economy of a country in terms of employment. In the UK in 2014 it provided employment of around three million people (Prospects, 2015). Indeed this sector is the UK's largest private employer.

One of the interesting aspects of retailing as a potential career rests with the scope and range of positions in this area. Many students taking a class in retailing currently work in a part-time capacity already. Ask your classmates whether they have any retail work experience and you will be surprised at the number of them who are currently or have worked over the summer in retailing. This provides a unique opportunity to directly relate and in some cases apply the concepts and underlying theories about the various aspects of retailing.

A career in retailing offers a diverse range of potential areas to work within. They include the following:

- in-store operations
- in-store sales
- marketing
- logistics
- IT
- web design
- social media
- visual merchandising
- customer relationship management
- procurement
- human resources (HR)
- finance.

Many people who have expertise in specific areas such as IT and logistics find that there are plenty of job opportunities in the field of retailing. As we mentioned earlier, retailers are pioneers in the adoption of technology. While most people associate a career in retailing with in-store selling, the reality is that the 'back-office' activities such as inventory management, logistics and procurement arguably are the most important elements of retail management.

As we note in this chapter, increasingly retailers are investing in the area of social media as shoppers, particularly those in the younger age bracket who use social media platforms to acquire information about products, engage in price comparisons and make purchases.

Many large retailers such as John Lewis, Sainsbury's and so on have well-established career development programmes in place that allow people to progress in a structured and coherent way. Opportunities also exist for short-term placements or internships as another mechanism for getting 'your foot on the ladder'.

Prospects (2015) identifies some of the main graduate suppliers in the UK.

In the clothing sector, employers include:

- Arcadia Group (includes Burton, Dorothy Perkins, Miss Selfridge and Topshop)
- John Lewis Partnership (includes Waitrose)
- Abercrombie and Fitch
- TJX Europe (includes TK Maxx).

In online shopping, large companies include:

- Amazon.co.uk
- N. Brown Group
- Shop Direct Group.

Supermarket retailers include:

- Tesco
- Aldi
- Lidl.

Other main retailers include:

- Dixons Retail (including PC World/Currys)
- Kingfisher (includes B&Q and Screwfix)
- Wilko.

Prospects (2015) notes that between now and 2020 there will be a greater demand for managerial positions. Overall forecasted growth is estimated to be around 55,000 in the UK, with the majority of these positions coming into the managerial area (41,700). Many of these positions will emerge in the supply chain area, customer service and managing 'big data'. This broadly reflects the trends and developments that we have identified in this chapter.

The websites listed here provide an indication of the range of jobs that are available in the retail sector. Please visit them to explore potential opportunities. If you are a student from outside the UK, you will find similar websites under the broad heading of retailing and retail careers.

www.retailcareers.co.uk

www.inretail.co.uk

1.6   Key trends in retailing

As we discuss in various chapters of this book, the retail sector has undergone major change over the last decade or so. We briefly highlight some of these trends here.

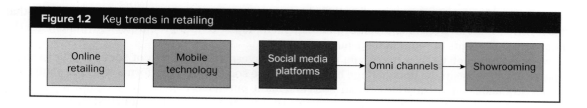

Figure 1.2   Key trends in retailing

1 *Online retail channels*: arguably the most profound shift in retailing has occurred with the development of online sales channels to complement and in some cases replace the traditional 'bricks-and-mortar' or physical retail stores. A report by the Centre for Retail Research (2014: 1) notes that:

> **"***E-commerce is the fastest growing retail market in Europe, with sales in the UK, Germany, France, Sweden, The Netherlands, Italy, Poland and Spain expected to reach a combined total of £111.2 bn in 2014 (€155.3 bn or $212.8 bn). We expect online sales in the USA to reach $306.0 bn (€224.0 bn) in 2014.***"**

These figures are based on a study conducted in eight European countries (UK, Germany, France, Spain, Italy, Netherlands, Sweden and Poland).

Growth in online retailing for 2013 and 2014 in Europe averaged 18 per cent. There is a variation, however, in the context of where this growth occurs. The UK, Germany and France are accountable for 81.3 per cent of online sales across Europe.

In the UK, online sales are around 13.5 per cent of overall sales. Table 1.1 provides a more detailed comparative breakdown.

We should treat these figures with some degree of caution as the growth of online sales is on an upward trajectory and is likely to have changed since the publication of this report. It also only focuses on a small number of European countries.

We consider the implications of online channels on overall retail strategy in later chapters.

2 *Mobile technology*: developments in this area are closely interlinked to the growth of online channels. This is particularly so when shoppers need to access and interact with retailers. When we refer to mobile technology we are considering the developments in the areas of smartphones, tablets and iPads. Shoppers are now extensively using these tools to seek out information on products, promotions, new merchandise, special offers and comparative prices. More importantly they can make

Table 1.1   Online retail sales home market 2014 (estimated)

United Kingdom	13.5%
USA	11.6%
Germany	9.6%
Sweden	7.6%
Netherlands	7.1%
France	6.9%
Spain	3.0%
Poland	2.8%
Italy	2.1%

Source: Centre for Retail Research (2014)

purchases using such technology and access all aspects of the retailer's offerings without necessarily having to make a visit to the physical store.

Retailers can also make use of these technologies to interact in a more proactive manner with their target shoppers. Retailers are using location-based techniques to more effectively customize their offers to shoppers. Systems such as Beacon are typical of the developments in this area. For instance if I have a specific app for a retailer and happen to be within 100 metres of one of its physical stores, I will most likely receive a message inviting me in. It might also (based on my previous shopping patterns) advise me that it has a new range of shirts in stock and that I should take a look. It might also say that because I am a loyal shopper I can take advantage of a 10 per cent discount. This type of situation in many ways changes the dynamics of the relationship between the retailer and the shopper.

3 *Social media platforms*: since 2014, platforms such as Twitter and Facebook tend to dominate in terms of how consumers interact and communicate with each other. Retailers have tracked this trend and we now see a plethora of Facebook groups that follow individual retailers. This has fundamentally changed and challenged the way in which retailers communicate with shoppers. Traditional media channels such as TV, print and radio involve a 'one-way' communication, where a message is sent to a target audience in the hope that it registers with them. Social media allows retailers to engage in a 'two-way' conversation. It can listen to its shopper's views, opinions and experiences, take note of areas of satisfaction and dissatisfaction and adapt its strategy accordingly. Retailers can customize offers and promotions in a more focused and effective way than before.

4 *Omni channels*: in response to these changes, retailers in many cases have had to develop a number of channels in order to fully interact with shoppers and more importantly provide a positive customer experience. In the early part of this decade many commentators predicted the demise of physical stores and for them to be replaced by online retail channels (e-tailing). In retrospect this was too simplistic a view. While pioneer retailers such as Amazon undoubtedly succeeded as pure online players, it became clear that shoppers in many cases required a more varied set of shopping options. While they might want to purchase a particular item online, they still required a customer experience that involved physical contact with a retailer. In response, retailers set up an online channel to complement rather than replace the bricks-and-mortar store. This became further complicated as shoppers tended to use various channels as 'touchpoints' during the purchasing process (problem recognition, search, evaluation, purchase and post-purchase). The term 'omni channel' emerged to describe a particular approach by retailers to deal with this challenge. This approach recognizes that we interact via numerous touchpoints throughout the buying process. It is about creating an integrated and seamless experience for customers as they interact with the organization. For instance a shopper at various stages in the process may interact with the retailer via email, a store branch, a call centre, a kiosk/ATM, mobile app and/or online channel. If there are discrepancies in terms of customer experience across these channels, then the likelihood is that the retailer will encounter a dissatisfied shopper.

5 *More dynamic and visual store designs*: increasingly, retailers are making use of technology to improve the design and layout of physical store outlets, both internally and externally. The concept of 'augmented reality' is used extensively. This essentially is a merging of mobile technology with in-store activities. For instance it is becoming quite common to see window displays or in-store displays where the shopper can interact with the 'visuals' being displayed on the screens. Topshop has developed an augmented reality app called Topshop Kinect Dressing Rooms that allow shoppers to try on items in a virtual space via their tablets or phones.

Digital technology also provides retailers with opportunities to highlight in-store promotions more effectively. Information on price alterations and special offers can be changed 'in real time' for instance. This reduces the delays that can occur when retailers have to alter pre-printed signage and information.

We can expect to see greater usage of virtual reality in the coming years. This allows retailers to provide a more 'connected' and immersive experience for the shoppers.

6 *Showrooming*: the increasing use of online channels by retailers, allied to social media platforms and mobile technology, has created the phenomenon of 'showrooming'. This occurs where shoppers

visit a store outlet to glean some information from the salespeople and benefit from demonstrations of the product's features (particularly with electrical products). They subsequently make a purchase on an online channel or website. In many cases this purchase may not have been made with the original retailer who they originally visited.

This can pose both threats and opportunities. It can be argued that retailers may have to review their portfolio of stores if shoppers are only using them for information acquisition and then purchasing items elsewhere, especially if they can be obtained at a lower price. Some retailers are currently going through this assessment exercise and a reduction in the number of stores operated by them may be the likely result.

However, it can be equally argued that shoppers use online channels, social media platforms and mobile technology to undertake their 'research' and then visit the store for reassurance from sales personnel and make their purchase. This only demonstrates the need for retailers to have in place a range of channels through which they can connect with the shopper and provide the necessary touchpoints.

1.7   Retail formats

Over the decades retailers have evolved and introduced a diverse range of formats in an attempt to develop some form of competitive edge. If we go right back to the early centuries we can see evidence of traders and merchants selling in souks or bazaars, where buyers come to the venue with the intention or buying or bartering. These formats have not disappeared. On the contrary they can be seen in many parts of the world and still attract shoppers and tourists as successfully as ever.

The nature and shape of retailing has changed over the centuries. We now have a plethora of business formats ranging from shopping malls, department stores, speciality stores to supermarkets, hypermarkets and on to non-store formats such as e-tailing and vendor machines.

Anitsal and Anitsal (2011) provide a comprehensive classification of store formats. They are outlined in Table 1.2.

Table 1.1 illustrates the diversity of the retail formats that exist in today's marketplace. We need to consider some of the trends and developments that have taken place in recent years.

1 *Enhancing the shopping experience*: increasingly, shoppers view shopping in a more hedonistic manner. This is particularly the case with shopping trips that are based on the principle of high involvement; that is, the consumer makes special efforts to assess alternative options and where they enjoy the experience of interacting with and consuming the product. This will have an effect on the type of format adopted by the retailer.

2 *The 'time-poor' shopper*: some shoppers do not have the time to allocate to the shopping experience and instead seek out a more convenience-based approach to the task of shopping. This is exemplified by the growth in online shopping across all of the retail sectors. Supermarket groups such as Tesco have invested heavily in such channels to address the needs of this particular group.

3 *Shopping as a leisure activity*: while some consumers view the challenge of shopping as a functional activity akin to brushing your teeth in the morning, other segments regard shopping as a leisure activity. In many countries shopping is listed as the most popular leisure activity, usurping entertainment and sport in the process. Retailers have had to respond to such demands by investing in store design and atmospherics to create an interactive and positive shopping environment. We have also seen the growth in large shopping malls, shopping centres and retail parks to capitalize on this development.

4 *Low touch versus high touch*: we have seen retailers develop and alter their business models to meet the changing demands of customers. Dell was one of the first companies to recognize that many shoppers did not require a large degree of personal interaction (high touch) when buying

Table 1.2   Store-based retail institutions

Format	Explanation
Speciality store	Narrow product line with a deep assortment
Drug stores	Walgreen, Body Shop, Gap, Boots, Superdrug
Department store	Several product lines with each operated separately
	Sears, Nordstrom, House of Fraser, Debenhams
Supermarket	Low-cost, low-margin, high-volume operation
	Tesco, Kroger, Morrisons, Ahold
Convenience store	Limited line with high turnover at slightly higher prices
Discount store	Lower prices with lower margin and higher volumes
	Lidl, Aldi, Poundland
Off-price retailer	Buy at less than regular wholesale prices and sell at less than retail prices
Factory outlets	T.J. Maxx, Miksasa, Sam's Club
Independents	
Warehouse clubs	
Superstore	Routinely purchased food and non-food items in large selling spaces
Category killers	Home Depot, Staples, Foot Locker, Toys 'R' Us
Supercentres	Wal-Mart Supercentres, Super Kmart
Hypermarkets	Carrefour, Continente, Meijer's
Catalogue showrooms	Broad selection of fast-moving brand names with high mark-ups
	Argos
Pop-up stores/vendors	Retailers take advantage of low rents or specific locations for a short period only
Non-store retail institutions	
Street vendors	Individual vendors
Catalogue/direct mail	Communicate through catalogue, mail, brochures
	Land's End, Spiegel
Vending machines	Indoor and outdoor machines for snacks and soft drinks
	Coke machines, Frito-Lay machines
Direct selling	Face-to-face product demonstration and selling
	Mary Kay, Anyway, Avon
TV home shopping	Customers watch TV and place orders by telephone
	QVC, HSN
E-tailer	Online retailer over the Internet
	Amazon.com, Asos

Source: Adapted from Anitsal and Anitsal (2011: 13–14)

goods. As a result they pioneered the selling of PCs, laptops and other related products via direct mail, then telephone selling and finally via the Internet. Retail banks have increasingly moved towards the development of low-touch channels such as Internet banking, ATMs and telephone banking. While cost considerations come into play in such decisions, there is also a recognition that shoppers in certain situations are moving away from the more expensive high-touch channels and are prepared to make purchases via remote channels. However, this is not a universal case. For instance, in China, many shoppers still require high levels of interaction and Dell has had to make adjustments to meet this requirement.

5 *Social media platforms*: the emergence of social media tools such as Twitter, Facebook, YouTube and blogs have changed the way in which retailers and shoppers engage with each other. Such tools allow shoppers to share experiences and opinions about products purchased and their experiences of shopping in stores. Retailers have responded by enhancing their online channels to include features that allow them to engage with shoppers. This trend is further explored in Chapter 7.

6 *Blurring of retail formats*: retailers can no longer be neatly allocated to a particular classification system such as the one depicted in Table 1.2. Over the last 25 years or so, retailers such as supermarket groups have extended their business operations from food across a diverse range of non-food operations. For instance, Tesco sells fuel, runs pharmacies, provides a range of financial services, sells books, clothing and household goods. It is even rumoured that Tesco wants to sell cars. As a result, many specialist, independent retailers have closed as they have been unable to compete on price with the large, multinational retailers.

7 *Omni retailing*: as retailers grapple with the challenge of providing a number of different retail channels for shoppers, they also have to be cognizant of the need to provide a relatively seamless and consistent experience for the shopper across the online and physical channels. This is referred to as omni retailing, which is explored in greater detail in Chapter 8.

8 *Corporate social responsibility*: this issue straddles a number of different areas in retailing and we look at it in greater detail in Chapter 11. However, retailers increasingly have to factor in ethical and corporate social responsibility considerations in their operations. Retailers such as Primark have come under close scrutiny as a consequence of its involvement with suppliers in Bangladesh, where a factory collapsed in May 2013 and called into question the way in which employees were treated there and the safety of the facilities used for production. In the quest to save costs, Primark and other clothing retailers have received criticism for the apparently less than comprehensive manner in which they select and monitor their suppliers.

9 *Environmentally conscious shoppers*: consumers are becoming more aware of 'green' issues and although this market segment is still relatively small, it is growing and retailers are responding with a number of initiatives to meet the demands from this source. This permeates through the supply chain issues in terms of sourcing suppliers, allocating space in stores to green products and employing policies and procedures with regard to the green segment of the market.

10 *Shop anytime, anywhere*: developments in technology have increasingly opened up new ways in which shoppers can engage in the buying process: from information search, comparative shopping through to the purchase. This is evidenced by the growth in mobile technology. This allows retailers to engage with shoppers as they pass by the store by sending messages to their mobile devices. Mobile retailing is likely to increase in popularity in the next decade.

We can see the challenges involved in trying to capture a framework that adequately identifies the different retail formats currently in operation. Some of the formats identified by Anitsal and Anitsal (2011) are becoming redundant or even more blurred as retailers address the developments that we discussed earlier. It may be more appropriate to consider the different retail formats in the context of what benefit or combination of benefits they address from the perspective of the target group of shoppers. They are summarized as follows:

1 *Convenience*: time-poor shoppers require a format that they can easily access either virtually or physically. The retailer has to ensure that it can meet the expectations and requirements of the shopper. Delivery time and the speed of delivery are crucial in this situation.

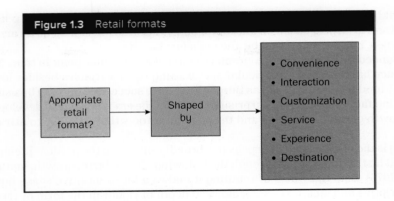

Figure 1.3 Retail formats

Appropriate retail format? → Shaped by →

- Convenience
- Interaction
- Customization
- Service
- Experience
- Destination

2 *Interaction*: this can vary depending on the extent of physical interaction the customer expects. In the case of the auto retail sector, many customers still place great emphasis on the need for physical engagement with the car showroom salesperson. By contrast, many purchases are 'low involvement' and do not require any interaction.

3 *Customization*: as noted earlier, technology now allows both retailers and customers to interact and engage more proactively than ever before. Some shoppers prefer to shop with retailers who have the relevant apps to allow for customized offerings, based on prior shopping habits or experiences.

4 *Service*: this can be viewed across a spectrum ranging from low to high. Aldi provides minimal service but focuses instead on price. In the high-end fashion sector, personal attention to the individual is critical and demands a strong level of investment.

5 *Experiential*: this relates to the type of shopping experience expected from the shopper. Apple and Nike are good examples of where they treat the store environment as part entertainment and part interaction with the merchandise. We discuss this in more detail in Chapter 5.

6 *Destination*: in some cases shoppers are willing to travel to shop. We discuss the case of IKEA in Chapter 6. It is a good example where shoppers are prepared to travel long distances to make purchases. This is in contrast to the first benefit mentioned here: convenience.

In summary, retailers are increasingly widening the range of formats – to connect and remain relevant to their target markets. We should not become too prescriptive with regard to which formats are more appropriate than others. The large retailers across the different retail sub-sectors tend to have a portfolio of formats. This is necessary to respond to and anticipate the changing shopping behaviours.

1.8 Theories of retail change

A number of concepts and theories have been put forward by researchers in an attempt to identify the rationale for the way in which retail formats evolve, become popular and slip into relative decline.

Perhaps the best known theory and one that still stands the test of time in many commentators' eyes is the wheel of retailing theory (McNair, 1931). He identified three phases in the development of a retailer's operations. Initially, the retailer moves into the particular sector with a combination of low prices and overheads. It captures a significant number of customers with this value proposition.

At a later stage, it 'trades up' and increases its prices and enhances the quality of the merchandise. In the third and final phase, it focuses on providing a range of services. This increases the cost of doing business and leaves it vulnerable to new entrants who tend to replicate the original model of low products and prices.

The theory still has intuitive appeal but over time has attracted some criticism. It has never been empirically tested and is largely based on anecdotal observation. While it may be an accurate reflection of what might happen, it is not supported by any evidence-based data.

It is firmly grounded in a particular geographic region at a particular point in time. Many innovative retailers for instance have entered a particular sector using other variables besides low price. It could be argued that fast-food restaurants such as Burger King have succeeded initially by using quick service as the differentiating factor. It also (not surprisingly – given the era when it was developed) cannot take account of the growth of online retailers and the particular tools that they use to attract customers to their websites.

Another theory is the institutional life cycle. It is broadly similar to the product life-cycle concept and suggests that retail institutions evolve through the following stages: birth, growth, maturity and decline (Davidson et al., 1976). Like the wheel of retailing it makes a lot of intuitive sense but it suffers from being overly descriptive and lacking in any empirical depth of rigour in the form of research studies. It is also difficult to predict with any certainty when a retailer is likely to move from one stage to another in the life cycle.

Other variations include the concept of 'the survival of the fattest' (Samli, 1998). This concept is a derivation of the Darwinian theory of the survival of the fittest. In the context of the retail sector, the stronger get stronger and the weaker get weaker and eventually disappear. The bigger (fatter) the organization, the more likely it is to succeed. Anecdotal evidence suggests that this is the case: in many retail sectors there exists a strong degree of concentration of power among a small number of 'large' retailers. These institutions have the economies of scale and scope to negotiate strongly with suppliers and, therefore, can reinforce their power and domination over time.

Anitsal and Anitsal (2011) make the point that more focus and attention needs to be paid to the way in which customers have changed. The concepts that we have looked at have the benefit of simplicity and pragmatism. However, they do not really address or consider the way in which shoppers have altered their purchasing patterns, changing their views and perceptions on a number of issues with regard to the ways in which retailers market their value propositions.

A more recent study by Levy et al. (2005: 85) put forward the concept of the 'big middle'. This is described as 'the marketplace in which the largest retailers compete in the long run, because this is where the largest number of potential customers resides'. As such, retailers like Target and Wal-Mart (USA) would be good examples. We see similar patterns in other countries in the case of retailers such as Tesco and Carrefour. Their thesis is based on the view that over time niche retailers will gravitate towards the big middle and adjust their value proposition accordingly. This usually consists of expanding the line of merchandise carried and by lowering product margins and eliminating certain aspects of customer service.

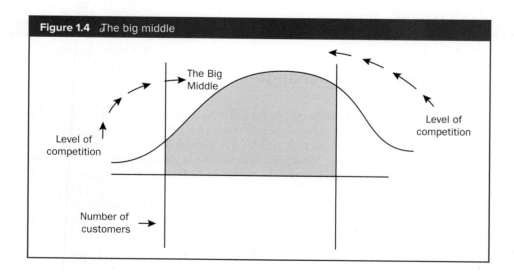

Figure 1.4 The big middle

Levy et al. (2005) argue that there are two ways in which they can compete in this retail space. The first strategy is described as 'low-price' where the retailer targets the 'price-conscious' shopper. Over time this category of retailer will reinvent itself by upgrading its product range. The second category of retailer targets the 'quality-conscious shopper' and over time will lower its prices and move downwards in terms of product development. Eventually these retailers become hybrids: falling into the middle on price and innovation.

As the retailers converge in the retail space known as the big middle, it can be argued that shoppers get the best of both worlds. The large retailers are in a position, due to their scale and scope of operations, to innovate in areas such as product development and price, to refresh their value proposition and retain the attention of shoppers. Reinvention is a key to the success of this strategy. Retailers do not want to be perceived as stale or stuck in a 'middle-of-the-road' position. If this happens, it is likely that some shoppers will tire of the product offering and seek an alternative option. If they remain static and resistant to change, it is likely that they will be usurped by other retailers who want to move into this space. Retailers such as Marks & Spencer have fallen into the trap of being 'stuck in the middle' and not being proactive in driving changes in their value proposition. It is arguable whether they will ever return to their dominant position of the 1970s and 1980s.

We can see similarities between this approach and the earlier theories of institutional change. It has intuitive appeal and can certainly be used as a pragmatic attempt to portray the way in which retailers evolve and develop their retail strategies.

In summary, the various theories about institutional change should be treated with caution. They serve a useful purpose in encouraging us to reflect on the underlying rationale for the way in which retailers evolve, develop and decline. They also reinforce the message that value propositions need to be innovative and relevant for shoppers in order to capture market share, but need to adapt to the drivers of change over time. Nothing remains static.

1.9 Case in point: Jessops

In January 2013, Jessops (founded in 1935) the UK photographic retailer went into administration. It had built up a strong reputation over the years for selling a broad range of photographic equipment at reasonable prices. It joined the stock market in 2004 with annual sales of £287 million and had a stated objective at that time of increasing its operations to over 400 stores in the UK. However, it encountered a steady decline in customer numbers. This was exacerbated by the acquisition of a number of stores. The chairman at the time, David Adams, embarked on a strategy of cutting stores and staff. He also recruited a CEO and between them they revised their strategy and attempted to turn the Jessops stores into 'one-stop-shops' that sold everything from expensive digital cameras, to bags, lenses and memory cards.

HSBC, the UK bank wrote off £34 million of loans in return for a 47 per cent equity stake.

They gained support from two of the main camera manufacturers, Canon and Nikon, who were keen to maintain a visible presence in shop windows. They obtained favourable credit terms and volume discounts from these companies and also benefited from store refurbishments and staff training programmes which were partially funded by these and other key suppliers.

Adams left in 2012. A new chairman adopted a more aggressive approach with its suppliers. Nikon tightened its credit terms in the run-up to the key Christmas period which deprived Jessops of much needed working capital. The company disappeared off the high street in January 2013. Jessops subsequently re-emerged again as a result of a buy-out and is currently trading again.

Source: Adapted from Shah, O. (2013) Jessops – over-exposed and now out of the picture. *Sunday Times* Business section, 13 January, p. 5.

Question

1 To what extent do you support the view that Jessops failed because it did not respond to the changing retail environment in this sector? Is there any reason why retailers such as Jessops should survive in this retail sector?

1.10 Structure of this text

Figure 1.5 depicts the structure and layout of this text.

In Chapter 1, we examined what we mean by retailing and its overall contribution to the economy. We also looked at the key trends and developments in this sector and the various retail formats that are used by retailers to deliver their respective value propositions.

Chapter 2: understanding the retail consumer, puts the shopper or consumer under the spotlight. In particular, we examine the way in which the consumer has changed in terms of behaviour, perceptions and attitudes. We look at shopping motivations and examine the concept of store loyalty. We also assess the concept of store image and how this is formed in the minds of shoppers. We consider how retailers respond to shopper needs and requirements by examining how they attempt to position their value proposition in an attempt to achieve differentiation over their direct and indirect competitors.

Chapters 3 and 4 assess the role and position of retailers within the context of the supply chain. Chapter 3 examines the main components of the supply chain and identifies how retailers in many cases have become the dominant player and in particular how power has shifted away from manufacturers and to the large retailers. We examine the components of the supply chain and discuss how supply chains have adopted a more 'customer-centric' approach, as opposed to the traditional view that tends to focus on 'pushing material and product' through the supply chain.

Chapter 4 investigates the specific relationship between suppliers and retailers. This has engendered much debate in the academic and business literature. We look at the nature of such relationships and

Figure 1.5 Chapter structure

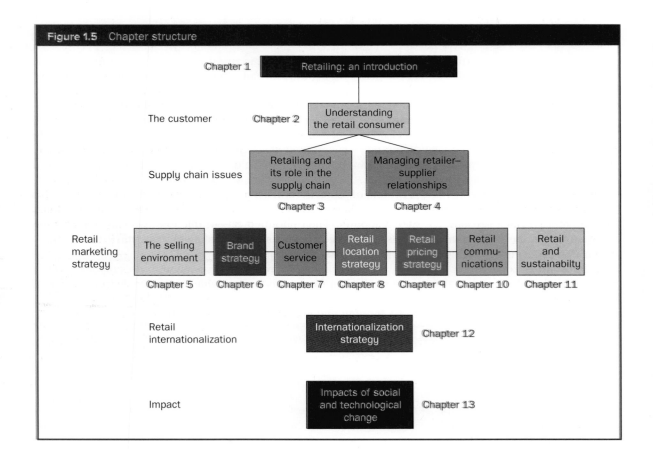

examine how power and conflict can occur. We also assess the areas where suppliers and retailers collaborate on various initiatives in order to derive benefits for both parties. We consider the criteria that retailers use to select suppliers and the sourcing policies that are employed in the retail sector.

Chapters 5–11 focus specifically on the retail marketing mix (programme) that retailers design in order to manage the value proposition successfully.

Chapter 5 addresses the overall challenge of managing the selling environment. Within the physical store, we look at the issues of store design and layout. We examine how technology has been used by retailers to enhance the customer experience and we consider the importance of experiential marketing as a proactive strategy for retailers in their quest to develop satisfied and loyal customers. We look at the challenges of designing online retail challenges and we also evaluate the ways in which the exterior parts of the store (entrances and windows) can be managed more effectively.

Chapter 6 focuses on the concept of branding and how retailers build and develop their brands to achieve a more meaningful position in the minds of shoppers. We examine different facets of branding from corporate branding and the role that social media platforms play in brand development to the way in which retailers develop their own brands (private labels or store brands). We also look at the effectiveness of store loyalty programmes.

Chapter 7 examines another key component of the retail marketing mix: customer service. We assess the different dimensions of managing customer service from the 'hard' elements (those that can be measured and quantified) to the 'softer' dimensions such as customer engagement and the relationship between the salesperson and the customer. We look at the challenges of motivating staff in a sector that is often characterized by the use of part-time staff and (relatively) low wages.

Chapter 8 assesses the role of store location in retail marketing strategy formulation and implementation. While some commentators argue that there will be less need for physical store outlets in the future, the reality is that physical retail space is increasing in many countries. We consider the criteria used by retailers when assessing potential retail locations. We look at the concept of shopping malls and assess the debate about out-of-town shopping centres and the attempts by policymakers to regenerate city/town centre shopping.

Chapter 9 considers the issue of pricing within the retail environment. We discuss some misconceptions held by business commentators about pricing and assess the specific challenges of pricing products in retailing – where in the case of the grocery sector, a retailer may carry over 30,000 different items. We evaluate the impact of social media platforms and technology on the pricing decision. We also investigate how retailers make use of IT enablers to more effectively manage pricing.

Chapter 10 addresses the ways in which retailers formulate and implement marketing communications strategies. We assess the various objectives behind such programmes and look at the potential shift in focus from the traditional communication tools such as TV, press and radio advertising to the more recent platforms in the area of social media and mobile. We also examine the role of in-store communications.

Chapter 11 focuses on the issue of sustainability and the role that it plays in the retail marketing mix. In the wider context we discuss the growing importance of corporate social responsibility and how this permeates through the initiatives used by retailers to address this challenge. We consider whether this is seen by retailers as a marketing tool or a phenomenon that will increasingly dominate overall management of the supply chain and in particular relationships between the key stakeholders in this process.

Chapter 12 considers how retailers address the challenge of internationalization. We examine the motivations for engaging in the pursuit of expansion away from domestic markets to other geographic regions. We look at the different models of internationalization and focus on the alternative modes of entry that are employed by retailers.

Finally, Chapter 13 in some ways acts as a synthesis of the main issues that we examined in our earlier chapters. We look specifically at the impact on retailing globally as a consequence of social and technological developments that have taken place over the last decade. We preview how retailers will further respond to these changes and adapt their strategies accordingly.

1.11 Conclusions

In this chapter we examined what is meant by the term 'retailing' and assessed the role that the retail sector plays within society as a whole and the economy in particular. We also looked at the retail sector in terms of providing career opportunities for graduates when they seek employment.

Retailing has undergone a major transformation over the last 15 years or so. This is noticeable in the way in which shoppers embrace social and mobile technologies in their various engagements with retailers. Retailers, in turn, have adapted their strategies to reflect the changes. The era of 'omni channels' has well and truly arrived and we are likely to see further and more strategic use of technology enablers such as augmented and virtual reality in the future.

In summary, this is a good time to study the field of retailing. Opportunities are emerging for employment across a number of different areas such as IT, web design, procurement, brand management and so on.

Chapter outcomes

- Retailers focus on the reselling of items to the final customer in the supply chain.
- The retail sector contributes significantly in terms of employment and contribution to the gross domestic product in the economy.
- Retailers have had to change their approach to connecting and engaging with shoppers as a result of developments in the area of digital and mobile technology.
- Issues such as sustainability are taking on greater significance in the formulation and implementation of retail marketing strategies.
- Retailers can no longer rely on a single channel to do business with their target market.
- Omni channels are and will in the future play a significant role in retail marketing strategy.

Discussion questions

1 Assess the view that physical store outlets will decline in importance over the coming decade.
2 The big middle theory has been put forward by commentators as an explanation for retail evolution and change. Assess the relevance of this theory. Use examples to support your point of view.
3 Examine the concept of showrooming and assess the implications for retailers.
4 Examine the concept of augmented reality. Using examples, demonstrate how a retailer can use it to enhance the shopping experience.
5 Evaluate the proposition that shoppers are becoming more difficult to do business with as a result of their increasing use of social media platforms.

References

Anitsal, I. and Anitsal, M. (2011) Emergence of entrepreneurial forms. *Academy of Entrepreneurship Journal.* 17(2): 1–17.

Centre for Retail Research (2014) *Online Retailing: Britain, Europe and the US 2014.*

Coughlin, A.T., Anderson, E., Stern, L.W. and El-Ansary, A. (2006) *Marketing Channels,* 7th edn. Upper Saddle River, NJ: Pearson, Prentice-Hall.

Dant, R.P. and Brown, J.R. (2008) Bridging the B2C and B2B research divide: the domain of retailing literature. *Journal of Retailing.* 84(4): 371–397.

Davidson, W.R., Bates, A.D. and Bates, S.J. (1976) The retail life cycle. *Harvard Business Review.* (November-December): 89–96.

Euromonitor International (2014a) *Retailing in Australia.*

Euromonitor International (2014b) *Retailing in South Africa.*

Euromonitor International (2015a) *Retailing in France.*

Euromonitor International (2015b) *Retailing in Germany.*

Euromonitor International (2015c) *Retailing in Sweden.*

Levy, M., Dhruv, G., Peterson, S., Robert A. and Connolly, B. (2005) The concept of the big middle. *Journal of Retailing.* 81(2): 83–88.

Levy, M. and Weitz, B.A. (2004) *Retailing Management,* 5th edn. Boston, MA: McGraw-Hill Irwin.

McNair, M. (1931) Trends in large-scale retailing. *Harvard Business Review.* 10 (October): 30–39.

Oxford Institute of Retail Management (2014) *Retail & Wholesale: Key Sectors for the European Economy: Understanding the Role of Retailing and Wholesaling within the European Union.*

Prospects (2015) Overview of the retail sector in the UK. Available online at: www.prospects.ac.uk/retail_sector_overview.htm (accessed 6 March 2013).

Rhodes, C. (2014) The retail industry: statistics and policy, p.3. Available online at: www.parliament.uk/briefing-papers/sn06186

Rosenbloom, B. (2013) *Marketing Channels: A Management Review.* Mason, OH: South-Western.

Samli, A.C. (1998) The changing retail population and managerial implications. In *Strategic Marketing Success in Retailing.* Westport, CT: Quorum Books, 43–68.

Shah, O. (2013) Jessops – over-exposed and now out of the picture. *Sunday Times* Business Section. 13 January, p. 5.

Chapter 2

Understanding the retail consumer

✓ Learning objectives

On completing this chapter you should be in a position to address the following objectives:

- ☑ Understand how consumers have changed in their opinions, attitudes and behaviour.
- ☑ Assess how these changes affect shopping motivations.

▶

◀ ☑ Examine the factors which shape store image.

   ☑ Understand the importance of store patronage and the underlying influences.

   ☑ Evaluate the importance of store loyalty.

   ☑ Understand the concept of store positioning and the ways in which retailers develop positioning strategies in response to target market needs and expectations.

   ☑ Identify the elements of retail marketing strategy.

2.1 Introduction

In this section of the book we consider the shopper or the retail consumer. We begin by looking at the motivations for shopping and the behavioural characteristics exhibited by shoppers. In order to design effective retail strategies, retailers need to have a clear understanding and insight into the way in which shoppers interact with their value proposition. More importantly they need to have an insight into the evaluative criteria that shoppers use when engaging with the various elements of the buying process: from the problem recognition stage, the search and evaluation stage, the purchase and ultimately the post-purchase considerations. We also consider how this is relevant to online retail channels.

We assess how shoppers form an image of a particular store and how this influences their buying behaviour. In particular, we evaluate the key factors that shape store image and how this affects the way in which retailers position their value proposition in the market space within which they compete.

The second part of this chapter assesses the general response of retailers to store motivations, patronage and image. We examine the concept of retail positioning. In order to make an impact on the relevant retail sector, retailers have to come up with a value proposition that is relevant and resonates with the target market. Positioning is a concept that recognizes that a retailer has to register on the radar and capture a meaningful position in the mind of the targeted shopper. We examine the ways in which retailers work on specific attributes in order to develop points of differentiation that can help to distinguish their value propositions from the competition.

We also consider when it might be necessary for retailers to reposition their value proposition. Every brand has a life cycle. At certain junctures, it may become a strategic imperative to reassess its overall strategy. It may be because it is no longer relevant to the target market or has been superseded by new or existing competition.

Finally, we consider the components of retail strategy and briefly look at the ingredients that go into the design and implementation of the retail programmes in response to the consumer demands and expectations.

2.2 The purchasing process

Before we address the trends and developments about shoppers and the shopping process, we should consider the overall steps in the purchasing process. This allows us to place the subsequent analysis and discussion within the context of the shopper and buyer behaviour.

The purchasing process includes the following steps.

1 *Problem recognition*: this is the first stage of the buying process that shoppers go through in the context of the purchasing decision-making process. Most purchases are triggered by a recognition

that some issue has occurred which needs to be addressed. For instance, in the case of grocery shopping, items need to be replaced/replenished, leading to a weekly or daily shopping exercise. This is a relatively low-involvement activity as staple items in the food and drink category (butter, milk and so on) do not require much time to be spent on assessing product alternatives or shopping around. However when we move into the fashion category, individuals may invest more time and shopping effort. We describe such activity as relatively high involvement.

2 *Search*: depending on the nature of the product or service, individuals may allocate time and effort to search for information that will help them to make a more informed decision about which brand to purchase or which store to patronize. Generally the more complex and expensive the item, the more time and effort will be spent on such activity. Consumers may utilize a number of sources in this respect. They may seek advice from family, friends and work colleagues. They may read relevant articles or visit websites to gain insight into issues such as price comparisons between brands, information on the various attributes and benefits associated with brands and so on.

3 *Evaluation*: consumers generally factor in a number of criteria that are relevant to them (often referred to as the 'consideration set'). Usually this will revolve around a combination of variables; for example, price, quality, convenience, customer service and so on. This is central to understanding how consumers make decisions as to what brands or services they purchase. It also provides the rationale for the concept of segmenting markets because it recognizes that consumers have different attitudes, perceptions and preferences. In the context of grocery retailing for example, some shoppers are very price conscious and patronize discount retail operators. Others focus more on quality branded products and shop in retailers at the higher end of the market.

4 *Purchase*: this is critical in the process because it means that the consumer engages in the transaction and makes a purchase. Increasingly the transaction is likely to happen online as opposed to the more traditional location of the physical store, showroom or outlet. Factors such as store design and layout, décor, and online web design and navigation play an important role in shaping how the transaction occurs.

5 *Post-purchase*: in many cases the process does not end with the purchase. In some situations, the retailer has to provide a range of services in support of the purchase. For instance in the case of electrical goods, servicing the product (e.g. cars), providing warranties in the event of product failure, dealing with complaints, returns and spare parts, all come into the post-purchase activities.

Understanding the purchasing process is central to our following discussion on how shoppers form an image of a particular retailer and how they subsequently engage with that retailer and its competitors.

2.3 The changing shopper

It can be argued that many of the traditional assumptions about how shoppers operate in the relationship with retailers have changed in the last decade or so. Traditionally marketers in general have tended to treat the consumer as a relatively passive individual: someone who receives communications from companies and who hopefully responds in a positive manner by buying either the product or service. However this landscape has changed significantly.

The emergence of the Internet initially and more recently social network platforms has created an environment where the consumer increasingly engages in a proactive manner with companies and organizations. This change in the relationship between shoppers and retailers is captured in Figs. 2.1 and 2.2.

The Internet has provided the opportunity to generate and assimilate information about brands, new products, and price and value comparisons without having to visit specific stores or outlets. Social networks allow consumers to engage with each other through blogging, sharing opinions and experiences on discussion forums and making recommendations to friends and other members in that specific community.

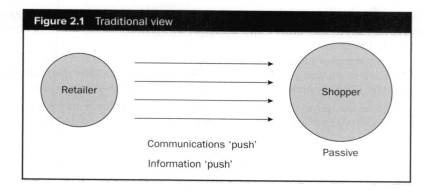

Figure 2.1   Traditional view

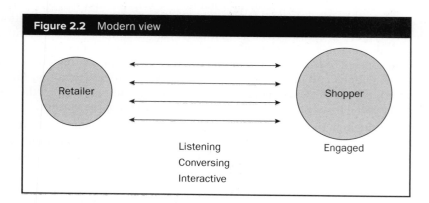

Figure 2.2   Modern view

While some of the information and comments made on such platforms may not necessarily portray an accurate perception or view, the reality is that consumers are more informed and better equipped to negotiate with companies and retailers, demand better levels of service and hold higher levels of expectations.

Companies have had to rethink many previously held assumptions and principles. For instance, they increasingly have to become more transparent with their pricing policies and strategies. It is becoming more difficult to manipulate and confuse shoppers – although utility companies, train operators and mobile phone operators still appear to design a bewildering array of price tariffs that are almost impossible to fathom out.

Discussion forums, Twitter, Facebook, LinkedIn and other such platforms have led to situations where some segments of customers can voice their anger and distrust of certain brands and organizations, causing at best some bad publicity and at worst, the need for such organisations to address the issues raised in these platforms. It also highlights the potential danger of losing control over the way in which an organization wishes to be perceived in the marketplace. Retailers such as Wal-Mart and McDonald's have had to deal with threats from 'renegade' consumers who are highly critical of various aspects of their operations. Similarly, Primark and Nike have engendered negative comments about their sourcing strategies.

The ability to hold dialogues with consumers has forced retailers to rethink their approach to advertising and promotion. Traditional methods such as TV, press and radio advertising may no longer appear as attractive as social media campaigns.

While in most developed economies shoppers have relatively more disposable income than they had 20 or 30 years ago (even allowing for recessions), some segments are increasingly 'time-poor' and seek more convenient and time-saving options when shopping. Conversely, other segments see the act of shopping as more than simply a functional activity. Instead they see shopping as a leisure, pleasure-seeking activity. The emergence of shopping malls, shopping centres and retail parks is a direct response to this development.

Shoppers lead ever-increasingly complex lives. This is most evident in the case of females. Over the last 50 years their roles have changed from the traditional 'stay-at-home' stereotype to one of professional career development. While this varies by geographic region, it has implications for the way in which this group approaches the challenge of shopping.

Increasing developments such 4G mobile technologies, tablets and other information technology (IT) devices change the way in which retailers and shoppers engage with each other. Personalized messages can be directed to mobile devices as a shopper enters a shopping mall. While there may be issues of intrusion into a person's privacy, the reality is that a broader array of opportunities arise for retailers in particular to target individuals.

Apart from communications, technology is likely to play an even greater role in the coming decades. Shoppers are unlikely to carry money with them and instead will make payment using technology. They will also expect much more interactivity and engagement with merchandise than has been the case in the past. Technology will allow retailers to change the way in which they present merchandise. It will allow them to personalize the engagement with shoppers and capture a much greater depth of information. These developments have changed the way in which the retailers and shoppers interact and communicate with each other. We examine this in greater detail in Chapter 10.

Technology such as 3D printing and more sophisticated forms of computer-aided manufacturing also allow manufacturers and retailers to bring more unique products and designs more quickly to the marketplace. In the case of 3D printing, a unique item costs the same as a one-size-fits-all item. This can enhance the degree of choice for the shopper and widen the shopping experience.

In summary, the landscape has changed in terms of the engagement between retailers and shoppers. Irrespective of whether opportunities or threats emerge for retailers, the reality is that they have to be proactive in terms of anticipating the likely impact of such changes and develop responsive strategies to address the demands of the market.

2.4 Motivations for shopping

Shopping motivations have been defined as 'the drivers of behaviour that bring customers to the marketplace to satisfy their internal needs' (Jin and Kim, 2003: 399). People visit stores for a number of reasons that have been well documented in academic and business literature.

One of the earlier researchers put forward the view that people shop for a variety of motives, some of which are not directly related to the actual purchase of a product (Tauber, 1972). He identified the following areas:

Personal motives

- *Role playing*: where people play an accustomed role in society. In the context of shopping, many women view grocery shopping as an integral part of their role.
- *Diversion*: where shopping is viewed as an escape from the mundane aspects of everyday life.
- *Self-gratification*: this would be situation-specific. In some cases it may be to buy something nice when a person is depressed.
- *Learning about new trends*: keeping up to date with fashion trends and developments is a common motive for many young people.
- *Physical activity*: the sheer act of walking to a store and spending time there can count as exercise for some people.
- *Sensory stimulation*: many shoppers enjoy interacting with merchandise or trying on items.

Social motives

- *Social experience outside the home*: provides the opportunity for a social experience outside of the home; for example, county fairs, market days and meeting at the shopping mall.
- *Communication with others having a similar interest*: having common interests in products or merchandise. People may meet in retail outlets to meet with friends and sales personnel to get advice and share opinions.
- *Peer group attraction*: being seen in a particular store may meet the desire for someone of being able to meet with a group of people to which they aspire.
- *Status and authority*: the situation may allow a shopper to command attention and respect; for example, being waited on in a restaurant.
- *Pleasure of bargaining*: for some categories of shoppers, the pleasure derived from haggling or negotiating on price with a sales representative is an attractive proposition.

Tauber's views stand the test of time and are still widely quoted by subsequent researchers. Much of the subsequent research carried out in this area either endorses these views or builds on them in an incremental way.

Impulse shopping

There is also a tendency for shoppers to take an impulsive decision to shop. This clearly is not a planned activity and one which could be stimulated by the retailer; for example, a special promotional activity, or by the individual; for example, nothing better to do. The most common manifestation of this can be found at the checkouts at supermarkets where items such as chocolate and snack products are conveniently located where shoppers are queuing to pay for their shopping. In essence, we can identify two general types of motivation: utilitarian and hedonistic.

In the case of utilitarian motivations, we recognize that in some cases shoppers are driven by a functional view of shopping. Certain items have to be purchased. This is exemplified in the way in which people shop for food items. The weekly shopping visit to the supermarket or the hypermarket is typically viewed as 'something that has to be done'. Many people do not like the trials and tribulations of trying to get parking accessible to the store and the consequent crowded shopping environment that exists in supermarkets, particularly at peak times. It is essentially a task-oriented activity: products have to be bought and shopping lists (in some cases) have to be drawn up. Babin, Darden and Griffin (1994) refer to this type of motivation as taking a largely rational view of the process of shopping. The overall objective here is to purchase the product or merchandise in question in an efficient and objective manner. However not all shopping activities are driven by these motivations.

In order to understand their motivations, we need to think carefully about the level of involvement of the shopper in the shopping situation. Low involvement suggests that the shopping exercise is relatively routine and does not demand high levels of extended problem-solving; for example, searching out for shopping alternatives or comparison exercises. Such items are likely to be purchased on a frequent basis.

High-involvement shopping takes account of the need for such extended problem-solving. If shoppers are buying a relatively expensive item and it is a purchase they make infrequently and have a lack of knowledge and information about the options, it is likely that they will invest time and shopping effort in making the purchase. Buying a new car would fall into this category.

Laurent and Kapferer (1985) pinpoint key factors that influence the level of involvement in such purchasing decisions:

- *Self-image*: this occurs in situations where the shopping activity and the purchase affect the self-image of the individual. Products like clothing and jewellery fall into this category. The slogan 'I am what I wear' encapsulates the essence of this level of involvement.
- *Perceived risk*: in cases where there is a high monetary value on the purchase or the product is technologically complex and there is a fear that a mistake could be made, it is more than likely that the shopping effort will be high and influence the shopping motive.

■ *Social factors*: this occurs where the individual is concerned about whether the purchase will be met with approval by peer groups. This is prevalent in the youth market where purchases of clothing items and entertainment-related merchandise are often influenced by peer pressure.

■ *Hedonistic influences*: this introduces the concept of pleasure-seeking into the discussion and recognizes that in many shopping situations, it is not so much about the product that is purchased but the experiential elements that play an equal if not more important influence on the shopping motive. Shopping malls in particular take this factor on board when designing their value offerings.

This concept of involvement is important because it provides us with some direction as to the likely nature of the shopping motivation across the different buying situations that shoppers have to address.

2.5 Shopping behaviour

Perhaps the single biggest advance in knowledge in the field of shopping motivations is the hedonistic nature of shopping. Jin and Kim (2003: 399) define hedonism as 'the drivers of behaviour that bring consumers to the marketplace to satisfy their internal needs'. Such a hedonistic approach takes shoppers away from the conventional utilitarian motivations and elevates retailing into the leisure arena where pleasure-seeking motivations take on greater precedence.

Arnold and Reynolds (2003) identify six dimensions of such shopping behaviour. They are as follows: adventure, social, gratification, idea, role and value.

1 *Adventure*: this refers to situations where shoppers seek active stimulation from the shopping trip with the emphasis placed on escaping from the real world and being part of another one. Tiso is a retail store that has a couple of outlets in the UK. It sells walking, mountaineering and adventure merchandise and accessories. As part of its store design it has designed a wall for shoppers to practise their climbing skills. This facility encourages shoppers to engage with the merchandise and the 'outdoor' life and builds on this concept of adventure as being an intrinsic part of the shopping experience and motivation for visiting the store.

2 *Social shopping*: this works on the principle that individuals do not like living in isolation. Socialization is an inherent part of everyday life. Shopping allows people to meet and congregate, discuss and have fun. Many of the large shopping malls in the Gulf States and large cities in Southeast Asia have a number of entertainment features built into the design and layout of the outlet. People can watch a movie, have a meal, engage in sporting activities, shop and so on. The Mall of the Emirates is one of the most popular shopping malls in Dubai. Due to a combination of weather conditions, a lack of propensity to participate in sports activities, a high level of expatriates and a focus on the family as a central part of life, shopping is the number one leisure activity in this region and in other Gulf States. This mall has created a large entertainment emporium in which you will find restaurants, nightclubs, multiplex cinemas, entertainment features for children and an authentic-looking ski slope. In essence, it is a haven for socialization.

3 *Gratification*: the focus here is on relieving stress and tension from everyday life. Shopping is an activity that can address such problems. It combines the elements of escapism and socialization within the overall belief that the act of shopping can bring relief and gratification to the individual. Retailers can address this type of motivation by developing an appropriate selling environment that makes it easy and relaxing for shoppers. The last thing they want to experience is further hassle, delays and queues to augment their existing feelings of tension! Retailers such as DKNY and Burberry have created a range of diffusion brands and accessories to appeal to the needs of shoppers and widen their use of and engagement with such brands. Such brand strategies work on the emotional appeal and play to the 'softer' feelings of shoppers. Christmas markets in many cities in Europe also work on this principle.

4 *Idea shopping*: this motivation appeals to certain segments of shoppers. Some people like to discover the latest trends and developments, be at the forefront of innovative products that appear on the shelves and gain some insight into the benefits and features of such products. This is evident in retail sectors such as electronics, fashion and entertainment. Some retailers such as Apple provide such a service and use some of their flagship stores worldwide to promote new products and train their sales team to demonstrate their features ahead of the formal product launch. By visiting such a store, shoppers can gain an insight into upcoming products, new features and areas of innovation. The purpose of such a visit is not necessarily to engage in the physical act of purchase, but to gain knowledge and insight. Eastlick and Feinberg (1999) identified a certain category of individual who acts as a 'market maven': someone who acts as a conduit of information about trends and developments in terms of new products and innovations that are on the market or are about to hit the outlets in the near future.

5 *Role*: some people can derive great pleasure from shopping for someone else. Buying gifts for instance can in some cases be more pleasurable than buying for themselves. Gift-buying allows individuals to engage with merchandise that may have no relevance to their needs or requirements. However by interacting with and purchasing such items, they can experience a range of pleasurable feelings without having to worry about the risk of making a mistake.

6 *Value*: some shoppers enjoy the challenge of bargaining for merchandise, haggling with sellers and deriving great pleasure from feeling that they have got themselves a 'good deal'. This is partly a cultural phenomenon. In some countries, haggling and negotiation over price is an intrinsic part of the purchasing and sales process: both parties enter the equation in the expectation that this will occur. In other countries, some shoppers experience discomfort at the possibility of having to negotiate with a seller. The following questions arise: Did I get a good deal? Am I being ripped off? What if I held out for a better deal or discount?

All of the above motivations are grounded in the belief that shopping effort is directed at pleasure-seeking and that shoppers enjoy the experiential elements associated with the process of shopping.

Further research in the area of shopping motivations endorses the work already covered in the preceding sections (see Parsons, 2002; Eastlick and Feinberg, 1999; Haanpa, 2005; and Lennon, Sanik and Labarbarbera, 2003).

Kaur and Singh (2007) carried out a study with young people in the Indian market and their findings reinforce the importance of hedonistic motivations for shopping as well as a diversion from the mundane features of everyday life.

We should be careful to avoid falling into the belief that shopping activity and the motivations for shopping are categorized as *either* utilitarian *or* hedonistic in nature. This is an unduly simplistic perspective and ignores a body of research that draws upon a sociocultural perspective of shopping, as opposed to the more traditional economic and psychological approaches.

Backstrom (2011: 201) captures the essence of this perspective in the following statement.

> **"**In sociocultural literature shopping is commonly regarded as an act of consumption which incorporates more facets than those present in the momentary visit and thus must be understood in relation to its wider social and cultural context.**"**

This approach suggests that we should take a more open and multifaceted view of the dimensions of shopping. For example, Backstrom's research considers the concept of shopping as a leisure activity and suggests 'that one and the same consumer may appreciate diverse aspects of shopping on different occasions, and thus engage in a wide repertoire of leisure shopping practices'.

In summary, we can say that shopping motives vary depending on the type of buying or shopping situation that faces shoppers. Some shopping motives are functional and relatively mundane; for example, the trips to the local convenience or corner shop for an emergency purchase such as milk or bread. Others involve a much higher level of involvement or engagement with the purchase/visit and involve more effort and planning; for example, a visit to a car showroom. Many shopping situations move the shopper into the area of pleasure-seeking and an escape from everyday life.

Since the early research by Tauber (1972), the findings from other work is remarkably consistent with his recommendations and these are summarized in Fig. 2.3.

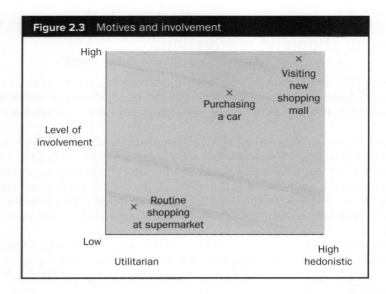

Figure 2.3 Motives and involvement

2.6 Case in point: Airport shopping

In a global context airports, with rare exceptions, have undergone a transformation over the last 30 years or so. They changed their business role and definition from that of government-owned centres for conveying passengers from A to B, to business service providers, with a focus on creating a positive customer-oriented experience. While delays and security problems have had a negative impact on some passengers' experience, the ubiquitous nature of airport retailing is evidence that airport providers see it as an antidote to such issues and an opportunity to encourage passengers to spend money as they wait for their flights or their connections.

In 2006, revenue from airport retailing generated on average 22 per cent of an airport's total business. In 2007 it was estimated that retail sales at airports touched $27.1 billion, making it the fastest-growing retail channel behind the Internet.

In general, such growth was driven by international tourist growth, economic liberalization, growth in passenger traffic and increasing flight delays. In many ways, it is perfect for the service providers: they have a captive audience that cannot leave the airport and are likely to be there for an average of over three hours.

The worldwide recession of 2008 onwards has reduced the number of passengers that fly. However in relative terms and in many countries, there is an increasing demand for airport expansion. This is particularly so in countries such as China, India and eastern Europe, as economies have developed and expanded more quickly than in other parts of the world.

Questions

1 Which shopping motivations do you think airport retailing addresses?
2 Assess how airport service providers develop their retail offerings to meet these shopping motivations.
3 In what ways do you think the shopping experience could be enhanced to address the hedonistic dimensions of the process of shopping?

2.7 Online shopping motivations

The research on shopping motivations has by and large focused on the traditional mode of shopping; that is, physical visits by shoppers to outlets. The upsurge in popularity of online shopping needs to be assessed in terms of motives. In recent years researchers have investigated this aspect of shopping motivation.

It would be easy to assume that online shopping appeals to that segment of the population that likes convenience and is time-poor. As we noted earlier, many people do not have the time to physically shop given their complicated and busy lives. The Internet presents an opportunity to carry out a range of shopping activities without having to physically move from the house, office or hotel. Rohm and Swaminathan (2004) developed a typology for online shoppers. They identified four categories: the convenience shopper, the variety-seeking shopper, the store-oriented shopper and the balanced buyer.

Noble et al. (2006) shed more light on the motives of the online shopper and identified a number of motives, some of which appear to be directly related to the online shopping experience. These included: information search, price comparison, uniqueness-seeking, product assortment, convenience-seeking, social interaction and browsing.

Some research has indicated that online shoppers differ in their motivations insofar as they are more concerned with convenience and are willing to pay extra in order to save time (Li, Cheng and Russell, 1999). Similar research in this area suggested that online shoppers are more driven by the need for information and more specialized or customized products. Mathwick, Malhotra and Rigdon (2001) advance the view that online shoppers are more driven by utilitarian motives and are not pleasure-seekers or motivated by escapism.

Kukar-Kinney, Ridgway and Monroe (2009) found that the issue of compulsive buying was an important consideration. Such shoppers get an emotional lift or boost from shopping. To this extent they may be seen as an extreme shopper, akin to people having an addiction like alcohol or gambling. The ease of access and immediacy of the Internet as a retail channel may further encourage such shoppers to make purchases. It also allows them to buy unobserved. Note that this research has limitations: it was based on a small sample and looked at shoppers of an upmarket ladies fashion online retailer.

Ganesh et al. (2010) undertook a more comprehensive survey of online shoppers. They identified seven online shopping motivations, which are as follows: web shopping convenience, online bidding/haggling, role enactment, avant-gardism (keeping up with trends), affiliation (interacting with other online shoppers), stimulation (interacting with interesting websites) and personalized services (being personally notified of new products or deals). Their study found that in overall terms online shoppers were more similar than dissimilar to traditional shoppers.

They also found areas of motivation that are more relevant to the online shopping experience which are difficult if not impossible to replicate by the traditional 'bricks-and-mortar' outlets. Statements from the qualitative phase of the research capture these differences:

- Shopping any time of day or night
- Avoiding crowds.

2.8 Store image

In this section we assess the importance of store image, both to the shopper in terms of influencing their store patronage decisions and to the retailer when it shapes its positioning strategy.

Du Preez, Visser and Van Noordwyk (2008) carried out a review of the various definitions of store image. They cite one of the earliest authors in the field (Martineau, 1958: 58) who defined store image as

'...the way in which the store is defined in the shopper's mind, partly by its functional qualities and partly by an aura of psychological attributes'.

Store image is formed by the cues or signals that the individual retailer sends out to its target market. This can take the form of visual cues such as store design, layout, location, merchandising and the various marketing communications tools employed. These cues can appeal to the functional and psychological aspects. The former refer to aspects such as the number of checkouts in a supermarket. Too few can cause delays and send a negative signal to a shopper – particularly if that individual is 'time-poor' and seeks speed of access and egress as the two main factors in the shopping experience. Other cues such as lighting, music and aroma can be used in a more subtle fashion to shape the store image.

Early research in this area by Lindquist (1974) reviewed the literature and identified nine different elements that form store image: merchandise, service, clientele, physical facilities, comfort, promotion, store atmosphere, institutional and post-transaction satisfaction. Further research by authors such as Bearden (1977) and Ghosh (1990) identified similar attributes and factors. The latter author pinpointed the merchandise carried by the store as the most critical element.

Baker et al. (2002) considered theories from cognitive and environmental psychology to develop a framework that proposes that the store environment dimensions (store employee perceptions, store design perceptions and ambient factors such as music and lighting) influence the consumer's perceptions of store choice criteria (interpersonal service quality perceptions, merchandise quality perceptions, time/effort cost perceptions, psychic cost (level of stress involved) and price perceptions), and that these perceptions in turn affect patronage intentions.

The store environment factors essentially are the cues, symbols and artefacts that shape store image and subsequently influence store choice criteria and subsequent store intentions. Put simply, store image is the composite picture built up in a shopper's mind as to how it is perceived, either positively, neutrally or negatively as the case may be. The visual cues outlined in Baker et al.'s model (2002) act as a powerful influence on how shoppers are likely (or not likely) to engage with that store. More critically, it influences the likelihood of shoppers coming back to that store on a regular basis and building up a level of brand loyalty and commitment to that store.

Du Preez et al. (2008) put forward a framework for understanding the dimensions of store image and these are captured in Table 2.1.

This framework emphasizes the relationship between the various attributes and store image. It stresses that the latter is formed by the consumer's perceptions of all the attributes associated with the store.

Pan and Zinkhan (2006) reinforce the importance of store image in shaping subsequent shopping patronage motives and behaviour. They stress the importance of visual cues as a significant influence as to how a shopper gathers information about the store and how they process this information. This helps them to form a judgement about the store and will affect their perceptions and opinions. This in turn acts as a predictor of whether they will engage in repeat visits to that particular store.

Much of the research in this area has focused on specific attributes in an attempt to describe store image. However, it does not necessarily capture the gestalt view of store image. The term 'gestalt' is defined as '...the idea that the individual's perception of any object incorporates innumerable bits of separate information that are combined in such a manner that the end result of the integration of inputs amounts to more than the sum of its constituent parts' (Chowdhary, Reardon and Srivastava, 1998: 73).

Attribute-based studies tend to capture a subset of store image (Zee-Sun and Good, 2007). Cognitive perceptions and emotional responses can emerge from attributes. They cite the example of a shopper hearing a piano playing in an immaculately clean store evoking images of friendliness, contentment or luxury.

In the context of e-tail channels, the engagement with the retailer tends to occur via PCs, laptops, tablets or mobile technology. Here, store image is formed by the way in which the website is developed in terms of layout, navigation, transaction areas and so on. Issues such as transparency and navigation in particular have a powerful influence on the formation of store image.

In the preceding sections we examined issues such as motives for shopping, store loyalty and store image. We conclude this part of the chapter by looking at how these issues interact. Bloemer and de Ruyter (1998) put forward the view that store loyalty is in essence all about store satisfaction management. The way in which shoppers form an image of a particular store will be shaped by their satisfaction levels. Thus, if they are to revisit the store on a regular basis, satisfaction levels have to be maintained

Table 2.1 Dimensions of store image

Dimension	Dimension names included from the literature
Atmosphere	Activity dimension; Clean and spacious atmosphere; Music/aesthetics dimension; Store atmosphere; Store atmosphere – aural; Store atmosphere – olfactory; Store atmosphere – tactile; Store atmosphere – visual
Convenience	Accessibility; Congestion; Convenience; Convenience (economic); Convenience – store location and mobility; Convenient facilities; Errand shopping; Facility convenience; In-store convenience and physical environment; Leisure activities; Location; Location and convenience; Price; Promotions/convenience; Proximity and familiarity; Service convenience; Variety under one roof
Facilities	Appearance; Congestion; Convenient facilities; Facilities; Facility convenience; Family shopping; Outside attractiveness; Physical facilities; Sensory/layout dimension; Servicescape; Service – store facilities; Store layout
Institutional	Clientele; Institutional; Institutional factors
Merchandise	Brand name; Fabric; Fashionability; Fashion goods; Focused shopping; Merchandise; Merchandise value; Merchandise variety; Merchandising; Popularity; Price; Price and quality aspects; Price competitiveness; Price/quality dimensions; Products; Quality/reputation; Rich mix of commodities and services; Status; Technical quality; Time/availability; Value; Value-added service
Promotion	Advertising; Interest shopping; Promotion; Promotions; Promotions/convenience; Sales and incentives
Sales personnel	Employee service; Functional quality; Personal interaction; Personnel; Preference for salespeople; Relational quality; Salesmanship; Salespeople service; Salesperson/service; Service – sales associates attributes
Service	After-sales service; Complaint handling; Core service; Credit; Credit facilities; Employee service; In-store service; Merchandise; Merchandise requests; Post-transaction service; Presence of related services; Rich mix of commodities and services; Salespeople service; Salesperson service; Service; Service convenience; Services; Service – sales associates attributes; Service – store amenities; Service – store facilities

Source: Du Preez et al. (2008: 52)

and from the perspective of the retailer, they have to be improved as customer attitudes and perceptions change over time. They conclude by noting that 'truly loyal customers are manifestly satisfied with the store and have a positive image towards the store' (Bloemer and Ruyter 1998: 512). In the next chapter we consider the ways in which retailers connect with their target market and develop store-loyal customers.

Retail positioning

Understanding how shoppers form an image of a store is central to the retailers in terms of designing appropriate strategies to encourage them to return to the store and, over time, build up a loyalty to shopping with that particular retailer. In order to put together a relevant value proposition, retailers have to position their points of differentiation clearly in their marketing communications with the target market.

So far in this chapter we have focused on building an understanding of the shopper with particular attention being paid to shopping behaviour and loyalty. We now consider the broad responses that retailers make in response to these factors and influences. We begin by examining the concept of positioning.

Ries and Trout (1986) wrote an influential text that examined the concept of positioning and highlighted its importance in shaping strategy for organizations. The key to understanding the concept of positioning is to recognize that it is not what companies and organizations 'do' to the product or service by means of marketing activities such as advertising or promotion. Rather the concept begins in the mind of the customer. It is about how the target market perceives the brand and how this perception is translated into specific attributes that are associated with this brand. This means that positioning is not about how the organization wishes its brand to be perceived in the mind of the shopper. Marketers have to be confident that they can influence the shopper's perceptions in a positive way.

Kalafatis, Tsogas and Blankson (2000) consider the various definitions that have been proposed by authors in this area and use the following definition to explain the concept. They suggest that an earlier attempt by Arnott (1992) to define positioning is an accurate view. He defines positioning as 'the deliberate, proactive, interactive process of defining, modifying and monitoring consumer perceptions of a marketable product...'.

The strength of this definition is that it explicitly recognizes the importance of engaging in longitudinal research to continuously monitor the changing landscape with regard to consumer perceptions. Competitive activities, new entrants, innovations and other factors all combine to ensure that the environment is not static. What may lead to a competitive advantage at one point in time can quickly disappear as consumers react to changes in the marker.

Differentiation is at the heart of positioning. Organizations are charged with the task of somehow differentiating their value proposition from the competition – both direct and indirect. Markets are becoming ever-more fragmented due to increasing customization and higher levels of expectations. We are witnessing increasing fragmentation within the media as the traditional means of communications are being challenged and supplanted by new media platforms (social media). It is becoming more and more difficult to carve out a clear point of differentiation in the mind of consumers across industry sectors. Unless a company has a clear and unambiguous point of differentiation, it is unlikely that its brand values will even register in the mind of the target market.

It can be noted that because positioning is based on the perceptions of the customer and not the organization, it is not fully in the control of the retailer.

In the context of retailing we are witnessing the emergence of greater numbers of more assertive, knowledgeable and questioning shoppers. Many retail sectors are moving from a functional view of what the customer wants to an experiential package of activities.

Creating and delivering customer value does not rest solely with marketing however. Knox (2004) recognizes that competition is in many cases based on the relative strengths of the respective supply chains rather than clever and creative marketing initiatives. He argues that positioning strategy design now encompasses all aspects of the organization.

Knox (2004) suggests a number of components to develop brand positioning. They are as follows:

- its overall reputation
- products/service performance
- product and customer portfolio
- networks.

He uses the example of airline brands to illustrate how these components interact and this is outlined in Table 2.2.

Table 2.2 The positioning of airline brands in the UK

	BA	EasyJet
Reputation	Reliable, predictable	Cheap
Product and service performance	Extensive routes, range of service, excellent recovery from problems	Fit for purpose, few routes
Product and customer portfolio	strong business class sub-brand Focus on long-distance business traveller	Corporate brand based on budget Traveller paying for own trips
Networks	Global alliances, deliver worldwide capability, Airmiles scheme a major part of loyalty strategy	Not as part of the brand

Source: Adapted from Knox, Maklan and Thompson (2000: 223)

In the context of retailing, Floor (2006: 82) engages in an extensive manner with the concept of retail brand positioning. He reinforces the importance of carving out a distinctive and meaningful position and cites the example of the US DIY retailer, Home Depot as a good example.

> **"***It got its original insight into how to revolutionise and expand its market by looking at the existing industries serving home improvement needs. It saw that people had two choices: they could hire contractors, or they could buy tools and materials from a hardware store and do the work themselves. Professional contractors only have one decisive advantage: they have specialised know-how that home-owners lack. Home Depot made it their mission to bolster the competence and confidence of customers whose experience in home repair was limited. The company now recruits sales assistants with significant trade experience, often former carpenters or painters. These assistants are trained to walk customers through any project: installing kitchen cabinets, for example, or building a deck. In addition, Home Depot sponsors in-store clinics that teach customers such skills as electrical wiring, carpentry and plumbing.*
>
> *Home Depot has also eliminated costly features that add cost. They have created a self-service warehouse format that lowers overheads and maintenance costs, generates economies of scale in purchasing and minimises stock-outs.*
>
> *Essentially Home Depot offers the expertise of professional home contractors at markedly lower prices than hardware stores. By delivering the decisive advantages of substitute industries and eliminating or reducing negative factors that held customers back, Home Depot has transformed enormous latent demand for home improvement into real demand.***"**

Source: Floor (2006)

2.10 Blending positioning attributes with shopping benefits

Retailers need to develop a positioning strategy to capture a position within the mind of their target market. In this section we consider how such a 'blending' exercise can be developed. Floor (2006) highlights how retailers form their brand positioning with respect to shopper need. This is captured in Fig. 2.4. Floor (2006) identifies four attributes that shape different retail brand positions. They are as follows:

- *Range brands*: the retailer focuses on developing a range of merchandise that is clearly stronger and better than the competition in that sector. This differentiation can be achieved either through the width and/or depth of the merchandise or through specialized merchandise. Examples would

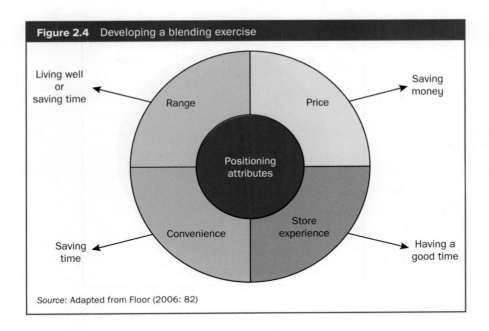

Figure 2.4 Developing a blending exercise

Source: Adapted from Floor (2006: 82)

include Foot Locker and Swatch. They appeal to a shopper who holds functional and/or emotional motives. From the point of view of convenience, such retailers provide a 'one-stop-shop'. They can also carry merchandise within their range that also addresses emotional needs.

- *Price brands*: the focus in this situation is on low price offerings that appeal to the price-conscious shopper. Such shoppers can be drawn from low and high-income circles. In many cases high-income shoppers, despite having a relatively large disposable income, still like to identify bargains and possibilities for savings. This is noticeable during the prolonged recession that occurred in the latter part of the first decade of this century. Aldi and Lidl present examples of such retail brands.

- *Convenience brands*: as noted earlier in this chapter, many shoppers are 'time-poor' due to busy professional careers combined with family commitments. This motive to save time can be viewed as functional in nature, although it does not ignore the fact that even in such circumstances some shoppers still have expectations of a high level of service and personal attention. In this respect, such a retail brand can appeal to both types of shopping motivation whether they be functional or hedonic.

- *Experience brands*: whereas the other three categories tend to focus mainly on the functional motives, this retail brand addresses the experiential dimension. An example would be Starbucks. At a functional level you can drink coffee in such an establishment. You can also use the WiFi facilities and browse the Internet. You can use the facilities to hold a business meeting or simply sit and watch the world go by. It is simply more than just a functional place where you drink coffee. Visiting an Apple store is also not about simply buying merchandise. You can try out new products, gain advice from sales staff and generally indulge in the atmosphere that is created in such stores. Increasingly retailers are developing flagship stores in key shopping malls to introduce customers to the latest designs and products.

Floor (2006) makes an important point when considering the attributes that retailers can use to position their value proposition in the minds of their target market. This is captured in Fig. 2.5.

Floor (2006) notes that it is impossible for a retailer to be excellent across a number of different attributes. Put simply, a retailer cannot satisfy everyone and be all things to all people. To this extent, it is important for a retailer to have a specific expertise or capability that is reflected in one particular area. This is referred to as a *differentiating attribute* by Floor. This particular attribute should form the central fulcrum of the retailer's overall marketing strategy. Outside of the marketing strategy it should form the genesis for the corporate mission and culture of the organization.

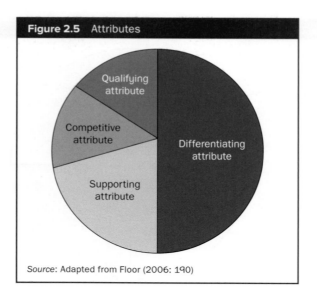

Figure 2.5　Attributes

Source: Adapted from Floor (2006: 190)

However, focusing exclusively on one attribute alone is not sufficient. In an increasingly competitive and complex market, it is difficult to base one's strategy on a single feature. Floor identifies the importance of having a *supporting attribute*. This should complement the differentiating attribute and provide the shopper with an extra reason for shopping at that store. For instance it can be argued that Zara's differentiating attribute is that of providing up-to-date, latest fashions, and it is complemented by the low, affordable price tags associated with the merchandise.

A *competitive attribute* recognizes that in order to be successful, this attribute is a minimum requirement. On its own, it does not provide any strong differentiating reason why a shopper should visit that particular store. For example, a discount retailer who uses low price as a differentiating factor does not have to worry unduly about the store experience. In this respect, the shopper is likely to view the low price as a compensatory factor for average to poor levels of customer service. Once the competition is around the same level on customer service, it will make little difference. However it is unlikely that the retailer would get away with an 'appalling' level of service. In this situation, the retailer has to be at a minimum, competitive on this attribute.

A *qualitative attribute* is similar to the previous one except that a retailer can afford to achieve less than the competition on this attribute, particularly if it is less relevant to the target market or the low rating on this feature is more than compensated for by the score on other attributes.

Table 2.3 summarizes the way in which these attributes can be implemented.

In overall terms we should recognize that the most appropriate positioning strategy is based on the overall capabilities of the retailers and more specifically the core competences; that is, the DNA of the business operations. This could be in any one particular area such as low price, quality, customer

Table 2.3　Using attributes to position against competitors

Attribute	Positioning against competition
Differentiating	Much better than the competition
Supporting	Somewhat better than the competition
Competitive	About as good as the competition
Qualifying	Acceptable versus competition

Source: Adapted from Floor (2006: 90)

Table 2.4 The positioning mix

Retail Brand	Differentiating	Supporting	Competitive	Qualifying
Wal-Mart	Price	Range	Convenience	Experience
Zara	Range	Price	Experience	Convenience
Starbucks	Experience	Range	Convenience	Price
Dollar General	Price	Convenience	Range	Experience
Nordstrom	Convenience	Range	Experience	Price
McDonald's	Convenience	Price	Experience	Range
Disney Store	Experience	Range	Convenience	Price

Source: Adapted from Floor (2006: 91)

service and so on. It is also critical that the chosen approach to positioning resonates with the needs, attitudes, perceptions and requirements of the target market. This latter point makes the brand *relevant* to the shopper and provides the rationale for visiting and (hopefully) revisiting that particular store. Thus, we have a mix of attributes that the retailer uses to establish a position in the mind of the shopper.

Table 2.4 provides some examples of how the four main attributes interact. We should look on this as the positioning mix which reflects the four categories identified by Floor (2006).

Activity

Select a retailer of your choice. Using the approach suggested by Floor (2006), identify the positioning strategy adopted by this retailer relative to the competition.

2.11 Repositioning

A brand goes through a life cycle like any product. At some point in its evolution it may need to be rejuvenated in order to adjust to the changing market environment. What might have worked well more than a decade ago may now appear to be 'stale' or 'dated'. Customers' attitudes and preferences may alter; new competitors arrive and 'change the rules of the game' or (in the case of retailing) new formats emerge.

If a retailer is experiencing a prolonged period of decline in term of decreasing sales and market share, it has to face up to a fundamental question. Where do we go from here? It may mean in the worst case scenario that it closes its operations and withdraws from the market. Some music stores such as HMV have closed due to their format and value proposition ceasing to be relevant to the customer. Independent retailers in some sectors have also had to close in the teeth of strong competition from the mega retailers who have infringed on their territory. This is notably the case with the large supermarket groups as they redefine their business from originally food to a range of non-food activities such as running pharmacies, selling fuel and financial services.

A less drastic strategy is to rethink the business and reposition the value proposition to take account of market and customer changes. HMV, for example, was subsequently acquired by Hilco UK; it redefined its value proposition and still retains a presence in the UK market. In the case of the travel sector, many travel agencies are repositioning their offering as travel consultants that can design bespoke package for corporate and personal travellers.

In some cases, a retail value proposition becomes 'lost' in the 'fog' of information and data that is directed at shoppers and it ceases to become clear as to what the retailer's key differentiating attribute is. Commentators suggest that this happens to retailers who end up in a 'middle-of-the-road' position. In such a situation, it can be argued that a retailer does not make any great appeal to any specific segment of shopper. At the bottom end, discount retailers have a clear position: low prices, basic customer service and store environment. At the top end, high-fashion retailers have an exclusive range of merchandise, customized and tailored customer service and luxurious facilities. A retailer who is caught in the middle may struggle to 'register on the radar'.

A decision to reposition the value proposition is not one that is made on a regular basis. It is relevant where there is a prolonged period of decreasing sales akin to the decline stage of the product life cycle. It will require changes across the broad dimensions of the retail marketing mix. For instance, if a fashion retailer makes a decision to reposition its offering to an older customer, it is not sufficient to introduce a new range of clothing to reflect this shift in focus. Changes will also need to be made to other elements of the retail marketing mix to support and reinforce this change in direction. Cosmetic or minor adjustments are unlikely to be effective. Indeed such tinkering with the existing value proposition may further confuse and alienate the target market.

For effective positioning and repositioning to work effectively, the following conditions should be present.

- The value proposition and the differentiating attribute need to be clearly identified and explained in the communications strategy adopted by the retailer.
- The value proposition and differentiating attribute must be relevant and credible to the target market.
- The value proposition and differentiating attribute need to be sufficiently different from the competitive value propositions. Otherwise, it simply becomes a copy-cat brand and is unlikely to make enough of an impression to capture the required sales and market share.
- The value proposition and differentiating attribute have to be consistent over time. Constant adjustment and alterations across the marketing mix are a major source of confusion and irritation to the target market.

2.12 Retail marketing strategy

In the previous section we examined the key strategic attributes upon which a retailer can set out its overall positioning strategy. The specific operational decision areas and tactics employed by the retailer to articulate the overall strategic positioning need to be considered.

Walters and Laffy (1996) identified four broad areas that make up the retail marketing mix. They are represented as follows:

- merchandise decision (range, width and depth of merchandise, branding and assortment profiles)
- store format, layout, space allocation, design and atmospherics
- customer service (pre-sales, sales and post-sales)
- customer communications: traditional (TV, press, radio, print and so on) and new (Internet, viral, social media and so on) forms of marketing communications.

Figure 2.6 identifies the elements of the retail programme in more detail and shows how this links up with the target market. We consider each element of retail strategy in Chapters 5–11.

The elements identified on the right-hand side of the diagram represent the retail marketing mix. We can see that it covers a broad range of areas and has been updated since it was originally developed by Davidson (1984) to include contemporary issues such as omni-channel coverage, social media platforms and issues such as sustainability and social responsibility.

Figure 2.6 provides us with a structure which we will use to examine each element of the retail marketing mix in the following chapters.

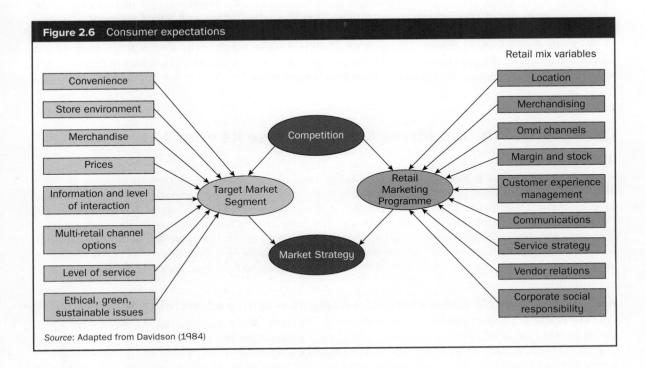

Figure 2.6 Consumer expectations

Retail mix variables

- Convenience
- Store environment
- Merchandise
- Prices
- Information and level of interaction
- Multi-retail channel options
- Level of service
- Ethical, green, sustainable issues

Target Market Segment

Competition

Market Strategy

Retail Marketing Programme

- Location
- Merchandising
- Omni channels
- Margin and stock
- Customer experience management
- Communications
- Service strategy
- Vendor relations
- Corporate social responsibility

Source: Adapted from Davidson (1984)

2.13 Conclusions

This chapter has focused on the consumer or shopper as the unit of analysis. We examined the motivations for shopping and concluded that shoppers are driven by functional needs such as the acquisition of food and clothing and also by more hedonistic needs such as the desire for a certain lifestyle, luxury and aspiration. The latter motives generally refer to shopping situations where there is a high level of involvement in the buying process. Shoppers are prepared to invest time and effort in the process in order to acquire the item (s) and get the expected pleasure or excitement from the exercise. By contrast, some shopping situations are more mundane and boring for some shoppers; for instance, in the case of the weekly trip to the supermarket.

We assessed the concept of store image and the ways in which shoppers form an image of a particular store. While much of the research in this area has been based on examining the range of attributes, we noted that a gestalt view of the store takes a broader view. This takes in cognitive perceptions and emotional responses and consists of a range of functional and psychological factors.

In the second part of the chapter we examined how retailers can respond to the motivations and patronage decisions of the shopper. In particular we evaluated the concept of retail positioning. This concept stresses the importance of retailers recognising the need to position their value proposition in the minds of the target market. Unless it captures a meaningful and relevant position in this space, it is unlikely the retailer will 'register on the radar' and gain a footprint in terms of market share and sales.

We established that the differentiating attribute is an important consideration in developing the positioning strategy. This attribute is in essence the rationale behind the value proposition and differentiates it from the competition. Without such a differentiating attribute it is unlikely that a retailer can gain a sufficient point of differentiation from the competition. It will inevitably become a 'me-too' or 'copy-cat' brand. It will not provide enough motivation or incentive for shoppers to visit that outlet on a regular basis.

We looked at the key areas where a retailer can shape the positioning of its offering. The main areas are merchandise, price, store environment and communications. We expanded on this to examine the various components of retail marketing strategy. This is a more varied and wider range of activities than the traditional '4 P's' framework that is so beloved of traditional marketing texts.

We made the important observation that retail marketing strategy on its own will not guarantee a successful outcome. Supply chain management is arguably more critical as weaknesses in this area will prevent many of the marketing initiatives from reaching fruition.

Case study: Why did Marks & Spencer lose its edge?

Introduction

Marks & Spencer is a UK food and clothing retailer and has enjoyed great success throughout the decades before losing market position in the late 1990s. Its St. Michael brand developed a strong reputation for good quality worldwide. In its successful period, it was perceived as being one of the most successful UK companies. It has introduced some initiatives since then to try and recapture its pre-eminent position; most notably with the launch of sub-brands in its clothing section such as Per Una and Autograph. In the following paragraphs we get the views of a few opinion formers and retail experts about the future for Marks & Spencer, particularly in the context of how they should position its value proposition.

Kirstie Allsopp, TV presenter, also designs a homeware range for M&S

I'm very proud to have a range in Marks & Spencer, although I think I can be honest about what I feel. I used to buy a lot of clothing from M&S – I've always been a fan, and I adored their Autograph range [famous fashion designers were brought in to collaborate on collections]. There are fashion designers whose stuff I wouldn't buy at the top end, but who did a diffusion line for Autograph when it first started, and I have some pieces from that range that I still wear. But M&S doesn't have that any more.

When I talk to the girls at work – many of them in their mid- to late-20s and on low incomes – they tell me they shop at Primark. I don't see them buying anything from Marks & Spencer. It has become about the food, which out-cools and out-sexes the clothes. Something, somewhere got a little bit lost.

I trust Marks & Spencer, but I don't have the sense any more that I will make a real discovery. My fashion advice mainly comes from weekend newspaper supplements, and I don't see a lot of M&S stuff in them. I know they do makeup, shoes, accessories – but I can't remember the last time I saw something in a magazine and thought, 'ooh', and then saw it was from M&S.

M&S can get its position back. The staff have a great attitude, and the company as a whole is a good one. I just think its womenswear has lost its edge.

Jess Cartner-Morley, *The Guardian* fashion editor

There is one straightforward factor contributing to M&S's woes. There is no one manning the tiller, fashionably speaking. The current collections fall between two reigns: they were conceived after Kate Bostock left last year, but have not been steered by her replacement, Belinda Earl – her influence will not be seen until the first autumn ranges land at the end of this summer. I have observed the dynamics at M&S for some time, and it strikes me that a healthy relationship between the CEO and the person fighting fashion's corner is key to good product. It will be fascinating to see what impact Earl has next season.

In part, the problem for M&S is that the competition has got so much better. The British high-street shopper is now thoroughly spoilt. Once, M&S filled a gap between fast fashion, which was cheap as chips but shoddily made, and the stodgy, elasticated-waistband fare of department store fashion. But the fast-fashion market has improved its production values, while a new category of grown-up high street stores, such as Reiss and Cos, has emerged. M&S, once front and centre of our clothing consciousness, has to fight for airspace. There has been a tendency to fight for attention by filling the rails with 'trend-led' clothes, which are often successful in winning media attention, but don't deliver strong sales on the shopfloor.

As a nation, we still identify strongly with M&S. It is a part of Britishness in a way no other brand is. Each of us has an opinion on what M&S should be selling, just as every football fan has a view on the team their manager should field. Here's my own tuppenceworth on how M&S should alter their offer: by refining the colour palette. Walk on to the womenswear floor and you find yourself in a hectic, multicolour world. Less pink, yellow and red, and more bottle-green, navy and off-white would instantly update the environment. Yes, you might annoy the odd customer who was hell-bent on fuschia, but you can't please all of the people all of the time.

The silver lining is that many women don't realise how much good stuff there still is in M&S. (I'm talking flagship stores. Sorry, provinces.) Recently I've bought a phenomenal leather pencil skirt with a gold zip, beautiful fabric and construction, for under £200, and a cream silk blouse with coral pocket borders that looks like it came from Paris for €200 rather than Oxford Street for £45.

Richard Perks, director of retail research, Mintel

There are two main drivers for M&S – womenswear and food. The food is doing well, but the problems are with the womenswear. They did the right thing in splitting it up into different sub-brands, but those brands are now insufficiently differentiated. They're also too 'old'. The great thing about Per Una when it launched was that it was young fashions engineered for older customers, but the 'young' look has gone. Historically, you were dragged in there by your parents and swore never to go in again, and then around the age of 30 you happened to go in and thought, 'Oh, that's quite good.' But it doesn't seem to be picking up those younger customers now. Debenhams is sitting where M&S should be, and does a good job, because its brands are differentiated.

There's a failure to understand what older people want. Sometimes you feel the merchandise is bought by a 25-year-old [M&S buyer] who has a caricatured granny in mind. Older people don't want to be sold down to. That is why Per Una did so well, because it looked young. That's what they've got to get back to.

M&S always did well in a recession – people went back to it because it was good quality and value. In boom times, it tended to over-engineer its products and they got too expensive. So it would have a bad start to the recession, but it would simplify its products, make them cheaper and clean up – that hasn't happened this time. I think Marc Bolland has to take responsibility for that.

Lead times are long – however much you like the idea of fast fashion, most things have to be planned in advance. Belinda Earl [former chief executive of Debenhams and Jaeger] joined in September, and she couldn't really have any significant impact until autumn/winter this year. Things have drifted; they need to take those sub-brands and give them their own personality.

Kim Winser, former chief executive of Pringle and Aquascutum, and director of womenswear at Marks & Spencer until 2000. Now runs Winser London

It's all about passion for product. That's what M&S has to turn its attention to – get back to really good, beautiful, quality products. I buy food from M&S, but not clothing – I haven't found that combination of fashionability, style and quality.

They do a number of different brand names – too many. By focusing on a few, they could use each brand to focus on a certain customer group, and gradually build up the value of that brand to that group – they will begin to love it and trust it and know it's for them.

When I was there we launched Autograph. It was about bringing in some of the best designers in Britain and capturing what they were good at. The designer collaborations can work, but only if it really does represent what that designer is famous for.

I don't think it's about the size of the company, I think it's about the people. There are too many excuses about business and bureaucracy, but the company is run by people, and I was definitely left to run womenswear, which at the time was a £2bn business. I was given that responsibility and account-ability. I loved it, and as a team of people, that was one of the reasons we had market-share growth, ▶

◀ because we really did love the customer and the product. So it can be done, whatever the size of the business, but I think it depends on the people.

Lifestyles change, and it's about a company constantly innovating, looking at what's happening and also predicting what's going to happen. To do that, you have to be absolutely in tune with your customer and what they want, and focus on what your brand is good at. I'm looking from the outside now, but that's where M&S was always a very successful business, because it put the customer first.

Source: Adapted from interviews by Emine Saner. *The Guardian*, 19 April 2013

Questions

1 Based on your understanding of issues discussed in this chapter, how effective in your view is the response of senior management in Marks & Spencer to the changing needs and requirements of the marketplace?

2 What in your view is the differentiating attribute of Marks & Spencer? How does this work in terms of its positioning strategy?

3 Do you think that Marks & Spencer needs a full repositioning strategy or some adjustments to its present approach?

4 Assess the ways in which UK shoppers have changed their shopping preferences and behaviours. What implications does it have for senior management at Marks & Spencer?

Chapter outcomes

- Shoppers have a wide range of motivations for shopping ranging from functional reasons through to hedonistic drivers.

- Much depends on the shopping situation. For high involvement shopping, shoppers are likely to view the activity as pleasurable and an antidote to the realities of life.

- In many countries, shopping is viewed as being the single biggest leisure activity, superseding sporting activities.

- Motivations for shopping on online retail channels are similar in many ways to those on traditional bricks-and-mortar outlets. However, website design, transparency and navigation play a significant role in creating a 'user-friendly' experience.

- Store image is made up of a composite picture of the retailer based on attributes. Cognitive perceptions and emotional responses emerge from the attributes.

- Retail positioning is critical for a retailer in capturing 'a slice of the target market's mind'.

- Positioning focuses on developing and shaping retail strategy around the differentiating attribute; that is, what benefit makes the retailer stand out from the competition? What benefit can give it a potential competitive advantage?

- Supporting, competitive and qualifying attributes have to be factored into the analysis and subsequent development of the positioning statement.

- Retailers at some point in the life cycle may have to consider a repositioning strategy in response to changes in market conditions and competitive activities.

- Effective positioning is based on the principles of clarity, focus and consistency.

- Retail marketing strategy focuses on key areas such as communications, merchandise and the store environment. We need to take a much broader view of these activities than the traditional 4 P's view of the marketing mix.

Discussion questions

1 If shopping patronage is in many cases all about leisure, how should retailers respond to this phenomenon?

2 Examine the extent to which you would agree with the view that store image represents the personality of the store. Use examples to support your point of view.

3 Identify the differences in shopping motivations between traditional bricks-and-mortar channels and online retail channels.

4 Select a retailer of your choice and critically appraise its approach to retail positioning.

5 Assess the reasons why a retailer might employ a repositioning strategy. What are the dangers associated with such a decision?

6 Evaluate the relevance of supporting, qualifying and competitive attributes when developing the positioning strategy for a retailer. Use a detailed example to support your line of argument.

References

Arnold, M.J. and Reynolds, K.E. (2003) Hedonic shopping motivations. *Journal of Retailing.* 79: 77–95.

Arnott, D. (1992) Basis of financial services positioning. Unpublished PhD thesis, Manchester Business School.

Babin, B.J., Darden,W.R. and Griffin, M. (1994) Work and/or fun: measuring hedonic and utilitarian value. *Journal of Consumer Research.* 20(5/6): 499–513.

Backstrom, K. (2011) Shopping as leisure: an exploration of manifoldness and dynamics in consumers shopping experiences. *Journal of Retailing and Consumer Services.* 18(3): 200–209.

Baker, J.A., Parasuraman, A., Grewal, D. and Boss, G.B (2002) The influence of multiple store environment cues on perceived merchandise value and patronage intentions. *Journal of Marketing.* 66 (April): 120–141.

Bearden, W.D. (1977) Determinant attributes of store patronage: downtown versus outlying shopping areas. *Journal of Retailing.* 53: 15–22.

Bloemer, J. and de Ruyter, K. (1998) On the relationship between store image, store satisfaction and store loyalty. *European Journal of Marketing.* 32(5/6): 499–513.

Chowdhary, J., Reardon, J. and Srivastava, R. (1998) Alternative modes of measuring store image: an empirical assessment of structures versus unstructured measures. *Journal of Marketing Theory and Practice.* 6(2): 72–86.

Davidson, W. (1984) *Retail Management.* Wiley: New York.

Du Preez, R., Visser, E. and Van Noordwyk, H.J. (2008) Store image: towards a conceptual model part 1. *SA Journal of Industrial Psychology.* 34(2): 50–58.

Eastlick, M. and Feinberg, R.A.A. (1999) The market maven: a diffusion of marketplace information. *Journal of Marketing.* 51(3): 281–290.

Floor, K. (2006) *Branding a Store: How to Build Successful Retail Brands in a Changing Marketplace.* Kogan Page: London and Philadelphia.

Ganesh, J., Reynolds, K.E., Luckett, l. and Pomirleanu, N. (2010) Online shopper motivations and e-Store attributes: an examination of online patronage behaviour and shopper typologies. *Journal of Retailing.* 86(1): 106–115.

Ghosh, A. (1990) *Retail Management.* 2nd edn. Chicago, IL: The Dryden Press.

Haanpa, L. (2005) Shopping for fun or for needs? A study of shopping values, styles and motives of Finnish consumers in 2001-2003. Paper presented at the *7th Conference of European Sociological Association,* Torun, September.

Jin, B. and Kim, J.O. (2003) A typology of Korean discount shoppers: shopping motives, store attributes and outcomes. *International Journal of Service Industry Management.* 14(4): 396–419.

Kalafatis, S.P., Tsogas, M.H. and Blankson, C. (2000) Positioning strategies in business markets. *The Journal of Business & Industrial Marketing.* 15(6): 416–437.

Kaur, P. and Singh, R. (2007) Uncovering retail shopping motives of Indian youth. *Young Consumers.* 8(2): 128–138.

Knox, S.D. (2004) Positioning and branding your organisation. *Journal of Product & Brand Management.* 13(2): 105–115.

Knox, S.D., Maklan, S. and Thompson, K.E. (2000) Building the unique organisation value proposition. In Schultz, M., Hatch, M.J. and Larsen, M.H. (eds) *The Expressive Organisation.* Oxford: Oxford University Press, 216.

Kukar-Kinney, M., Ridgway, N.M. and Monroe, K. (2009) The relationship between consumers' tendencies to buy compulsively and their motivations to shop and buy on the Internet. *Journal of Retailing.* 85(3): 298–307.

Laurent, G. and Kapferer, J.N. (1985) Measuring consumer involvement profiles. *Journal of Marketing Research.* 12 (February): 41–53.

Lennon, S.J., Sanik, M.M, and Labarbarbera, P.A. (2003) Motivations for television shopping: clothing purchase frequency and personal characteristics. *Clothing and Textiles Research Journal.* 21(2): 63–74.

Li, H., Cheng, K. and Russell, M.G. (1999) The impact of perceived channel utilities, shopping orientations and demographics on the consumer's online buying behaviour. *Journal of Computer Mediated Communication.* December: 5.

Lindquist, J.D. (1974) Meaning of image: survey of empirical and hypothetical evidence. *Journal of Retailing.* 50: 29–38.

Martineau, P. (1958) The personality of the retail store. *Harvard Business Review.* 36: 47–55.

Mathwick, C., Malhotra, N. and Rigdon, E. (2001) Experiential value: conceptualisation meassurement and application in the catalog and Internet shopping environment. *Journal of Retailing.* 77 (Spring): 36–59.

Noble, S.M., Griffith, D.A. and Adjei, M.T. (2006) Drivers of local merchant loyalty: understanding the influence of gender and shopping motives. *Journal of Retailing.* 82(3): 177–188.

Pan, Y. and Zinkhan, G.M. (2006) Determinants of retail patronage: a meta-analytical perspective. *Journal of Retailing.* 82(3): 229–243.

Parsons, A.G. (2002) Non-functional motives for online shoppers: why we click? *Journal of Consumer Marketing.* 19(5): 380–392.

Ries, A.L., and Trout, J. (1986) *Positioning: The Battle for your Mind.* London: McGraw-Hill

Rohm, A.J. and Swaminathan, V. (2004) A typology of online shoppers based on shopping motivations. *Journal of Business Research.* 57(7): 748–757.

Tauber, E.M. (1972) Marketing notes and communications: why do people shop? *Journal of Marketing.* October: 46–49.

Walters, D. and Laffy, D. (1996) *Managing Retail Productivity and Profitability.* London: MacMillan.

Zee-Sun Y. and Good, L. (2007) Developing customer loyalty from e-tail store image attributes. *Managing Service Quality.* 17(1): 4–22.

2

Supply chain issues

Part contents

Chapter 3

Retailing and its role in the supply chain

☑ Learning objectives

On completion of this chapter you should be in a position to address the following objectives:

- ☑ Understand the concept of the supply chain and the trends and developments that have occurred in that area.
- ☑ Examine the link between retailing, marketing and the supply chain.
- ☑ Evaluate the position of the retailer in the context of the supply chain.
- ☑ Examine the concept of a demand chain as opposed to a supply chain.

Examine the different retail formats and how they have evolved.

 Recognize the reasons for the growing importance and influence of the retailer in modern supply chains.

3.1 Introduction

In this chapter we define what is meant by retailing and identify its position within the context of the overall supply chain.

The retail sector in general is arguably the most 'visible' area in the economy. In boom periods, retailers tend to do well as consumers have money in their pockets and are prone to purchase a range of items from essential products (food and clothing) through to discretionary items (cars, home entertainment and electronics). By contrast when the economy encounters a recessionary period, the first area to 'take a hit' is retailing. Not surprisingly, many consumers 'tighten their belts' and are reluctant to purchase items that can be postponed to a later date or which might be viewed as non-essential and discretionary purchases.

It is important to place retailing in context and as a consequence we examine the overall concept of a supply chain and trends and developments in that area. Retailers do not operate in blissful isolation from other key parties in the supply chain. Without an appropriate and well-managed supply chain, retailers cannot hope to address the needs of shoppers in a relevant and timely manner. We assess the implications for retailers and shoppers as a result of these changes. Supply chains in general and retailers in particular have to be increasingly customer-focused in the design and implementation of their strategies.

As the management of supply chains has evolved and developed, it is becoming increasingly clear that organizations are moving away from the traditional approach of 'pushing' products through the system and on to the final customer. Instead the 'leading-edge' organizations are adopting a 'customer-centric' approach where supply chains are designed specifically with the needs and requirements of the customer in focus. Instead of driving the supply chain from the perspective of the organization, it is shaped by the customer. In essence supply chain management has embraced the marketing ethos. There is now a considerable overlap between the two disciplines of supply chain management and marketing.

We address what is meant by the concept of the supply chain in the early sections of this chapter. In particular we focus on the components of the supply chain; that is, the key stakeholders in the process. We examine the functions that are performed by the various organizations that operate in a supply chain.

We examine the shift from the traditional 'supply-push' approach to supply chains that are based on the principle of 'demand-pull'. This is significant because it heralds a change in business philosophy: from one based on organizational issues to one that is based on the customer. In the context of our investigation of retail marketing, it highlights the importance of understanding the link between retailing, marketing and the supply chain.

3.2 The concept of the supply chain

Retailers are one of a number of key stakeholders that are involved in creating, managing and delivering value to the shopper. Retailers on their own are not in a position to achieve these objectives. They depend on key stakeholders such as manufacturers and logistics companies. These stakeholders operate within what is known as a supply chain. In this section, we consider what is meant by this term.

Lambert and Cooper (2000: 65) define supply chain management as 'a series of activities and inputs that produce specific value outputs to customers'. A traditional supply chain is depicted in Fig. 3.1.

Gattorna (2006) demonstrates that a supply chain is essentially a collection of interconnected links. These links cover the broad spectrum of activities from the procurement and supply function to the

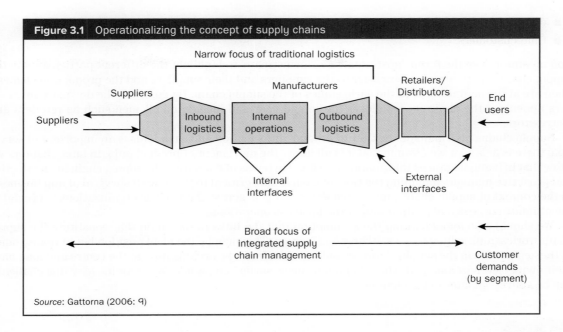

Figure 3.1 Operationalizing the concept of supply chains

Source: Gattorna (2006: 9)

production process and the subsequent moving of product or services to channel members and ultimately on to the final purchaser or consumer.

The supply chain is only as strong as its weakest link: there is no point in having a 'state-of-the-art' manufacturing plant if the supply base is inefficient or unreliable. Likewise, a poor channel system also weakens the ability of the supply chain to deliver value to its target market.

The supply chain involves external and internal parties. For instance the suppliers and their suppliers, although external and in most cases independent from the manufacturer (or the organization at the hub of the supply chain), are equally if not more important players in the shaping and implementation of overall business strategy. Thus, we should take a broader view of what constitutes the concept of the enterprise or business. The enterprise is made up of internal and external operations and in effect becomes an 'extended family' – incorporating all parties involved in the creation, management and delivery of value.

The term 'supply chain management' emerged as a popular term in the 1990s and replaced the somewhat narrower concept of logistics management. As we can see from Fig. 3.1, logistics tends to focus on the movement of materials, components and finished product from suppliers to the production functions (internal operations) and then onwards from the factory gate to the various middlemen who handle the merchandise.

Authors such as Christopher (1992, 1998), Cooper, Lambert and Pugh (1997) and Hagel and Singer (1999) were in the forefront in advocating the need for a broader view of what constitutes the supply chain. Instead of focusing on the logistics aspect only, they argued that it was more relevant to take an integrated view of this concept. This recognizes that it covers the full range of activities from the supply base and their suppliers right through to the engagements and interactions with the final consumer of the product or service.

Since the 1990s the focus within the literature on supply chain management has been on an integrated and holistic view of how it operates. We elaborate on this point in the next sections of the chapter.

3.3   Components and functions of the supply chain

The key stakeholders in the supply chain that we referred to earlier consist of the following parties:

- supplier network (upstream members and activities)
- enterprise (internal business functions)

- distributive networks (downstream members and activities)
- final customers.

Commentators use the terms 'upstream' and 'downstream' to highlight the different participants in the supply chain. Upstream members refer to the suppliers and their suppliers and the production element. They are at the beginning or at the early stages of the supply chain. By contrast, the downstream members appear as the chain moves closer to the end user and include middlemen such as retailers and distributors.

Supply chains also manage the flow of product, information and cash. This is an important observation: there is a danger we assume that it is all about the movement of product only. In later chapters we show that in many instances information is critical in terms of managing the supply chain in an effective and proactive manner. Managing the flow of cash is also critical to the overall survival of any business. In the context of supply chains, managing the cash cycle across the various organizations is crucial to the ultimate success and profitability of the business operations.

We should also avoid making the assumption that the links in the chain that constitute the supply chain work seamlessly and in a synchronous fashion. This may be the ideal position but in reality some of the key parties in the supply chain are independent from the organization at the centre and may have their own objectives and goals that may not be necessarily compatible. We examine how this challenge can be addressed later in the chapter.

3.4 Trends and developments in supply chain management

Over the last two decades or so supply chain management has moved to the forefront of many organizations' agendas when focusing on overall business strategy development and implementation. Why has this happened?

Organizations have had to grapple with the following challenges:

- be faster to market
- provide better service
- deliver better sales processes
- lower operational costs
- lower production costs
- lower inventory costs.

These challenges appear to be somewhat contradictory. For instance how can you improve customer service while at the same time lowering your costs? The reality is that all of these challenges interact with each other. Decisions on lowering inventory costs will have implications for decisions in other key areas. Organizations that invest in supply chain management can address cost, service and responsiveness issues by critically assessing each element in the supply chain to seek out areas of improvement where efficiencies and increased capabilities can be identified.

A key recurring theme runs across all of the challenges that we have identified: the customer. Gattorna (2006) puts forward the view that many organizations traditionally adopted an operations management view when managing the supply chain. This focus on costs covers all of the elements in the supply chain processes from supplier management and relationships, manufacturing, warehousing inventory and transportation management to managing relationships with the middlemen.

While this is a commendable approach insofar as it makes an organization potentially more competitive, it embraces a philosophy that is largely internally focused and to some extent ignores the realities of what may be happening in the market; that is, changing customer behaviours, attitudes and perception.

The pressures from the marketplace (higher customer service levels, quicker response to customer demands, lower inventory and so on) have forced organizations to take a more strategic view of the role of supply chain management. Instead of using internal considerations as the driver for supply chain management, organizations have had to rethink the process and base their decisions in this area on the demands of the market. This represents a fundamental shift in thinking and has implications for how we view the position of the concept of the supply chain in overall business strategy formulation and execution.

3.5

From supply-push to demand-pull

Increasingly the customer is the focal point for the design of supply chain strategies (Hines, 2013). Jacobs (2006) noted that in the 1980s the average lead time in the apparel industry – from the raw materials to the customer – was around 66 weeks. By the mid-2000s this had been reduced to an average of 12 months. Over the past decade or so, retailers such as Zara have reduced the lead time to around five to six weeks. In the context of delivering value, this represents a shift in thinking from a supply and manufacturing focus to a customer focus.

Many commentators use the terms 'value chain' and 'supply chain' interchangeably. The use of the term 'value' reinforces the message about the importance of delivering a 'value proposition to the end user and brings us closer in many ways to the customer-focused view of the supply chain as advocated by Hines (2013).

In Fig. 3.1 (on page 51) the demand side is represented by the retailers that have to make decisions on what to sell based on their knowledge and feedback from shoppers. The suppliers and manufacturers have to put together the package that makes up the final product for the retailers to sell to the target market. We can see that the two elements (demand and supply) cannot operate effectively without co-operation and collaboration. Otherwise there is a breakdown in communications, a lack of feedback on market demands, discontinuities in the flow of information and product. The end result is a disjointed and unwieldy supply chain that is not responsive to the market demands.

From a marketing perspective, it makes more sense to refer to this process as the demand chain; not the supply chain. This view is reinforced by Christopher (1998). Indeed he advocates that the term 'chain' should be replaced by 'networks' as this more accurately reflects the fact that there are multiple suppliers, channel members and customers involved in the process.

In essence, this view of the supply chain being based on a demand-pull framework reinforces the relationship between marketing and supply chain management. This philosophy places the customer at the heart of supply chain design and implementation. It also stresses that no single business function such as marketing, procurement, manufacturing, logistics and so on can operate in isolation. Creating, managing and delivering a value proposition is a process that involves strong interaction, integration and collaboration across the business disciplines.

This emphasis on integration also extends outside of the organization to the external partners that are involved in the supply chain. In the context of retailing, this means working closely and in a collaborative manner with a retailer's supply base. While some of the relationships will be transaction-oriented (no real emphasis placed on long-term relationships), key suppliers in product categories are critical to successful in-store promotions for example.

Developments in the area of information technology (IT) have helped in no small measure to capture information on shopper patterns of purchase behaviour. The ability to use 'real-time' information and make this available to suppliers also helps to develop effective initiatives in the context of management of the supply chain. We explore this aspect more closely in Chapter 4. Table 3.1 provides us with a comparison of the two approaches.

The term 'demand' explicitly places the customer and the market at the heart of decision-making. However, as most of the authors in this area still use the term 'supply chain management', we will continue to adopt this phrase in the relevant chapters of this book.

Moreover, this increasing focus on demand highlights the close relationship between the marketing function and supply chain management. Without an adequate understanding of the final customer, it is unlikely that the management of the supply chain will have a resonance and coherence. More importantly, it is uncertain as to whether there is any alignment between supply chain decisions and the demands of the marketplace.

Table 3.1   From supply-push to demand-pull

Supply chain	Demand chain
Efficiency focus (cost per item)	Effectiveness focus, product-market fit
Processes are focused on execution	Processes are focused more on planning
Cost is the key driver	Revenue is the key driver
Short-term oriented, within the immediate controllable future	Long-term oriented, within the next planning cycle
Typically the domain of tactical manufacturing and logistics personnel	Typically the domain of marketing, sales and strategic supply chain managers
Focuses on immediate resource and capacity constraints	Focuses on the long-term capabilities, not short-term constraints
Historical focus on manufacturing planning and controls	Historical focus on marketing and supply-chain realignment

Source: Langabeer and Rose (2001)

Figure 3.2 depicts a framework for designing and managing the value chain (Walters and Rainbird, 2004: 474). Walters and Rainbird note that the demand chain can be described as 'an understanding of current and future customer expectations, market characteristics, and of the available response alternatives to meet these through the deployment of operational resources'.

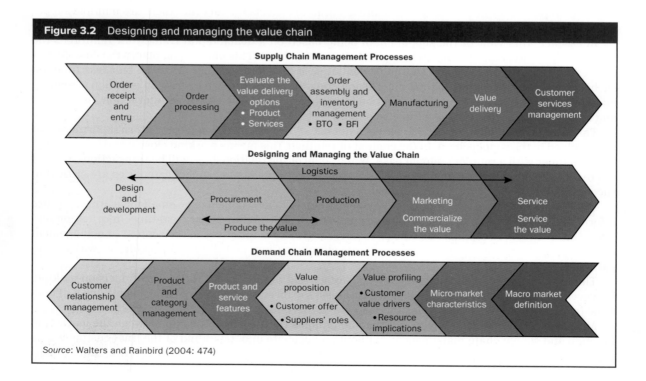

Figure 3.2   Designing and managing the value chain

Source: Walters and Rainbird (2004: 474)

Vignette: Supply chain key to Gap's global growth plans

The specialty retailer Gap Inc. announced plans to expand its Old Navy stores overseas, particularly in China, and aim for an omni-channel experience.

The chief executive officer (CEO), Glenn Murphy, stated that speed to market was a critical factor in achieving these ambitions. To this end the company has reduced its core pipeline by one-third and is now turning its attention to 'fabric platforming'. This involves not hundreds of fabrics, 'but the right amount of fabrics, because they can be washed and treated in many different ways. Fabric platforming is a big change that's coming in the business.' It also feeds into vendor-managed inventory. Murphy stated that 'vendor-managed inventory is a style that's around 52 weeks, the fabric is platformed, the vendor sits on six weeks of finished goods, you've got two weeks in the distribution centre, you've got two weeks in a store, done, it's a continuous cycle'.

The next step in the model is rapid response. This is a 'style that's four to six weeks. You don't buy it all at once. The fabric is sitting there. You go and do a short, some are pleated, and some are not pleated, get a read, make your adjustments. Fabric is sitting there, it is not rocket science.'

Gap is also seeking out opportunities in the area of seamless inventory and a global assortment.

'Today we have pools of inventory trapped around the world. It first gets trapped in a country. So Japan inventory, when the PO gets cut and goes to a vendor and it goes to Japan, it is Japan's inventory. It's trapped in Japan. Then it goes to stores, and is trapped in 150 stores. We are now going to unlock the power of our inventory where any unit that leaves a vendor should go to where that unit could be maximized the most. It starts with having a global assortment.'

Gap has moved from seven regional merchandising teams, all feeding ideas direct to the design teams, to a global centre in New York which channels this regional information into 'one global vision'. The company is seeking to have 70–80 per cent of its products the same consistently globally, with the remainder open for local requirements.

The company operates 3300 stores under the Gap, Banana Republic, Athleta, Old Navy, and Intermix brands. It wants to create an end-to-end experience that merges online and bricks-and-mortar shopping.

Source: Adapted from Barrie, L. (2012) Supply chain key to Gap's global growth plans. Available online at: www.just-style.com (accessed 13 May 13)

3.6 Obstacles to designing and implementing demand chain management

As organizations move to a customer-oriented, demand-driven approach and away from the traditional supply-push approach, we need to consider some of the challenges and hurdles that have to be addressed.

Jacobs (2006) makes a criticism that in the context of fashion retailing, much of the marketing activity is about promoting the merchandise to customers and less so in the case of collecting marketing intelligence from the customer. He cites the example of female shoppers who are increasingly becoming bored with the 'me-too' approach of many retailers and shopping malls in terms of creating the shopping experience. He exempts smaller and more creative retailers that are more customer-focused and can gain some differentiation over their competitors. He is critical of the use of the term 'demand chain management' as a result of the lack of investment in customer intelligence.

The single biggest obstacle to effective implementation centres on the challenge of collaboration and integration across the different business functions. Unfortunately, in many organizations, internal business functions still operation in 'silos'. This means that there is little or no collaboration between the functions: each one trying to protect its own 'empire' and being suspicious of colleagues from other business disciplines. The challenge for supply chain managers is to 'crash through' this mentality to create an environment where multi-functional teams flourish and a spirit of collaboration is fostered and encouraged.

A 'product champion' is also critical to the successful implementation of effective supply chain strategies. With full support from senior management, such an individual can establish initiatives with internal staff and external organizations. Increasingly, we are seeing companies recruiting people to work exclusively in this co-ordinating role.

Notwithstanding these criticisms, there are persuasive arguments to suggest that companies cannot ignore the customer when designing supply chains. We can see a joining together of the demand and supply processes. We now consider the different types of supply chains.

In the context of retailing, effective supply chain management is becoming even more critical due to the emergence of multi channels and omni-channel frameworks. In the latter case it is critical that inventory is available to shoppers no matter which channel they eventually frequent in order to complete the purchase. If there is an intermittent availability of stock across the channels, that is, an item may be available on the e-channel but unavailable in some of the physical stores, this is most likely to result in a dissatisfied and unhappy shopper.

It becomes a strategic imperative to ensure that the different retail channel members work in an integrated manner in order to deliver a consistent and seamless experience for the shopper.

3.6.1 Designing different supply chains for different segments

Gattorna (2006) argues that a 'one-size-fits-all' approach to supply chain design and implementation ignores a basic principle of marketing: customers have different needs and requirements which mean that markets need to be segmented to reflect the fact that different groups exist with different requirements. While segmentation is intrinsic to the marketing function, Gattorna puts forward the view that the information collected by marketing personnel is not necessarily fed back to the other business functions, particularly at the upstream end of the supply chain.

Gattorna (2006) notes that the four generic supply chain 'types' that he identifies may combine in different ways; for example, lean with agile, collaborative with agile and so on.

Continuous replenishment supply chain: this approach requires collaboration with suppliers to meet the requirements. It tends to be used in situations where the demand is relatively predictable and the overall focus is on the retention of customer relationships.

Lean supply: the focus here is on removing cost wherever possible. It works well in situations where the main evaluative criteria used by customers centres around cost and efficiency. There is less emphasis on service and the relationships tend to be relatively loose.

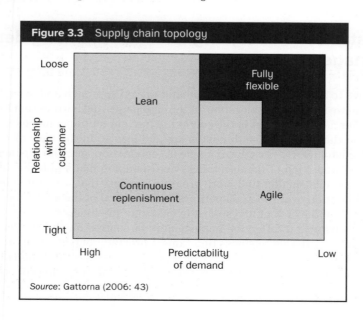

Figure 3.3   Supply chain topology

Source: Gattorna (2006: 43)

Agile supply chain: this approach is appropriate in situations where the demand is unpredictable and it is driven by customer pull (as opposed to supply push). The key word here is responsiveness: supply chains have to respond to unplanned or unanticipated demand. The cost of doing so will naturally be higher but customers are willing to pay. The focus is on speed and capacity.

Fully flexible supply chain: this is an extreme example of an agile supply chain approach. A minority of customers may expect this demanding level of service and are willing to pay for it – particularly in crisis situations where potential supply is threatened by some event; for example, a strike, a tsunami or earthquake. They will be prepared to pay a premium price for such a service.

The onus, therefore, is on having the capacity to implement multiple supply chain strategies in order to best address the needs of the customer base. It makes intuitive sense to accept that customer and market preferences and expectations are likely to differ and that segments can be identified, each having specific requirements.

Gattorna's framework introduces a number of key concepts that we need to consider. First, some supply chain strategies are based on close and collaborative relationships with other organizations in the supply chain. In order to be in a position to be able to replenish product and inventory, it is predicated on trust and collaboration between the parties involved. This covers areas such as transparency in terms of sharing information and having open access to production schedules.

The issue of collaboration is pertinent in the case of retailing. Chapter 4 outlines that the nature of the relationship between retailers and suppliers is one that is often characterized by collaboration and the need for joint programmes between them, particularly in the area of in-store promotions.

Second, the concept of agility enters into the equation in many situations. This approach is relevant in situations where there is a strategic imperative to get the product to market as quickly as possible. In the context of retailing, Zara provides a good illustration. It captures ideas for designs from fashion catwalks, movie premières and student campuses. It aims to get the idea into a design and ultimately into its stores within a period of three to four weeks. The ability to develop an agile supply chain is predicated on the use of IT to create real-time information that can be shared across the partners in the supply chain.

Third, we need to understand the concept of lean supply chains. In contrast to speed of response and flexibility, a lean supply chain implies a focus on costs and efficiencies. Ryanair provides a good example in this instance. Let us consider the Ryanair business model from the starting point where a customer seeks out flight information and attempts to book a ticket online to when the individual arrives at the point of destination (hotel or residence). Over the years, Ryanair has systematically addressed the issue of eliminating cost. This is exemplified in specific areas such as: the elimination of travel agents and middlemen through direct booking on the Internet, the elimination of formal check-in desks, self-printing of flight tickets, removal of covered bridges to gain access to the plane and so on. While it also seeks to identify areas for increased revenue generation, it has succeeded in reducing costs across its supply chain, particularly in terms of its negotiations with aircraft manufacturers, where it has developed a modern fleet at a very reasonable price.

This section has highlighted the importance of multiple supply chains. Due to the increasing complexity of the marketplace, a one-dimensional approach is unlikely to cater for the varying requirements and demands of customers.

3.7 Retail supply chains

The retail sector has been at the forefront of developments in terms of innovations in supply chain management over the last 30 years or so. Retailers have pioneered the use of IT such as electronic data interchange (EDI), product replenishment programmes and similar collaborative arrangements with suppliers (see Chapter 4 for a more detailed discussion on these matters).

We should not be surprised at the role that retailers have played in instigating improvements in this area. Large retailers in particular are characterized by multiple site locations (in terms of retail outlets), multiple distribution centres and a large and diverse supply base. In order to improve their competitiveness they have constantly sought improvements and efficiencies across the supply chain operations. In particular, they have focused on the strategic management of information, store and shelf space and the supply base. We examine both areas in greater detail in later chapters.

3.8 The shift in power

Perhaps the single biggest development in retailing over the last few decades has been the shift in power from manufacturers to retailers. In developed economies through to the 1960s, the power structure rested with large manufacturers such as Procter & Gamble, Coca-Cola and Unilever. They developed the products, invested large amounts of money in building and promoting the brand and controlling the price at which the product was sold.

However, the emergence of powerful retailers such as Wal-Mart, Carrefour and Tesco, combined with category killers such as IKEA, Toy 'R' Us and numerous other 'big box' operators, has led to a distinct shift in power. Authors such as Davies (2009), Srinivasan (2004) and Arnold (2002) have supported this view through their research into this topic.

Wheeler and Hirsh (1999) identify the main reasons for the shift in power and this is highlighted in Table 3.2.

As the scale of retailers grew, they were able to increase their demands on the supply base. This mainly took the form of price discounts and more focused levels of service. In some cases they demanded a specific payment for placing a supplier's products on their shelves. While this has been banned in many countries, large retailers can get around this problem by seeking bonuses or discounts. They argue that they provide access to a large percentage of the total market (in the UK, the top three food retailers hold about 70 per cent of the total food sales) and suppliers should pay for this privilege. They also 'encourage' certain categories of suppliers to manage the inventory issue by participating in initiatives known as 'vendor managed inventory' (VMI).

It is debatable whether retailers can leverage such power on the powerful brands; that is, those holding the number one position in terms of market share. If Tesco refused to stock Coca-Cola, a public outcry from brand-loyal customers would create problems. We examine the nature of the relationships between manufacturers and retailers in Chapter 4.

We should avoid making the mistake of interpreting this shift in power as one that has created only problems and difficulties for suppliers. Studies such as one carried out by Morrison and van Assendelft (2006) demonstrate that top performing retailers held one-third less inventory than those of the average performing retailers. While these benefits accrue mainly to the retailer, suppliers can also benefit

Table 3.2 Shifts in power

Traditional manufacturer ⟶ Retailer	
Sources of power	**Sources of channel power**
Good product	Purchase and selection service
Brand pull	After-sales service
Installed base	Convenience and variety
Broad product line	Private labels
Fragmented channel	Lower cost format
Consolidation of purchasing power	
Availability	

Source: Wheeler and Hirsh (1999: 9)

from participating in such programmes. Their own capabilities in the areas of inventory management are raised as are their abilities to forecast demand patterns and make use of relevant and sophisticated information technology.

3.9 Case in point: UNIQLO

Along with Zara and H&M, Uniqlo has been one of the pioneers of fashion retailing. This company was established by Tadashi Yanai in 1984 as the original outlet of Fast Retailing, and was originally founded by his father. Its main customers initially were junior and senior high school students who were attracted to the store by the extremely low prices, relative to competitors in the apparel sector.

Its early approach revolved around a marketing strategy that stressed the following: clothing must be promoted as (1) basic tone, meaning that the clothing design is not changed with the seasons, (2) casual clothing that people generally wear at home or on holidays, (3) clothing for all ages and (4) unisex. The advertising was based around inserts into the national newspapers in Japan. The strategy worked as people were attracted to its merchandise because of the low prices.

Japan in many ways is very traditional and tied to long-standing practices. This was no different in retailing. First, retailers had the right to send merchandise back to manufacturers on an unconditional basis. As a consequence there was no risk to the retailer in terms of overstock. Second, the manufacturers set the price for their products. Retailers were also unable to make decisions to reorder merchandise that was in high demand.

Uniqlo challenged these conventions by developing a business model known as a SPA model (Special store retailer of Private label Apparel). It was based on the approach used by Giordano, the Hong Kong clothing retailer, which was a subcontractor of The Limited, a major US apparel company. Uniqlo's main objective was to be able to set prices on products sold in its stores. The new model was based around the concept of an innovative manufacturing retailer that handled all procurement, logistics and merchandising functions and was no longer dependent on the traditional middlemen such as wholesalers and independent manufacturers.

Over the years this model has been continuously refined. In contrast to competitors such as Zara, it does not concentrate on chasing the latest fashion trends. Instead Uniqlo focuses on technology and invests in the long term of the business. Its product offerings focus on basic items such as fleece, slim down jackets, synthetic thermal underwear and denim. The company believes its customers care more about quality and value than about a quick response to changing styles. Rather than rushing to market, Uniqlo uses long development cycles in which it tests new materials and designs. Instead of operating on the basis of a transactional approach to its suppliers, it enters into long-term partnerships with material manufacturers. This is similar in many ways to the approach used by the automotive manufacturers.

These relationships are exemplified in terms of the way in which it sources material such as denim from the industry's top denim producer, Kaihara Corporation. Likewise it works closely with the synthetic fibre maker Toray Industries Inc. on new materials such as HEATTECH and Silky Dry.

Overall, it has around 70 partner factories, 90 per cent of which are located in China. As the company expanded it has also sourced production in neighbouring Asian countries. Its current aim is to source one-third of its production outside of China. This allows Uniqlo to offer customers reasonably priced garments with luxury materials such as cashmere, Suprima cotton, Merion wool and premium down.

The charismatic CEO, Tadashi Yanai, identifies styles within product categories that will not go quickly out of fashion, differentiates these styles and sets up a supply chain that delivers these styles to the consumer. Like the car manufacturers, Yanai also uses the concept of 'planned obsolescence'. In other words, he drives consumers to update their wardrobes based on changes in technology. These changes are determined by Uniqlo, rather than the company initiating change by responding to the latest fashion trends captured from the catwalks or film premières. He has set the retailer a target of $50 billion in revenue by 2020.

He has struggled in the UK when in the early 2000s the objective was to establish 50 stores in the first three years. It failed for a couple of reasons. First, it was a rushed strategy and failed to take account of the UK approach to management. The shop assistants were not adequately trained in customer service and second, the feasibility studies failed to pick up on obvious issues such as the different climate between the UK and Japan. This resulted in poor sales for merchandise such as polo shirts. Many of the shops were closed.

▶

◄ In 2005, he opened three flagship stores in New York. They failed to make much of an impression and Yanai felt that you have to have brand recognition before you can make an impression in such a market. He relaunched again in New York a year later with a 36 000 square-foot store in the trendy part of Manhattan. He followed this up with two more very large stores: a 64 000 square-foot store on 34th Street and an 89 000 square-foot store on Fifth Avenue.

Many commentators express the view that the business model employed by Uniqlo is reminiscent of Gap Inc. back in the 1990s. It has used sports personalities such as Novak Djokovic, the tennis player, to act as an ambassador for its products. It opened a massive store in San Francisco in late 2012 and runs its e-commerce platform entirely from the USA.

Source: Various

Questions

1 To what extent do you think the supply chain strategy used by Uniqlo is innovative?
2 Can this model be transferred successfully to other geographic regions?
3 How does the model stack up with that of retailers like Zara?

Vignette: IKEA's approach to global supply chain planning

IKEA is a Swedish household and furniture retailer with global operations spanning around 25 countries and over 250 stores. It also has 32 external franchisees in over 16 countries.

The stores are supplied through 31 distribution centres or directly from the 1350 suppliers that are located in over 30 countries. It operates on the premise of opening around 10–15 new stores on an annual basis.

The IKEA supply chain is mainly made-to-stock and only a few products are made to customer orders. It is heavily reliant on forecasts. The individual stores and regions have traditionally held a strong degree of power and freedom in terms of planning and replenishment requests. This has led to a fragmented supply chain planning approach with a lot of local optimization and manual intervention. Local stores have tended to over-order to compensate for the possibility of stock-outs or delays in supply of merchandise. This is symptomatic of disorganization, with different partners (stores, suppliers and distribution centres) tending to operate from different objectives.

The company realized that it had to do something to redress the problems caused by this approach to supply chain management.

Source: Adapted from Jonsson, P., Rudberg, M. and Holmberg, S. (2013) Global supply chain planning at IKEA. *Supply Chain Management: An International Journal.* 18(3): 337–350.

Question

1 How would you address the problems caused by the approach to supply chain planning at IKEA? Specifically, what initiatives would you consider introducing?

3.10 Collaboration in the retail supply chain

Collaboration is an ever-recurring theme in our discussion on supply chains in general and retail chains in particular. Without relevant and committed collaboration, it would be impossible to implement the initiatives that we highlighted earlier. In order for such collaborative initiatives to work, mutual benefits should be there for the parties involved.

Anbanandnam, Banwet and Shankar (2011) identify a series of steps for initiating and implementing such ventures. This was based on work carried out with apparel retailers and suppliers in the Indian market. The key issues to emerge from their work are:

1 *Top management commitment*: in order for any initiatives to work in the area of collaborative relationships, it is a requirement that top management from the parties involved commit time and resources to nurture and develop the initiatives; without this feature, it is unlikely that the developments will move much beyond the drawing board.

2 *Information sharing*: we have identified this element in earlier paragraphs and its importance is reinforced here. The requisite IT systems need to be requisitioned to act as an enabler for the data to be transformed into relevant, real-time information.

3 *Trust among supply chain partners*: running through all of the initiatives is the basic requirement of trust between the partners that are actively engaged in this process. If trust exists then it reduces the potential for individual partners behaving opportunistically at the expense of others within the supply chain. This is perhaps the most difficult aspect of collaborative-building as in practice selfish behaviour is common in many situations.

4 *Long-term relationships*: if collaboration is expected to last, then the parties involved need to commit to lasting relationships. This may not be necessary for certain supply chain strategies (as discussed earlier in this chapter) but for strategies that focus on responsiveness then long-term relationships are essential.

5 *Risk and reward sharing*: this reinforces the message about 'win-win' situations. If collaboration is to work, then there is an expectation that improvements and benefits will accrue to all parties. Of course, this ignores the reality that in many cases there is a power-dependency position where one party is vulnerable to another and may be forced to comply with requests and requirements that do not necessarily benefit it.

In summary, a number of priorities can be identified that act as drivers for collaborative initiatives such as those indicated in the preceding paragraphs. A survey by Randall et al. (2011) of over 200 supply chain managers and leaders from retail, manufacturing, logistics, transportation, consulting and information service providers identified the following factors as key drivers of competitive advantage. They are identified in Table 3.3. Future issues are pinpointed in Table 3.4.

Table 3.3   Retail supply chain management drivers of competitive advantage

Issue	Percentage of respondents
Responsive operations to meet changing requirements	49.2
Coordinated product flows all the way to the store	34.9
Precise supply chain cost knowledge and control	6.4
Enhanced visibility across the supply chain	4.8
Rigorous inventory management and rationalisation	4.8

Table 3.4   Future issues

Issue	Percentage of respondents
Emphasis on sustainability and related costs	30.7
Rising oil prices and their impact on network design	30.7
Government regulation and compliance costs	17.7
International carrier's financial health and loss of capacity	14.5
Domestic carrier's financial health and loss of capacity	6.5

Table 3.3 highlights the importance of responsiveness and coordination as potentially the key differentiators in identifying those organizations that are at the forefront of innovation in the retail sector.

Table 3.4 unambiguously identifies the issue of sustainability as a key issue in the next decade. We will examine this theme in greater detail in Chapter 11. The ongoing world recession (2008–present) is reflected in the respondents' concerns about costs and viability of international and domestic carriers. This is not surprising given the rising costs in areas such as fuel.

3.11 Conclusions

In this chapter we identified the role and function of retailers within the context of the overall supply chain. Retailers resell merchandise that is supplied to them by manufacturers and suppliers. However, this would be a very narrow and limited view of the retailer's contribution to creating, managing and delivering value to the shopper. Retailers, for instance, play a critical role in developing a selling environment that appeals to the shopper and encourages them to revisit the store on a regular basis. Retailers have to be responsive to the ways in which consumers wish to engage with the shopping process. This may be through visits to physical stores or outlets or via online and virtual channels. In certain retail situations shoppers demand 'high-touch' (high levels of personal interaction); in other cases, 'low-touch' retail channels can address consumer needs. We look at the role of the marketer in engaging the customer in the following chapters.

We examined the different retail formats adopted by retailers and how retailing has evolved over the last decades. The changes in format are driven by changing market conditions and the need to develop differentiating factors that can give a retailer a potential competitive advantage. The biggest single change in format in recent years has been the emergence of online retail channels that now provide a real alternative to the traditional 'bricks and mortar' channels.

We assessed the concept of the supply chain and the changing role of the retailer. Supply chain management refers to all of the various parties involved in the creation, management and delivery of value to the end user. It covers the broad spectrum from the supplier's suppliers (upstream) to the internal operations of the organization and then on to the external (downstream) partners such as retailers, distributors and other forms of middlemen or intermediaries and finally to the end user.

We examined the close interaction between the marketing function and the overall management of the supply chain. Instead of adopting the traditional view of pushing product and material through the supply chain, the leading-edge companies are beginning with the demand patterns and requirements from the end user and using this information as the basis for designing supply chain strategies. The term 'demand chain' is a more accurate portrayal than the term 'supply chain'.

We assessed the shift in power from the manufacturers to the retailer. While this is the main subject of our next chapter, we established that there are positive and negative consequences for the various parties in the supply chain. The retailer can negotiate very favourable terms in terms of discounts and bonuses from suppliers. This may be perceived as using the power position in an aggressive and coercive manner. However, suppliers can benefit from participating in a number of collaborative initiatives through gaining expertise in inventory and quality management and increasing their capabilities in the area of IT.

Chapter outcomes

- Retailers do more than simply resell merchandise; they add value by creating and managing attractive selling environments, both in a physical and virtual sense.

- We cannot assess retailers in isolation: they operate within the wider context of the supply chain and are dependent to a greater or lesser extent on the performance of the various parties that operate within the specific supply chain.

- Within the supply chain, we are seeing leading-edge retailers operating a demand chain philosophy as opposed to the traditional, supply-push approach.
- Large retailers increasingly are able to gain benefits from the scale of their operations.
- This is exemplified through the way in which they negotiate special discounts and bonuses from suppliers.
- Power can be used through a mixture of coercive, aggressive tactics and a consensual approach with the supply base.
- Effective supply chains operate on the basis of collaboration and co-ordination in an attempt to derive mutual benefits for all parties.
- In the future, issues such as sustainability will take on greater significance in managing retail supply chains.

Discussion questions

1 Assess the view that marketing plays a critical role in shaping and managing retail supply chains.
2 Examine the extent to which you would agree with the view that a retailer is only as strong as its weakest link in the supply chain.
3 Some commentators argue that supply chain management and marketing management are increasingly overlapping. How accurate is this perception? Use examples to support your point of view.
4 The key to successful retail supply chain management is to drive costs out of the operations. How accurate is this view?
5 Identify areas within the retail sector where it is essential to design and implement an agile supply chain.
6 Collaboration is seen as an essential ingredient of responsive retail supply chain management. What are the obstacles to operating this approach? Use examples to support your line of argument.
7 How would you respond to a supplier that feels that it has nothing to gain from entering into a long-term relationship with a retailer where it is asked specifically to manage the inventory function?

References

Anbanandam, R., Banwet, D.K. and Shankar, R. (2011) Evaluation of supply chain collaboration: a case of apparel retail industry in India. *International Journal of Productivity and Performance Management.* 60(2): 82–98.

Arnold, S.J. (2002) Lessons learned from the world's best retailers. *International Journal of Retail & Distribution Management.* 30(11/12): 562–570.

Christopher, M. (1992) *Logistics: The Strategic Issues.* London: Chapman & Hall.

Christopher, M. (1998) *Logistics and Supply Chain Management.* London: Financial Times/Prentice Hall.

Cooper, M.C., Lambert, D.M. and Pugh, J.D. (1997) Supply chain management: more than a new name for logistics. *The International Journal of Logistics Management.* 8(1): 1–14.

Davies, M. (2009) Identifying the real challenges. *Logistics Management.* 7(1): 5.

Gattorna, J. (2006) *Living Supply Chains: How to Mobilise the Enterprise Around Delivering What your Customers Want.* London: FT/Prentice Hall.

Hagel, J. and Singer, M. (1999) Unbundling the corporation. *Harvard Business Review.* March/April.

Hines, T. (2013) *Supply Chain Strategies: Demand Driven and Customer Focused,* 2nd edn. Abingdon: Routledge.

Jacobs, D. (2006) The promise of demand chain management in fashion. *Journal of Fashion Marketing and Management.* 10(1): 84–96.

Lambert, D.M. and Cooper, M.C. (2000) Issues in supply chain management. *Industrial Marketing Management.* 29: 65–83.

Langabeer, J. and Rose, J. (2001) *Creating Demand Driven Supply Chains.* Oxford: Chandos Publishing.

Morrison, G.P. and van Assendelft, A. (2006) Charting a new course: the retail merchandising supply network. *Supply Chain Management Review.* 10(8): 54–60.

Randall, W.S., Gibson, B.J., Defee, C.C. and Williams, B. (2011) Retail supply chain management: key priorities and practices. *The International Journal of Logistics Management.* 22(3): 390–402.

Srinivasan, M.M. (2004) *Streamlined: 14 Principles for Building and Managing the Lean Supply Chain.* Mason, OH: Thomson Business and Professional Publishing.

Walters, D. and Rainbird, M. (2004) The demand chain as an integral component of the value chain. *The Journal of Consumer Marketing.* 21(7): 465–475.

Wheeler, S. and Hirsh, E. (1999) *Channel Champions: How Leading Companies Build New Strategies to Serve Customers.* San Francisco, LA: Booz-Allen and Hamilton, Jossey-Bass Publishers.

Chapter 4

Managing retailer–supplier relationships within the supply chain

✓ Learning objectives

On completion of this chapter you should be in a position to achieve the following objectives:

- ✓ Understand the key factors that shape and influence the relationship between suppliers and retailers.
- ✓ Gain an insight into the concept of power and the issue of power dependency.
- ✓ Identify the criteria used by retailers to select potential suppliers.
- ✓ Examine the mechanism used by retailers to monitor supplier performance.
- ✓ Evaluate the role of co-operation and collaboration in the relationship between suppliers and retailers.
- ✓ Assess the implications for the shopper.

4.1 Introduction

This chapter examines the relationships and the managerial challenges between two of the key stakeholders in the retail supply chain: the retailer and the supplier base. Such relationships are characterized by a range of characteristics ranging across power, conflict, co-operation, collaboration, coercion and manipulation. In many cases there is a disparity between what is publicly promoted: collaboration and co-operation, and what happens in practice: the use of power to apply pressure by one stakeholder on another.

We examine the recent trends and developments in the management of retailer–supplier relationships. We also assess the concept of power and its influence on the relationship. We consider the ways in which retailers source their merchandise and the factors that influence global versus local sourcing. We assess how retailers and suppliers by using collaborative approaches can establish efficiencies and cost reductions. We also examine the relationship from the perspective of shoppers. Do they derive benefits from the way in which the retailer manages supplier relationships? Do they get more choice in terms of products and better price deals?

4.2 Trends and developments in stakeholder relationships

Much of the research in the area of relationship management in a business-to-business (B2B) context has emphasized the need for a shift from transactional and adversarial relationships to ones that are characterized by collaboration and co-operation between the key stakeholders in the supply chain (Hansen, 2009). Authors such as Berry (1983), Gummesson (1999) and Webster (1992) put forward the view that the benefits of stakeholders in the relationship working closely together to achieve objectives that are mutually beneficial far outweigh the benefits that may accrue from the traditional 'arm's-length' nature of transactional relationships. Such collaborative relations are grounded in the partners taking a long-term view of their business dealings, engaging in highly interactive activities; for example, joint cost-reduction programmes, joint quality management initiatives and collaborating on product development.

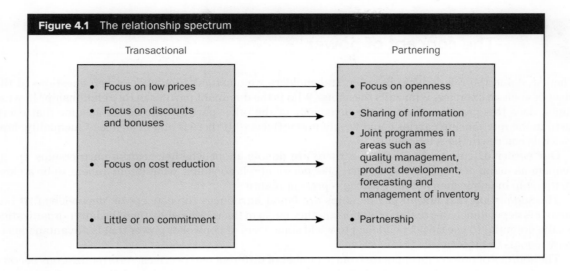

Figure 4.1 The relationship spectrum

Transactional

- Focus on low prices
- Focus on discounts and bonuses
- Focus on cost reduction
- Little or no commitment

Partnering

- Focus on openness
- Sharing of information
- Joint programmes in areas such as quality management, product development, forecasting and management of inventory
- Partnership

It can be argued that this focus on relationship management has crossed virtually all aspects of marketing management and is evidenced by the plethora of research and publications on customer relationship management, relationship marketing and so on.

It has also been aided by developments in information technology (IT). This has allowed stakeholders in the supply chain to share relevant information with each other and in theory provide the platform for more accurate and effective forecasting, management of inventory and store replenishment programmes. In the latter case, leading retailers ask some categories of suppliers to manage the process of restocking merchandise on their shelves. Such practices reinforce the concept of integrated value chains that we discussed in Chapter 3. Leading-edge companies at the forefront of supply chain management are ardent practitioners of such openness in their relationships and it can be argued that without such levels of trust and co-operation, such value chains would not achieve their objectives.

Sako (1992) argues that a shift to this collaborative approach that involves commitment – often in the form of a contractual relationship – requires a major alteration in mind-set.

The key driver in this form of relationship is mutuality; that is, the expectation that by engaging in such close relationships both parties will gain from the experience in the form of improvements in areas such as general competitiveness, profitability and increased sales. In theory, partners can focus on their areas of competence by jointly addressing key managerial issues to achieve common objectives.

However, Hingley (2005) points to a number of researchers who challenge the view that companies in general and marketers in particular have fully embraced the basic premises of relationship management. Welsh and Zolkiewski (2004) point to a 'darker side' in such relationships. They argue that there are potential negative consequences associated with such close relationships. Instead of blithely assuming that trust and co-operation are a natural outcome, some organizations will be driven by self-interest and will behave in an opportunistic manner if they can derive individual benefit from a particular activity. Instead of mutual interest being the guiding light, organizations are focusing instead on self-preservation and will engage in all manner of activities to achieve this goal.

Palmer (2000) introduces the word 'selfishness' into the discussion on this issue. He notes that many organizations reinforce their position in the relationship, particularly if they are in a more advantageous position than their 'partner' and can wield their power to put pressure on the other party to act and behave in a manner that meets their respective agendas. We should, therefore, consider terms such as 'mistrust', 'suspicion', 'greed', 'selfishness' and 'self-interest' when examining the nature and scope of relationships in general. We explore these contrasting positions within the context of the retail sector in this chapter.

4.3   The concept of power

When studying the relationship between stakeholders we must ask a number of key questions at the onset of such an exercise. Who calls the shots? Who is the dominant partner in the relationship? In what way(s) does this partner influence the behaviour of the other parties? Should we assume that every party in the relationship carries equal weight and influence? If there is any evidence of inequality, how does this emerge in the relationship?

Our earlier discussion suggests that there are doubts about whether healthy partnerships are as frequent as many commentators suggest. Like personal relationships, what might appear to be a close partnership in public may not necessarily represent reality.

The suggestion that not all partnerships are equal introduces the concept of 'dependency'. If one partner is dependent to a greater extent on another party in the relationship, then the latter organization has the potential to use this dependency to wield some form of control or power that is advantageous to its own goals or objectives.

The sources of power can emanate from a number of different perspectives. As organizations become larger, they gain economies of scale that allows them to demand better deals and discounts from suppliers. Market share also increases and allows them to hold a dominant position in their respective market sectors.

Power can also emerge from some original product development or proprietary design that allows an organization to rise to the top and consequently leave it in a position where it can exert pressure on other stakeholders in the supply chain.

Information can also lead to a power position. With the adoption of IT in general and database software, companies, by dint of the information that they capture, can leverage pressure on other parties to comply with their requirements.

Power can also exist because of an organization's reputation or historical influence in the market. For years Guinness, the brewery company (now part of the Diageo group), wielded power based on its dominant and historical position in the beer market and was in a position to put pressure on pubs to fall in line with their strategy.

Power can be used in an aggressive and coercive manner. This is often evidenced in one party putting pressure on a supplier to introduce a cost reduction programme, carry certain products in its portfolio, accept reduced margins, increase customer service levels and so on. If the party does not fall in line with such demands, contracts are cancelled and the other party will select another supplier. This is referred to as a 'win–lose' situation where only one party gains benefits and the other has to make sacrifices if it wishes to continue in the relationship.

Power can also be wielded in a more subtle way. One party can provide incentives so that the other party adheres to their requests. This may take the form of a long-term contract (ensuring some form of consistency or stability for the other party), or larger and more lucrative contracts. It can also be argued that such an incentivized approach can lead to longer-term benefits for the other party. This could result in greater efficiencies in production and logistics or a stronger knowledge base with regard to quality management. This is often described in the literature as a 'win–win' situation where there are no losers and each party derives some benefits from the relationship.

4.4   Power in the context of the retail sector

We now turn to an examination of how the concept of power works within the retail sector. Amato and Amato (2009) state that in an examination of the US retail sector, the 'emergence of mega-retailers such as Wal-Mart, Toys 'R' Us, Home Depot, Walgreen Drugs, Office Depot and Best Buy signals a likely shift in channel power in some markets from manufacturers to large retailers'. They cite research by Oliver and Farris (1989), Blattberg and Neslin (1990) and Burt and Sparks (2003) in support of this view.

In many developed economies, we have witnessed a greater concentration of power resting in the hands of a small number of very large retailers. As far back as 1999 Dobson and Waterson highlight the growing importance of retailers in the USA and Europe. They noted that the fourth largest company in the world was the US retailer Wal-Mart. In the context of the UK, two supermarket chains rank in that country's top 10 companies (Tesco and Sainsbury's). In Belgium the largest company is a retailer, the Colruyt Group. In virtually all of Europe, there is still strong evidence of retail concentration across all of the major retail markets (Nicholson and Young, 2012). Table 4.1 highlights this concentration of power in the food sector in Europe, Australia and the USA.

The concentration market share among so few retailers indicates the extent of the bargaining power that resides with them in respect of their dealings with the supply base.

Dapiran and Hogarth-Scott (2003) consider the issues of retail concentration and supplier dependency as two critical variables and develop a model that is addressed in Fig. 4.2.

This suggests that when retail concentration is high and there is low retail dependence on the supplier, retailers are more likely to employ coercive methods to drive through their strategy. When both variables are high, retailers are more likely to use expert power, often through initiatives such as category management. Such an approach can encourage trust and co-operation. Aggressive use of coercive power can lead in the worst case scenario to a total breakdown in relationships.

Table 4.1 The concentration of national food market shares

Country	Year	Number of supermarkets	Combined food market shares
Australia	2011	2	71%
Austria	2009	3	82%
Belgium	2011	5	71%
Canada	2011	5	75%
Denmark	2009	5	80%
Finland	2011	3	88%
France	2009	5	65%
Germany	2011	4	85%
Greece	2009	5	50%
Italy	2009	5	40%
Netherlands	2010	5	65%
Norway	2011	3	81%
Portugal	2011	3	90%
Spain	2009	5	70%
Switzerland	2011	4	76%
U.K.	2011	4	76%
U.S.A.	2006	4	35%

Source: Nicholson and Young (2012: 2)

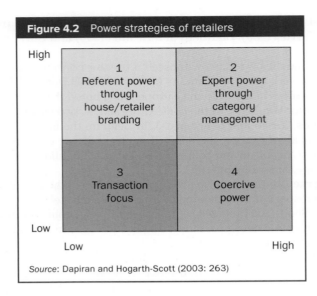

Figure 4.2 Power strategies of retailers

Source: Dapiran and Hogarth-Scott (2003: 263)

Radaev (2013) conducted research in the context of two areas within the retail sector in Russia (grocery and home electronic appliances) and identified a number of areas where retailers use their market power in negotiations with suppliers. These are summarized as follows:

Pricing requirements

- Price discounts that allow a retailer to offer the lowest price of a commodity in the region while maintaining a standard gross margin
- Guarantees of the best minimal price at the market
- No increase in price until the agreed-upon date
- Delays in payments for delivered commodities for more than 40 days after the date of invoice

Slotting allowances

- Payments for access to chain stores
- Payments for the enlargement and change of the product assortment
- Payments for obtaining additional shelf space
- Payments for an increase in sales (retro bonuses)

Unpaid services to retailers and penalties

- Additional discount during promotion campaigns
- Penalties for breaking delivery schedules, mistakes in documentation and distortion of transportation and storage standards
- Providing complementary samples of new products
- Providing quarterly promotion plans and fixing promotion budgets
- Penalties for observing a product's shelf life

Compensation for retailer's services

- Payments for advertising commodities in retailer's media
- Payments for advertising commodities in the mass media

■ Payments for replacing commodities with a low level of sales
■ Payments for losses from shoplifting

This study was carried out in one specific country and, therefore, may display certain characteristics and behaviours that might not be representative of other economies. It is also possible that responses from suppliers to surveys may use it as an opportunity to play the 'victim' on such demands that are placed on them by retailers but in reality may be satisfied to accept a request for slotting fees in order to guarantee contracts and sustain their business.

4.5 Case in point: Recession pits retailers against suppliers

The relationship between retailers and suppliers has always been a heated issue, including retail giant Wal-Mart's massive clout to press suppliers for continued lower costs and stores' growing push for their own store brands, analysts said. For those that supply to department stores, the steep discounts that stores such as Saks Inc. gave during the holiday season to spur demand were for a big part a burden to be shouldered by their suppliers in the form of what is called markdown support, they said.

'In this downturn a lot of suppliers got pressed pretty hard by the retailers to cut prices more than the suppliers thought would happen,' said David Abella, who helps manage about $2.4 million in assets at Rochdale Investment Management, which owns retail stocks from Wal-Mart to Target Corp. without any exposure to apparel suppliers. 'With some of the fierce competition, they really leaned hard on the suppliers to bear the brunt of it.'

The apparel industry has been among the worst hit in this downturn because of its discretionary nature. Industry-wide apparel sales in the first half of the year declined 7 per cent, the research firm NPD Group said Wednesday.

Suppliers such as Polo Ralph Lauren Corp. have been able to fare slightly better in the relationships between retailers and vendors not only because its brand is more resilient but also because it has been able to offer a wider assortment such as full home furnishing lines in its stores that shoppers would be able to find by going to a department store, Abella said.

Liz Claiborne also has been opening more of its own stores and is adding more products such as jewellery in its stores such as Juicy Couture.

The parties also have been signing more exclusive deals. A rival of Liz Claiborne, Jones Apparel Group Inc., for instance, has unveiled exclusive l.e.i. line of clothing for teens at Wal-Mart and Rachel Rachel Roy at Macy's. Liz Claiborne's exclusive tie-ups include Liz & Coat at J.J. Penney Co.

'It'll always be somewhat of an issue' between retailers and suppliers, Abella said. 'Suppliers are in a tough spot. I'm not too optimistic.'

Source: Recession pits retailers against suppliers: Downturn prompts suppliers such as Liz Claiborne to rethink relationships. *MarketWatch*. 12 August 2009

Question

1 Is the message from this example suggesting that the only option for suppliers is to open their own retail stores in competition with existing retailers?

4.6 How valid is the view that a shift in power has taken place?

The evidence from the retail trade and the academic research undertaken in this area provide some contrasting views and opinions.

Kadiyali, Chintagunta and Vilcassim (2000) investigated two specific product categories, refrigerated juice and tuna, and found that retailers generated more profit from total channel sales than the manufacturers.

Research by Bloom and Perry (2001) showed that for small suppliers in a relationship with Wal-Mart, their financial performance suffered. However, in the case of larger suppliers they found evidence to suggest that they may benefit from being involved. These benefits could include the ability to restrict a supplier's competitor from gaining access to shelf space or heighten recognition of their brand as it appears across the various Wal-Mart stores. They concluded by noting that 'our results show that it is not possible to identify the impact of Wal-Mart upon supplier profits unambiguously' (Bloom and Perry, 2001: 391). This would appear to at least challenge the commonly held view by many commentators that Wal-Mart unequivocally damages suppliers.

Mottner and Smith (2008) undertook a study with suppliers to Wal-Mart and their initial results suggested that these suppliers have lower margins than non-Wal-Mart suppliers. They are unclear whether this is as a result of Wal-Mart negotiating lower margins from them or if it is a result of a strategic decision to be a low-cost provider of merchandise to that retailer. They further observe that 'the relationship between Wal-Mart and suppliers is not one of dependency but rather one of partnering such that Wal-Mart provides a strategically aligned selling venue for manufacturers of low-cost goods' (Mottner and Smith, 2008: 539).

More recent research by Huang et al. (2012) examined one supplier's involvement with Wal-Mart across thousands of retail stores and hundreds of products for a period of five years. Their findings identify three managerial implications:

1 The study shows that selling to Wal-Mart can boost a supplier's bottom line in addition to other benefits such as improved distribution processes and inventory management systems.

2 While the supplier benefits from the additional volume that Wal-Mart generates, performance is best when post-entry shipments to incumbents (existing retailers) increase or remain unchanged. While Wal-Mart can beat incumbents on price, they can only do so on items that everyone sells. Wal-Mart cannot beat them if it does not sell those items stocked by the incumbents.

3 To enhance an incumbent's assortment options, manufacturers should maintain product lines. The danger is that suppliers gear most of their marketing resources to serve the retailer and Wal-Mart is the primary retailer. This can create a 'lose-lose' situation because the retailers' only option is to carry the same merchandise as Wal-Mart. Suppliers need to study shoppers' preferences and also cater for other retailers beside Wal-Mart.

This research is by no means conclusive but probably represents the most detailed and complete study of the relationship between a large retailer such as Wal-Mart and one supplier. The biggest problem in this area of research, however, is gaining proper access to the key personnel and data to allow for meaningful analysis.

4.7 Retailer–supplier relationships: an Asian perspective

Much of the research on this topic has emanated from a North American perspective. We need to consider work that has been carried out in other geographic regions. Chung, Sternquist and Chen (2006) point to previous work by Sternquist (1998) that characterizes Japanese culture as one that endorses loyalty, harmony and a long-term focus on the business relationship. In the latter case the focus is on a long-term view of the various stakeholders in the supply chain and not on any one specific dyadic relationship.

The findings from Chung et al. (2006) strongly identify the importance of this long-term perspective. Once a relationship is established (which may take some time) between a supplier and a retailer, trustworthiness is seen as an obligation towards partners in equation. If suppliers are seen to infringe, then retailers employ social sanctions and refuse to become involved again. This effectively ostracizes channel members that have broken their obligations.

The influence of culture is critical towards gaining an understanding of how relationships are established, develop and evolve over time. What may work well in a North American or western European environment may fail in an Asian culture. This is explored in greater detail in Chapter 12 on retail internationalization.

4.8 Retailer–supplier relationships: an industry perspective

Academic research on this topic has not provided any clear results on the implications that arise from the shift in power from suppliers to retailers. Certain retail sectors, most notably grocery/food retailing have featured prominently in the business and general press over the last decade or more. Many commentators are critical of the way in which powerful retailers such as Tesco, Carrefour and Wal-Mart have created major problems for a number of different suppliers. This is noticeable in the agri-business sector in the UK.

Duffy, Fearne and Hornibrook (2003) conducted research with a number of suppliers to the food retailers drawn from a number of key commodity sectors such as lamb, beef, pork, apples, potatoes, liquid milk and cheese. The findings were inconclusive mainly due to a number of the respondents being reluctant to engage in discussion on some topics for fear of reprisal, despite being assured of anonymity. The evidence from the research suggested that the retailers tended to use their power dependency position to drive initiatives, although some respondents felt that retailers were becoming more open and transparent in terms of explaining strategies and policies.

In a European context, there is evidence of regulatory bodies and governments becoming more proactive (Moore, 2008). The main focus of such initiatives has been targeted towards possible breaches of competition law in such areas as supplier pricing and collusion.

Retailers can put pressure on suppliers due to their ability to leverage their expertise in the industry. This may manifest itself through deep understanding of shopping patterns, purchasing habits and shopping behaviour with regard to special promotions. This in turn can translate into pressure being placed on suppliers to deliver on certain product categories that are identified as being strategic to the retailer. This identifies one of the potential negative outcomes for suppliers in such relationships.

The relationships between retailers and suppliers are not totally based on the expectation of punishment if the latter does not comply or fall in line with the agenda of the former. Retailers can grant a special status to a supplier who confers potential competitive benefits. This reflects one of the positive outcomes to emerge.

As stated earlier, suppliers can gain in terms of efficiencies and expertise as a consequence of being a part of a leading-edge supply chain. This can occur in areas such as logistics, customer service and quality management.

4.9 Impact on the shopper

Perhaps the key constituent member of the supply chain is the shopper. What then are the consequences for this party in light of the trends and developments in relationships between suppliers and retailers?

Retailers argue that they offer the consumer a wide range of product that offers great value for money. By addressing cost issues with suppliers and setting high demands and expectations, they are in a position to put together a value proposition that addresses the needs of the shopper. Slogans such as 'Every little helps', which was used by Tesco in one of its advertising campaigns, illustrates how the concept of getting better value can be communicated to shoppers. The issue of retail marketing communication strategy is examined in detail in Chapter 10.

Some suppliers in retail sectors such as grocery put forward the counter-argument that the unceasing pressure placed on them to reduce costs and pare margins right down to the bare minimum restricts their opportunity to grow their business and invest in new products and development. In the worst case scenario, it can lead to suppliers going out of business, creating higher levels of unemployment and as a consequence damaging the overall economy.

4.10 Case in point: Food fights

In the food sector, supplier relations have been a contentious point for more than a decade.

A plethora of food suppliers allege that late payment, retrospective charges for promotions and last-minute changes to terms remain commonplace in the grocery world. Suppliers complain such factors mean that they are unable to gain a sustainable margin or plan investment for the future.

Sainsbury's former chief executive Justin King long defended the retailer's position by pointing out that many of its suppliers, including Coca-Cola and Mars, are bigger than Sainsbury's and wield more power.

He told *Retail Week*: 'No supermarket can do the right thing for its customers without great relationships with suppliers. A lot of our suppliers are as big if not bigger than we are.'

And departing Tesco boss Richard Brasher, in one of his final speeches to Tesco suppliers, asked for their help and ideas to turn around the UK business.

Some suppliers believe big retailers of all sorts exert great power over suppliers, and late payment has been a key issue. The Forum for Private Business (FPB) pointed the finger at a number of retailers including Matalan, Alliance Boots, House of Fraser and Argos for late payment at the height of the credit crunch in 2008/9. The FPB claims suppliers are unwilling to come forward to report abuse in the supply chain.

An FPB spokesman says: 'If you squeeze the suppliers then they will go out of business and then the number of suppliers you can choose from reduces, ultimately impacting on customer choice.'

Vital support

But in many cases, retailer–supplier relationships are strong. A number of retailers ranging from pound stores to value fashion rely on good relations with suppliers that can offer large volumes quickly.

In some cases, as with George at Asda's acquisition of Turkish supplier GAAT's sourcing division this month, this can lead to the retailer buying up the business and working directly.

JJB Sports chief executive, Keith Jones, says the support of suppliers was critical in its fight for survival. Big brands such as Nike and Adidas backed the sportswear chain when it was at its lowest ebb, and continued to supply JJB even when it was revealed it was likely to breach its banking covenants last January. Adidas even provided the retailer with a £15 million loan so it can push ahead with its store revamp programme.

Source: Adapted from Lawson, A. (2012) Suppliers and retailers: the difference between partnership and confrontation. *Retail Week*. 18 May, pp. 1–6.

Question

1 In the case of JJB, identify the main benefits that accrue to the shopper as a result of this retailer's relationships with its main suppliers.

It can be argued that shoppers are now in a stronger position than ever as the Internet plays an ever-growing role in shopping behaviour. Shoppers are better informed about the options open to them in terms of price, quality and promotional offers. They can use a variety of channel options to make their final purchases. As a result, retailers have to be vigilant about transparency of their pricing and provide a portfolio of merchandise that is competitive.

In summary, the evidence from academic research and business commentary suggests that the shift in power from suppliers to retailers has undoubtedly occurred in the case of most of the retail sub-sectors.

Nobody can conclusively claim that the use of power by the dominant retailers automatically leads to negative consequences for suppliers. While small suppliers are more likely to experience pressure from retailers and in the worst case scenario, struggle to survive, others can derive benefits from becoming involved in a relationship with a powerful retailer; for example, improved efficiencies and capabilities.

For the shopper, there are also mixed experiences. While they may benefit from very competitive prices as a result of retailer–supplier relationships, it can be equally argued that the closure of a large number of small, independent retailers has restricted the degree of choice open to them. The reduction of traditional shop formats such as corner shops, butchers, specialist retailers and so on has led to a decline in choice as the large retailers increasingly redefine their business and move into retail areas that are far removed from their original retail format. This is exemplified by food retailers such as Wal-Mart, Carrefour and Tesco that now populate a range of retail sectors, from banking, pharmacy, clothing and electrical goods, as well as their original business, to food.

4.11 Retailer sourcing strategy

Retailers exist because their core function is to sell on merchandise to the end user. In order to be in a position to do so, they are required to compile a range of products that address the needs of their specific target market.

In this section we consider the options open to retailers when sourcing merchandise and look at the rationale for sourcing in a global context as opposed to relying on domestic suppliers.

Monczka and Trent (1991: 3) define global sourcing as '. . . the integration and coordination of procurement requirements across world-wide business units, looking at common items, processes, technologies and suppliers'.

The main driver for the move to global sourcing has been the 'cost imperative'. As organizations come under increasing competitive pressure to be more efficient in their overall operations, they seek opportunities to reduce cost across all areas of the supply chain. If lower cost alternatives can be identified, then they are likely to pursue such strategies. Sourcing and procurement is one such area. By sourcing globally, retailers can establish relationships with organizations that offer a low-cost alternative. Suppliers in certain regions, by dint of lower wages, can provide retailers with access to a wider range of merchandise that simply could not be produced at an equivalent cost in their own domestic economies. However, it would be inaccurate to focus simply on cost as the main imperative for a global sourcing strategy. Kusaba, Moser and Rodrigues (2011) point to research that suggests that such an approach allows companies to access a wider range of suppliers, higher quality products and new technologies.

In the context of retailing we need to consider recent developments in some sub-sectors such as fashion retailing. While the cost imperative still exists, retailers face the challenge of getting merchandise into stores as quickly as possible to match competition and satisfy the demands of shoppers.

Retailers such as Zara have changed the business model in this respect. Traditionally fashion retailers worked on the premise that there are 'four seasons' in the year and each season is 'announced' with the release of a range of merchandise that reflects the mood of summer, autumn, winter and spring.

Zara regularly changes its merchandise on a three to four weekly basis. They do this to create a sense of excitement among shoppers and provide an ever-changing degree of choice. They work on the principle that if shoppers see something that they like in the store when they make a visit, then they should buy it as it is unlikely to be there when they make their next trip to the Zara outlet. While this, on the face of it, challenges conventional marketing thinking (products should always be available to meet the demands of consumers), in fact it works in reverse. Shoppers become accustomed to this pattern and make more frequent visits to see the latest items on the shelves. It is estimated that 'Zara-loyal' shoppers make three times as many visits as shoppers of competitive stores such as Next and H&M.

While it might be fanciful to suggest that Zara creates 52 seasons in the year, this retailer has turned the conventional 'four seasons' model on its head, and this approach is now increasingly being adopted by its main competitors.

This example highlights the challenge facing retailers in the context of sourcing material for their stores. It is not just about the cost imperative any more. Retailers have to ensure a quick turnaround in terms of getting merchandise to their outlets in a quick and responsive manner.

Doyle, Moore and Morgan (2006) argue that for retailers in the fast fashion sector, a balance has to be achieved between the need to achieve lower cost operations and the need for maintaining customer responsiveness and also maintaining margins. The fast fashion sector by definition is based on the characteristics of a high degree of unpredictability with regard to demand (and the implications that this has for forecasting), very short product life cycles and an expectation on the part of shoppers of variety and choice in the merchandise presented at the stores.

In essence, retailers operating in this sector have to address the issue of rapid store replenishment. In such circumstances, it is not realistic to employ a sourcing policy that can take weeks or months for merchandise to get to individual stores. This seriously calls into question the efficacy of employing a global sourcing strategy where the lower costs associated with such a practice can be lost if retailers cannot meet the demand patterns and shopper expectations. In this case, it can be argued that retailers need to have their sources of supply in relatively close proximity to their core market. In the case of Zara for instance, they have a state-of-the-art logistics centre at their headquarters in Spain, with many of their suppliers close by or in neighbouring countries. While the costs of labour and production may be higher than in other parts of the world, Zara retains tighter control over its supply base and can employ rapid replenishment strategies with regard to its portfolio of stores in Europe. It typically can get inventory to stores in three to five days in this geographic region.

Cho and Kang (2001) identify a number of benefits and challenges associated with global sourcing strategies. These are summarized in Table 4.2.

The challenges involved in sourcing globally cannot be underestimated. Different cultures and behaviours can create problems for retailers used to dealing with domestic suppliers. We have previously looked at the Japanese approach to relationship-building. In that case a long-term view of the relationship can be difficult to comprehend for retailers who are used to quick decision-making.

Retailers who are used to sophisticated IT and telecommunications infrastructures can encounter problems in certain regions that cannot meet the level of expectations of retailers who are relying upon ease of transfer of information and communication.

Exchange rate fluctuations can seriously threaten predetermined cost estimations and in practice can create lower than anticipated savings from pursuing a global sourcing strategy. Such imperfections can lead to a fall in profitability based on prior assumptions about the performance of the currency in question.

A failure to understand customs procedures and documentation can lead to inordinate delays in expediting material from the supplier to the domestic market. This becomes a serious problem in situations where the retailer is operating in a 'rapid replenishment' scenario. Such delays can lead to stock-outs and dissatisfied shoppers who are likely to go to competitors.

Table 4.2 Benefits and challenges of global sourcing

Benefits	Challenges
Non-availability of products locally	Cultural, political and legal differences
Cost savings	Lack of technology
Access to higher quality product	Poor infrastructure (IT, communications)
Cost reduction (labour, facilities and infrastructure)	Customs procedures
Shortening of product development time	Exchange rate fluctuations
Satisfying counter-trade obligations	Instability (economic, political)

Source: Adapted from Cho and Kang (2001)

When considering the balance to be achieved between the benefits of global sourcing and the difficulties associated with such a strategy, we need to consider the following factors:

- the nature and structure of the market sector (degree of competition)
- the level of predictability of demand (low versus high)
- the lead times involved in shipping product to the local market and then on to distribution centres and/or individual outlets
- the nature of the product life cycles
- the degree of specialism of retailer (for example, grocery versus niche retailing)
- costs of labour, facilities and infrastructure in the domestic versus offshore markets
- importance of quality with regard to the merchandise
- availability of suitably qualified labour in domestic versus offshore regions.

The issue of exposure to risk is a constant theme running through this discussion.

Risk in the context of the global supply chain has been defined as '. . . the distribution of performance outcomes of interest expressed in terms of losses. Profitability, speed of event, speed of losses, the time for detection of the events and frequency' (Manuj and Mentzer, 2008).

Christopher et al. (2011) identify a risk classification system that looks at the following issues. These are outlined in Table 4.3.

Global sourcing policy inevitably leads to longer supply chains and creates an even more complex structure involving many partners. Peck and Juttner (2002) point to issues over which organizations have little control, such as natural disasters, strikes and political unrest.

In trying to mitigate these areas of risk, Christopher et al. (2011) propose the following model.

- *Network re-engineering*: companies need to consider criteria other than cost and customer service when (re)designing supply networks.
- *Collaboration between global sourcing parties*: closer working relationships within the supply network based on trust, transparency and co-operation are necessary.
- *Agility*: companies need to be in a position to respond quickly to unpredictable change in demand or supply. This agility is needed also in suppliers so that the overall supply chain can react in such a rapid fashion to mitigate risk.
- *Creating a global sourcing risk management culture*: developing a risk management culture in an organization can only happen if it is driven by senior management. This requires a focus and a vision that can create a business-wide awareness of the issues.

In summary, risk is a critical concern for organizations within the context of sourcing strategies that embrace the global dimension. As they grapple with the challenge of achieving a balance between cost considerations and responsiveness to the market demands, it is important that they have a formal set of

Table 4.3   Global sourcing risk classification

Global sourcing risks	Examples
Supply risk	Supplier disruptions, unreliable suppliers
Environmental and sustainability risk	Fluctuations in interest rates, quota restrictions Unanticipated resource requirements, high levels of CO_2, carbon footprint emissions during the global sourcing activity
Process and control risk	Inefficient supply teams in the organizations
Demand risk	Variations in demand, uncertainties in demand

Source: Adapted from Christopher *et al.* (2011)

procedures in place for evaluating the potential risks involved and a process for mitigating the problems that may arise.

Global sourcing achieved great heights of popularity among retailers in the 1980s, 1990s and the first decade of this century. The lure of low-cost labour and material on the face of it allowed them to become more efficient in terms of managing the cost base and protecting margins.

Platts and Song (2010: 329) show that in the context of sourcing product from China, 'on average, companies have to add about fifty per cent to the quoted price to get an indication of the total cost of outsourcing from China'. While this is subject to significant variation across different industry sectors, it highlights the dangers of assuming cost savings from global sourcing without proper and detailed assessment of the breakdown of the cost components. Cost savings can quickly turn into overruns and destroy preconceived budget calculations.

The advent of quick response in general and 'fast fashion' in particular has encouraged retailers to rethink their approach to sourcing and instead consider the benefits that can accrue from adopting a more localized approach. While certain aspects such as cost may increase, improvements in areas such as risk, unreliability, delivery and quality issues can be achieved. This can lead to a more balanced approach to sourcing and a more effective and responsive supply chain.

4.12 Selecting and evaluating suppliers

We have discussed the issues and challenges involved in local versus global sourcing. We now consider the rationale used by retailers in selecting suppliers and the criteria that they use in this process.

Before we look at the specific criteria, we begin by assessing the nature of the different relationships between retailers and their supply base. Relationship management theory suggests that there is no such thing as a 'one-size-fits-all' approach to dealing with suppliers. It is not financially viable or necessary to have a close, intimate relationship with each supplier. In some cases, it will be critical for retailers to work closely with certain suppliers. This will happen where there is an expectation that the supplier will play a role in product design or where the particular merchandise in question plays a critical role in the overall product portfolio of the retailer's value proposition.

In other cases, where cost is the driver, retailers are more likely to adopt a transactional (arm's length/adversarial) approach. In this case, they will use a range of suppliers over a period of time that can meet their cost requirements. As a result there is no loyalty or attachment established with any one specific supplier.

In retail sectors where high levels of responsiveness are critical, retailers may establish long-term relationships with certain suppliers that have the core competences and capabilities to meet such demands. Such relationships are critical if suppliers are to meet the requirements of flexibility in the context of the product mix and volume and the ability to meet a diverse range of delivery requirements and expectations.

Kausik and Mahadevan (2012) highlight the growing importance of sustainability in the supply chain and the need for retailers to audit existing and potential suppliers carefully in the expectation that they are capable and compliant in this area. This will become even more critical in the coming years as governments and policymakers introduce more stringent legislation in the area of sustainability, social responsibility and the environment.

4.13 Criteria for selecting suppliers

When retailers select suppliers they utilize a number of criteria to assess potential suppliers and evaluate the performance of existing ones. A number of areas can be identified as detailed in Table 4.4.

Table 4.4 attempts to capture all of the key issues that retailers may take into account when selecting and reviewing the performance of suppliers.

Retailers will customize this list depending on the following considerations:

- the nature of the products they sell
- the nature of demand for these products (predictable versus unpredictable)
- the level of complexity in terms of manufacturing and logistics

Table 4.4 Criteria for selecting suppliers

Product-related issues:
- Production capacity
- Input to product design and development
- Innovation capabilities

Quality-related issues:
- Quality assurance programmes in place
- Continuous improvement programmes
- Modern processes and technologies
- Modern production facilities

Responsiveness-related issues:
- Ability to meet required lead times
- Flexibility in terms of meeting a diverse range of lead times
- Evidence of IT capabilities to meet forecasting and inventory requirements
- Capabilities in participating in initiatives such as ECR and inventory management programmes

Network-related issues:
- Evidence of working with other suppliers (1st, 2nd and 3rd tier categories)
- Level of experience of working with similar retailers
- Subcontracting capabilities
- Evidence of working in a full service or production-only scenario

Price and cost-related issues:
- Flexibility and adaptability
- Ability to conform to payment schedules set by the retailer
- Willingness to participate in cost-reduction programmes

Sustainability-related issues:
- Evidence of policies and procedures in areas such as social responsibility, the environment, treatment of the workforce, 'green' initiatives and energy conservation
- Willingness to comply with sustainability programmes and initiatives developed by the retailer

Management-related issues:
- Evidence of managerial capabilities that measure up to the expectations of the retailer
- Objectives and strategies that are compatible with those of the retailer
- Formal systems and procedures that are consistent with the expectations of the retailer

- the extent to which the sector is characterized by fast response
- the balance between cost, quality and service considerations
- the nature of the anticipated relationship with the individual supplier.

Vignette: Company B

Company B (its name is not revealed due to issue of confidentiality) is a leading department store for brands in the UK with a reputation for quality and with retail stores in all the major cities throughout the UK. The target market consists of top-end customers. A focus is placed on identifying exclusive niche brands.

For women's wear, the company buys in brands and also develops a number of brands in-house. Customers range from 'fashion lover' to 'traditional' with traditional customers' needs being met solely by concessions. Bought-in brands include Diesel and Miss Sixty through to Jerry Weber and MaxMara. Own brands are designed for the younger consumer; another line for career customers and a third category for classic customers.

The company works closely with suppliers when developing ranges. Information is generated from Worth Global Style Network, catwalk shows and information held by the designers themselves. Teamwork plays a key role, and buyers and designers meet on a weekly basis to share ideas. Suppliers provide up-to-date market and trend information.

Manufacturers work closely with suppliers in terms of either responding to ideas put forward by buyers or developing a collection for consideration by the buyers.

The retailer visits manufacturers (mostly based in Hong Kong) having sent them sketches earlier. Manufacturer samples are inspected and delivery phasing is worked out.

The company liaises directly with the manufacturers and has used the same supply base since the range was introduced five years earlier and has developed strong relationships. Often buyers and designers recommend suppliers on the basis of their experience in this sector.

To meet the demands of fast fashion consumers, the company is building relationships with 'up-and-coming' artists from areas including Spitalfields and Portobello markets in London in order to invest in a local supply base. This allows the company to introduce weekly changes to its collection.

From the perspective of one Hong Kong-based manufacturer, people are an important relationship factor. Communications can often be difficult, which is why they choose to deal directly with their clients. Relationships between organizations enable them to define the critical path and order confirmations together. Trust is important as suppliers intuitively know the company's product and quality requirements.

Source: Adapted from Bruce, M. and Daly, L. (2006) Buyer behaviour for fast fashion. *Journal of Fashion Marketing and Management*. 10(3): 327–328

Retailers can employ a range of evaluation approaches to the task of selecting new suppliers or evaluating performance of an existing one. These can be based on simple five-point rating scales (or similar scales) that can be weighted according to the perceived importance of the selected variable.

4.14   E-procurement in the context of retailer–supplier relationships

Many areas of the retail sector are characterized by low margins and an ever-increasing pressure to reduce costs and 'do more with less'. Since the 1990s electronic or online procurement has created both opportunities and challenges in terms of seeking such efficiencies.

Online purchasing systems evolved from the concept of electronic data interchange (EDI). This emerged in the 1980s and allowed companies to electronically communicate via computer both internally (across departments and in the case of retailers: store outlets and distribution points) and externally (with suppliers and other relevant organizations in the supply chain). The retail sector and the automobile sector were at the forefront in adopting this technology. It ran into significant problems however. First, different standards and protocols emerged that were only applicable in a particular sector or in the case of a particular manufacturer or retailer. For instance Ford developed its own bespoke systems for its supply base. If a supplier also had a contract with another automobile manufacturer it was likely to find a different set of protocols in existence. This added significantly to the cost of purchasing the necessary software and also added to the complexity of doing business with different customers via different software systems. It also led to situations that accentuated the dangers of one party being more dominant than another. For example, a powerful retailer would try to force its suppliers to participate in the EDI system thus running the considerable risk of abusing its dominant position and antagonizing individual suppliers that were faced with the costs of investing in the necessary technology.

By contrast, electronic procurement systems rely on the Internet and are not faced with the same level of restrictions and costs that were associated with EDI. Internet-based technologies also step outside of procurement and can be used to manage all aspects of the retail supply chain from logistics to store inventory replenishment, customer service management and transportation.

In the context of the retail sector retailers and suppliers operate in a B2B environment. Retailers are challenged with the task of seeking out appropriate suppliers that can meet the criteria set by them in terms of supplying merchandise. We examined the criteria for selecting and evaluating suppliers in the preceding section. Online or electronic procurement allows both parties to interact with each other and perform a number of essential functions within the nature of the relationship. Retailers can use such systems for ordering merchandise, replenishing inventory, forecasting, invoicing, payment and taking delivery of merchandise.

By using electronic means to carry out these tasks, significant benefits can accrue to the retailer. Effendi et al. (2013) identify the following areas. It creates greater market transparency by 'allowing buyers to discover new sources of supply, gauge product availability and obtain more accurate and lower market prices. It improves purchasing control by 'allowing inclusion of corporate purchasing policies (approval procedures and purchasing limits), lists of preferred suppliers, and volume purchasing agreements to be incorporated within the platform. Most companies have poor control over spending; they allocate total budget amounts but in fact have limited control over exactly what and when employees buy'.

It is expected to decrease administrative costs. Effendi et al. (2013: 60) state that:

> **"***the reduction of administrative costs derived mainly from a transfer of activities from corporate central procurement to the requisitioner as corporate policies can be incorporated into the system. As a consequence, companies save costs in central purchasing that helps to reduce processing cost for each requisition / purchase order. Reduction in administrative costs can also result from faster approvals and easier, asynchronous communication with suppliers.***"**

However, there are significant challenges to overcome as well. Perhaps the biggest challenge is to get 'buy-in' from suppliers. Although the costs of becoming involved in an online procurement system have decreased substantially since the heyday of EDI, suppliers need to be convinced that they too can benefit from participation. The use of real-time information for example can lead to more accurate forecasting on the part of the retailer and lead to efficiencies also for the supply base. Retailers and suppliers can also collaborate over specific promotional campaigns. Resistance to change is another consideration when establishing such an online system.

4.15 Areas of collaboration and co-ordination

Within the context of retailer–manufacturer relationships, we can identify a number of specific initiatives where the parties involved work closely together with potential benefits accruing to both parties. We consider some of the main developments in this section.

4.15.1 Efficient consumer response (ECR)

This concept has its genesis in research that was carried out in the 1990s between Wal-Mart and Procter & Gamble in the North American retail market. The findings showed that there were a number of clear deficiencies and inefficiencies in the supply chain, resulting in large inventory levels and clear evidence of a lack of co-ordination in the supply chain. More importantly, it became clear from the analysis that a broad range of savings could be generated: an important benefit in the context of a retail sector driven by the need to generate cost reductions.

Fernie (Fernie and Sparks, 2009) reflects on a number of similar initiatives undertaken by various interested parties in Europe in the mid to late 1990s.

Efficient consumer response (ECR) has been defined as 'a global movement in the grocery industry focusing on the total supply chain – suppliers, manufacturers, wholesalers and retailers, working closely together to fulfil the changing demands of the grocery consumer better, faster and at least cost' (Fiddis, 1997: 40).

The general focus of these studies was primarily on reducing cost in the supply chain and identifying areas where there was unnecessary duplication with the overall objective of becoming more efficient and effective across the supply chain.

Fernie (Fernie and Sparks, 2009) refers to work done by Coopers & Lybrand (1996) which puts forward a framework that identifies the main areas of focus for the research studies in this area. These are identified in Fig. 4.3.

Such ECR initiatives have focused in general on the following areas: the development of collaborative arrangements, joint business plans, shared sales forecasts and continuous replenishment from orders generated.

The studies carried out in this area, which were undertaken mainly in the 1990s, were before the developments with the arrival of the Internet. Since then, particularly in the last decade, we have seen the emergence of intranets and extranets that make it relatively easier for organizations in a supply

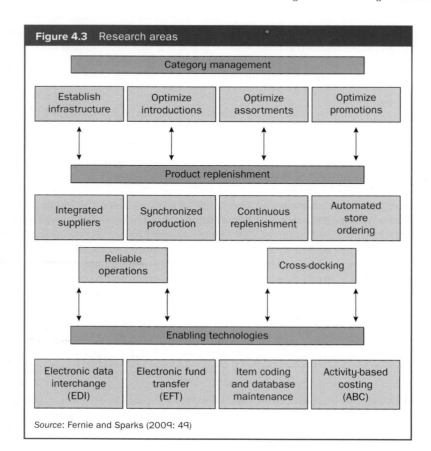

Figure 4.3 Research areas

Category management

| Establish infrastructure | Optimize introductions | Optimize assortments | Optimize promotions |

Product replenishment

| Integrated suppliers | Synchronized production | Continuous replenishment | Automated store ordering |

Reliable operations | Cross-docking

Enabling technologies

| Electronic data interchange (EDI) | Electronic fund transfer (EFT) | Item coding and database maintenance | Activity-based costing (ABC) |

Source: Fernie and Sparks (2009: 49)

chain to share information and communicate with each other in real time as opposed to relying on historical data. This arguably has improved efficiencies in supply chains and has certainly led to a more open and transparent approach.

We should inject a note of caution here and recognize that such studies by their nature are difficult to carry out (due in the main to the sensitive nature of the data and the consequent reluctance of organizations to become involved).

Corsten and Kumar (2005) carried out a study that in their view provides 'qualified' evidence to suggest that collaborative ventures benefit suppliers in their relationships with large retailers. As discussed in earlier sections of this chapter, much depends on the power-dependency position in the particular relationship. Corsten and Kumar speculate, however, that over time suppliers become dependent on the capabilities of smart retailers.

4.15.2 Category management

The nature of retailing, particularly in the food sector, is one of a large array of merchandise that appears on the shelves. The question arises: how do you manage such a large volume of product in an effective manner? The concept of category management is one option. Instead of trying to manage each individual item, this approach groups each brand into specific categories or strategic units.

Rashid and Matilla (2011: 64) define category management as 'the way of managing retail operations by classifying the assortment of the retailer into categories on the basis of consumer preference, not just on the basis of individual brands or items'. Both retailers and suppliers jointly develop and manage these category plans. This extends also to the buying and merchandising decisions where a category manager takes on this responsibility. The essence of category management is that it is a collaborative venture between manufacturers and retailers with the overall objective of satisfying the needs of the customer. It revolves around optimizing the role of the particular category (for example, body care products) over time across the areas of price, promotion, merchandising and shelving. From a strategic perspective, a retailer identifies the portfolio of categories within the retail format and category managers would be tasked with the responsibility of managing an individual category.

The process of category management is based on an understanding of industry trends allied to 'big data' management. In the latter case we refer to data on a broad range of issues such as shopping patterns, preference, reactions to special promotions and price reductions, and so on.

Gooner et al. (2011) identify two key aspects of category management. The first relates to category management intensity, which can range from a simple 'resupply' situation to a detailed category analysis, planning and execution. The second part relates to the lead supplier influence. This refers to the supplier who has the most influence on the retailer in that particular category. This latter relationship will vary: in some cases the retailer will initiate activities and manage the category through to the supplier playing a bigger role in this task.

Gooner et al.'s (2011) research shows that retailers engage in this activity in a diverse manner. In cases where the retailer does not have the resources to plan and implement a particular category area, they engage more fully with the retailer. Likewise, when they have the resources, they are less likely to increase the intensity of their category management efforts. They also indicate that there can be 'win-win' situations where retailers actively use effective suppliers to serve as category captains to manage the product categories that they are involved more intensively.

The role of the lead supplier can raise questions of whether that supplier, by virtue of its role as category captain, can leverage an unfair advantage over its competitors in that particular category due to its close relationship with a key retailer. They can influence what appears on the shelves of the retailer and potentially can restrict competitive activities.

Gooner et al. (2011) argue that the overall benefits that can accrue from such a collaborative activity tend to outweigh the negative aspects such as potential collusion and anti-competitive issues.

As retailers try to optimize their return on investment, category management provides them with an opportunity to manage their selling space strategically within the physical store in order to maximize the profit on each square foot or metre. By working closely with suppliers in each category and basing decisions on shopper-centred data, retailers can improve their competitive position. Suppliers can also benefit from greater returns on sales and overall performance.

4.15.3 Vendor-managed inventory (VMI)

Inventory represents one of the highest costs inputs in any supply chain. This is particularly the case in a retail context where excessive inventory, in an environment that in many cases has a limited shelf life, increases the costs further. Poor forecasting can result in retailers building in buffers in their order patterns to allow for the unpredictability in demand. While this might ensure that stock-outs of product may not happen, it places great pressure on the cost of holding such inventory. What if the projected demand for these products does not happen? If we consider the retail clothing sector, this may be a relatively common occurrence. This means that inventory is built up in the supply chain and will either have to be destroyed or sold off at knock-down prices, ensuring that margins will be reduced substantially.

An effective retail supply chain is one where there is little or no inventory resting in the supply chain. Ideally, both retailers and suppliers would prefer it if nothing was produced until an order was placed.

Vendor-managed inventory (VMI) programmes are one response to the challenge of reducing inventory in the supply chain. By entering into collaborative arrangements with key suppliers and making use of IT systems and sharing real-time information, retailers can manage inventory more effectively. In the case of VMI, retailers pass on the responsibility for managing inventory on the shelves of its stores to key suppliers.

One of the key challenges facing retailers is to maximize selling space within their store operations. Sophisticated software allows for detailed appraisal of the optimum returns per square metre of space. Such key performance indicators can be achieved if a more strategic approach with regard to inventory management is implemented.

By collaborating with suppliers and involving them intensively – to the extent of managing the inventory – it can be argued that benefits accrue to the retailer in terms of increased profits and to the supplier in terms of more accurate forecasting, allowing them to also benefit in greater production efficiencies. Kim and Park (2010) suggest that this initiative is also linked to the pricing strategy adopted by the retailer. Where the pricing strategy is flexible, it is less likely that there will be fluctuation in the inventory levels.

Critics of such initiatives as VMI take the view that it presents a convenient way for retailers to pass on the costs of inventory holding and replenishment to their suppliers.

4.15.4 Radio frequency identification (RFID)

Radio frequency identification (RFID) is essentially an extension of the barcode concept that has long been a feature of retailing. This technology creates 'intelligent' barcodes that can 'talk' to a networked system and track a specific product item, pallet or case as it moves from the point of manufacture to the time it ends up in a shopper's basket at the retail store. In its early stage of development it was originally used in the agricultural sector to track and identify cattle.

In the retail sector, one of the biggest challenges and costs revolves around managing inventory. As products move from suppliers to the retailer's distribution centres and then on to individual store outlets, items can be lost and disappear. Retailers also have to face the challenge of frequently and accurately replenishing inventory across their portfolio of stores. It is also time-consuming if inventory has to be visually checked. Radio frequency identification (RFID) creates a situation where such information can be captured via the tag on each item, therefore reducing the time factor.

Around 2004 Wal-Mart, the US food retailer, first introduced RFID. In the first two years it required its top 100 suppliers to use RFID. It then tried to extend it to all its suppliers. Results were mixed. Many suppliers were unhappy at having to incur the expense of using this system (O'Connor, 2014). In 2007, Wal-Mart changed its RFID strategy. It diluted its original objective of having the most sophisticated supply chain in the world. Given that most of its suppliers already had sophisticated IT systems in place, it was unrealistic to expect major improvements as a result of implementing RFID.

In the new era of omni channels, however, RFID is likely to play a critical role, particularly in terms of managing inventory and tracking items across different channels. If an item is available in a physical store but is not available on the online website, the net result is an unhappy shopper.

4.15.5 Price promotions and advertising campaigns

We examine this area in greater detail in Chapter 9. However, both retailers and suppliers seek out opportunities to maximize their respective return on sales. This is a central element in B2B marketing.

One such area is that of special promotional campaigns. These can involve existing brands or new product launches by suppliers. As a retailer increasingly captures more and more data about its shoppers, it is in a position to share this information with selected suppliers and develop targeted price promotions. The technology allows for detailed analysis; for example, the propensity of shoppers to respond to special offers, price cuts and so on. We should note here that we are referring to B2B marketing.

4.16 Case in point: The horse meat scandal

In early 2013, in the food sector, it was discovered that horse DNA was found in a range of ready meals and burgers sold by some retailers. This initially occurred in the Republic of Ireland where one supplier was suspected of putting horse meat into a range of its products and passing it off as beef. It quickly spread to the UK where a number of retailers such as Tesco, Iceland and Aldi, and fast-moving consumer goods suppliers also found traces of horse meat in their range of items.

As further investigations took place, it quickly became apparent that the practice of using horse meat in the supply chains was very prevalent across Europe. Serious questions were raised about the level of security and monitoring that existed in the supply chain.

For instance, Tesco had a plethora of controls in place to ensure the quality of its meat products, including regular audits and tests on the species of animal used, as well as approved subcontractor lists backed by the British Retail Consortium's accreditation. Tesco told the environment, food and rural affairs select committee (UK government) that it carried out 22,000 specific tests a year, covering 40 per cent of its products, for quality and adherence to strict product specifications. It had visited Silvercrest, part of the ABP group that produced burgers found to contain horse meat, three times in 2012 to audit the company's practices. Yet the supplier somehow slipped through the net, apparently buying meat from an unapproved Polish supplier for as long as a year. Tesco's technical director, Tim Smith, told the select committee: 'It was impossible to check the supplier in Poland as we didn't know it existed.'

Keeping the supply chain simple is a challenge. Dalton Philips, the chief executive of Morrisons, who avoided being implicated in the scandal, suggested that the supply chain had become 'far too complex'.

In the case of the supplier, Findus, its beef lasagne products were found to be made almost entirely of horse meat. In some of these cases the meat was reported to have come from a factory in Luxembourg belonging to the French food supplier, Comigel. It reached there from Spanghero, a food plant in France, which apparently bought horse meat from Romania, although this was challenged by the Romanian government.

In contrast, Morrisons has been largely insulated from the horse meat scandal because it sources the bulk of its own-label meat in the UK and processes it at its own network of abattoirs.

How feasible is it to monitor members of the supply chain? Tesco, for example, is promising to carry out regular DNA tests on its meat products. It estimates the new regime could cost between £1 million and £2 million a year with each test costing about £450. Other grocers might follow suit. Already, Iceland has said it will change its processes to include tests for horse meat; before, it stuck to testing for contamination by other meats that were processed in the same factory, which is a common practice.

Source: Adapted from: Butler, S. (2013) Analysis: horse meat scandal delivers supply chain lessons. *Retail Week*. 21 February

Questions

1 Assess the nature of the relationships between retailers and suppliers in this particular sector.
2 What in your view are the reasons for the emergence of this scandal?
3 How can such a problem be eliminated?

The practitioner view
Managing retailer–supplier relationships

Kevin McNally, National Account Manager with Procter & Gamble

Kevin McNally manages a number of products for Procter & Gamble, such as Pampers, and over the last few years has worked closely with the main grocery retailers in the UK.

We asked Kevin for his views on a number of issues relating to the relationship between retailers and suppliers in a highly competitive retail sector.

How would you describe the typical relationship between retailers and suppliers?

Kevin notes that the typical relationship, from P&G's perspective, can best be described as one of 'trying to build very collaborative long-term, win-win relationships. We are in it for the long term. It involves building a joint business plan that will drive sales and profitability in the long term.

'P&G's approach is one of building joint value: we are not in it for the quick buck. We want to work with retailers over 2–3-year planning cycles and have a vision of where we want to go with our businesses, together.'

Is this approach typical of other suppliers?

'For the bigger suppliers like P&G, I believe this is typical. For the smaller and less developed suppliers, it is likely to be more transactional, short-term. They might not have the resources to have a multi-functional team-based approach in terms of generating business insights, or having a dedicated finance analyst for that particular retailer.'

Kevin observes that a supplier of the size and scale of Procter & Gamble would have a dedicated team to develop the joint business plan with an individual retailer like Tesco and manage the day-to-day operations of the relationship.

'We would have around 40–50 personnel who would be 100 per cent dedicated to working on a particular retailer business across our brands. The extent of the team would depend on the volume and scale of business with that particular retailer and the categories we operate in with them. For smaller retailers (outside of the top four or five grocery retailers), there might be some crossover; one account manager looking after all categories. One salesperson might be responsible for six categories at any one time.'

We asked Kevin if conflict exists in the relationship as this is often identified as being a characteristic of retailer–supplier relationships.

Kevin, while obviously reluctant to go into too much detail, noted that when it does occur it tends to be because of 'the nature of the high pressured retail environment where significant pressure exists on all sides to hit key performance indicators (KPIs) in terms of profitability, sales or inventory targets. That breeds conflict, especially where the supplier's KPIs are not aligned to the retailers'. For example, if we are trying to drive sales where in fact the retailer is more about the balance between sales and profitability, that can cause conflict in terms of the relationship. The key factor is how we manage through this in the joint business planning; how we agree joint goals and joint measures so both retailer and supplier are working in the same direction and measuring success in the same way. Retailers and suppliers will never have 100 per cent common business goals and strategies. But many ARE the same and where our goals are compatible we can work on the common threads that tie them together.'

How do retailers and suppliers liaise over the issue of information?

Kevin observes that it depends on the approach of the retailer to the issue of information and IT.

'UK retailers are very advanced in this area. So, on a weekly or daily basis we are sharing data between retailer and manufacturer to look at how all of our categories are performing in areas such as volume / value sales, the levels of inventory and how much stock has gone to waste. We can really get detailed information in real time.

'I would say we have got that in place with all of our big retailers.

'Beyond that when you start getting into the really rich data about customers, a lot of the big retailers will have a separate agency within their business or a part of their business, that manages it. For example in Tesco the company that manages it is called Dunnhumby. They are owned by Tesco but they manage all of the Clubcard issues. Generally the supplier would need to enter into a contract with that agency to access the data and at that stage it becomes a relationship with that agency – Dunnhumby account managers work with us on a weekly basis, providing analysis for us on request. This allows us to truly understand shopper behaviour and tailor our offering better for them in stores.'

In the case of smaller retailers, Kevin notes that much would depend on the resources of the supplier concerned. Most retailers would make use of such information that is made available by agencies such as Dunnhumby. However, the capability to access such detailed and 'rich' data would largely be determined by the financial capability of the supplier to pay for such information. 'Suppliers would access that information on a daily or weekly basis.'

How do you use differentiated promotional plans with retailers?

Kevin highlights this aspect as being crucial in building relationships with retailers:

'This will increase in usage. The reason is that shoppers are looking for an enhanced retail experience. Shoppers don't just consider price when they look for VALUE. The value equation for people is much broader than that – it includes consideration of product performance, the trust or equity that the brand has, the experience in store as they shop, even down to the ease and convenience of access to the shop itself. When shoppers go to a supermarket, they are looking for something above and beyond the promotional message; in other words an amazing shopping experience. If we can bring in some of the marketing, e.g. brand ambassadors or sponsorship of events, for example built around sporting themes, and bring them into the store, this resonates with customers. From the retailer's point of view, we also really need to try and change the game a bit in terms of how we sell the product. It is unsustainable to be always offering big price promotions. We need to find a message over and above price that attracts people into the stores to buy our products.

'Another aspect to consider is that this is a good way of building the area of corporate social responsibility, for both parties. For example, in Asda during certain promotional periods, on every one of our products that is bought, we donate one day's clean drinking water to the developing world through our P&G Children's Safe Drinking Water Programme (which has provided more than 7 billion litres of clean drinking water since inception). This has had huge reach across all media, in-store and above the line. This helps to build warmth towards both parties and get consumers excited about shopping in the store.

'A similar campaign which started in the UK but is now global is our partnership between Pampers and UNICEF. For every pack of Pampers nappies bought during the campaign, P&G donates one vaccine to help protect mums and babies in the developing world from newborn/neonatal tetanus. Our mission with UNICEF is to try to eliminate this disease altogether. So far we have eliminated neo-natal tetanus from 15 countries. This is a flagship brand/NGO CSR partnership that others in the industry and in the third sector have identified as an example to follow. It's run for nearly a decade now and we get fantastic support from our retailers on it.

'This provides huge differentiation opportunities and there is a big win-win for everyone.'

Do you use digital marketing to build links with customers?

'We are using geo-targeting on mobile devices. So if a shopper is within a two mile radius of an Asda store, we can send them a message asking whether they know that Asda is donating towards clean drinking water. We could use it also for promotionally-led messages, e.g. "Pampers is now half-price at Asda for a limited period only". This is very much central to the joint business plan with the retailers.'

How do you manage and implement the joint business plan?

'We work with multi-functional teams. All of these things would be agreed in the business plan. We agree with the retailer for the year what sales target we both want to hit; for instance, the profitability matrix ▶

◀ that we want to hit; how we will support the UNICEF campaign. The idea of a joint business plan is really important. Everything we do is structured around this plan.

'When the plan goes off course it can put a strain on the relationship. In other circumstances it can help to keep the relationship on track.'

Kevin notes the multi-functional team would negotiate and agree the plan with the senior buying teams at the retailer:

'It takes quite a while . . . a good couple of months to negotiate it with the retailer. It is not a simple process.

'Within that we would try and have building blocks with different multi-functional aspects, e.g. a project to reduce inventory. We would be looking for in-store support for that business.'

4.17　Conclusions

In this chapter we have focused on the relationships between retailers and suppliers: two of the critical stakeholders in the supply chain process. We have looked at how power, and the way in which it is used, plays a significant role in establishing the 'ground rules' in these relationships. The research shows that there is no conclusive evidence that the power of retailers ensures that suppliers tend to suffer in their engagements with them. However, evidence from the retail industry strongly suggests that certain categories of suppliers, for example small ones with relatively low market share, have to fall in line with the demands and requirements of the large retailer.

We have also investigated areas where suppliers and retailers can collaborate and potentially derive mutual benefits from such initiatives. In particular we considered policies such as ECR, category management and VMI policies and procedures. These policies are aimed at reducing the cost of inventory management and seek other efficiencies such as more efficient replenishment within the supply chain. We noted that sophisticated IT systems act as facilitators and allow the parties involved to share information in real time.

We considered the sourcing strategies employed by retailers and in particular investigated the challenges of sourcing in a global context versus sourcing from a localized supply base. While low cost has been the traditional factor in encouraging retailers to source globally, the evidence suggests that such a one-dimensional approach runs the risk of ignoring other imperatives such as the ability to engage in quick response and rapid replenishment strategies.

We also examined the criteria used by retailers when selecting and evaluating suppliers for their supply base. In particular we looked at the core factors such as product-related, quality-related, responsiveness-related, network-related, price and cost-related and sustainability-related issues. The importance of these factors and their relative weighting will vary depending on the nature of the merchandise sold, the demand patterns and lead times and the level of responsiveness demanded by customers.

In summary, the relationship between retailers and suppliers is more complex than is often portrayed in the business press and the academic literature. Articles that identify suppliers as the victims in the relationship tend to gloss over the fact that benefits can accrue to them from being involved with a large supplier. Undoubtedly smaller suppliers that do not hold any key differentiating features to their product offering suffer and in many cases go out of business. It is difficult to be prescriptive about the nature of these relationships. In some cases, collaboration and co-operation can lead to significant mutual benefits for both parties. In other cases, the coercive wielding of power can place enormous pressure on suppliers to comply with the demands and in the worst case scenario lead to practices that damage the credibility of the supply chain and mislead the shopper.

Chapter outcomes

- Retailers will develop a portfolio of relationships with their supply base.
- These relationships will vary from transactional, adversarial engagements to close partnerships with key suppliers.
- The power-dependency position will ultimately shape the nature of the relationship between the individual supplier and the retailer.
- Power can be used in a number of different ways ranging from coercive and aggressive initiatives to collaborative and interactive practices.
- Retailers use a number of different criteria for selecting and monitoring suppliers. Their relative importance and weighting will vary according to the nature of the demand and the merchandise sold.
- When sourcing suppliers it is dangerous to use low cost as the sole criterion. Other factors such as responsiveness and rapid replenishment may be equally if not more important
- As retailers seek a more integrated and aligned supply chain, more emphasis is being placed on seeking areas of collaboration.
- This is driven by cost and efficiency factors. The desired result in many cases is a leaner, more agile and cost-effective supply chain.
- Generating published research in the area of retailer–manufacturer relationships is difficult given the sensitive and proprietorial of the data and practices between the key parties involved in the relationship.

Discussion questions

1 Assess the view that retailers have an unhealthy influence over their suppliers and that ultimately this means that the shopper suffers as a consequence.
2 Examine the benefits that can emerge from collaborative initiatives such as VMI and ECR for retailers and suppliers. Is it feasible or desirable to pursue such strategies with all suppliers?
3 Assess the extent to which you would agree with the view that power corrupts and leads to unethical and dangerous practices by suppliers in the supply chain.
4 Evaluate the view that the key criterion for selecting and evaluating suppliers is their ability to implement cost reduction programmes.
5 Examine the view that inventory is the single biggest cost factor in the retail supply chain and the focal point for determining the relationship between the retailer and the supplier.
6 Identify and discuss the main points you would cover on the following topic: 'The dangers of sourcing globally'.
7 Select a retailer of your choice and from using published data, assess the strategy that it adopts in term of its relationships with its supply base.

References

Amato, L.H. and Amato, C.H. (2009) Changing retail power and performance in distribution channels. *International Journal of Retail & Distribution Management.* 37(12): 1057–1076.

Berry, L.L. (1983) Relationship marketing. In Berrly, L.L., Shosack, G.L. and Upah, G.D. (eds). *Emerging Perspectives on Services Marketing.* Chicago, IL: American Marketing Association, 25–28.

Blattberg, R.C. and Neslin, S.A. (1990) *Sales Promotion: Concepts, Methods and Strategies.* Englewood-Cliffs, NJ: Prentice-Hall.

Bloom, P.N. and Perry, V.G. (2001) Retailer power and supplier welfare: the case of Wal-Mart. *Journal of Retailing.* 77: 379–396.

Bruce, M. and Daly, L. (2006) Buyer behaviour for fast fashion. *Journal of Fashion Marketing and Management.* 10(3): 329–344.

Burt, S.L. and Sparks, L. (2003) Power and competition in the UK retail grocery market. *British Journal of Management.* 14(3): 237–254.

Cho, J. and Kang, J. (2001) Benefits and challenges of global sourcing: perceptions of US apparel retail firms. *International Marketing Review.* 19(5): 542–561.

Christopher, M., Mena, C., Khan, O. and Yurt, O. (2011) Approaches to managing sourcing risk. *Supply Chain Management: An International Journal.* 16(2): 67–81.

Chung, J., Sternquist, B. and Chen, S. (2006) Retailer–buyer supply relationships: the Japanese difference. *Journal of Retailing.* 82(4): 349–355.

Coopers & Lybrand (1996) *European Value Chain Analysis Study – Final Report.* Utrecht: ECR Europe.

Corsten, D. and Kumar, N. (2005) Do suppliers benefit from collaborative relationships with large retailers? An empirical investigation of efficient consumer response adoption. *Journal of Marketing.* 69 (July): 80–94.

Dapiran, G.P. and Hogarth-Scott, S. (2003) Are cooperation and trust being confused with power? An analysis of food retailing in Australia and the UK. *International Journal of Retail & Distribution Management.* 31(5): 256–267.

Dobson, P. and Waterson, M. (1999) Retailer power: recent developments and policy implications. *Economic Policy.* 28. Oxford: Blackwell Publishers.

Doyle, S.A., Moore, C.M. and Morgan, L. (2006) Supplier management in fast moving fashion retailing. *Journal of Fashion Marketing and Management.* 10(3): 1361–2026.

Duffy, R., Fearne, A. and Hornibrook, S. (2003) Measuring distributive and procedural justice: An exploratory investigation of retailer-supplier relationships in the UK Food industry. *British Food Journal.* 105(10/11): 682–694.

Effendi, J., Kinney, M.R., Smith, T.K. and Murphy, L. (2013) Marketing supply chain using B2B buy-side ecommerce systems: does adoption impact financial performance? *Academy of Marketing Studies Journal.* 17(2): 57–83.

Fernie, J. and Sparks, L. (eds) (2009) *Logistics and Retail Management: Emerging Issues and New Challenges in the Retail Supply Chain,* 3rd edn. London: Kogan Page, 38–62.

Fiddis, C. (1997) *Manufacturer-Retailer Relationships in the Food and Drink Industry: Strategies and Tactics in the Battle for Power.* London: FT Retail & Consumer Publishing, Pearson Professional.

Gooner, R.A., Morgan, N.A. and Perreault, W.D. Jnr. (2011) Is retail category management worth the effort (and does a category captain help or hinder)? *Journal of Marketing.* 75 (September): 18–33.

Gummesson, E. (1999) *Total Relationship Marketing: From the 4Ps – Product, Price, Promotion, Place – of Traditional Marketing Management to the 30Rs – the Thirty Relationships – of the New Marketing Paradigm.* Oxford: Butterworth-Heinemann.

Hansen, J.M. (2009) The evolution of buyer-supplier relationships: an historical industry approach. *Journal of Business and Industrial Marketing.* 23(3/4): 227–236.

Hingley, M. (2005) Power imbalance in UK agri-food supply channels: learning to live with the supermarkets? *Journal of Marketing Management.* 21: 63–88.

Huang, Q., Nijs, V., Hansen, K. and Anderson, E.T. (2012) Wal-Mart's impact on supplier profits. *Journal of Marketing Research.* XLLX (April): 131–143.

Kadiyali, V., Chintagunta, P. and Vilcassim, N. (2000) Manufacturer-retailer channel interactions and implications for channel power: an empirical investigation of pricing in local market. *Marketing Science.* 19(2): 127–148.

Kausik, U. and Mahadevan, B. (2012) A review of strategic sourcing literature during 1997-2010: trends and emerging issues for research. *South Asian Journal of Management.* 19(2): 78–98.

Kim, B. and Park, C. (2010) Supply chain coordination between supplier and retailer in a VMI (vendor-managed inventory) relationship. *The Business Review.* Cambridge. 15(2): 165–170.

Kusaba, K., Moser, R. and Rodrigues, A.M. (2011) Low-cost country sourcing competence: a conceptual framework and empirical analysis. *Journal of Supply Chain Management.* 47(4): 73–93.

Manuj, I. and Mentzer, J.T. (2008) Global supply chain risk management strategies. *International Journal of Physical & Distribution Management.* 38(3): 192–223.

Monczka, R.M. and Trent, R.J. (1991) Global sourcing: a development approach. *International Journal of Purchasing and Materials Management.* 27(2): 2–8.

Moore, B. (2008) Open-market powerplay in supplier-retailer relationships. *Retail Policy Issues. The Retail Digest.* Autumn: 16–20.

Mottner, S. and Smith, S. (2008) Wal-Mart: supplier performance and market power. *Journal of Business Research.* 62: 535–541.

Nicholson, C. and Young, B. (2012). *The Relationship Between Supermarkets and Suppliers: What are the Implications for Consumers?* Consumers International.

O'Connor, M.C. (2014) Can RFID save bricks and mortar retailers after all? *Fortune.* 16 April.

Oliver, J.M. and Farris, P.W. (1989) Push and pull: a one-two punch for packaged products. *Sloan Management Review.* 31(1): 53–61.

Palmer, A. (2000) Co-operation and competition: a Darwinian synthesis of relationship marketing. *European Journal of Marketing.* 34(5/6): 687–704.

Peck, H. and Juttner, U. (2002) Risk management in the supply chain. *Logistics and Transport Focus.* 4(10): 17–21.

Platts, K.W. and Song, N. (2010) Overseas sourcing decisions – the total cost of sourcing from China. *Supply Chain Management: An International Journal.* 15(4): 320–331.

Radaev, V. (2013) Market power and relational conflicts in Russian retailing. *Journal of Business and Industrial Marketing.* 28(3): 167–177.

Rashid, S. and Matilla, H. (2011) Study on the scope and opportunities of category management for aligning the supplier-retailer business strategy. *South Asian Journal of Management.* 18(4): 62–89.

Sako, M. (1992) *Prices, Quality and Trust: Inter-Firm Relations in Britain and Japan.* Cambridge: Cambridge University Press.

Sternquist, B. (1998) *International Retailing.* New York: Fairchild Publications.

Webster, F.E. (1992) The changing role in the corporation. *Journal of Marketing,* 56 (October): 1–17.

Welsh, M. and Zolkiewski, J. (2004) Barriers to virtue: exploring the dark side of dyadic relationships. In *38th Academy of Marketing Conference Proceedings.* University of Gloucestershire. July.

3

Retail marketing strategy

Part contents

Managing the selling environment

☑ Learning objectives

On completion of this chapter you should be in a position to address the following objectives:

- ☑ Understand the importance of managing the selling environment in the context of retail strategy formulation and implementation.

- ☑ Examine the components of store layout.

▶

☑ Assess the components of store design.

☑ Gain an insight into the concept of retail as theatre and its role in shaping customer experience and expectations.

☑ Identify the ways in which retailers can maximize selling space in terms of profitability.

☑ Recognize the importance of the retail selling environment in establishing the retailer's brand identity and its points of differentiation over its competitors.

☑ Examine the relationship between managing the selling environment and the positioning strategy of the retailer.

☑ Form opinions on the use of psychology as a mechanism for managing the selling environment.

5.1 Introduction

This chapter examines the concept of the selling environment. This term refers to the physical and virtual spaces that are available to retailers as they attempt to attract customers to their product offerings, encourage them to browse, hopefully make a purchase and ultimately revisit that space on a regular basis.

In the early part of this chapter, we assess the challenges involved in developing the layout of the store. We introduce the notion of 'retail as theatre'. It is crucial that, in managing the selling environment, the retailer makes the space as attractive and inviting as possible for the shopper. There are some exceptions; that is, discount retailers. Their mission is to provide value in terms of low prices. It does not make sense as a consequence to invest heavily in store atmospherics and decor as this would add significantly to the overall cost of operations. Retail as theatre is an analogy that recognizes the importance of adapting some of the basic principles of drama; that is, evoking certain moods, role-playing and creating a lasting and memorable experience for visitors to the retail space.

We also assess the importance of 'atmospherics' and examine its components. In terms of store design, atmospherics play a critical role in shaping and influencing the behaviour and mood of the shopper. If a retail space has no atmosphere, it is akin to a football match taking place in an empty stadium. In the latter case, the game will take place but will suffer as a result of the absence of fans.

Some commentators argue that the selling environment presents opportunities for retailers to use psychological ploys to enhance the customer experience. Others put forward the notion that retailers manipulate shoppers in terms of influencing their behaviour. We engage in this debate and make some observations.

We evaluate store design and layout considerations from the perspective of managing and raising customer experience and expectation in the context of retail as a form of leisure and entertainment.

5.2 The retail selling environment

The battleground for attracting shoppers, encouraging them to browse and purchase and ultimately develop commitment and loyalty to the retailer rests firmly with the selling environment. This refers to the space that is available to the retailer in terms of presenting its merchandise. The selling space also acts as a potent form of in-store communication: the retailer can use various cues to reinforce its brand identity and value proposition in the minds of shoppers. The role played by visual merchandising, employees and layout can make an indelible mark in terms of shaping the shopping experience. It also, if used appropriately, communicates the brand identity of the retailer.

Floor (2006: 266) develops this theme more fully and suggests that 'the design of a store is broadly comparable to the packaging of a manufacturer brand. It should communicate the positioning and personality, add value to the merchandise and be efficient and effective.'

The space used by retailers to engage with shoppers is often described in the literature as the *servicescape*. Bitner (1992) describes this concept as a physical setting in which a marketplace exchange is performed, delivered and consumed within a service organization. Bitner identified the following three elements to the servicescape:

- ambient conditions (atmospherics)
- special layout and the functionality of the store
- signs, symbols and artefacts (used to create and manage the brand personality and how it is perceived by shoppers.

Critics of the original servicescape concept note that it fails adequately to acknowledge that many of the stimuli used by organizations are subjective and difficult to measure and are capable of being interpreted by (in the case of retailing) shoppers in different ways.

Rosenbaum and Massiah (2011) argue that more focus is needed in other areas besides the physical dimension such as the aspect of social interaction that takes place in such settings and the interactions with store employees. They identify four environmental dimensions: physical, social, socially symbolic and natural. Figure 5.1 provides more detail on the framework.

Physical dimension: this is perhaps the easiest of the dimensions to understand from the perspective of the retailer. Technology, atmospherics and layout are designed by management and to some extent are controlled.

Social dimension: shoppers are not only influenced by the physical dimension however. Social aspects play a role, a key element being the interaction between the customer and the employee in the store. One issue: social density refers to the degree of crowding that may exist in a servicescape environment. Not surprisingly, physical spaces that are overcrowding lead to negative feelings and perceptions.

Socially symbolic dimension: this dimension broadly refers to the signage, symbols and logos used by the retailer to convey messages to the shoppers and reinforce the brand personality of the store. Such symbolism can evoke feelings of nostalgia, patriotism and positivity and lead to purchases in the particular store.

Natural dimension: this is perhaps the most difficult of the dimensions to relate to within the context of the retail sector. Much of the empirical research in this area is drawn from psychology and medical sciences. Rosenbaum and Massiah (2011) cite the example of health researchers who investigated the impact of hospital gardens on patient wellbeing. In the context of retailing, retailers may use elements of the green environment within their store design and layout to capture the natural aspect.

Rosenbaum and Massiah (2011: 482) note some implications for management as a consequence of this expanded view of the servicescape.

> **"***This expanded definition of a servicescape results in new managerial implications. That is, from a customer's perspective, an ideal servicescape would be one that is physically appealing, socially supportive, symbolically welcoming, and naturally pleasing. Yet, not all customers will perceive all four servicescape dimensions or consider them equally important.***"**

Retailers have to take account of their target markets and the reasons why they visit their stores. If shoppers see the purpose of the shopping visit as an escape from everyday life, then the natural dimension may take precedence in the way in which the servicescape is developed and used. For more functional purposes, the physical dimension may play the greater role in the servicescape design.

Figure 5.1 Expanded servicescape

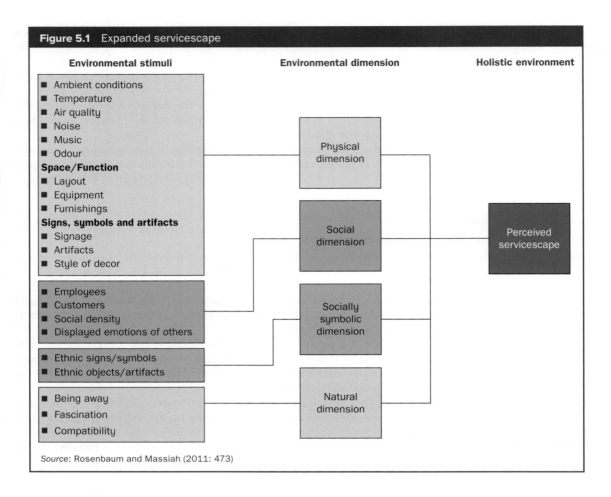

Source: Rosenbaum and Massiah (2011: 473)

The space can be physical (a store or outlet), virtual (an online retail fulfilment channel), direct mail channels such as the IKEA and Argos books or a combination of all of these options. In this chapter we focus mainly on the physical and online spaces as they represent the most commonly used selling environments.

The physical selling environment refers to the *internal and external* dimensions. In the context of external aspects, we need to consider features such as the entrance to the outlet, the use of logos and window displays to encourage shoppers to enter the store in the first instance. Unless they come into the store, a sale will not take place. Once they are inside the store, we need to consider the ways in which retailers can manage and enhance the experience. How do we display our merchandise? Where do we display the different categories of product within the store? Should we provide a clear 'signpost' for shoppers as they walk around the store? How do we influence and shape the mood of the shopper? How do we manage the entrance and exit of shoppers? How can we ensure that shoppers spend as much time as possible in the store? How can we encourage shoppers to spend more than they originally intended? These questions in essence will influence the approach that retailers will adopt when developing and managing the selling space.

The same challenges face online retailers. Although there is no physical space for shoppers to invade, the website must also consider the importance of encouraging them to visit and navigate their way around the key features and areas. Websites that confuse and irritate customers are unlikely to encourage repeat visits. Transparency, clarity and ease of access are central to creating successful virtual selling environments.

The key word in this section is 'selling'. The ultimate challenge for retailers is to convert customer visits and browsing into a sale. This is the 'acid test'. Without sales, store design and layout strategies can be deemed to fail. It is not just about getting a sale however. Once in the selling space, effective strategies should recognize the importance of purchases that are unplanned; that is, where the shopper buys merchandise that they had not set out to purchase.

Successful retailers also work on the principle of encouraging shoppers to 'trade up'; that is, purchase a more expensive, higher quality item than they had originally intended. A shopper may enter an electrical store to purchase an HD TV set. A price tag of £1,000 may be the initial plan in terms of expenditure. A combination of visual merchandising and the influence of the salesperson can lead to a purchase of an HD TV of £1,400. An attractive selling environment can enhance the shopping experience but can also ensure that the shopper visits parts of the store that was not planned. The positioning of salespeople offering samples for tasting such as cheese or wine can lead to additional purchases. The placing of 'adjacencies' (wine beside the cheese counter) can lead to complementary purchases that were not pre-planned. These examples highlight how the selling environment can be maximized to ensure that conversion rates (visits: sales) are high and more profitable.

5.3 Store layout decisions

The physical retail selling environment begins with an 'empty shell'. This applies to large spaces such as hypermarkets or small concession areas in department stores. If it is left as an empty shell, it will serve no purpose. It will be impossible to create interest in the minds of shoppers; it will fail to create any sort of mood or atmosphere; it will fail to provide any signpost or guide for shoppers to identify relevant product categories or the ability to navigate with ease around the selling space. The layout of the selling space provides coherence and logic for the shopper. It acts similarly to a 'satnav' in the sense that it provides a reference point and generates a form of familiarity on subsequent revisits to the outlet.

Aghazadeh (2005: 31) identifies a number of guidelines for making store layout decisions. They are as follows:

1 Locate high-draw items around the periphery of the store.
2 Use prominent locations for high-impulse and high-margin items.
3 Distribute what is known as 'power items' to both sides of an aisle and disperse them to increase the viewing of other items.
4 Use end-aisle locations for high exposure rate.
5 Convey the impression of the store by careful selection in the positioning of the lead-off department.

We must inject a note of caution at this stage however. The principles identified in the preceding paragraph are more appropriate for a large store such as a supermarket or hypermarket. Much will depend on the nature of the merchandise sold and the shopping motives.

Store layout decisions are heavily influenced by the nature of the products sold. For instance, supermarkets tend to sell products that are largely utilitarian. This recognizes that many of these products are low-involvement purchases (for example, cereals, baked beans and coffee). Retail banking could also be described as largely utilitarian. Customers are not seeking or expecting high levels of pleasure or enjoyment by making such purchases or visits. Clearly, there may be certain product categories in a supermarket that may engender higher levels of hedonistic behaviour (for example, electronics and clothing sections). However, the shopping experience is one that is based on convenience: a weekly visit to the supermarket is seen as a functional activity by many shoppers. Ease of access to the store, clear signposting to the various product sections, ease of payment and ease of exit feature prominently in the shopping process for the majority of shoppers.

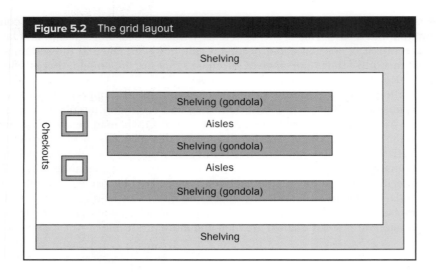

Figure 5.2 The grid layout

At the lower end of the scale we see the approach of discount retailers such as Aldi and Lidl. A visit to such retail outlets shows that while the layout typically follows a logical 'grid' layout, the merchandise is displayed in a simple and rudimentary fashion. In some cases the items are left in their boxes and the shopper has to extract the individual items. Little emphasis is placed on visual cues such as lighting and floor material. In every sense, the focus is on simplicity and cost.

In situations where the focus is on a utilitarian shopping experience, layout decisions have to address issues such as the flow of 'footfall' through the store, the management of queues at the checkout and speedy access to the different sections of the store. Generally in such shopping situations, there is a lack of focus on encouraging shoppers to browse. Aisles need to be sufficiently wide to reduce crowding and delays. The grid system is adopted by many retailers in such situations. Figure 5.2 presents the typical grid layout.

The main benefit of the grid approach to layout design rests with its logical approach. Each aisle or gondola is labelled. This provides a clear signpost to the shopper and in the case of revisits generates reassurance that desired items can be easily traced in terms of their location within the store. The shopper becomes familiar with the placement of merchandise and can quickly gain access to the relevant areas within the store.

The disadvantage of such an approach is that it is mechanical in terms of its approach and can convey a sense of repetition and boredom with regard to the shopping experience. However, as we noted earlier, the shopper is not necessarily seeking a hedonistic shopping experience and such a functional approach to layout is compatible with shopping expectations for the majority of supermarket shoppers.

As we see later in this chapter, the use of visual cues such as lighting, colour and aroma can create interest and curiosity even with such a mundane approach to layout.

In other situations, the retailer is positioned at the high-end or luxury segment of the market. The store layout has to reinforce this approach. The layout has to engender interest and curiosity. It has to stimulate the shopper and heighten the experience. It must complement the decor and atmosphere that is appropriate to the desired store image and positioning strategy. The hedonic nature of this shopping experience cannot be ignored. In such situations the level of expectation among shoppers is higher. They exhibit hedonistic behaviour in this regard: pleasure and engagement with the retail brand is foremost in their expectations. All of the elements of the selling environment have to address such criteria. Store layout in particular should reflect empathy with the needs and requirements of the shopper.

In contrast to more utilitarian shopping experiences, one of the challenges for hedonistic shopping environments is to encourage browsing and create pockets of interest for shoppers. Any initiative that encourages shoppers to engage and interact with the merchandise adds value to the experience and is more likely to generate sales and repeat visits.

Figure 5.3 identifies an approach that is often referred to as 'free form'.

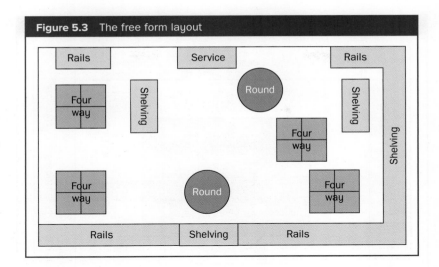

Figure 5.3 The free form layout

We can see that this approach utilizes a combination of small gondolas, hanging rails and shelving units. Free form layouts break up space into various areas. When combined with other visual cues, the retailer has the opportunity to highlight certain product categories and draw shoppers to these areas of the store. Instead of the mechanistic approach associated with the grid system, the retailer can encourage browsing and interaction with the items. By working on the issues of curiosity and interest, such an approach can encourage shoppers to 'trade up' and also make an impulse purchase.

The free form approach can create the impression of 'organized chaos'. By focusing on certain areas within the store, retailers can make it difficult for shoppers to easily locate the sections that they wish to visit. While this may create some irritation, it can work to the advantage of the retailer. They can force shoppers to visit displays and shelving units that they had no intention of investigating. This can lead to additional purchases or trading up to a more expensive brand or item. A balance has to be achieved between irritating customers and drawing them to as many pockets of interest as possible within the store. Some retailers, particularly supermarkets and large specialty retailers, alter and move around the product categories. Again this can create irritation, particularly for shoppers who visit on a relatively frequent basis and who have become accustomed to expecting certain items to be located in a specific part of the store. Moving around merchandise takes shoppers out of their 'comfort zone' but can address the 'boredom factor'.

The 'racetrack' layout (sometimes referred to as the loop) also represents a popular approach for retailers. This is depicted in Fig. 5.4.

This figure shows that various departments are located on the outer rim of the store. They are grouped within the centre space. This type of layout allows the shopper to move around the store in a relatively easy and free-flowing manner. The groupings ideally should represent a logical form and provide some complementarity; for example, the paint section should be adjacent to the home section. This may stimulate extra purchases where the shopper goes into the store with the intention of buying paint but may see some home furnishings that have a high level of appeal. This approach offers maximum product exposure to the shoppers.

In summary, store layout decisions should consider the following factors from the perspective of both the retailer and the shopper:

- *Managing the flow of footfall*: where possible, retailers should have aisles that allow for comfortable negotiation on the part of shoppers. Areas of congestion cause irritation at peak shopping times.
- *Create pockets of interest*: combined with atmospherics, retailers ideally would like shoppers to visit as many areas of the store as possible. Clever positioning of certain items of merchandise, for example low-ticket items towards the back of the store so that shoppers have to pass more expensive higher-ticket items, can generate higher levels of purchases.

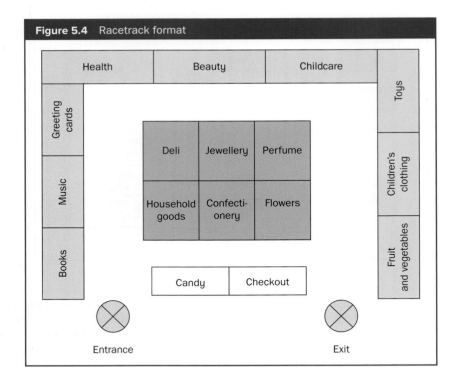

Figure 5.4 Racetrack format

Activity

IKEA uses software to analyse traffic patterns through its stores. It has been criticized for designing a layout that forces shoppers to follow a predetermined path through the store that makes it very difficult for them to exit sections that they do not particularly wish to visit. There are exits but they are placed in such a way that they are difficult to find and the majority of shoppers follow this pre-planned route. Almost like robots. The displays and use of 'slice of life' to present various facets of their merchandise; for example, kitchen settings, bedrooms and so on, add value to the shopping experience and it can be argued that this counterbalances the dangers of causing irritation. It can be further argued that IKEA addresses the issue of high-involvement purchases where shoppers enjoy the experience of shopping for household products and that they are more than willing to put up with the inconvenience of having to follow a set path through the store. The issues of queuing to pay for products as well as potential delays resulting from waiting to pick up merchandise is of more concern to customers and IKEA has attracted some stinging criticism for shortcomings in this area of store design and layout.

Task

Make a visit to your local IKEA store and assess the effectiveness of its store design and layout from the point of view of a retail marketing expert and as a shopper.

■ *Inject excitement*: retailers who stick rigidly to grid layouts run the risk of making shopping boring and repetitive for shoppers. A variation of display units and shelving can break up space in the store and tempt shoppers to linger and inspect merchandise in certain areas of the store. For example at the end of a long aisle in a supermarket it may be prudent to have a display unit with demonstrators promoting new soft drinks or perfumes.

- *Encourage the purchase of additional items*: a layout that places complementary products side by side is more likely to generate extra sales. Buying a suit for an interview for example would be considered as a major purchase by many males. A layout that also places shirts and ties close to the suits section is likely (prompted by gentle persuasion from sales personnel) to result in extra purchases without putting undue pressure on the customer.

- *Encourage impulse purchases*: similar to the previous observation, shoppers can be tempted to buy items that were not originally part of their shopping list or plan. In supermarkets, for example, retailers will place snack items as close as possible or right beside the checkout areas. This has prompted much criticism from consumer groups; they claim that retailers are manipulating both children and parents. Placing toothpastes aimed at children at the lower end of the shelving is also an example of either manipulation or clever psychology on the part of the retailer depending on your point of view!

- *Encourage loitering*: this is relevant to retail environments where the retailer wants to encourage shoppers to linger and spend some time in a particular section or category of the store.

Vignette: Apple Store

Recently Apple was granted a trademark for the glass-fronted, rectangular-patterned design of its Apple Store by the US Patent and Trademark Office. It has been pursuing this strategy since 2010. After initial rejection, it submitted additional materials and drawings and gained the trademark on its mall-centric, rectangular store layouts.

The registered trademark certificate details the brand's approach.

'...a primarily glass storefront, rectangular recessed lighting traversing the length of the store's ceiling. Cantilevered shelving and recessed display spaces along the front side walls, rectangular tables arranged in a line in the middle of the store parallel to the walls and extending from the storefront to the back of the store, multi-tiered shelving along the rear walls, and an oblong table with stools located at the back of the store below video screens in the back wall.'

Microsoft has also acquired a trademark on the design of its stores. Its certificate describes the layout as '... three-dimensional trade dress depicting the interior of a retail store with four curved tabletops at the front and rear walls and a rectangular band displaying changing video images on the screens'.

Both of these trademarks prove that architectural layout as a form of intellectual property can be owned and branded, no matter how simple or 'intuitive' it may be.

Source: Adapted from: Palladino, V. (2013) Apple store receives trademark for 'distinctive design and layout'. Available online at: www.wired.com/design/2013/01/apple-store-trademark/ (accessed 9 July 2013)

In summary, store layout literally sets the agenda for managing the selling environment. Pine and Gilmore (1999) highlight the importance of creating memorable experiences for consumers. We have examined the factors that influence the store layout decisions. The challenge facing retailers is to achieve a balance between satisfying the needs and expectations of the shoppers and creating a chaotic and disorganized structure that can lead to dissatisfaction and customer defection to competitors.

5.4 Retail as theatre

In Chapter 7 we examine the trends and developments with regard to customer experience management. In the context of the retail sector (as is the case in many service-related industries) the shopper has become a more proactive player in relationships with retailers. They no longer act as passive recipients of the value proposition developed by the retailer. Increased expectations, combined with a greater degree of choice and knowledge, has led to greater interaction with all aspects of the retailer's offering.

The services marketing literature in general contains a number of seminal articles that use the theatre metaphor. Studies by Pranter and Martin (1991), Broderick (1998) and Zeithaml and Bitner (1996) articulate words that are synonymous with drama and theatre. Baron et al. (2001) cite terms such as 'backstage', 'front stage', 'scripts', 'roles' and 'settings' to convey the analogy between retail design and theatrical performance.

In the context of retailing, Baron et al. (2001: 103) note that the use of theatre 'is international and covers many different product categories: food, shoes, perfume/toiletries, children's clothing and toys, electrical goods, sports goods, home furnishing, garden products and cars'.

However, Harris, Harris and Baron (2003: 186) also note that 'there is little evidence that there has been any serious attempt by retailers or their advisors to go beyond the use of the theatre metaphor as a purely literary device that creates a theatrical vocabulary for generating attractive sounding ideas'. They identify four different roles for shoppers within the context of using some of the principles of theatre and drama.

1 *Customer as voyeur*: in this situation customers recognize a realistic setting. They are observing and participating in a slice of real life. An example is that of the Kotva department store, based in Prague. They ran a competition for a family to spend a month living in the store, making use of the kitchen and living room setting located in prime street-level display areas. At the end of the month they could take away all of the furnishings. This initiative attracted high levels of publicity and crowds watched the family all day. This is a somewhat contrived example however. A more sophisticated approach would be one where the employees would undertake some of their activities in a real-life setting or where a fashion retailer would present some of its design in a party setting.

2 *Customer as 'spect-actor'*: this occurs where employees and customers interact with each other, share opinions and views from friends and colleagues. Baron et al. (2001) cite the example of a retailer selling climbing and walking gear, located near the Peak District in the UK (a popular area for these activities). The store is divided into two sections. The front area sells books, maps and craft items. The back section has become a meeting place for climbers and a strong and vibrant community has developed for sharing views and opinions with employees and fellow enthusiasts. Since this article was published over 10 years ago, we can see how online retailers have adopted this approach by creating communities where their customers are encouraged to post views and opinions. This approach addresses the challenge of recognizing that customers are no longer passive individuals. Increasingly, they prefer interaction with retailers, other customers and opinion leaders.

3 *Customer as 'sense-ceptor'*: as the title suggests, the sensory aspect of the shopper's experience is paramount. The case of Albert Heijn, a Dutch retailer specializing in food and groceries, provides a case in point. The central area of its outlet has specialist food counters, similar to a local market. Customers can purchase fresh products and receive advice from staff on cooking and preparation. They can participate in tasting sessions to 'whet their appetite' and stimulate them into purchasing items. Employees play a critical role with their expertise.

4 *Customer as connoisseur*: this role is drawn from the concept of absurd theatre. It is designed to provoke an individual and it depends on that individual's prior knowledge and experience. An example cited by Baron et al. (2001) is that of On the Wall Productions of St. Louis. Inside the store there is an apparent art theme. Or is there? The self-portrait of Van Gogh has a set of 12 ears alongside it to 'pin the ear on Van Gogh'. It is, therefore, a game shop. Or is it? There are rubber clocks, inflatable ancient Egyptian mummies and tubes of various shapes that make thunder-like noises. Models of modern space rockets and ancient medieval treasures glow in the dark. This approach is designed to challenge and engage the shopper.

The concept of retail as theatre has relevance for the way in which retailers interact with their customer base. In cases where retailers are selling merchandise that evokes hedonistic behaviour and where the shopper engages and interacts with both the product and sales staff, retail as theatre can enhance the experience and add value. As we have already noted, the extent to which retailers make use of theatre can vary. At one end of the spectrum it can be introduced in a simple and straightforward manner. For instance some supermarkets dress their operatives at the fish and meat sections in white coats and hats to convey the impression of expertise. At the other extreme, retailers may venture into the theatre of the absurd to create a dramatic setting that challenges the shopper.

In tandem with the use of atmospherics (which we examine later in this chapter), the use of drama can work on issues such as interest, arousal, pleasure, entertainment and interaction. This can contribute in a positive manner to the overall experience for the visitor to the store and develop a level of commitment and loyalty that might otherwise be difficult to cultivate.

As customers across all categories of the services sector wish to participate, interact and share experiences (either physically or virtually) and become part of a community, the adoption of dramatic initiatives can reinforce these desires.

De Nisco and Napolitano (2006) identify the importance of treating many aspects of the retail sector as being in the entertainment category. Many retailers have built entertainment firmly into the design and layout of their stores and shopping malls. For instance the Mall of the Emirates shopping mall in Dubai has installed a realistic ski slope within its complex. Live music, multiplex cinemas, events related to entertaining children and other initiatives also reinforce the view that shopping for many people is a key element in their desire for entertainment and recreation.

We end this section by making some observations about how to use the retail as theatre metaphor in an effective manner.

1 **The nature of the retail format**: although not necessarily confined to large retail selling spaces, shopping malls, department stores, category killers (for example, Toys R Us) and specialist retailers (B&Q, Bunnings, Apple and Nike) need to create a frisson of excitement and energy to make full use of the available selling space. Entertainment-related initiatives can combine with atmospherics to address these issues.

2 **The nature of the merchandise**: high-involvement items need to be presented in an imaginative and creative way to encourage shoppers to engage and interact with them. Products that are aspirational and lifestyle-oriented are prime candidates for the use of theatre to promote them to shoppers. The luxury brand sector is a good example.

3 **The type of shopping behaviour**: as noted earlier, hedonistic, pleasure-seeking behaviour generates expectations that are geared around entertainment and indulgence. Retail as theatre can work on these desires and provide a positive and pleasant backdrop.

4 **Launching and promoting new products**: international fashion, electronics and sports equipment retailers use flagship stores to introduce new designs to their customer base. Moore, Doherty and Doyle (2010) examine such formats from the perspective of market entry. These stores are usually located in prime retail locations in large and influential cities (New York, London, Paris, Milan, Shanghai, Dubai and so on) and also serve as an important mechanism for promoting the latest designs and technological improvements. Shoppers use such stores as a reference point and make shopping trips to learn, inform, discuss with salespeople in the store and share views with colleagues. Retailers can make imaginative use of theatre to display and promote new products and designs.

5 **Activating customer engagement and interaction with merchandise and staff**: the concept of experiential marketing advocates that organizations should encourage the consumer to become proactive in engaging with merchandise, particularly in the case of items that are geared to hedonistic behaviours. Retail as theatre can be used to provide stimulation for interacting with products. The Hamleys case in point vignette provides some examples to support this approach.

5.5 Case in point: Hamleys toy shop

Hamleys is a well-known toys retailer that was established in London in 1760 by William Hamley. It has grown to twenty-five stores worldwide and its flagship store is located in London. It is the largest toy shop in the world.

In terms of store layout and display it follows four basic methods: its displays are arranged by theme, brand, promotion and multimedia. In the case of developing a theme, we can see sections such as the 'wild animal' area. Hamleys augments this section by including trees and leaves and the inclusion of a life-size figure of a camel to convey the appropriate background 'theatre'. It also uses displays to highlight certain brands such as the 'Hello Kitty' collection and Lego brands. In terms of displays that focus on promotions, Hamleys locates discounted items, promotional products and new launches at conspicuous points within the store beside the main pathways.

The retailer makes extensive and proactive use of multimedia displays. Video instructions are placed on the display unit beside the screen and are designed to encourage children and parents to interact with the clips. Staff are on hand to help where necessary.

Because of the nature of the product (toys are the epitome of interaction) much of the in-store strategy is built around engagement. A piano mat encourages shoppers to play music! A test track allows them to engage with toy motor cars. Costume fitting rooms encourage them to try on clothing.

Staff engage and interact proactively with shoppers. They carry out magic pen demonstrations. They participate in a mystery UFO demonstration in the 'performance' area of the store (such demonstrations vary throughout the year). Staff also engage in story-telling with children at the 'tables and fables' bandstand. They encourage kids to take part in getting their pictures taken with them (staff dressing up in costumes and so on).

The party room plays an important part in bonding with parents and kids. This is available for birthday parties, visits of characters from children's movies, general activities and competitions. Retail as theatre in this case is aimed at children and parents. This recognizes that while kids are the primary target, it is also critical to engage with parents in terms of building interest, enthusiasm and excitement. After all, it is the parents who pay for the ultimate purchases in the store.

Question

1 Assess the view that 'retail as theatre' can be overused and can deflect attention away from the primary objective of selling merchandise.

5.6 Managing sensory marketing considerations

Atmospherics play a critical role in shaping and influencing shopping behaviour. In addition, it heightens the shopping experience, something that we have recognized throughout the book as being of increasing significance for many shoppers.

Much of the research on atmospherics has its basis in the context of environmental psychology. In particular, the stimulus-organism-response model (S-O-R) is utilized to structure the work in this area.

Mower, Kim and Childs (2012: 443) note that this model 'assumes that consumers' emotional responses to a physical environment mediate the influence of the environment on their behaviors'. Building on this model, Mehrabian and Russell (1974) identified three aspects of emotion that influence people's responses to the environment: pleasantness, arousal and dominance. The term 'pleasantness' focuses on the extent to which the consumer feels happy and content within the context of the experience. Arousal relates to the extent that the individual is stimulated or excited by the experience. Dominance addresses the feeling of being in control (or not). They further explored the relationship between pleasantness and arousal as a critical factor in determining an individual's approach or avoidance behaviour. The former refers to the extent and desire to visit and stay within the environment and engage with people. By contrast the latter relates to the unwillingness of the consumer to remain in the environment and stay away from it in future. This research was carried out within the context of general services marketing encounters.

Donovan and Rossiter (1982) addressed these issues within the context of the retail sector. They found that the pleasure experienced by shoppers played a strong role in approach–avoidance behaviour. Arousal also was a critical factor influencing the amount of time spent in the store and the level of interaction with sales staff. Interestingly they saw no relevance for the concept of dominance in the context of the retail sector.

There are lessons here for retailers. Pleasure and arousal are critical in terms of attracting shoppers to either a physical store or an online e-tail channel. The general layout of the store allied to the use of visual cues plays a significant role in addressing these twin challenges. As we note later in this chapter the S-O-R model has equal relevance for the design of e-tail operations. Visual and aural cues apply here as the retailer entices the shopper to visit the site and spend some time visiting the different areas.

In the next section we explore in more detail the issue of experiential marketing and the role of atmospherics.

5.7 Experiential marketing

Hauser (2006: 1) defines experiential marketing as 'connecting customers with your brand through one or more meaningful and relevant experiences while appealing to both rational and emotional behaviors'. This highlights the importance of creating emotional connections with the shopper. Why would a customer come back to your store? A critical factor is the type of experience encountered by that shopper. Experiential marketing contributes significantly to the relationship between the retailer and the target market.

What aspects of retail strategy does experiential marketing address? Morton (2009) identifies the following areas:

- build relationships
- raise awareness
- increase loyalty
- establish relevance
- encourage interaction and product trial
- create memories
- stimulate positive word of mouth
- change the mind of dissatisfied customers
- create product desire
- verify the target audience
- increase return on marketing investment.

When we use terms such as 'atmosphere' and 'atmospherics' within the context of retailing, we are essentially focusing on a range of cues (signals) that work on the senses. These include sight, sound, smell, touch and taste. The task facing the retailer is one of designing and implementing cues that accentuate positive and pleasurable experiences while at the same time avoiding the dangers of intruding into shopper's personal space and irritating them. Figure 5.5 captures the dimensions of multisensory communication.

Research by Hulten (2011) also emphasizes the importance of sensory marketing in shaping the retail brand and the overall personality of the store. For instance, the use of the colour 'green' on many aspects

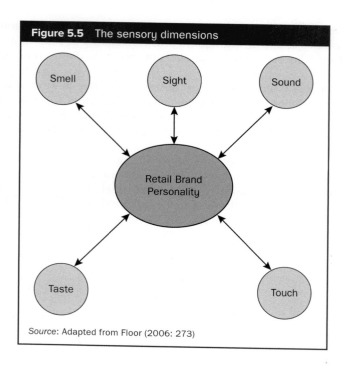

Figure 5.5 The sensory dimensions

Source: Adapted from Floor (2006: 273)

of the Body Shop's interior and exterior fixtures and fittings, fascia, packaging and so on reinforces the 'natural' environmental considerations, a key element of its value proposition and mission statement.

When we consider the various elements of atmospherics, retailers should adopt a holistic approach to develop a strategy. Colour, lighting, aroma, music and sampling demonstrations need to be integrated into an overall strategy that addresses the desired objectives such as engagement, interaction, mood-setting and pleasure-seeking. We now consider each element in turn.

5.7.1 Colour

This is perhaps the most visual way in which retailers can engage with shoppers. There is a perception that a neutral approach to using colour is the most appropriate way to display merchandise. Neutral shades – black, white, creams, browns, greys – are useful in store design because there is no danger of the merchandise clashing or having to compete with the store's decoration.

Clearly, it depends on the nature of the retail format and the value proposition. Colours that are too garish can create the effect of irritating shoppers. On the other hand, bright yellow, orange or lime colours can be used effectively in order to highlight special offers or discounted items. Over time, shoppers become accustomed to the fact that areas in the store where these colours appear, are the places to go to make purchases of bargains or offers such as 'buy one get one free' (referred to as BOGOFs). Tesco, the UK food retailer, makes extensive use of yellow to highlight such promotions.

Colours are capable of being interpreted differently by people and have different associations across different cultures. In a European context, for example, the colour blue evokes associations with cleanliness, hygienic and coolness. Purple suggests an element of sophistication and luxury. Red is often associated with something that is dynamic and aggressive. In the case of China, red and gold are considered to be symbolic of prosperity and wealth. Purple signifies nobility.

5.7.2 Lighting

The use of lighting has the same impact as in the way it is used in theatrical productions. The stage director wishes to highlight certain areas of the stage more fully than other parts. Different coloured lighting can also play an active part in creating a certain desired mood in the minds of the audience. Likewise, retailers can also generate similar effects. The level of ambient light needs to be such that the customer can see the merchandise clearly.

Virtually all stores need to look bright and inviting. Lighting can be used to create interest in the store design itself. It can also influence the propensity of shoppers to examine and handle merchandise.

Wall lights and spotlights can play an integral role in any shelf display and enhance the dramatic effect – suspended lighting or pin spots can play a significant role in augmenting the design and shape of the items. A visit to a jewellery store or even a brief perusal of the window display can clearly demonstrate how items such as rings, watches and bracelets can be highlighted to great effect. The glistening allure of gold and silver can generate very positive thoughts and stimulate a purchase.

Different coloured lighting can also work on mood management. Blue lighting is often used in the case of pharmacies. This reinforces the hygienic and clean nature of the premises and the products sold there.

Vignette: Hollister – a step in the dark

Hollister, a subsidiary label of the US retailer Abercrombie and Fitch, makes a virtue of deliberately using low levels of lighting within its stores. It focuses on casual clothing for young people and its designs are heavily influenced by the lifestyle of the Californian coast. In some ways it is a throwback to the Beach Boys generation. Its store design encourages shoppers to hang out and discover their clothing. A visit to one of their stores creates the feeling that you are in a nightclub or a trendy bar. The lighting is very dark and helps to cultivate a 'club-like' atmosphere where people can mingle and interact with each other. This approach has attracted criticism from visitors to their stores however. The following quotes capture these perceptions more fully.

'I went in a couple of times and couldn't see anything properly. I assume they have something to hide since they don't want their clothes to be seen in good light. They claim it's meant to be "casino-like". If a casino were that dark then it would be perfect for pickpockets and thieves.'

'It's because if the lights were turned up people would realise how awful their clothes are.'

Some Facebook groups have challenged the retailer. *'Hollister, you're a store, not a maze. Turn the lights on.'*

The use of lighting by this retailer certainly evokes controversy and criticism.

Source: Adapted from 'Shoppers left baffled by Hollister store's dim lighting policy'. *Daily Telegraph*. 27 October 2011. © Telegraph Media Group Limited 2011

5.7.3 Sound

Some people take the view that there is nothing as perfect as the 'sound of silence'. This may be appropriate if somebody wants to engage in a period of reflection or study in a library. How appropriate is it for shopping, however? Retailers face the challenges of encouraging shoppers to browse, interact with merchandise, visit as many parts of the store as possible and shaping shoppers' moods in such a way that they will be receptive towards the notion of making a purchase. Store patronage and loyalty are influenced in many cases by the store environment (Turley and Milliman, 2000).

As most of us who enjoy listening to music will readily recognize, our general mood, attitudes and general outlook on life at a particular point in time are significantly influenced by the type of music we play. Broekemier et al. (2008: 60) note that 'music is ordinarily highly controllable, ranging from loud to soft, fast to slow, vocal to instrumental, heavy metal to hit-oriented rock, or classical to contemporary urban'. It is relatively cheap to use and can be varied to suit different times of day and when there is low or heavy footfall within the store. While this level of control is attractive for retail strategists, it also presents problems. For instance what music should be played? How loud should it be? How do we get the balance right between capturing the attention of the shoppers on the one hand and intruding into their personal space on the other? These are easy questions to pose but rather difficult to answer.

A classic case in point is the playing of 'Christmassy' music in the weeks leading up to what is a key shopping period in certain parts of the world. Advocates argue that such music creates a 'happy', 'family' mood among shoppers. Others suggest that the constant playing of 'White Christmas', 'We wish you a merry Christmas', 'Have yourself a very merry Christmas' and 'Driving home for Christmas' is boring, repetitive and irritates some shoppers.

Some supermarkets make use of music that is there in the background but is difficult to attribute to any specific group or artist. This is often referred to as 'muzak' because of its banality. It is seen by some shoppers as a major irritant. Apart from this negative feature it can be argued that the retailer is missing out on an opportunity to use music that is more in line with its core brand values and link the emotions and perceptions of shoppers to these features. All Saints, the UK fashion retailer, targets mid- to high-income young people who have an interest in rock and roll. Not surprisingly, it makes constant use of fast and energetic rock and roll music in its outlets to infuse shoppers with its brand ethos.

In many cases the focus of the retailer is on encouraging shoppers to spend a greater amount of time in the outlet than originally planned. Bookstores are a prime example. As a consequence, classical slow tempo music relaxes shoppers and tempts them to linger in the store. By contrast, quick tempo music such as German quick march music has the opposite effect and would encourage a fast flow of shoppers through the store and to the exits!

In summary, music presents the retailer with opportunities to affect the mood and movement of the shopper within the store. Careful attention needs to be paid to the target market. The nature of the retail value proposition also influences the approach to the use of music within the various outlets. Strategists should also assess the core brand values of the retailer and appropriate music formats that complement the brand ethos. The challenge lies in capturing the correct balance between stimulating arousal in the minds of shoppers and irritating them.

5.7.4 Smell

This is another key element of atmospherics that can be used to good effect by retailers. Clearly some retail value offerings are strong users of aroma as they attempt to shape the mood and behaviour of shoppers as they approach and enter the store.

Coffee shops, perfumeries, bakeries and florists are prominent users of aroma. Enter a supermarket and the first smell you are likely to be assailed with is that of fresh bread baking in an oven. For many people this conjures up the image of their mother baking cakes and scones at home. It induces a warm, sentimental and happy feeling and can set the agenda for the subsequent shopping experience in that store. Abercrombie and Fitch go a step further and create an artificial aroma. It pumps this smell throughout each of its stores and for many regular shoppers it is regarded as an 'institutional' aroma that is automatically associated with this retailer.

The type of scent used by retailers can also impact on the response of shoppers. Tischler (2005) ran an experiment in the women's and men's sections of a US clothing store. In the women's section, a smell of vanilla was diffused through the store. By contrast, in the men's section, a spicy, honey-like fragrance was released. The results generated the doubling of turnover in both sections on the days when the scents were used. Interestingly when the scents were reversed in both stores, customers spent less than the average daily take.

The use of artificial aromas to arouse interest and set the mood can be criticized for being overly cynical. However, as discussed earlier, research demonstrates the impact that it can have not just on the mood of the shopper but on sales, which is the acid test for such initiatives in the area of atmospherics.

When making decisions on aroma, retailers also need to consider the ambient factors that can affect the experience for shoppers within the store environment. Such issues address areas such as the air temperature and quality, humidity and the degree of circulation and ventilation throughout the store. A complementary factor is the relative cleanliness of the outlet. A fresh, natural aroma can quickly lose its lustre if the floors and display units are dirty.

5.7.5 Touch

The ability to engage and interact with merchandise is for many retailers central to obtaining a purchase. This is particularly the case for items that are relatively high involvement and encourage hedonistic behaviour. From a pragmatic perspective, items such as electronic goods, where there is some degree of complexity involved on the part of the shopper, need to be demonstrated and explained. Interaction with such items reduces any anxiety shoppers may hold about their ability to use the product and bolster confidence.

Perfumeries can combine aroma with engagement as, for example, sales demonstrators can spray new or existing perfumes on customers to allow them to try out the product. Jewellery items can be made more alluring and attractive if the shopper can try on a ring or a bracelet and assess its merits in a mirror, with some timely advice from a sales assistant. In an earlier case vignette we considered how Hamleys, the toy retailer, actively encourages engagement and interaction. We also look briefly here at the approach of Tiso, an outdoor specialist retailer based in the UK.

Vignette: Tiso

Tiso was established in 1974 by Graham and Maude Tiso in the UK. It currently runs 11 stores throughout Scotland, England and Ireland. It also operates four outdoor experience stores in Edinburgh, Glasgow, Inverness and Perth. It is still family-owned. It was established at the outset because the owners felt that there was a gap in the market. Nobody, in their view, was providing quality outdoor gear and equipment in Scotland.

Within the experience store in Glasgow, they make use of technology to allow the shopper to try out items and gain information about various aspects of outdoor pursuits. For example the store operates a 'Run 4 It' lab, where an individual can try on various outdoor shoes and measure their running styles and patterns. The resulting data can help the individual to select the most appropriate shoe in terms of design, weight distribution and configuration.

Tiso also has an in-built climbing wall which is designed to encourage active participation and experimentation for visitors. Trained staff are available to provide advice on the suitability of equipment and so on.

A large authentic rock outcrop is used to provide a background to the store and is devoid of any trees, plants or fauna, thereby stimulating the outdoor experiences.

The use of such props and technology allows the visitor to interact in a meaningful and relevant way with the various items of outdoor clothing and equipment and is more likely to stimulate sales. Unobtrusive and knowledgeable staff play a critical role in providing advice and guidance where requested by the shopper. Tiso presents a good illustration of how a retailer can recognize the importance of the shopping experience and introduce initiatives to make the concept of experiential marketing work well.

Technology plays an important role in allowing shoppers to interact with merchandise. Nike allows shoppers to interact with sports equipment such as tennis rackets to simulate the feel of playing tennis shots. Large golf equipment retailers also make use of similar simulation tools to encourage shoppers to try out golf clubs so that they can be measured in order to purchase customized equipment.

Fashion retailers use technology that allows shoppers to virtually try on fashion items which can be varied by colour and can save them time in terms of physically trying on merchandise.

Visit an Apple store and it does not appear as if they are selling any products at all. Instead it almost resembles a science laboratory where staff are actively engaged in demonstrating products, addressing problems and queries raised by shoppers and, in effect, providing solutions. Many subsequent purchases are not made within the store. Instead, shoppers will then visit the Apple website and make their relevant purchases in the knowledge and confidence that they now understand how that product works. Any subsequent problems that they encounter can be addressed by means of another visit to the physical store.

5.7.6 Taste

Food and beverage retailers can make extensive use of this element to stimulate sales, introduce shoppers to new flavours and complement other products being sold in the outlet or store.

Retailers across a range of sectors such as music, books and fashion use simple beverages such as coffee and confectionary to create a relaxed environment where shoppers are encouraged to browse and engage with products.

Micro-breweries integrate the production of beer with retail selling. It is not uncommon to visit the retail premises of a beer company and witness the production of beer at the various stages of manufacture through glass partitions and/or via a guided tour by one of the employees. At the end of the tour, the visitors are encouraged to sample the various beers that are made on the premises. Bottle shops often also make strategic use of 'taste'-oriented initiatives to promote and sell various elements of their merchandise. Wine tasting and whisky sampling nights, often run by 'an expert' invited in by the retailer, can form a very effective mechanism for boosting sales, establishing new wines or selling off excess stock.

5.8 The use of materials within the selling environment

We should not underestimate the importance of using flooring, ceiling, fixtures and fittings and display units as an important shaper of the shopper's store experience. Such materials also send out signals or cues to visitors to the store. We briefly consider these elements.

Flooring, ceilings and partitions: although it is unlikely that a shopper will be fixated by the floor material or the ceiling, they can influence the perception of the shopper of the store and its merchandise. Carpet, polished wood (dark, light, stained), unpolished wood, terracotta tiles, linoleum, marble or stone tiles and textured rubber/plastics all represent options for the retailer in terms of store design. Individually they can communicate different brand associations and values.

For instance, marble flooring can be used to reinforce the 'luxury' aspect of the merchandise sold in the store and the core values of the brand. The colour and quality of carpets can also suggest certain associations. Trims such as chrome, stainless steel, metals – polished, matt, brushed, galvanized – and, for example, aluminium, textile and coloured acrylic also affect the store image.

For example, AllSaints, the UK fashion retailer, presents some good illustrations of what we mean in the preceding paragraphs. The product displays used by AllSaints and the use of appropriate lighting convey the impression of being on stage.

In terms of ceiling and walls, we can see that the desired impression is that of an 'industrial warehouse setting'. The walls are bare and show the bricks originally used to build the wall. The ceilings consist of 'stage' lighting that pinpoints and illuminates the merchandise.

Extensive use is made of traditional sewing machines that are displayed prominently on walls and display units. This is designed to reinforce the quality and originality of the designs. The overall approach, using a combination of lighting, a warehouse effect combined with the use of unique artefacts (for example, sewing machines) manages to convey a consistent store image that aligns effectively with the core values of the retail proposition.

Decisions with regard to the use of materials on flooring, walls, ceiling and fixtures and fittings will be heavily influenced by the following factors.

- *The nature of the product sold*: food-related items will require materials that are hygienic and easy to maintain. Jewellery outlets make use of plush carpeting to reinforce the perception of luxury.

- *The cost involved*: discount retailers will, relatively speaking, spend considerably less on materials and fixtures and fittings. First, consumers do not hold high expectations about the quality of the selling environment. Second, spending money on expensive materials reduces the ability of the retailer to offer bargains and discounted items. Expensive materials would also send 'mixed messages' to shoppers.

- *The level of store traffic*: heavy footfall in supermarkets and large 'category killer' outlets requires durable, long-lasting flooring material. Due to the large extent of selling space, it should be capable of being easily maintained and withstand 'wear and tear'. A large department store might be well advised to use wood block or tiling on the main walkways throughout the selling environment.

- *Hedonic versus utilitarian shopping motives*: the more the retail value proposition appeals to the pleasure-seeking desires of shoppers, the greater the requirement for more expensive and luxurious materials across these areas. Such retail propositions will require more frequent refurbishment and updating as the store image is likely to become 'stale' more quickly.

■ *Environmental and safety criteria*: in an age where 'health and safety' concerns impinge on many aspects of people's lives, the retail sector is no different. Retailers have to comply with a raft of safety issues and none more so than in the case of store design and layout. Clearly this had relevance for the type of material used on floors and fixtures and fittings. Increasingly retailers are recognizing the importance of using eco-friendly material. Apart from any safety considerations, it can reinforce the impression that the retailer has environmental concerns at the forefront of its brand values.

5.9 In-store marketing communications at point of purchase

Retailers make extensive use of a range of materials to encourage shoppers to visit various sections of the store, to highlight special promotions or price deals and reinforce the retailer's value proposition.

As we see a convergence of information management allied to the use of technology, retailers are increasingly in a stronger position to maximize sales in each and every area of the store. This extends to the shelf positioning of the merchandise; the particular location on the shelf (high, eye level or bottom); return per square metre of selling space; and the location of specific product categories within the store. We examine the communications aspect of in-store marketing in greater detail in Chapter 10. In this chapter we consider the different materials used by the retailer in-store.

■ *Banners*: retailers often place banners in key places within the store; for example at the front of shopping aisles or hanging from the ceiling, to attract the attention of the shopper and get across a particular message to them in the form of a slogan. Such banners are often placed at the entrance to the store. The objective is usually based around providing information; for example, a special promotion or comparative price advertising. It also has a persuasive element to it and in many cases it is designed to reinforce the key points of differentiation of the retailer. The banners can take many forms, including 'pop-up' banners (often referred to as Toblerones). Such a banner has the benefit of being light in weight and easy to assemble and can be moved around. Banners can be vertical, horizontal, circular or rectangular in shape.

■ *Shelf-edge labels*: retailers place such labels on the shelves to inform the shopper about issues such as price comparisons with other retailers. This typically would highlight a specific item; for example, a yoghurt, its price (as audited at a specific time) and its weight versus an identical item from a competitor. These materials are often referred to as 'shelf-talkers'. Typically they are designed with bright 'beacon' colours (for example, yellow or orange) and attempt to engage with the shopper and impart information that can help in making a purchasing decision.

■ *Cart (trolley) talkers*: this is a variation of the shelf-talker and is located on the shopping cart. The same objectives apply to the shelf-talker.

Digital technology in particular creates further opportunities for retailers to drive improvement in the use of such shelf and cart labels. Much greater levels of information can be included in digital signs. It can also capture the attention of the shopper more clearly because the information is not 'fixed' on a label. In this case it contains moving material. The downside of this is that it may irritate shoppers and distract them. This is similar to the technology that is used in sports stadia with perimeter advertising.

■ *Augmented reality*: retailers are making much greater use of the concept of augmented reality in terms of making the shopping experience more positive and helpful for shoppers. This concept works on the basis of the merging of mobile technology with in-store and exterior activities. Scan the QR codes to access YouTube videos demonstrating the full effects of AR in action.

This technology allows the shopper and the retailer to engage with each other in a more meaningful way. For instance the shopper can use augmented reality to visualize how items of clothing can look on their bodies, playing around with different sizes and colours in the process. Retailers can run various interactive initiatives that attract shoppers into the store, and while there, encourage them to engage with various items of merchandise.

5.10 External dimensions

In addition to the interior dimensions associated with managing the physical selling environment, we need to consider the external aspects. Communicating the values of the retail brand and the value proposition is at the centre of retail strategy. In the context of the selling environment, the external aspects – window displays, awnings and the entrance to the store – can be used as an effective method for targeting customers.

5.10.1 Windows

Many retailers fail to take up the opportunity to make effective use of the window displays at their disposal. This is often evidenced by the cluttering of badly presented inventory that fills up the available space but does little to attract the attention of people as they pass by the windows. On busy high streets or in shopping malls, one of the primary functions of window displays is to catch the eye of the passer-by. This is not enough however. It should stimulate their curiosity and ideally 'pull them' towards the entrance to the outlet. Hammond (2011: 181) identifies three functions of window displays.

1 **Intrigue**: abstract but largely focused images that pique the customer's interest. AllSaints displays rows and rows of old sewing machines in its windows. It raises questions. Why are they in the window? Let us go and find out. It has the psychological effect of stimulating the shopper's subconscious. It suggests tailoring, hand-making and quality – attributes that reinforce AllSaint's premium positioning strategy.

2 **Inform**: simple and sharp messages. 'Sale now on'. 'Everything must go'.

3 **Inspire**: a window that gets shoppers thinking about the store and its contents. Gap ran a window display where it featured three fun dresses in the window with a slogan on the window that said 'Flirty Dresses are the Key to Spring'. This encourages the customer to think about ditching the winter blues and jumping into a fun spring wardrobe.

In a European context, the shopping period leading up to Christmas often produces some outstanding window displays from retailers, capturing the essence of the sentiments behind Christmas and attracting the attention of people on the high street.

In 2014 Harrods, the upmarket UK retailer, invited 11 luxury goods designers to create a series of bespoke, hand-crafted pieces for the various window displays. They focused on the concept of oversized vintage toys. For example the well-known UK furniture designer, Amy Somerville, created a giant wooden musical box with an art deco mirror and a spinning ballerina dressed in a Zuhair Murad tutu.

Designers are also making use of technology to use plasma screens in windows and digital-related tools to create movement and the effect of energy. Flashing messages, of course, can irritate shoppers but have the undoubted ability to capture the eye and attention of passers-by.

As mentioned in the previous section, augmented reality can create a much more dynamic, visual and engaged usage of window displays. Scan the QR code to see this in action.

5.10.2 Awnings

Awnings refer to the covering that is often placed over the entrance to the outlet or store. On high-street locations in particular this fulfils the basic function of providing shelter to shoppers from the elements. In warm climates it provides welcome relief from the sun and in wetter climates some protection from the wind and rain. Lush, the toiletries retailer, makes use of its awning to communicate the essence of its value proposition: 'fresh handmade cosmetics'. Retailers can combine colour to also make their outlet stand out in the high street.

5.10.3 Signage/fascia

This refers to the logo, name, graphics and colours. This can be integrated with the awnings to reinforce the brand message and subconsciously work on the shopper's associations with the logo or design of the

Figure 5.6 External displays at Lush

retailer. Figure 5.6 shows how Lush combines a number of its external features with its overall brand identity.

5.10.4 Door entrances

The entrance to the store should not be underestimated in terms of its role in influencing shopping behaviour. Decisions have to be balanced with some pragmatic issues however. For instance a wide entrance to the outlet has the effect of 'welcoming' people but also raises some concerns about inviting shoplifters into the outlet!

Some retailers, particularly if located in interior shopping malls, do away with any form of door at all. This is based on the view that a door can be seen as an obstacle or barrier to entry. Subconsciously some shoppers feel threatened and intimidated as they approach the entrance. A door, particularly when it is closed, can exacerbate these feelings and may lead to them turning around and walking away. Open doors are more prevalent in interior locations such as shopping malls. In many parts of the world, wet and windy conditions prevail and make the concept of open doors problematic: merchandise can be damaged, shelving can be blown down and the wind can make it an unattractive place to be for both shoppers and store employees.

Retailers also have the option of using a funnel entrance. This is effectively a recessed entrance: the door is not located directly on the street. Instead shoppers have to go through a funnel to access the door. Usually on either side, the retailer can make use of window displays to attract the attention of shoppers, providing further temptation as they contemplate entering the store. The door is potentially intimidating, but the display of items on the adjoining windows can hopefully overcome the reluctance of the shopper.

In summary, retailers should be proactive in terms of using the external dimensions of the store environment to communicate their brand values and promises. In many ways the external positions of retail outlets on busy high streets, shopping centres and retail parks resemble TV advertisements. In both cases the challenge is to attract the attention of shoppers/viewers in a world where people are constantly bombarded by messages and communications. The external elements of the selling environment can play a significant role in capturing attention, creating curiosity, reinforcing brand values, evoking conscious and subconscious feelings and drawing shoppers to the entrance to the store. When linked to the use of various aspects of the senses (colour, lighting and aroma in particular), retailers can differentiate their retail location in a cost-effective manner.

5.11 Conclusions

In this chapter we have considered the challenges involved in managing the physical selling environment. This involves both internal and external aspects. We can identify a number of key objectives for retailers when grappling with this challenge. The external dimensions provide an opportunity to capture the attention of people on the high street or within the shopping centre/mall. The next step is to create a welcoming background as they consider the items in the window displays and contemplate entering the store.

Once inside the store, the retailer has a number of dimensions to address when putting together an effective selling strategy. Store layout sets the agenda for the subsequent shopping experience. The layout has to consider the requirements of the shopper (comfort, easy access to the different categories of merchandise, as little delay as possible and so on) with the retailer's desire to encourage shoppers to visit as many parts of the store as possible.

Atmospherics play a critical role in shaping and influencing shopping behaviour. When we use this term we refer specifically to addressing the senses: smell, sight, sound, taste and touch. We considered the various initiatives that retailers can use to design focused and effective selling strategies. We also noted that again a balance has to be struck between the retailer's and customer's requirements. By going too far with psychological ploys to encourage people to spend more money, retailers can be criticized for manipulating shoppers and engaging in unethical behaviours. Such instances include the placing of confectionery items at the checkouts so that children can pester their parents to put items in the shopping basket.

Decisions with regard to the use of atmospherics depend on the nature of the retail proposition and the shopping behaviour involved: hedonistic versus functional shopping. Hedonistic shopping behaviour revolves around the shopping experience. Customers expect to see an exciting and stimulating environment when they visit retail outlets. They like to engage with merchandise in an interactive way. They seek pleasure from the shopping experience and retailers have to respond accordingly.

We assessed the concept of retail as theatre; that is, the use of dramatic initiatives can add richness to the shopping experience and allow the retailer to heighten emotions and reinforce brand values. Such an approach can also allow shoppers to engage with various aspects of the merchandise and, when combined with the involvement of sales personnel, can inform, solve problems, entertain and challenge shoppers.

Case study: Lush

Lush is a soap and toiletries company that holds the following values as being central to its value proposition: making products by and using little or no preservatives or packaging, fighting against the use of animals when testing products and inspiring a culture of employing happy people who make happy soaps.

Lush recognizes the importance of managing the selling environment in order to drive footfall and sales. You smell the company before you arrive at the entrance to its stores. Its lingering aroma of scent and soap assails your olfactory senses from a radius of about 15 yards or so in the approaches to the outlet.

The shelving within the store displaying the merchandise is made from natural wood and the internal signage and information about the items is handwritten on blackboards.

The merchandise is displayed in an unusual manner (see Fig. 5.7). At first glance, they appear like pastries would be presented in a confectionery shop. Figure 5.7 depicts what appears to be a cheese-wheel except it is not. Instead it contains soaps from which the customer can cut off a wedge. Shoppers are encouraged to try the products. Bowls of water are placed on each stand to reinforce the concept of hygiene and preservative-based products are placed in ice.

Figure 5.7 Merchandise display at Lush

The packaging (gift wraps, bags and so on) all depict the slogan 'Fighting Animal Testing'. This reinforces one of the central platforms of the brand's ethos.

The mugs and merchandise also attempt to convey the concept of 'happy employees'. Pictures of individual staff members are featured on the wrapping to demonstrate that they have been handmade and hand-crafted.

Unconventional wrapping such as the use of scarfs is used to make the items stand out.

In summary, Lush makes extensive and strategic use of the key dimensions of store layout and design to promote its items and communicate the core values of its brand.

Questions

1 From the brief description of its strategy and the accompanying photographs, assess the merits and weaknesses of Lush's approach in its management of the retail selling space.

2 Do you believe that this approach needs to be changed from time to time or should it remain a consistent strategy?

3 If you were a competitor of Lush, what would you do to achieve greater differentiation?

Chapter outcomes

- The physical selling environment refers to both internal and external dimensions that can be used to create a selling environment which satisfies the customer's needs and requirements.

- Store layout should provide a logical and coherent road map for shoppers as they negotiate their way around the selling space.

- Effective store layout can encourage shoppers to spend more time in the store, visit more pockets of interest, trade-up their expenditure to more expensive items and visit specific pockets of interest in the store.

- Retailers can embrace the concept of retail as theatre and employ a range of initiatives to heighten the shopping experience.

- We need to delineate between the different categories of shopping motivations: hedonistic versus functional. This will largely determine the approach to be adopted by retailers in terms of managing the store environment.

- Multisensory marketing relates to the way in which retailers appeal to the senses (sound, sight, taste, touch and aroma).

- In hedonistic shopping behaviour, shoppers wish to engage and interact with the product. Strategies that encourage such behaviour can significantly heighten the experience for shoppers in this type of buying situation.

- Managing the selling environment also addresses the need to reinforce brand values and associations.

- Developing the online selling environment needs to focus on creating a positive experience for the visitor.

Discussion questions

1 Assess the extent to which you would agree with the view that managing the selling environment is largely about communicating the brand values of the retailer.

2 Make a visit to a retail store of your choice. Carry out an observation audit (making notes of the way in which the retailer addresses the internal and external dimensions of the selling environment). Assess the strengths and weaknesses of the strategy adopted by the retailer. What recommendations would you make to the store manager?

3 Evaluate the proposition that the concept of 'retail as theatre' lacks substance when it comes to applying it.

4 Some commentators believe that retailers manipulate shoppers in order to generate increased sales. Is this a valid argument?

5 How can a retailer make more strategic use of window displays?

6 Evaluate the notion that bright and garish colours used in interior and external store design only serve to irritate shoppers. Use examples to support your point of view.

References

Aghazadeh S. (2005) Layout strategies for retail operations: a case study. *Management Research News*. 28(10): 31–46.

Baron, S., Harris, K. and Harris, R. (2001) Retail theatre: the 'intended effect' of the performance. *Journal of Service Research*. 4(2): 102–117.

Bitner, M.J. (1992) Servicescapes: the impact of physical surroundings on customers and employees. *Journal of Marketing.* 56(2): 57–71.

Broderick, A.J. (1998) Role theory, role management and service performance. *Journal of Services Marketing.* 12(5): 348–361.

Broekemier, G., Marquardt, R. and Gentry, J.M. (2008) An exploration of happy/sad and liked/disliked music effects on shopping intentions in a women's clothing store service setting. *Journal of Services Marketing.* 22(1): 59–67.

De Nisco, A. and Napolitano, M.R. (2006) Entertainment orientation of Italian shopping centres: antecedents and performance. *Managing Service Quality.* 16(2): 145–166.

Donovan, R.J. and Rossiter, J.R. (1982) Store atmosphere: an environmental psychology approach. *Psychology of Store Atmosphere.* 58(1): 34–57.

Floor, K. (2006) *Branding a Store: How to Build Successful Retail Brands in a Changing Marketplace.* London: Kogan Page.

Hammond, R. (2011) *Smart Retail: Winning Ideas and Strategies From the Most Successful Retailers in the World.* London: Prentice Hall.

Harris, R., Harris, K. and Baron, S. (2003) Theatrical service experiences: dramatic script development with employees. *International Journal of Service Industry Management.* 14(2): 184–199.

Hauser, E. (2006) The many faces of experiential marketing. Available on line at: http://www.chiefmarketer.com/the-many-faces-of-experiential-marketing/

Hulten, B. (2011) Sensory marketing: the multi-sensory brand-experience. *European Business Review.* 23(3): 256–273.

Mehrabian, A. and Russell, J.A. (1974) *An Approach to Environmental Psychology.* Cambridge, MA: MIT Press.

Moor, E. (2003) Branded spaces: the scope of 'new marketing'. *Journal of Consumer Culture* 3(1): 39–60.

Moore, C.M., Doherty, A.M. and Doyle, S.S. (2010) Flagship stores as a market entry method: the perspective of luxury fashion retailing. *European Journal of Marketing.* 44(1/2): 139–161.

Morton, J. (2009) Latest survey of marketers reveals plans for increased spend on experiential marketing for 2009. *Marketing Weekly News.* 11 July: 31.

Mower, J.M., Kim, M. and Childs, M.L. (2012) Exterior atmospherics and consumer behaviour: Influence of landscaping and window display. *Journal of Fashion Marketing and Management.* 16(4): 442–453.

Pine, B.J. and Gilmore, J.H. (1999) *The Experience Economy: Work is Theatre and Every Business is a Stage.* Boston, MA: Harvard Business School Press.

Pranter, C.A. and Martin, C.L. (1991) Compatibility management roles in services performers. *Journal of Services Marketing.* 5: 43–53.

Rosenbaum, M.S. and Massiah, C. (2011) An expanded servicescape perspective. *Journal of Services Management.* 22(4): 471–490.

Tischler, L. (2005) Smells like brand spirit. *Fast Company.* August, 56.

Turley, L.W. and Milliman, R.E. (2000) Atmospheric effects on shopping behaviour: a review of the experimental evidence. *Journal of Business Research.* 49: 193–211.

Zeithaml, V.A. and Bitner, M.J. (1996) *Services Marketing.* New York: McGraw-Hill.

Chapter 6

Retail brand strategy

☑ Learning objectives

On completion of this chapter you should be in a position to address the following objectives:

- ☑ Understand the concept of brand and how it applies to the retail sector.
- ☑ Examine the components of brand-building and strategy development.
- ☑ Gain an insight into the concept of store brands and the role they play in overall brand strategy.
- ☑ Assess the impact of digital marketing and social media on brand-building.
- ☑ Assess the advantages and disadvantages of store brands for the various stakeholders: retailers, shoppers and suppliers.
- ☑ Evaluate the importance of relationship-building between the retailer and the customer.
- ☑ Examine the importance of brand loyalty and the role that store loyalty cards play in retaining customers.
- ☑ Assess the effectiveness of loyalty programmes.

6.1 Introduction

In this chapter we evaluate a critical aspect of retail marketing strategy: brand-building and development. As we discussed in earlier chapters, one of the biggest challenges facing retailers is identifying points of differentiation over their competitors and establishing and building awareness levels among their target markets. The subsequent task is that of attracting them to their outlets (physical and/or virtual) and developing loyalty and commitment towards shopping with them.

In a global retail environment where competition is becoming increasingly more intense and diverse, it is critical that retailers establish some form of awareness, recognition, preference and positivity in the minds of their target market. Otherwise they are likely to sink without trace in the confusing and overcrowded retail market sectors that shoppers have to operate within. Retail brand strategy development provides the retailer with the opportunity to carve out a meaningful and relevant position in the market. The anticipated outcome is one where the retailer can achieve targeted sales, market share and profitability. Without such a focused approach it is unlikely that the retailer will make any significant impact within the mind of the shopper.

Retailers have invested greatly in brand development and brand-building to attract and retain customers. The benchmark is to satisfy and where possible exceed customers' expectations. If this is not achieved then shoppers will go elsewhere in order to satisfy their needs and requirements.

In the early sections of this chapter we examine the concept of the brand and its components. We evaluate the challenges involved in building the brand and increasing brand equity in order to attract and primarily build brand loyalty. We examine the relationship between brand strategy and positioning and revisit some of the concepts discussed in Chapter 3.

We then examine the concept of store brands. This is also referred to in the business literature as private labels or own labels. These are brands that are owned and marketed by the retail store and provide an alternative option for shoppers. We assess the ways in which such brands have evolved and adapted to changing market conditions and demands. We consider the benefits and potential downsides for the key stakeholders in the process.

In the latter stages of this chapter we examine the concept of store loyalty and how brand strategy plays a strategic role in cultivating commitment and repeated visits to the store on the part of shoppers.

Over the last 20–25 years retailers have made extensive use of loyalty cards to encourage shoppers to remain loyal to the store. We evaluate the usefulness and appropriateness of such tactics from the perspective of the retailer and the shopper.

What is a brand?

When we use terms such as 'brands' and 'brand strategy', we are explicitly recognizing the importance of differentiating and distinguishing one product from another. Back in the 19th century cattle ranchers in the USA seared a mark on their cattle to differentiate one ranch from another as a means of simple identification. In the context of business, a brand is a combination of a name, a logo and a symbol to provide recognition and awareness of a product. If we consider the plethora of products and services available in modern business sectors today, it is critical that a brand makes some attempt to register in the minds of consumers and that they associate certain benefits and features that are attributed to it.

As brands develop and become established in the specific industry sector, the objective is to gain more than recognition in the minds of consumers. Awareness hopefully leads to consumers trying out the brand to discover its features and potential benefits. If it is perceived as something that simply replicates and copies what is already available (often referred to as a 'me-too' product), then consumers will most likely revert to their original preferred choice. In the longer term such brands will disappear from the market. After all, why would people buy such a product if it offers nothing beyond what is already on the market to their benefit?

If a product gets over the initial hurdle of breaking into the 'mind-set' of its target market and an increasing number of customers continually purchase it, it begins to develop a reputation, largely built around a couple of relevant attributes. This may revolve around factors such as low price, high-quality merchandise, excellent customer service and so on. As well as garnering a stronger reputation, consumers begin to trust the brand and have confidence that it will deliver on its promise that is relevant to that particular segment. The keyword here is 'relevant'. A food retailer such as Waitrose, for example, provides a range of items that tend towards the 'high end' in terms of quality. This point of differentiation is reflected in its pricing strategy. Thus, segments that are concerned with low prices are unlikely to be attracted to this type of value proposition.

The role that brands play in the context of consumers and organizations is captured in Table 6.1.

Table 6.1 The role of brands

Consumers
Identification of a source of product
Assignment of responsibility to product maker
Risk reducer
Search cost reducer
Promise, bond, or pact with maker of product
Symbolic device
Signal of quality
Manufacturers
Means of identification to simplify handling or tracing
Means of legally protecting unique features
Signal of quality level to satisfied customers
Means of endowing products with unique associations
Source of financial returns

Source: Keller (2008: 7)

While our main interest is directed towards the retail sector, we should recognize that brands cover a wide range of levels and categories. Many people associate branding with traditional physical products. However, branding is critical for the marketing of a wide spread of services in such sectors as tourism (the marketing of countries and cities), sport (the marketing of clubs, organizations, sporting events and competitions), education (universities, colleges and schools), religion (churches and beliefs) and individuals (athletes such as Tiger Woods, Roger Federer and Lionel Messi). Branding is also crucial in business-to-business markets where companies have to address issues such as corporate reputation, reliability, service, price and quality in order to also differentiate their offering from the competition.

6.2.1 Branding and retailers

For retailers, branding is also a critical component of their overall retail marketing strategy. As we discussed in Chapter 3, building store image is a key challenge. Shoppers will patronize stores that are in line with their expectations and which address their key evaluative criteria. An image that is out of line with these factors will simply not appeal to that target market. Therefore the careful development and cultivation of a store image is essential for the future of any retailer.

A positive and relevant store image allows the retailer to also retain customers and develop loyalty and commitment to that retail value proposition. We examine this in greater detail later in the chapter. As well as retaining customers and generating loyalty, retailers have the opportunity to capitalize on this by targeting shoppers with personalized offers and rewards based on the nature and extent of their shopping patterns. This reinforces the importance of customer relationship management that creates the potential to cement the interaction between both parties.

In addition to compiling a range of merchandise and designs from a supply base, many large retailers have developed a portfolio of their own or store labels to further reinforce their image and relationships with their customers. We investigate this aspect of branding later in the chapter.

6.3 Brand equity

Keller (2008) has written extensively on the topic of branding. He developed a model that was called the *customer-based brand equity* model (CBBE). This is depicted in the shape of a pyramid and is highlighted in Fig. 6.1.

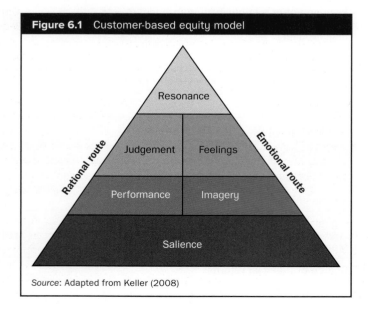

Figure 6.1 Customer-based equity model

Source: Adapted from Keller (2008)

Keller (1993: 8) defines the CBBE as 'the differential effect of brand knowledge on consumer re to the marketing of the brand'. It is based on the principle of building the brand over a period of tin moving through a number of steps or stages (six) from the base of the pyramid up to the pinnacle We now consider each of these six steps.

The term 'salience' addresses aspects of the brand that are noticeable and recognizable to the consumer. This does not necessarily mean all elements of the brand, but aspects which mean that the consumer includes the brand in the 'consideration set' when evaluating brand alternatives in the early stages of the purchasing process.

The next level on the pyramid covers the issue of 'performance'. This refers to the ability of the product/service to meet the functional needs and requirements of the consumer. This covers product characteristics such as quality, durability, customer service, price and so on.

'Imagery' refers to social and psychological needs. It considers the relationship between the brand's and the consumer's characteristics. For instance, in the case of luxury brands, the product may allow the consumer to relate their desired social position in society by purchasing such an item.

The third step in the process takes us to two elements: the cognitive and affective. In the case of the former it is referred to in the model by Keller as 'judgement'. In the latter he uses the term 'feelings'. This stage builds on the second one. Here, the shopper is in a position to make some observations and opinions about a particular brand in relation to aspects such as quality and credibility. The second element relates to the ability of the brand to engender feelings such as excitement, happiness, fun, social approval and so on. It can be based on the individual reaction or as part of the social desirability and approval of the social set to which the individual belongs.

The concept of 'resonance' represents the strongest level of commitment of the individual to a particular brand. It takes the relationship between the consumer and the brand to a new level and is ideally where the brander wants to be. With such a high level of commitment and intensity on the part of the consumer, it is the ultimate in terms of customer relationship management. The consumer has a very strong loyalty to the brand, will continue to buy more of that brand and trade up to more expensive versions (where relevant). They will also act as strong ambassadors and advocates of the brand and spread 'the good news'.

6.4 Building the brand

Although products can emerge on the marketplace relatively quickly, it takes time and considerable financial and managerial effort to turn a product into a well-established and recognized brand. For instance, customers may be initially suspicious and distrustful of a new brand that appears on the market, particularly if the company is not well known or is entering a new and geographically dispersed market. As we mentioned earlier, brands develop on the basis of customers having confidence and trust in the brand's promise and its value proposition.

The reverse can also apply. Brands that hold a strong position in their domestic markets can leverage that power through word-of-mouth and the social media. When they enter new international markets, customers are already familiar with the brand and look forward to its arrival with great enthusiasm and anticipation. For example, when IKEA opens a new store in a new market or even in an existing one, people often queue overnight in order to be first into that store when it opens in the morning. In some cases fighting and riots have happened in such circumstances! However, even in these cases, we should remember that it took time for the organizations to develop the build the brand in the first instance.

In Chapter 3 we examined the concept of positioning and its importance for setting the agenda for the subsequent marketing strategy. There is a very close relationship between brand development and positioning. The latter refers to the way in which the brander wishes to be perceived in the mind of the targeted customer and how it compares with its competitors on the evaluative criteria that the customer adopts when making purchasing decisions. The wider the gap between how the brand is actually perceived and how the brander wants it to be perceived, the bigger the problem and the challenges.

Decisions regarding the positioning of a particular brand force decision-makers to address some fundamental questions. These can be summarized as follows.

- What does our brand represent?
- In what ways does our brand differentiate itself from our existing and potential competitors?
- Do we have a clear understanding of the needs and requirements of our target market?
- What position (if any) do we currently occupy in the minds of our target market?
- Do we have a sufficient marketing budget to address the challenges involved to capture (or retain) prime position in the minds of our target market?
- How consistent is our approach to positioning?

The answers to the above questions shape the subsequent retail strategy and influence the ways in which the elements of the retail marketing mix are used to reinforce the value proposition. Keller (2008) identifies four stages in the brand management process.

1 *Identifying and establishing brand positioning*: the positioning exercise generates analysis about the brand and its core brand associations. This gets to the heart of what the brand is all about. How would somebody describe it in one sentence? This is often referred to as the essence or DNA of the brand.

   For instance, Lush, the handmade cosmetics retailer, established its presence in the hair, skincare and body treatments market by making fresh products by hand using little or no preservative or packaging. By using creative designs and only using materials that have not been tested on animals, it has carved out a relatively distinctive position in the minds of shoppers. Since its inception, this has been the consistent message in all its product development, store design and marketing communication activities.

2 *Planning and implementing brand marketing programmes*: as the brand gains traction by gaining more and more positive comment and perceptions from its target market, it can develop what is referred to as 'brand equity'. Roper and Fill (2012: 162) define this as 'the marketing benefits and outcomes that would accrue due to its brand name compared with those that would accrue if the same product did not have the brand name'. The benefits are reflected in higher market share, premium prices, stronger customer loyalty and less chance of brand-switching. This situation of strength and power does not happen immediately and the development of marketing activities needs to reinforce the central differentiating point(s).

   In the case of Lush, the gradual evolvement of the brand has focused on the efforts of the founders to position it as an 'ethical brand'. This is evidenced in areas such as 'store design and layout' where it uses natural wood that is sustainably sourced, eco-paint and energy-efficient LED lighting. It has supported a number of eco-led initiatives to further reinforce its brand image, even to the extent of refusing to open stores in Israel.

3 *Measuring and interpreting brand performance*: marketing research is critical in this stage of strategic brand management. Areas such as brand awareness, brand associations, brand attitudes, degree of brand attachment and the ways in which customers use the brand and discuss it with others need to be audited on a regular basis to establish how well the brand is performing relative to competitive offerings. This type of longitudinal research allows companies to track performance and identify areas where slippages have occurred. It also identifies areas that can help to improve the level and extent of brand equity.

4 *Growing and sustaining brand equity*: this addresses the need to take a long-term view of the brand and how it can be further developed. For some companies this involves managing a portfolio of brands and the consequent opportunities and challenges in managing the interaction and synergies across the brands to the greater benefit of the company. In the context of the retail sector, those involved in international markets have to manage the challenges of operating in diverse cultures with different levels of infrastructure and different shopping patterns, expectations and perceptions.

When retailers transfer a format from one country to another, big decisions have to be made about the degree of standardization in terms of the brand message versus the need to customize the overall marketing campaign to reflect local needs and concerns. Some retailers such as IKEA arguably sell merchandise that has a universal need. In the case of IKEA, that might be interpreted as affordable and functional furniture and household items for young people purchasing or renting a flat or house for the first time. While this lends itself towards standardization, some form of adaptation is necessary. For instance, the size of flats in Asian countries such as Japan and China is much smaller and compact than in North America and many parts of Europe. This has implications for design of household items to take account of the reduced space. While the overall points of differentiation in this case remain the same (lower prices than the competition and functional yet modern designs), the size and shape of individual items such as furniture should be in proportion to the space dimension. This is captured in IKEA's corporate mission statement:

> "*Our company vision is this: To create a better everyday life for the many people. We do this by offering a wide range of well-designed, functional home furnishing products at prices so low that as many people as possible will be able to afford them.*" (*IKEA Corporate reports*)

We will examine the wider issues involved in internationalization and retailing in Chapter 12.

6.5 Case in point: Ted Baker

Ted Baker is an international clothing retailer. It was established by Ray Kelvin in the city of Glasgow in Scotland in 1988 and initially commenced trading as a specialist men's shirt retailer. In the intervening years to the present it has established its operations as a global lifestyle brand and has succeeded in bucking the recession as it continues to grow its business across Europe, the Middle East, North America, Asia and Australasia. At the end of 2013, Ted Baker had representation in over 35 countries.

It has expanded its product range across menswear, womenswear, accessories (for example, shoes) sleepwear and childrenswear. It makes use of a number channels including physical stores through concessions, its own stores, licencing, wholesaling and through the medium of e-commerce.

In the first eight years of its existence the company struggled to survive and largely did so because Kelvin ploughed every penny he had into the business to keep it afloat. It finally achieved a degree of success during the 1990s. This was the era of 'acid house' music. The bright shirts produced and designed by Ted Baker fitted neatly into the lifestyle and aspiration of young males who were into this music. Demand grew exponentially for the shirts and accessories and put the retailer on a firm footing.

On the strength of this success in the UK, Kelvin developed a range of womenswear that took off in the North American market.

In 1997 Kelvin took the company out of its private status and it operated as the 'No Ordinary Designer Label Limited'. He still retained a substantial part of the business however.

Ray Kelvin is still CEO of the firm and he describes himself as 'the closest thing to Ted'. In many ways he represents Ted's alter ego and he continuously asks himself the question, what would Ted do? When faced with decisions on new product launches and designs, he is quirky in many respects: covering his face during interviews and demanding that journalists do a number of press-ups if they turn up late for briefings or meetings.

Many of his stores are customized and have unique features. When he opened his store on 5th Avenue in New York, he designed a collection based on his love of fly fishing.

When asked the reasons for the continued success of Ted Baker, Kelvin stated, 'better product, better design, it's that simple'. This reflects the obsession that the retailer has with the focus on design, patterns and tailoring. It is perhaps the main reason why it can command higher prices than competitors, appealing as it does to the fashion-conscious individual who is prepared to pay a bit extra for these benefits.

As it expands internationally, Ted Baker makes the most of the 'quintessentially British' emphasis. This is most notably highlighted in its store design, particularly in its Tokyo store where it includes a booth fashioned like the back of a London black cab (taxi) to present some of its merchandise. This lifestyle dimension to its brand image was also exemplified when it opened a new store in 2011 in the Bluewater shopping centre in the UK. The store was styled as the fictional village of Tedbury complete with a country pub, apothecary, a baker and cake shop. This quirky and 'fun' approach to its brand ▶

◀ would appear to appeal to its target market. It was one of the first fashion retailers to provide free in-store WiFi and touch screens and interactive installations in its outlets.

It was also one of the first retailers who entered the 'e-tail' era in 1999, when it launched a transaction-based website. It carried out major upgrades to this site in 2009 and also upgraded its North American web channel in 2014. It worked closely with a multi-channel consultancy firm to drive major improvements to the site by creating separate customer journeys for men and women in order to maximize the customer experience.

It has over 180 stores in the UK and has expanded across Europe (Netherlands and Ireland in addition to its existing stores there). It has launched concessions in South Korea and opened the store on the iconic 5th Avenue in New York in 2012.

This store was designed along the following lines: 'The store, which is the brand's largest unit in the US, has been designed to replicate a traditional London townhouse of the Twenties. It features Art Deco design details including an elaborate metal staircase with messages written on the steps and bespoke printed wallpaper, along with exposed brick walls, a three-story glass chandelier and an elaborate digital window installation that includes a huge clock with pendulums and moving cogs and a screen that will display movies, photos and animation'.

The 5th Avenue flagship marks the eighteenth store for the brand in the USA and its third in Manhattan, following the Meatpacking District and SoHo. Each store is unique and designed to fit into the neighbourhood in which it is located. This store brings to life the company's interpretation of 'Ted's Grand House'. Shoppers enter the grand hall where men's and women's apparel and accessories share the space. Vintage-looking portraits with a twist hang from the walls and include images of women with moustaches or tea cakes on their heads and a young child with a Mohawk.

Menswear has its own home on the lower level in a space designed to mimic a scullery complete with dozens of butler's bells on the walls, pots and pans at the bottom of display racks, upside down jelly moulds hanging from the ceiling and a silver service at the cash wrap. The store opened with the company's fall collection of tailored clothing and sportswear in heritage fabrics that recall the great English outdoors.

The women's department is upstairs and is reminiscent of a lady's boudoir with fans on the walls and a cash wrap that looks like a vanity table. Fitting rooms feature floor to ceiling velvet curtains. The fall women's collection features a 'town meets country' theme and includes everything from the Working Title tailored pieces to eveningwear.

 Ted Baker's reputation for being a 'fun and quirky' retailer extends to its approach to marketing. It has relied mainly on word-of-mouth and various marketing stunts to drive its brand forward. Two typical campaigns reinforce this perception. Over the course of the Easter period a few years ago it ran a 'giveaway' that consisted of a chocolate bunny hotpot to customers who purchased items in the store. During the 2006 World Cup Football tournament, it created a range of football cards featuring players. It has not invested (in comparison to its competitors) in traditional advertising media. Instead it makes use of 'new media' such as YouTube. Scan the QR code to view the YouTube video for Ted Baker's collection.

Sources: Adapted from: *Retail Week*'s 25th anniversary: Ted Baker celebrates 25 years in retail. Holland, T. *Retail Week* (21 Jun 2013): Ted Baker Opens On Fifth Ave. Palmieri, J.E. WWD204.27 (8 August 2012)

Questions

Before addressing these questions, please engage in an online search for updated articles and videos on Ted Baker.

1 Assess the approach of Ted Baker in terms of building its brand.
2 Was its success largely built on luck rather than a preplanned strategy design?
3 Do you expect to see this brand around in 10 years' time?
4 What recommendations would you make to senior management in this operation about maintaining its success?

Dimensions of brand equity

We referred earlier to the concept of brand equity and the role that it plays in developing a strong brand. Brand equity revolves around a number of key dimensions: awareness, loyalty, perceived quality, brand associations and other proprietary brand assets (Aaker, 1991).

6.6.1 Brand awareness

This aspect is the building block for developing a strong brand. Without high levels of brand awareness and brand recall, it is virtually impossible to capture a position in the mind of the shopper. In order to be considered as an option for a purchase, the brand must register 'on the radar'. Brands that engender high levels of recognition are much more likely to generate a sale and in instances where the shopper is not that familiar with a range of brand options, the brand with the highest level of recall is likely to be selected as the preferred choice.

6.6.2 Brand loyalty

Strong equity revolves around loyalty and commitment to that brand. It is more cost-effective to retain customers than it is to chase new ones. Loyal customers are less likely to switch to another retail brand. Retailers can also benefit from loyal shoppers through positive word-of-mouth and sharing of such experiences on social media platforms and blogs. If shoppers are tempted by a new retailer appearing on the scene, the retailer may have sufficient time to adapt its strategy to prevent loyal customers from switching their allegiance.

6.6.3 Perceived quality

This refers to the shopper's perception of the overall quality or superiority of a brand in relation to others that are considered in the purchase decision. This is not unidimensional and considers aspects such as performance, reliability, serviceability, style and design, conformance to shopper expectations and so on. In the context of the retail sector, which is largely service-dominant, the issue of conformance to expectations in general and to the desired shopping experience in particular is of critical importance in shaping the perception of quality.

6.6.4 Brand associations

When reflecting on a particular brand, it is normal for shoppers to have certain associations with that brand. A typical example (outside of the retail sector) that is often cited in the literature is Volvo. When that brand name is mentioned, most people associate it with 'safety'. This happens mainly because through the decades Volvo has stressed this attribute in its marketing communication strategy and features it strongly in the context of product design and ergonomics. This does not imply that other cars are less safe or indeed that it is the defining influence that people consider when buying a car. However, it reinforces the importance of the concept of brand association. If it is salient or relevant in terms of the benefits that people seek when making a purchase decision, it is more likely that that brand will feature highly as a favourite option for shoppers. For ethically concerned shoppers, retailers such as Body Shop and Lush inculcate strong associations with issues such as using natural ingredients that have not been tested on animals. Such value propositions resonate strongly with this segment of shoppers and are more likely to attract them into their retail stores and online channels than more mainstream retailers operating in the body care market.

6.6.5 Other proprietary brand assets

This refers to the issue of being able to leverage the brand and build on its strengths. An example would be an exercise in co-branding. This involves two branders with similar brand values coming together to engage in various marketing exercises such as joint promotions or the creation of a new product. Nike's involvement with the US basketball player, Michael Jordan, is an early example of how both parties can benefit from the positive associations of each other. Companies such as Louis Vuitton that made its name in the travel luggage and handbag sectors used the power of its brand equity to move into the jewellery sector.

6.7 Brand personality

When developing the brand, it is important to consider the concept of the brand as a personality. We have already discussed the relevance of brand associations and the role that they play in shaping an overall perception and image of a brand. Aaker and Fournier (1995) define brand personality as 'the set of meanings constructed by an observer to describe the "inner" characteristics of another person'. In subsequent research, Aaker (1997) developed a personality scale that could be used across different product categories.

In the context of retailing, store image refers to the combination of dimensions that shape a shopper's perception of a particular store. As we noted in Chapter 2, this is made up of factual and emotional variables. The former refers to objective and observable issues such as store layout, number of changing rooms, car parking facilities, merchandise and so on. The latter refers to subjective variables such as aspiration, lifestyle and so on. It is easy to assume that store personality and store image are one and the same phenomenon. However, Das, Datta and Guin (2012: 98–99) draw a distinction between the two and suggest that store personality refers to the 'consumer's perception of the human personality traits attributed to a retail brand'.

Most of the studies on brand personality have been conducted in non-retail sectors. Studies such as one conducted by Geuens, Weijters and Wulf (2009) developed a personality scale based on five factors: responsibility, activity, aggressiveness, simplicity and emotionality. However, it can be argued that retail brands are different from traditional brands insofar as influencing factors such as store design can play a critical role in shaping the perceived personality of the retail outlet.

Willems et al. (2011) examined the fashion retail sector and developed a specific scale that included the following dimensions. *Innovativeness* (trendy, hip, boring, youthful and modern); *chaos* (chaotic, careless, tidy, calm and busy); *conspicuousness* (special, extravagant and striking); *agreeableness* (approachable, reliable, successful and friendly) and *sophistication* (classy, elegant, stylish, distinguished and chic). Such scales need to be considered from a holistic perspective: the level of interdependency, however, needs to be investigated more fully examined.

Das et al. (2012) argue that more research needs to be conducted on the impact of brand personality on favourable brand intentions (such as brand loyalty and positive word-of-mouth). Similarly, more investigation is also required on the impact of antecedents such as store design, atmospherics and layout on the brand personality dimensions.

It is important in the context of retail strategy formulation and implementation that the personality of the store is understood by management. In forming associations with a brand, research indicates that shoppers either consciously or subconsciously link personality traits with the store and this influences their shopping patronage behaviour.

6.8 Corporate branding in the retail sector

In the preceding sections we focused our discussion on branding with particular emphasis on the relationship between the brander and the consumer/shopper. In this section we broaden our discussion and consider the importance of corporate branding and reputation. This explicitly recognizes that there are wider audiences and stakeholders than the consumer. Large retailers are generally not privately owned and as a consequence are answerable to their shareholders and the stock market. Their strategies are examined intently by financial journalists and experts and their overall reputation can be enhanced or damaged by the reactions and interpretations of such stakeholders in the process.

The reputations of retailers such as Primark and Benetton have been adversely affected by some of their actions such as allegations of using child labour to produce merchandise and controversial advertising strategies that have potentially offended religions. Such responses from the wider business community and society in general can affect the reputation and standing of retailers and ultimately hit them where it hurts in terms of reduced profitability and sales.

It can also affect the morale of employees who may have to encounter criticism and abuse from shoppers. The role of the internal employee is crucial in corporate branding within the context of the retail sector. Retailers are primarily service providers. While physical merchandise is presented and sold, much of the interaction between customers and staff revolves around the delivery of a range of services such as advice and guidance, processing payments, dealing with queries and complaints and actively selling items. Deficiencies in these areas by employees or in the website design (in the case of online channels) can lead to customer dissatisfaction and ultimately a reluctance to visit that store or website in the future.

King (1991) argued that customers increasingly make their judgements on the basis of the overall corporate culture as opposed to functional benefits highlighted in various marketing communications strategies. This reinforces the message that brand-building does not reside with the marketing department and brand managers any more. Instead, branding is the responsibility of the whole organization and must permeate throughout all of its corporate objectives and activities.

Van Riel and Fombrun (2007) highlight some benefits associated with this approach. They can be summarized as follows.

- It creates coherence and provides a framework for internal co-operation.
- It signals the strength and size of the organization to its key audiences.
- It is more cost-effective to operate an overall corporate brand than it is to develop a range of different product brands.

Roper and Fill (2012) identify some potential limitations with such an approach however.

- Corporate branding implies that the large sums spent on building product brands have been a waste of time.
- It can damage the impact and contribution of local brands.
- It can potentially upset and alienate customers if well-loved and favourite brands disappear from the shelves.

In the context of the retail sector, the use of corporate branding can extend in a number of different ways. For instance, food retailers such as Tesco have a number of different retail formats to cater for the demands and shopping preferences of its customers. This can range from the very large hypermarket format through to the Metro format (city-centre-based and focused on convenience) and Express (petrol forecourt format). It can reflect itself in terms of different product offerings at different price-points; for example, Tesco's Finest (high price) through to Tesco Value line (low prices).

The more recent emergence of online and mobile channels also provides opportunities for retailers to bring them under the overall umbrella of the corporate brand. As we discussed in Chapter 1, if inconsistencies and variations occur in terms of the customer experience, there is a danger that customers become confused and ultimately dissatisfied with the overall value proposition and their attitudes and perceptions of the overall brand will become more negative as a consequence.

Burghausen and Fan (2002: 98) conducted some qualitative research with seven retailers and their findings indicated that corporate branding is the main 'tenet of the corporate brand [and] acts as a strategic reference point aligning internal capabilities and resources with external factors and demands, thus guiding corporate strategy'.

In summary, corporate branding recognizes the need to adopt a wider perspective. The multiple stakeholders can play a significant role in shaping the perceptions that consumers hold about the store image. As we discuss in Chapter 11, retailers are coming under increasing pressure about their overall role in the community and in the wider society. In addition to the profit objective, retailers have to recognize that they also are expected to act as 'good corporate citizens' particularly in areas such as the environment and social responsibility. Managing ongoing relationships with customers, suppliers, opinion formers, the business press and shareholders is central to shaping and building the corporate brand.

6.9 Impact of social media on the retail brand

In recent years the major adoption of social media platforms by consumers has transformed the way in which they engage with brands. As we note in Chapter 10, social media opens up opportunities for branders to more effectively 'talk' and 'listen' to their customer base. Davis, Piven and Breazeala (2014) make the observation that in the context of developments in social media we have witnessed 'a shift from marketer-led brands to customer ownership and co-creation of meaning'. This reinforces the changing role of the customer in relationships with brands. Consumption is a 'two-way' process. In the context of retailing, shoppers share views, perceptions and experiences with each other within brand communities; for example, Facebook pages. They also participate vigorously in social media platforms created by the branders.

We have seen the emergence of what is termed 'brand communities'. While the initial engagements on social media were driven by PCs and laptops, the exponential growth in smartphones, tablets and Androids has led to greater mobility and flexibility. As we discuss in Chapter 13, retailers have developed location-based applications which mean that they can engage with shoppers when they are 'on the move'. Shoppers can also engage with the brander and with each other with much greater degrees of mobility and freedom than ever before.

Davis et al. (2014) identify five core elements of brand consumption in a social media setting. They are as follows.

- *Functional brand consumption*: consumers make use of social media to address a number of problems or issues that require some clarification. These include: (1) solving problems; (2) sending specific inquiries; (3) searching for information; (4) evaluating service before purchasing; and (5) gaining access to a brand's special deals and giveaways.

- *Emotional brand consumption*: this emotional involvement with the brand involves some enjoyable connections. Examples include: (1) alleviating personal problems or situations; (2) feeling privileged, recognized, and valued by a brand; and (3) escapism and satisfaction of curiosity.

- *Self-oriented brand consumption*: this aspect replicates some of the functional and emotional elements but will tend to vary due to the individual's lifestyle and the goals that drive them forward. Three primary motivators contained in this core value include: (1) self-actualization; (2) self-perception enhancement; and (3) self-branding. They reveal that consumers often seek self-actualization in their experiences with brands and other consumers in a social media community.

- *Social brand consumption*: this refers to the level of interaction between consumers in the brand community. In particular, this form of brand consumption is exhibited by the willingness of consumers to share their experiences with each other, make recommendations and indeed act on recommendations by members of the particular brand community.

- *Relational brand consumption*: this focuses on the level of interaction between the consumer and the brand. In many ways social media shortens the gap between the brander and the individual. The web page or Facebook group brings the individual in close and intimate contact with the 'people behind the brand' on an instant and '24/7' basis. It also allows for a degree of personalization in terms of the level of contact and interaction between both parties.

Davis et al. (2014) observe that social media platforms create opportunities for branders to engage with their target markets in a proactive and interactional manner. The design and 'feel' of the website play a critical role in addressing a diverse range of needs: from information-seeking to escapism.

6.10 Challenges in online branding

The existing research on building brands through an online presence is less developed or robust than in the case of the 'bricks-and-mortar' channels. Early work by authors such as De Chernatony and Christodoulides (2004) suggested that branders developed an online presence to complement the existing brand image and gradually expanded the features of the website to allow for greater engagement with their customer base. Issues such as loyalty schemes and the ability to engage in a two-way dialogue (as opposed to a traditional monologue) opened up opportunities for branders to engage more fully, develop loyalty and trust, and work more closely on relationship marketing. Similarly, in the early part of online channel development, the issues of trust and confidence proved to be critical potential hurdles that had to be addressed. While such issues are still there, they have largely been addressed in terms of greater measures introduced by retailers.

More recently (as we discuss in Chapters 1 and 13), the emergence of omni-marketing strategies means that branders have to ensure consistency across the different marketing channels. This is particularly relevant for retailers who make use of a number of such channels to connect, interact and transact with their target markets. Any variation in terms of the customer experience means that the overall brand image is likely to be damaged if the shopper finds differences in terms of service quality, or the ability of the retailer to have stock available or capable of being delivered within the requisite time-frame that was promised.

Ruparelia, White and Hughes (2010) undertook research on the attributes that shape trust within the context of the online environment. They identified a number of such influencing factors as shown in Fig. 6.2.

Ruparelia et al.'s findings suggest that security and privacy issues are not as critical as before. However, we should treat this with some degree of caution as previously studies have highlighted their importance to customers. We are also likely to find some variation based on geographic location: some regions are more advanced with regard to Internet usage and the Internet architecture also varies in terms of sophistication.

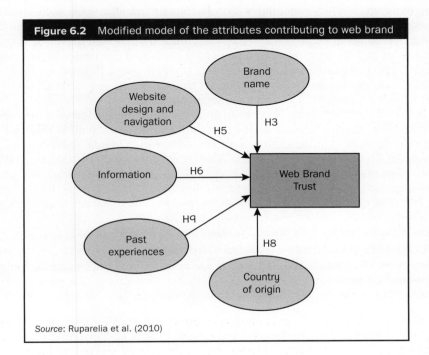

Figure 6.2 Modified model of the attributes contributing to web brand

Source: Ruparelia et al. (2010)

The issue of control is important in the context of online brand management within the context of social media platforms. While retailers can learn much from the discussions and experiences of shoppers that are posted and shared on Facebook, Twitter and so on, there is a real danger of losing control over the content. This is particularly so in the case where negative comments and views are expressed. Retailers have to grapple with the challenge of managing such a situation. While it may be desirable to employ an open approach to such postings, the reality is that in cases where the comments become vitriolic, the image of the brand can suffer and it may be necessary to intervene and moderate such discussions.

6.11 Case in point: Brand-building at Amazon.com

Amazon was not the first online retailer but when it was formed in 1994 in the state of Washington (USA) by Jeff Bezos, it challenged the way in which traditional and online retailers did their business. While it started as an online bookstore, it quickly branched out into a broad range of activities ranging from CDs, consumer electronics products, toys, jewellery and furniture, and more recently, to Amazon e-book readers, Fire Tablets and Fire TV. It claims to offer the 'earth's biggest selection of products' through its websites. In essence, it has moved from having a narrow value proposition (online bookselling) to being one of the world's largest shopping destinations.

It has consistently adapted its business model. For instance, it allows other suppliers and manufacturers to sell items on its websites, offering them a gateway to the global marketplace and ensuring that Amazon.com can concentrate on the more profitable product lines and keep away from the slower-moving items. Thus, we can see that it operates in the business-to-business as well as the business-to-consumer marketplaces.

Pure e-tailers like Amazon bring like-minded individuals together in a community setting. Amazon can provide a number of value-adding services such as reviews of different books, highlighting to customers in advance of publications or items that may be of interest to them based on their previous buying history and optimized search processes. They can do so at a significant cost reduction compared with other competitive retailers that is mainly due to the nature of the business model: elimination of intermediaries and direct relationships with suppliers.

Lindic and da Silva (2011) refer to the concept of affectivity. This relates to the feelings or emotions that consumers experience when engaging with a particular brand. As we have already mentioned, emotional considerations play a significant role in bonding the consumer with the brand with the end product resulting in feelings of positivity and passion. Amazon addressed this issue through its launch of the Kindle e-reader in 2007. This generated numerous blogs and discussion forums where shoppers could share their experiences and feelings about this product. Also, through its Author Central service, Amazon facilitates its customers by creating a mechanism for them to interact with their favourite authors and get advance information about upcoming publications.

User-generated content (UGC) is also taking on greater significance in terms of interactions between retailers and customers. Amazon was one of the first online retailers to avail of this tool. Such reviews allow the customers to share opinions and benefit from other individuals' observations. It also allows Amazon to monitor such views and, in the wider context of other retailers, adjust marketing strategy, merchandise offerings and so on in response to both positive and negative comments (Klaus, 2013).

Questions

1 Examine how Amazon has built its brand over the last two decades or so.
2 In what ways has the online presence contributed to this exercise?
3 Does a pure e-tailer like Amazon have advantages over traditional bricks-and-mortar retailers when it comes to brand-building?

6.12 Store brands

In this section we consider a phenomenon that has grown significantly within the retail sector over the last 20 years. Traditionally, retailers emerged because of the need of manufacturers to make their products available to the ultimate end user: the shopper. Clearly, this would be impossible without the emergence of resellers, hence the emergence of retailers.

Over time, as retailers became bigger and more powerful, they developed a range of their own brands or labels. This was motivated by the desire to provide for their customer a cheaper alternative to the manufacturer's or supplier's brands. Various terms are employed in the literature to describe this type of brand. Private labels, own labels and store brands are the most common. We use the term 'store brand' in this chapter.

Store brands (as the title suggests) are products that are marketed by the retailer as opposed to the manufacturer's brands (which are produced and marketed by the manufacturer). The history of store brands originated in the US market as far back as the 19th century. The emergence of powerful brands such as those developed by Procter & Gamble and Unilever in the 1950s led to a decline in the concept of store brands. Shoppers were enthralled by the clever and creative promotion of consumer goods, and manufacturers held a very dominant position in the supply chain.

The emergence of large food retailers such as Wal-Mart, Tesco and Carrefour in the 1970s and 1980s led to a shift in power from the manufacturers to the retailers. This was exacerbated by the growing concentration of power in the food retail sectors – larger sales and market share residing with fewer retailers. The 1970s also witnessed a major worldwide recession that prompted the large retailer to develop a range of merchandise under the name of the supermarket in order to provide a cheaper alternative to the manufacturers' brands. The lower price was achievable because the retailer did not have to invest in the same level of marketing as the international manufacturers. They could also approach manufacturers and get them to produce the products and negotiate very favourable terms: manufacturers seldom work at 100 per cent capacity and they are in a position to use up excess capacity to generate extra income. In many cases manufacturers of well-established international brands will produce store brands for retailers under contract.

Typically, these 'first-generation' store brands were of inferior quality to established national and international brands. For instance, the syrup and sauces used in the ingredients would not contain the same level of consistency. Paper-based products such as toilet rolls and tissues would be of a thinner ply. They sold at anywhere from 20 per cent to 40 per cent lower than the manufacturer brands. Thus, the shopper had a real alternative to the more expensive (but higher quality) brands. During this period the term 'generic brand' was often used to describe products that only used simple black-and-white packaging to further reduce costs.

Over time, the retailers increased the quality of the products and reduced the gap in this area with the established national and international brands. This led to 'second generation and third generation products which largely reflected this improvement in quality and led to store brands which were essentially "me-too" products' (Laaksonen, 1994).

Zielke and Dobbelstein (2007) identify three categories of private labels that are captured in Table 6.2.

Table 6.2 Categories of store brands

Classic store brand	Positioned similar to or slightly below producer brands
Generic store brand	Basic, plain packaging, cuts in quality, no advertising
Premium store brand	Positioned like leading national brands

Source: Zielke and Dobbelstein (2007: 113)

Since 2000 store brands have fluctuated in popularity. As recessions disappeared and periods of prosperity emerged, shoppers who purchased store brands veered back to the established national and international brands. However, it would be wrong to believe that a shift in disposable income is the sole influence on people's attitudes to store brands. Shoppers, as we know, include a number of evaluative criteria in their purchasing decisions. Price is certainly one of these factors. However, factors such as quality, value for money, country of origin, status and so on also come into play in such an exercise.

We should also recognize that, in the context of supermarkets, variation in attitudes occurs across different product categories. Store brand items that are based on taste, flavour and richness of ingredients are potentially less popular with certain shoppers than 'commodity-based' items such as tissues, toilet paper and shoe polish.

Generally, retailers have reduced the perceived gap in quality as they seek to attract customers to their store brands.

Vignette: Store brands are here to stay

The adoption of store brands by shoppers varies by country and by region. A study of private labels by the Symphony IRI Group (2011) across a number of European countries found that over 30 per cent of overall market share was made up of private labels. Table 6.3 presents selected findings from the study.

Table 6.3   Private label market share (by value) 2011

Country	Market share
United Kingdom	49.2%
Germany	37.7%
France	31%
Spain	40.4%
Netherlands	27%
Italy	16.1%

Source: Symphony IRI Group (2011: 7)

In summary, the Symphony IRI Group (2011: 5) study generated the following key findings.

- The market share of private label has increased across Europe. Value varies from as much as 49.2 per cent of all FMCG products sold in the United Kingdom to 16.1 per cent in Italy. This compares to around 18.5 per cent in the USA.
- Retailer own brands command on average a 30 per cent price advantage over national brands that provides real value to cost-conscious shoppers in the current economic environment.
- Although private label promises good value for the best price, consumers still prefer to buy national brands if they can do so at the same price.
- Private label products are now available in 9 out of every 10 categories giving consumers more options on brand choice.
- Private label brands benefit from a well-developed merchandising strategy and still command the biggest share of many FMCG categories.

Benefits and challenges arising from store brand development

6.13.1 Benefits to manufacturers

- Making more efficient use of production capacity
- A source of cash generation
- Facilitating relationships with powerful retailers
- Affords an opportunity to improve efficiencies by learning from the experiences of retailers (particularly for small manufacturers).

6.13.2 Challenges to manufacturers

- Designing an appropriate response as store brands close the gap in areas such as quality and become well-recognized and established brands in their own right
- Developing innovative products that will lure shoppers away from store brand alternatives
- Seeking cost reductions to their production processes in order to close the gap on price with store brands
- Second-tier branders (manufacturers who do not hold a strong position in the market are likely to lose out as they will find it difficult to differentiate their value proposition from store brands)
- Introducing their own range of discount price brands to compete directly with store brands
- Protecting and growing the equity of their own brand in order to further develop loyalty among shoppers
- Differentiating their brands from store brands by addressing non-price factors such as quality, originality and appeal.

6.13.3 Benefits to retailers

- Store brands can further enhance store image and develop confidence and trust in the minds of their target market
- Increase brand loyalty
- Provide a wider range of alternatives for the shopper. In Europe store brands are available in nine out of every 10 FMCG categories (Symphony IRI Group, 2011)
- Because they control shelf-space and shelf positions in the store, they can optimize their placement of store brands
- Less marketing budget required to promote store brands
- Increase traffic through the store outlets
- Opportunities to widen the scope and range of store labels (for example, cigarettes, nappies and alcohol
- By improving quality levels, they can compete more aggressively with established manufacturers' brands.

6.13.4 Challenges to retailers

- As the shift to higher quality occurs, the marketing investment may also have to rise in order to position the store brands more effectively
- Protect margins on store brands (particularly if investment has to increase)

- As quality improves across the store brand portfolio, retailers will be hoping for greater levels of loyalty from their target market(s).

6.13.5 Benefits to shoppers

- Store brands provide a clear and distinctive alternative to manufacturer brands
- Initial suspicion and cynicism about the quality of store brands has been reduced due to improvements in quality and packaging
- As retailers drive quality improvements in their store brands and manufacturers respond to such developments, the shopper can benefit from lower prices, greater variety and degree of choice.

We should recognize that the developments with regard to store brands will not mean the elimination of manufacturer brands. Powerful and dominant brands across the FMCG categories will continue to hold their position. Retailers need brands that are number one in terms of market share and to a large extent are dependent on their continued availability. In this respect, the relationship between suppliers and retailers is symbiotic (they both derive benefits). This is demonstrated in the context of the support that manufacturers can provide to retailers in areas such as sales promotions in stores. Retailers can reciprocate by sharing data with the manufacturer in order to maximize their respective positions. Glynn et al. (2012) conducted research which suggests that the value of manufacturer brands to retailers is not simply financial or transactional. Joint efforts by both parties can derive synergies from managing the degree of channel support for the products. We examined the nature of such relationships in greater detail in Chapter 4.

6.14 Shopper's response to store brands

In the previous section we examined the evolution of store brands from basic, low-price, low-quality products to ones that in some cases are the equal of or better than manufacturer brands. In this section we consider the propensity of shoppers to engage with and purchase store brands.

When purchasing store brands, research has shown that the perceived risk associated with purchasing such a brand can impact on the shopper's willingness to buy (Zielke and Dobbelstein, 2007). They assessed the issue of risk across a number of product categories. Their findings indicate that in certain cases, for example sparkling wines, shoppers are more prone to avoid such brands. This might be explained by the social risk associated with this product. In many cases such a brand is consumed in the company of relatives or friends, and shoppers may be concerned about the possible negative impression that might ensue if they offer someone a glass of such wine.

Products such as butter, on the other hand, did not have any such social risk connotations. Their research also suggests that respondents reacted favourably to store brands priced 40 per cent below a comparable manufacturer brand or at around a 10 per cent reduction. If items were priced at around 20 per cent below however, there was a lower willingness to purchase a store brand. This suggests that retailers should avoid a 'stuck-in-the-middle' approach to positioning on price.

The issue of attitudinal effects also did not appear as clear-cut as one might expect. In some cases (sparkling wine brands), acceptance by friends and satisfaction were regarded as very important. In other cases value for money and quality featured prominently.

While it would be dangerous to generalize from such research, it highlights the fact that shoppers hold different perceptions and attitudes to purchasing store brands across different product categories. It also reinforces the notion that such decision-making is not grounded solely on the basis of price.

We are also witnessing the increasing tendency of retailers to be more innovative with regard to the development of store brands. The focus on improving quality and packaging of store brands has helped to reduce the perceived risk associated with purchasing store brands.

In the context of fashion retailing, operators such as Zara have demonstrated their ability to closely follow high-fashion design and come up with imitation items (that skirt around, but avoid, any copyright issues) and get them on the shelves quickly and at a lower price than the proprietary designers and branders.

Abril and Martos-Partil (2013) suggest that a strong manufacturer brand that holds a high reputation may not necessarily dominate a product category as much as one might expect. They cite the example of the cereal market where store brands hold a market share of 44.9 per cent. Depending on the product category, price advantage and familiarity with store brands can more than compensate for the reputation that a manufacturer brand might hold.

In summary, we should avoid becoming overly prescriptive about the impact of store brands: in an earlier section we noted a large variation in terms of market share across a number of countries in Europe.

In the last decade the increased focus by retailers on improving product quality and packaging has led to store brands competing more aggressively with manufacturer brands across different FMCG categories. In many cases 'blind-testing' of brands shows that it is difficult to identify the well-known international brands from store brands.

While lower price is still seen as being the strongest motivator for purchasing store brands, it can equally be argued that shoppers are including other factors in their purchasing decisions; for example, value for money. In some ways the global recession of the late 2000s and the early half of this decade has forced shoppers to manage their budgets more tightly. When they switch to store brands they are often pleasantly surprised by the quality of such items and the savings they can make as a consequence.

6.15 Case in point: UK supermarkets and store brands

Tesco

Tesco has worked hard to revive its own brand offer since issuing a shock profit warning in January 2012. Its strategy began by ditching the iconic blue and white stripes of its Tesco Value brand after 20 years in favour of a new line, Everyday Value, which featured improved packaging and product specifications. Tesco is now on track to reformulate and repackage 8,000 products across its ranges this year.

The retailer officially relaunched its top-tier Finest range that is worth £1.4 billion annually and 12 million products from which are consumed each week. The 1,500 product range, first launched 15 years ago, is now sponsor of ITV drama Downton Abbey and could spur Tesco shoppers to trade-up.

It has also thrown its weight behind product innovation. *Retail Week* revealed that the grocer is targeting 10 per cent of its sales in 2015 coming from products it does not already sell. In the first half, Tesco has begun the strategy in earnest as more than 1,750 brand new products were introduced.

However, the grocer was at the centre of the media's coverage of the horse meat scandal, so Tesco will have to work twice as hard to ensure its own brand appeal is revived.

Asda

Asda has put the majority of its own label focus on its 'Chosen By You' range, which tests products via consumer panels before they hit the shelves. Asda expanded its offer to a 180-strong product line called Chosen By Kids, which includes breakfast, lunch and evening meals. Furthermore, its partnership with West London cookery school, Leiths, has added clout to its Extra Special premium offer.

Asda has also used its links with parent Walmart to export its offer globally. It has enjoyed some success in surprising areas; for example, its Extra Special Golden Ale has become the second best selling in the Japanese supermarket chain Seiyu.

Its George clothing brand remains the UK's largest supermarket clothing brand and a refit of its in-store offer has formed the basis of a snappy strategy to 'dial up our fashion credentials', according to non-food boss Andrew Moore.

Sainsbury's

Chief executive Justin King has extolled the virtues of Sainsbury's own label offer throughout the economic downturn as shoppers combine its premium and basic lines in the same basket. King said: 'Our ▶

own-brand offer continues to grow at over twice the rate of branded goods, with Taste the Difference growing particularly strongly and 'by Sainsbury's' performing well following its relaunch.'

That Tesco's Price Promise promotion, which matched its prices on branded and own label goods, provoked the ire of Sainsbury's is perhaps unsurprising as the latter believes its combination of value and values, that is ethically sourced low-price goods, is a winner. While Tesco focuses purely on price, Sainsbury's says the straight price comparison is not a fair one as it does not reflect the value its ethical principles bring.

In non-food, Sainsbury's moved to bolster its offer last month by relaunching its Tu brand into nearly 400 stores. The brand has been refocused on clothing, away from its general merchandise products, as it aims to outmuscle rivals and build on its position in the market. Tu is the eleventh biggest clothing brand in the UK by value and seventh by volume.

Morrisons

Morrisons is in the process of a wide-ranging own brand overhaul. By the end of 2013 it had refreshed 2,500 lines since kicking off an own label project in October 2011, and plans to have refreshed 10,000 by January 2015.

Chief executive Dalton Philips has pinpointed its M Savers brand, launched last year, as a strong point of difference and claims it is the fastest growing value own label in the market.

At the premium end, its 400-line M Kitchen range, developed by executive chef Neil Nugent at the grocer's kitchen at its head office in Bradford, has been relaunched. Last week, Morrisons kicked off a marketing campaign for the lines and took celebrity chefs on the road to display the products' quality.

The reach of its Nutmeg clothing range has also been expanded. It launched in 100 stores in early 2015 and is now in 172 stores in dedicated shop-in-shops.

Source: Lawson, A. (2013) Analysis: How grocers' own-label brands are faring as Sainsbury's triumphs. 2 October.

Question

1 Assess the various approaches used by the four UK retailers. Which of the approaches in your view (having read the preceding section on store brands) is likely to be the most effective?

6.16
Retail store loyalty

The concept of brand loyalty is well documented in the literature. All businesses recognize the benefits that derive from having loyal and committed customers and the retail sector is no exception. We can summarize the benefits of such loyal customers as follows.

- Loyal customers tend to buy more goods.
- They tend to be more predictable in their purchasing behaviour and patterns.
- It is cheaper to retain existing customers than it is to seek new ones.
- They speak positively about the brand/company/store.
- Loyal customers tend to spend more and become more profitable over the life span of their involvement with the company.
- They are less likely to switch to competitive offerings.

In order to generate loyalty and commitment, retailers have to consider how they should manage their relationships with customers. Morgan and Hunt (1994) note that while most organizations lose around 10 per cent of their customers annually, a 5 per cent reduction in this figure can increase profits by somewhere between 25–85 per cent.

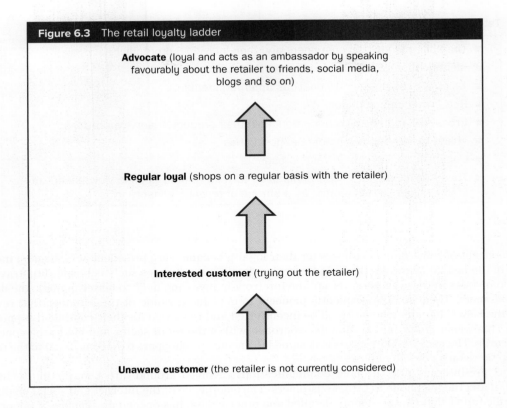

Figure 6.3 The retail loyalty ladder

Advocate (loyal and acts as an ambassador by speaking favourably about the retailer to friends, social media, blogs and so on)

Regular loyal (shops on a regular basis with the retailer)

Interested customer (trying out the retailer)

Unaware customer (the retailer is not currently considered)

In the context of the retail sector, the challenge is to move the shopper up the loyalty ladder. This is represented in Fig. 6.3.

Customer relationship management (CRM) has emerged over the last 20 years or so as a mechanism for addressing the question of what is the most effective way to manage relationships with customers. Information technology (IT) has helped in no small measure to facilitate organizations in capturing data about their customers and translating such data into meaningful information that can be used to design more effective marketing programmes that can be customized to meet the personal expectations of the customer base. We will examine developments in IT in Chapters 9 and 13.

Although CRM has tended to dominate the agenda in many organizations in recent years, the major challenge that companies have struggled to cope with revolves around what to do with the masses of data that is captured on their customer base. Data is meaningless unless it can be analysed and interpreted in a meaningful way and disseminated to the relevant personnel in the organization.

The CRM challenge is further exacerbated by the fact that customers generally are more sophisticated, more demanding and more knowledgeable than ever before. Greater choice allied to access to information on the Internet and the sharing of views and opinions on social media platforms has led to a change in the way that companies in general and retailers in particular engage with their customer base.

In the context of the retail sector, such organizations can capture information on the shopper's individual shopping patterns such as average amount spent on a shopping visit, number and categories of items purchased, length of time spent in the store, reactions to special promotions and offers, method of payment and so on. If used properly, such information affords the retailer the opportunity to design and implement personalized communications with the individual shopper, special offers and rewards that are relevant to that person across a number of different channels and media platforms.

Customer relationship management (CRM) programmes recognize that not all customers are equal: some customers are more valuable to the retailer than others; they spend more and demonstrate greater degrees of loyalty and commitment. A basic analysis of customer databases inevitably highlights that the 'Pareto Principle' is in evidence. This occurs where 20 per cent of the customers may generate around 80 per cent of the sales. The benefits accruing from CRM programmes are summarized in Table 6.4.

Table 6.4 Benefits of CRM programmes

- The ability to identify customers and their individual profitability
- Identification of individual customer's specific needs
- Tailored products to individual customer requirements
- Retain customers longer
- Cross-sell and up-sell other products in their product or service portfolio
- Ability to identify new product opportunities
- Capability to target high value prospects
- These developments allow companies to take a more holistic view based on the lifetime value of a customer as a stream of revenue generation

The concept of rewarding customers for their loyalty became very prevalent across many industry sectors in the last 20 years, particularly in service-dominant industries such as hospitality, travel and retail. Companies in these sectors were to the forefront in investing in IT to better manage the data on their customers. They were subsequently pioneers in devising a range of programmes that revolved around the belief that customers should be incentivized and rewarded for their continued support and loyalty. This was a prevalent and popular approach within the retail sector and led to the concept of loyalty cards. The use of loyalty cards is designed to encourage shoppers to become loyal to the retailer and shop there on a consistent basis.

In the 'pre-Internet' era, targeted communications revolved around direct marketing techniques using mail and the telephone to target customers. The emergence of the Internet and social media platforms, allied to IT that captured more detailed and precise data, has opened up avenues of opportunity for retailers in terms of how they interact and engage with their customer base. Traditionally, marketing communications have been based on the 'information-push' principle where the company pushes out messages to a passive customer. The new era is based on the principle of two-way communication where both parties (organization and customer) interact and share information.

6.17 Loyalty programmes

Waarden-Meyer (2008: 89) defines a loyalty programme as 'an integrated system of marketing actions that aims to make customers more loyal by developing personalized relationships with them'. The objective of such a programme is to further develop the degree of loyalty and commitment across the customer base with a view to retaining customers.

The use of the loyalty card acts as a connection point between the retailer and the customer. Noordhoff et al. (2004) note that the card acts as a mechanism for registering and transferring dynamic information about the shopper's buying behaviour over time. What then are the advantages and weaknesses of such loyalty programmes from the perspective of the retailer and the shopper?

Benefits to the retailer

- The identification and storage of individual purchasing behaviour
- Customized segmentation – 'segments of one'
- Identification of shoppers who are more (or less) price-sensitive and who are more (or less) prone to respond to special offers
- A greater understanding of buyer behaviour leaves the retailer in a stronger negotiating position with suppliers

- Optimization of space within the retail outlet in terms of positioning of merchandise on shelves and in specific areas of the store
- More effective management of processes such as peak time and off-peak times
- Proactively target certain customers (based on shopping behaviour) in advance
- The ability to upsell (encourage the shopper to consider buying a more expensive alternative) and cross-sell (complementary products).

Potential disadvantages to the retailer

- Failing to turn the masses of data collected into usable and relevant information
- 'Paralysis by analysis'
- The prevalence of store loyalty cards means that shoppers 'collect' cards and use them extensively where a particular retailer has a special offer, thus weakening the possibility of building loyalty
- Cynicism from the 'card-carrying' shoppers, particularly about the nature of the incentives and rewards
- Failure to provide meaningful rewards to shoppers; often evidenced in situations where it takes major shopping effort and expenditure before any benefit accrues to the shopper
- Making the reward process too complex.

Benefits to the shopper

- Getting a reward (usually in the form of vouchers and discounts) for shopping with a particular retailer
- Invitation to special events and activities organized by the retailer (for example, a preview evening featuring upcoming new designs in the case of fashion retailers)
- Getting rewards that are relevant and meaningful to the shopper's personal brand preferences.

Potential disadvantages to the shopper

- Having to provide personal information in order to acquire the card
- The danger that such information may slip into the hands of other companies or service providers
- Intrusion into a person's privacy
- Very little real and tangible reward
- 'Fatigue': they become collectors of cards and make little use of them.

6.18 Loyalty cards: the evidence

The use of loyalty cards and loyalty programmes has generated great debate and disagreement over the last 20–25 years. For instance, research conducted by Bellizzi and Bristol (2004) suggests that loyalty card programmes do not engender store loyalty. In part, this was because many of the respondents to their survey also carried cards from the other main supermarkets.

It is difficult to make statements about the efficacy of store cards and loyalty programmes due to the diverse nature of shopping and retail value propositions. Waarden-Meyer (2007: 234) makes the pragmatic comment that 'overall, consumer segments are likely to react differently to loyalty programs, as occurs with sales promotions'.

The prevalence of such loyalty programmes has created a degree of fatigue and cynicism among shoppers and arguably weakens their resolve to be completely loyal to any one store or outlet. Given the degree of choice and options that are available to shoppers, it is inevitable that 'promiscuity' exists: where shoppers are likely to have a repertoire of 'two or three' retailers that they patronize on a regular basis. In the case of some shopping situations, for example at the functional rather than hedonistic end of the spectrum, shoppers may become loyal to a particular retailer on the basis of factors such as convenience as opposed to any incentives that might accrue from a loyalty card.

Retailers are often guilty of providing inadequate rewards where shoppers have to collect a very large number of points before they get any form of reward in the form of vouchers or discounts on items. To some extent retailers do not show much imagination or creativity in rewarding customers.

Research by Ou et al. (2011) in Taiwan reinforces this view that customers become cynical and disillusioned by minimal perceived rewards.

A tiered system of reward, where the very loyal customers are treated differently to regular or occasional shoppers, may lead to stronger levels of response and commitment from certain categories of shoppers.

Developments in mobile technology such as smartphones can create opportunities for retailers to introduce imaginative loyalty programmes.

6.19 Case in point: Tesco Clubcard and MoneySavingExpert.com

Tesco was one of the first pioneers of the loyalty card. First established in 1995, the Tesco Clubcard has evolved over the years. MoneySavingExpert.com explains how the system works for shoppers (http://www.moneysavingexpert.com/shopping/loyalty-scheme-tricks, accessed June 2015):

You accumulate Tesco Clubcard points at a rate of one per pound spent. You earn them in-store at Tesco, or via partners such as E.on.

Each point is worth a penny if used for in-store shopping, and they're sent out in vouchers (if you've at least 150 points on your account) every three months.

It's possible to get back lost or unclaimed Clubcard vouchers if they're less than two years old. Follow the steps in our Reclaim Tesco Vouchers guide to see if you've got any hiding from you.

Clubcard Boost Partners. *Triple or quadruple points value when redeemed elsewhere.*
This is the powerhouse of the Tesco points boosting method. Trade in normal vouchers for Tesco's special Clubcard Boost tokens, and each £10 voucher becomes worth up to £40 in exchange and rewards with Boost partners.

Clubcard Boost includes offers for train tickets, days out, magazine subscriptions such as *Cosmopolitan*, travel, including holidays, gifts, hotel rooms and more. Among the options are an £18 RAC membership (see Breakdown Rewards), an adult cinema ticket for £4.50 in points, or a year's Merlin theme parks pass for £50. See our top 10 deals under the Boost scheme for more info.

The list price of goods in the brochure is sometimes higher than the market price, so you may not always get 3× or 4× value. Yet if you're exchanging to buy something you would've bought anyway, it is a great deal.

Earn Tesco points with E.on. *Earn points when paying your energy bill.*
Customers of E.on can earn Tesco Clubcard points, if you're on one of its tariffs with rewards. You can choose to receive your E.on rewards either as vouchers for high street retailers or Clubcard points.

Customers can earn up to 1,500 E.on reward points each year which can be exchanged for an equivalent number of Clubcard points. This is only £15 off Tesco shopping but can be worth up to £60 in Clubcard Boost Rewards. Choose to take your E.on rewards as Clubcard points and register your Clubcard with E.on. It's NOT worth switching to E.on purely for this, see Cheap Gas & Elec for how to find the cheapest provider.

Tesco Credit Card. *An additional 1 point per £4 spend.*
The Tesco Clubcard Credit Card pays you 1 point per £4 you spend anywhere outside Tesco (5 points per £4 spent at Tesco), which if redeemed in-store at Tesco is a rather paltry 0.25% return on spending. Trade them in for Clubcard Boost tokens and it becomes a more respectable 0.75% or 1%.

Ordinarily, you should repay IN FULL every month to avoid interest. However, Tesco offers 21 months' 0% on new spending – the longest available. This means you could do ALL normal spending on it to rack up the points, stashing away the cash you'd normally spend, then pay it off in full within 21 months. More info in the 0% Cards and Stoozing guides.

Compared with the top cashback card, which pays up to 5% cashback initially (see Top Cashback Cards), this is weak. Following the 0% period, if you don't pay the Tesco card off in full, you'll pay 18.9% representative APR.

Join Tesco's clubs. *They send special extra points vouchers.*
If you join one of Tesco's clubs, such as its Baby Club or Christmas Savers, you'll get vouchers in its emails to earn extra points when buying relevant products.

Watch out for in-store promotions. *Tesco could pay you to shop.*
Look out for any Tesco promotions offering extra Clubcard points. These can open up loopholes where it's worth buying the goods even if you don't want them.

The best examples are the famous Johnson's Baby Powder and beef-in-gravy loopholes which originated on this site and ended up in all the papers. They worked like this:

When you bought any two Johnson's products, you got 100 extra points. The cheapest item was baby powder, at 76p. This meant you could spend £1.52 to get 101 points, worth £4.04 of Clubcard deals vouchers, making more than £2.50 PROFIT.

With the similar beef-in-gravy episode, one MoneySaver bought a few hundred pounds' worth, donated it to a homeless shelter and used the points for a return trip for two to New Zealand. Be careful with these loopholes, as Tesco reserves the right to block people for fair usage breaches. All major loopholes will go in the free weekly email.

Even if you can't make a profit, the bonuses can lead to serious discounts. For instance, Tesco once sold iPod Shuffles for £49 – a good price – adding 999 bonus points on top of the usual points. These were worth £42 of Clubcard Deals, so the iPod effectively cost £7.

Visit http://www.moneysavingexpert.com/shopping/loyalty-scheme-tricks for more including:

- **Tesco Bank current account.** *Earn extra Clubcard points on all debit card spending.*
- **Tesco Bank mortgage.** *Earn extra Clubcard points on mortgage repayments.*
- **Earn points with your mobile.** *Bonus points for Tesco Mobile customers.*

The practitioner view
Managing the own label with retailers

Russell Donaldson, Director of Marketing at Dawnfresh Seafoods Limited

Russell Donaldson has worked with Dawnfresh Seafoods Limited in his capacity as Director of Marketing. We spoke to Russell about the challenges of developing and managing own labels and branded products and dealing with the major supermarket groups.

The company is a family-owned business and its origins can be traced back over 300 years. It is the largest trout producer in the UK and the largest supplier of loch trout in the world. It sells chilled, frozen and finished fish products to a wide range of customers, both in the branded and own label categories. Its customers include Tesco, Sainsbury's, Asda, Morrisons, Marks & Spencer, Selfridges and a range of restaurants, farm shops and distributors. You can find out more about the company by visiting its website at: http://www.dawnfresh.co.uk/

We asked Russell to give us an insight into the role that own label brands play in Dawnfresh Food's strategy.

Russell noted that 'all of the "big four" supermarket groups (Tesco, Sainsbury's, Asda and Morrisons) are customers. We also have M&S. It is our major customer. We deal with the discounters as well, but in a much smaller way.

▶

◀ 'We are producing predominantly trout products, both simple wet fish and value-added product. It will look different depending on which retailer you are talking to.

'In the case of discounters, they are looking for a very small product range: only a few products that will sell. With Marks & Spencer, they are taking inspiration from restaurants and what's out there in gastronomy and what's happening in other countries . . .what's innovative and new. So we are looking at very different ends of the scale in terms of product development.'

What about the nature of relationship with retailers when managing own label issues?

Russell notes that this will vary across the different retailers and will depend on a number of factors.

'With some of our retailers we have a very good, strong relationship where we almost own the category. This would be the case with Marks & Spencer, where we sell some of our smoked fish, hot smoked salmon and flavoured – added-value salmon and trout. We work very closely with our salesperson and their buyers. Also our developers and their developers know each other well and they would be working on what should we be doing for Christmas 2016 and beyond. We look almost two years, eighteen months ahead.

'With some of the others it is far more transactional. In this situation the attitude would be as follows. We want to buy your product. We want to take a look at it. You have a minimum grocery scope (GSCOP). They work within the legislation which says that they have to give a supplier twelve weeks' notice of any removal (of product from the shelves). So they will launch a product and they may tell us pretty much straightaway: we have launched it. We have four weeks data. It is not working. We want to withdraw. So they can almost withdraw as soon as it goes on. Then you are back in and you are trying to say that didn't work; let's try something else.

'What you ideally want to do is get something onto the shelf that is a big seller and they really want to have it. Trout is a very big product for us but it is not something that everyone wants to eat. So we have a perception issue.

'We have to do other products besides trout. If you can get on the shelves with a simple cold-smoked salmon . . .everybody wants that. It is a line that is out there. It is almost a "must have" product. The challenge for that product is that it will be driven by price. And that goes into the operations management side of life. It is about being the low cost producer. It is very competitive.'

What is the relationship between quality and own labels versus branded products that are on the shelves in supermarkets?

Russell observes that this has been an evolving area.

'The quality levels are a lot better now. There is tiering within it now. They are a lot better at defining what their value brand is: their entry level brand. So an example would be the Everyday Value own label at Tesco. Or Sainsbury's Basics. Even Marks & Spencer are doing it now – Simply M&S.

'So there is an entry level tier. There is a mid-tier and then there is a top tier, for instance Tesco's Finest.

'So as a supplier, we will pitch into a tier. We will go to them and say to them, we think it fits here. Here is where our inspiration came from and here is where we think you should price it.

'We can't tell them how to price it or position it. That is up to them. But we will also benchmark and say that this compares favourably with top tier or middle tier own labels in these retailers and this is also where it compares.

'The retailer top tier is very close to the top brands out there. They definitely pose a threat to the brands that are number two or three in terms of market share. But it is category dependent. Categories make a big difference. The likes of P&G and Unilever, the big branders, probably operate in categories where branding is important.

'We operate in the fish category – a sub-category of meat, fish and poultry. There is less branding in chilled food than you would think, especially within fish. Which makes our other side of the business – setting up a brand, more difficult.'

In that context what about your strategy for developing branded products?

Russell highlights RR Spink as being one of its key branded products.

'We can trace the RR Spink brand back to three hundred years in fact. 1715 was when the Spink family started catching and smoking fish in Arbroath. So it gives us a lot of heritage and a good brand story. A lot of our brand is about the story. But it wasn't doing a lot; it was sitting on the shelves of Sainsbury's in Scotland – ticking over and virtually doing no sales. So we looked at rebranding it, revitalising it and modernising it about mid-2013. So we decided to focus on fish and premium. It was originally positioned as an original Scottish smoked fish. A multiple retail brand. But to be fair, it had probably never defined its consumer group. It had never identified its design or its values. It was a label more than a brand. It was a name that came out of the family business. RR Spink was Bob Spink, who owned it with his father. The factory was the RR Spink site. So they put the factory name onto some packaging and they sold it.

'Dawnfresh decided that it wanted to get into branded business. So given that the RR Spink brand owns a Royal Warrant (the stamp of approval from the Queen), it should be a premium, prestige brand. That gave us a bit of differentiation.

'I think the research that we did was right – the targeting was right. Where we went wrong was the route to market. We deliberately kept away from multiple retailers; which is fine as a strategy – there is nothing wrong with that. But we need to get the scale and the volume that we need. We need a fair amount of volume.

'To get that scale of volume out of independents is really difficult. You either have to work through distributors and there is not that many distributors that distribute chilled food for a start. And those that do are more used to chilled meats; so fish is difficult and it is not a massive seller. We were finding that we were sending out small amounts infrequently to different places, so it was getting in the way of the operation.

'As a business we are trying to do own-label, put pallet loads onto trucks and distribute them to the Tesco type business: that's one type of skill-set. And then at the other end, we send five packs of really expensive smoked fish to a farm shop in the middle of England somewhere. The logistics and operations behind these two models is very difficult to marry up.

'Mind you, Selfridges are a customer and a fan. Caviar House and Prunier, who run shops in the airport, are also fans and we are now building those relationships to try and push more through those types of channel: to push it into high end food service rather than farm shops.

'We are now looking at taking it internationally, because a niche in the UK, you're getting so tightly into micro-niching that it's a really small pool that's going to buy 60 kilos of fish – smoked fish. People are getting used to seeing cold smoked fish from Lidl for £15 a kilo or equivalent or £1.50 for a pack. We are selling a pack of a similar size that is £6 or £7 a pack. That's a difficult sell. There is a tangible story as to how the fish is grown, fed and so on plus there is a tangible story around the brand: the Royal Warrant, the heritage and so on – the skills, the hand-cutting and so on.'

We take up the issue of internationalizing the brand and the business with Russell in Chapter 12.

6.20 Conclusions

In this chapter we have examined the role that brand strategy plays in shaping and implementing overall retail marketing strategy. The approach by the retailer towards branding is intertwined with the way in which it wishes to position itself in the minds of its target market.

We considered the concept of corporate branding and noted that this exercise is linked closely to the overall corporate culture and the ethos of the organization; that is, its DNA or reason for being in existence.

The challenge of building the brand was discussed in some detail and we recognized the benefits of achieving a position where the brand has strong levels of equity. This means that shoppers are willing to pay a premium for the brand.

Store brands are a key feature in many retail sectors. They reflect the power of retailers and offer a viable alternative to manufacturer brands from the point of view of the shopper. We examined the way in which such brands have evolved over the last 20 years and noted that the gap in real and perceived quality has reduced significantly.

In the final part of the chapter we considered the issue of store loyalty and the focus on developing, managing and sustaining ongoing relationships with the customer base. As is the case in many industry sectors, customer retention is at the heart of such retail strategy programmes. By engendering loyalty from key segments, retailers are in a stronger competitive position and make it difficult for competitors to poach or tempt shoppers to switch allegiance.

We examined one particular approach that has become endemic across retail sectors: loyalty programmes and the specific use of loyalty cards as a mechanism to incentivize shoppers to remain loyal and continue to patronize a particular store. We assessed the pros and cons associated with such initiatives and highlighted areas of opportunity and areas of deficiency.

Chapter outcomes

- Retail brand strategy is linked closely to the positioning statement of the retail value proposition. The key points of differentiation in such a statement form the basis for shaping the branding strategy.

- Developing the personality of the brand is an equally important challenge. It can be argued that it is difficult to sustain points of differentiation alone. For certain shopping situations – particularly those of a hedonistic nature – building the personality of the brand through the shopping experience is crucial in generating future loyalty and commitment from shoppers.

- Increasingly, retailers have to take a wider view of their operations rather than just the bottom line of profitability. They have to act as responsible corporate citizens and factor in environmental issues and their general conduct into their corporate social responsibility objectives. The notion of corporate branding and reputation plays a critical role in this respect.

- Corporate branding affects all aspects of the retail operation not just the marketing department.

- Store brands have undergone a number of generations of development over the last 30–40 years. In the context of food retailing, such brands generally offer three tiers of offerings in terms of price points and quality levels: low, medium and high. At the top end many store brands compete aggressively with manufacturer brands.

- Information technology (IT) systems and software have afforded retailers the opportunity to capture vast amounts of data on their customers.

- The challenge is to interpret the data and transform it into relevant and actionable information for its key personnel in the organization.

- Store loyalty cards have been used extensively in the retail business over the last 20 years.

- The extent of their use has led to a certain level of cynicism among shoppers.

- Their usefulness is questionable and will only develop brand loyalty if meaningful rewards and incentives are used by retailers.

- With further developments in mobile technology, retailers need to focus their efforts on using loyalty programmes in a more creative and imaginative manner.

Discussion questions

1 Assess the role played by internal staff in building the retail brand.
2 Examine the extent that you would agree with the view that store brands only work effectively in periods of recession.
3 Evaluate the proposition that store loyalty cards only benefit the retailer.

4 Some commentators argue that shoppers will increasingly be influenced by the retailer's approach to managing its social responsibility obligations and this will play a more significant influence on their purchasing behaviour than branding issues. Examine the extent to which you would agree with this view.

5 Store loyalty programmes are a major intrusion into people's privacy and annoy shoppers. Detail how you would respond to such a claim.

6 The increasing adoption of mobile technologies will mean that retailers can target customers with incentives more effectively than in the past. Examine the extent to which you would agree with this perception. Use examples to support your line of argument.

References

Aaker, D.A. (1991) *Managing Brand Equity*. New York: Free Press.

Aaker, J.L. (1997) Dimensions of brand personality. *Journal of Marketing Research*. 34: 347–356.

Aaker, J.L. and Fournier, S. (1995) A brand as a character, a partner and a person: three perspectives on the question of brand personality. In Kardes, F.R. and Sujan, M. (eds) *Advances in Consumer Research*. Provo, UT: Association for Consumer Research, 391–395.

Abril, C. and Martos-Partil, M. (2013) Is product innovation as effective for private labels as it is for national brands? *Innovation: Management, Policy and Practice*. 15(3): 337–349.

Bellizzi, J.A. and Bristol, T. (2004) An assessment of supermarket loyalty cards in one major US market. *Journal of Consumer Marketing*. 21(2): 144–154.

Burghausen, M. and Fan, Y. (2002) Corporate branding in the retail sector: a pilot study. *Corporate Communications: An International Journal*. 7(2): 92-99.

Das, G., Datta, B. and Guin, K.K. (2012) From brands in general to retail brands: a review and future agenda for brand personality measurement. *The Marketing Review*. 12(1): 91–106.

Davis, R., Piven, I. and Breazeala, M.l. (2014) Conceptualising the brand in social media: the five sources model. *Journal of Retailing & Consumer Services*. 21: 468–481.

De Chernatony, L. and Christodoulides, G. (2004) Taking the brand promise online: challenges and opportunities. *Interactive Marketing*. 5(3): 238–251.

Geuens, M., Weijters, B. and Wulf, K.D. (2009) A new measure of brand personality. *International Journal of Research in Marketing*. 26: 97–107.

Glynn, M.S., Brodie, R.J. and Motion, J. (2012) The benefits of manufacturer brands to retailers. *European Journal of Marketing*. 46(9): 1127–1149.

IKEA, About. Available online at: http://www.ikea-group.ikea.com/corporate/about_ikea/index.html (accessed March 2015).

Keller, K.L. (1993) Conceptualizing, measuring, and managing customer-based brand equity. *Journal of Marketing*. 57 (January): 1–22.

Keller, K.L. (2008) *Strategic Brand Management: Building, Measuring and Managing Brand Loyalty*, 3rd edn. New York: Pearson.

King, S. (1991) Brand building in the 1990s. *Journal of Marketing Management*. 7: 3–13.

Klaus, P. (2013) The case of Amazon.com: towards a conceptual framework of online customer service (OCSE) using the emerging consensus technique (EXT). *Journal of Services Marketing*. 27(6): 443–447.

Laaksonen, H. (1994) Own brands in food retailing across Europe. *Oxford Reports on Retailing*. Oxford: Oxford Institute of Retail Management.

Lindic, J. and da Silva, C.M. (2011) Value proposition as a catalyst for a customer-focused innovation. *Management Decision*. 49(10): 1694–1708.

MoneySavingExpert.Com. (2013) Loyalty points boosting. 13 June.

Morgan, R.M. and Hunt, S.D. (1994) The commitment-trust theory of relationship marketing. *Journal of Marketing*. 58(2): 20–38.

Noordhoff, C., Pauwels, P. and Odekerken-Schröder, G. (2004) The effect of customer card programs: a comparative study in Singapore and the Netherlands. *International Journal of Service Industry Management*. 15(4): 351–364.

Ou, W., Shih, C., Chen, C. and Wang, K. (2011) Relationships among customer loyalty programs, service quality, relationship quality and loyalty: an empirical study. *Chinese Management Studies*. 5(2): 194–206.

Roper, S. and Fill, C. (2012) *Corporate Reputation: Brand and Communication.* Harlow: Pearson.

Ruparelia, N., White, L. and Hughes, K. (2010) Drivers of brand trust in Internet marketing. *Journal of Product & Brand Management.* 19(4): 250–260.

Symphony IRI Group (2011) *Retail Private Label Brands in Europe: Current and Emerging Trends.*

Van Riel, C.B.M. and Fombrun, C.J. (2007) *Essentials of Corporate Communication.* Abingdon: Routledge.

Waarden-Meyer, L. (2007) The effects of loyalty programs on customer lifetime duration and share of wallet. *Journal of Retailing.* 83(2): 223–236.

Waarden-Meyer, L. (2008) The influence of loyalty programme membership on customer purchase behaviour. *European Journal of Marketing.* 42(1/2): 87–114.

Willems, K., Swinner, G., Janssens, W. and Brengman, M. (2011) Fashion store personality, scale development and relation to self-congruity theory. *Journal of Global Fashion Marketing.* 2(2): 55–65.

Zielke, S. and Dobbelstein, T. (2007) Customers' willingness to purchase new store brands. *Journal of Product & Brand Management.* 16(2): 112–121.

Chapter 7

Managing customer service

☑ Learning objectives

On completion of this chapter you should be in a position to achieve the following objectives:

☑ Understand the importance of customer service in the overall context of retail strategy implementation and design.

▶

◄ ☑ Assess the relevance of the various elements that make up customer service within the retail environment.

☑ Set appropriate customer service levels for different categories of retailers.

☑ Recognize the importance of conducting research with customers in order to monitor changes in attitudes and perceptions towards customer service.

☑ Identify the specific constraints facing retailers with regard to developing and implementing customer service programmes.

☑ Evaluate the relevance of customer service in the context of online retail operations.

7.1 Introduction

Customer service represents one of the critical elements in the retail marketing mix. In this chapter we begin by examining the main dimensions of customer service and its role in shaping the shopping experience.

We assess the critical influences that shape the design and implementation of customer service strategy. We also assess the critical decisions that retailers have to make about the approach to customer service. Should it form the central focus for overall retail strategy? Should it play a more peripheral role? What approach should be adopted in those areas where there is discretion with regard to setting appropriate customer service levels?

We identify the key success factors necessary to develop effective customer service channels. We examine the challenges involved for retailers as they design appropriate customer service strategies within the context of multi-channel retail platforms.

In the latter stages of this chapter, we consider the challenges involved in customer service management, not least the balancing act behind setting customer service levels and the associated costs.

7.2 Customer service in context

Retailers are tasked with the challenge of providing positive and attractive shopping environments for customers. In other chapters we consider such issues as store design and the use of atmospherics. However, one key issue that affects customer perceptions of the retailer's operations is the management of the customer's experience. Grewal et al. (2009: 1) note that 'understanding and enhancing of the customer experience sits atop most marketing and chief executive's agendas both in consumer packaged goods manufacturing and retailing fields and it remains a critical area for academic research'.

Cognito (2012) conducted research with UK homeowners and found that:

- 67 per cent of UK consumers believe service has deteriorated or stayed the same across the last three years

- 22 per cent of UK consumers believe customer service has improved a little over the last three years

- 3 per cent of UK consumers believe customer service has improved a lot

- 21 per cent felt service is becoming increasingly fundamental, stating it is growing in importance as a factor affecting market share.

These figures suggest that customer service is perceived as being an important influence on buying behaviour. However, there still exists a marked gap in performance between what organizations are doing in this area and how consumers perceive it.

The key to customer service design, that is to say how service is planned and organized, and how it is implemented, rests on the assumption that the retailer understands the needs and requirements of its target market. Without adequate and relevant marketing research, it is difficult to 'second-guess' what is the most appropriate combination of service provision. Although retailers handle, present and sell physical products, much of their operations fall into the service dimension.

Some commentators hold the view that companies are all about people and not about buildings or associated technologies. This succinctly encapsulates the view that all organizations whether product-dominant or service-dominant depend on their employees to convey the value proposition and implement the service strategy.

7.3 Customer value propositions

Before looking in detail at customer service, it is useful to revisit the concept of customer value propositions with regard to retailing. Rintamaki and Kuusela (2007) observe that value largely revolves around the benefits that come to the customer as a result of consuming the offering and the potentially negative consequences associated with making the effort or sacrifice (monetary and time-based) to acquire the benefits. When the benefits are perceived to outweigh the sacrifices, then it can be argued that value is created.

Recent research in this area suggests that 'value propositions are reciprocal promises of value, operating to and from suppliers and customers seeking an equitable exchange' (Ballantyne and Varey, 2006). This view emphasizes the interactive nature of the relationship.

The challenge facing all retailers, therefore, is to make sufficient use of resources and capabilities to create and implement a value proposition that is relevant to the target market and potentially develops a competitive advantage.

Rintamaki and Kuusela (2007: 624) conclude by suggesting that a customer value proposition should:

- increase the benefits and/or decrease the sacrifices that the customer perceives as relevant
- build on competencies and resources that the company is able to utilize more effectively than its competitors
- be recognizably different (unique) from competition
- result in competitive advantage.

The extent and level of customer service clearly plays a role in the design of the overall value proposition.

7.4 Customer service defined

Sparks (1992) observes that despite the plethora of definitions abounding in the literature, customer service ultimately is about attracting, retaining and enhancing customer relationships. This encapsulates a more strategic view of its role in retailing marketing and recognizes the importance of capturing and building store loyalty among shoppers over a prolonged period of time. Thus, shopper perceptions from that first point of contact with the retailer, the 'moment of truth', are critical in shaping either positive or negative attitudes and can be very difficult to subsequently change.

In the context of 'bricks-and-mortar' retailers (stores with a physical presence), the role of the employee/salesperson is highlighted as playing a critical role in the customers' perception of the encounter (Carlzon, 1987). Further seminal research in the area of services marketing (Bitner et al., 1990; Shostack 1985) reinforces the role of the interaction between the retailers' representative and the shopper in shaping positive and negative perceptions.

In this chapter the terms 'customer experience' and 'customer service' are used interchangeably. While some may argue that there are significant differences, they can also be viewed as being synonymous. It might be more appropriate to recognize that when we examine the topic of customer service, we are not merely referring to the activity that takes place from the time that shoppers arrive at the store to the time they leave. We should take a more holistic view of the process and view it as the 'touchpoints' that occur from the time shoppers become aware of the retailer (either online or in a physical sense) to the various activities that occur long after shoppers have made a purchase; for example, warranties, returns, complaints and subsequent revisits to the store or the website. In this sense, the term 'customer experience' may be more appropriate as it would appear to take a more general view of the process of engagement between retailers and shoppers.

7.5 Customer experience management

Increasingly, consumers are moving away from treating the process of shopping as a functional activity that has to be completed, to one which is experiential in nature. This is demonstrated by the fact that for many people, shopping is viewed as a leisure-based activity. In this context, retailers and shopping mall developers have to respond by creating retail infrastructures that build upon the simple function of buying and selling merchandise and instead provide an 'entertainment-focused environment'. This allows shoppers to socialize with friends, have a meal, watch a movie, use WiFi facilities and shop as well.

The implications of this move towards creating a retail environment that is essentially experiential in nature affects most if not all aspects of retail marketing. The role of employees in this process cannot be underestimated.

Verhoef et al. (2009: 32) define customer experience as 'holistic in nature and involving the customer's cognitive, affective, emotional, social and physical responses to the retailer'. Some of the responses by retailers can be controlled, indeed manipulated, by them. These include the range of merchandise on display: atmospherics, price points and the service interface (level and extent of employee – customer engagement). Other factors such as the influence of friends and colleagues on the shopper, the nature of the shopping visit (functional versus experiential) and social media influences are largely outside the control of the retailer.

In order to understand the customer experience, it is important that retailers identify the key touch points in the process. This refers to those points of engagement by the shopper with the retailer in the pre-sales, sales and post-sales dimensions of the purchasing process. This is depicted in Fig. 7.1.

We can see throughout the buying process that the retail employee plays an important role in the following areas:

- information provision
- displaying product knowledge to the shopper
- establishing trust and confidence
- sales skills
- cross-selling (encouraging the shopper to buy complementary items)
- up-selling (encouraging the shopper to trade up to a more expensive item)
- dealing with disinterested customers
- dealing with 'problem' shoppers
- handling complaints
- implementing policies and procedures associated with returns and warranties.

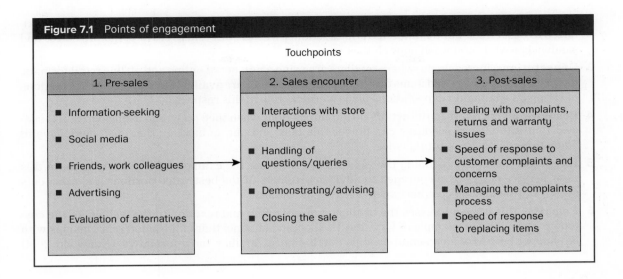

Figure 7.1 Points of engagement

Touchpoints

1. Pre-sales	2. Sales encounter	3. Post-sales
■ Information-seeking	■ Interactions with store employees	■ Dealing with complaints, returns and warranty issues
■ Social media	■ Handling of questions/queries	■ Speed of response to customer complaints and concerns
■ Friends, work colleagues	■ Demonstrating/advising	■ Managing the complaints process
■ Advertising	■ Closing the sale	■ Speed of response to replacing items
■ Evaluation of alternatives		

Most of the above activities take place when the customer visits the store and highlight the role of the employee in both shaping the customer experience as well as enhancing the opportunities for sales from the perspective of the retailer.

Dixons Retail plc is Europe's largest specialist electrical and services company. Its overall mission is to bring the latest technology at the best prices to its customers combined with great advice and after-sales care. Due to the nature of its product portfolio, some items are relatively complex from the perspective of its customers and may be of high monetary value (for example, HD TV). Therefore, shoppers may have some anxieties and fears about purchasing such items. The role of the employee is critical in terms of shaping the experience for the shopper.

Dixons has developed what it calls a 'customer plan' to address the challenge of enhancing the shopping trip for the customer and taking out some of these fears and doubts. The plan is designed to meet the following issues.

■ It's an exciting place to be.
■ It's easy to shop.
■ I can get what I want when I want it.
■ The prices are good.
■ They make things work and keep them working.
■ They deal with queries and complaints brilliantly.
■ They're interested in working out what's right for me.

This strategy focuses on the role of the employee in providing customer service levels that specifically address the requirements of the shopper and meets (hopefully exceeds) customer expectations. Visit the following link to acquire more detail about this approach: http://www.dixonscarphonegroup.com/media-centre/video-library/videos/ (accessed March 2015).

7.5.1 Underpinning customer experience excellence in retail

Nunwood (2014), an experience management consultancy firm, identify six key pillars that act as the drivers for customer experience excellence in the retail sector. They are summarized as follows.

1 **Personalization**: this addresses the need to make the product as relevant and customized as possible for the shopper. For example in the case of Lush, the soap and cosmetics company, great emphasis is placed on the sales staff engaging fully with customers before directing them to particular products. Such conversations allow them to recommend appropriate products.

2 **Time and effort**: this focuses on how shoppers spend their time and how the latter can be maximized to best effect. For instance, a German retailer, Wash&Coffee, delivers high-quality coffee and sandwiches while you wash your clothes.

3 **Expectations**: increasingly, where retailers are using a number of online and offline retail formats, it is critical that advertised items on websites or in the store are available and meet the expectations of shoppers. Managing expectations plays a critical role in this respect.

4 **Resolution**: this refers to the art of putting things right when they go wrong. Nunwood (2014) suggest that inflexible procedures can hinder this task and put up barriers that customers have to 'jump through' to get natural justice.

5 **Integrity**: this refers to 'doing the right thing'. They cite the example of Domino's Pizza. In this case, service staff are encouraged to advise customers of the best value portions and pizza cuts even if this means the customer spends less in the outlet.

6 **Empathy**: this issue addresses the challenge of reflecting and reacting to the feelings of the customer. They cite the example of QVC, the TV shopping channel that builds good relationships with its shopper by dint of a presentation style that is chatty, familiar and informative. (Nunwood, 2014)

7.6 Setting appropriate service levels

7.6.1 Strategic questions

Before moving on to the practicalities of setting customer service levels, the retailer should consider the following questions:

- What level of service is proper to complement a firm's image?
- Should there be a choice of customer service?
- Should customer service be free?
- How can a retailer measure the benefits of providing customer service against their costs?
- How can customer services be terminated?

The approach to retail positioning will shape the policy with regard to customer service strategy design. There is no standard level of customer service. A discount retailer such as Aldi and Lidl will, in relative terms, place less emphasis on customer service in its value proposition and instead focus more fully on low prices as the fulcrum of its overall business model. By contrast, Waitrose will invest more heavily in customer service to reinforce its overall approach to positioning in that sector.

This raises the issue of whether customer service is viewed as a cost or as an investment. It is too simplistic to fully support either argument: a retailer cannot completely ignore customer service as there are basic levels that have to be provided in order to meet essential 'health and safety' standards.

Figure 7.2 shows that continually investing in customer service does not necessarily lead to automatic increases in customer satisfaction.

Beyond a certain point, the costs of increasing customer service levels outweigh any potential benefits that may accrue to the retailer in terms of enhanced customer satisfaction levels.

It is critical that retailers engage in longitudinal research (research that is carried out on a regular basis as opposed to a survey that captures information only at one point in time) to monitor and assess customer expectations in relation to what they want by way of customer service. Continuous and ongoing research provides the retailer with the opportunity to see if changes are occurring in this area. It is dangerous to assume: (a) that customer expectations will remain the same over time; (b) that retailers need to constantly increase levels of customer service; and (c) that customer expectations cannot be altered.

Without such investment in marketing research, there is a danger that retailers overestimate the level of service expected by customers. While it is true to say that in general shoppers are becoming more

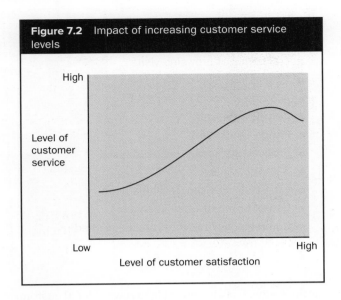

Figure 7.2 Impact of increasing customer service levels

demanding and knowledgeable, that does not necessarily translate into automatically assuming that service levels have to increase accordingly.

Customer expectations can change due to a number of factors such as competitive activities, new entrants to the market adopting different business models and the general state of the economy (recessionary times versus boom times).

Retailers can also reduce the level of customer service provided. This may occur due to a couple of reasons. For instance, research may indicate that customers have reduced expectations about the level of service that they require. This might happen where retailers increasingly rely on technology; that is, a website (low touch/remote) to provide information as opposed to the more expensive (high touch) retail store employees. In this context 'low touch' refers to situations where the shopper does not require a high level of personal interaction (high touch) and instead prefers a less personal means of interacting with the retailers. As shoppers increasingly become more comfortable with these sources of information, they no longer place as strong an emphasis on personal interaction with representatives from the retail organization. Retail banks globally have moved away from high touch channels such as bank branches to web-based services and call centres. While there is a danger that such a move to low-cost channels can alienate certain segments; for example, older people, low-income or rural-based customers, it can also significantly reduce the cost structure of the retail operation.

As well as reacting to changes, retailers can impose changes in customer service levels on their target market. While this is potentially a dangerous strategy (it may lead to customer defections), if the business model and position of the retailer in the market is sufficiently strong enough, it can lead to cost reductions. Low-cost airlines such as Ryanair have successfully managed a reduction in customer expectations in recent years by imposing charges on baggage and the booking process without apparently consulting with its customer base. Table 7.1 highlights critical areas where the retailer needs to capture information from its customer base in order to facilitate decision-making with regard to customer service strategy.

Marketing research on the issue of customer service will also help a retailer to identify different segments that may have different attitudes, perceptions and needs in this area. It may quickly become apparent that a 'one-size-fits-all' approach may not be the most appropriate strategy. This leads to the question of whether or not a retailer should provide different levels of services to different segments. The answer to this rests very much with the nature of the retail operation, the complexity of the products sold and the ability to bundle the services; that is, provide a streamlined basic service or 'wrap' additional layers or dimensions and charging accordingly. We see this in many service organizations such as airlines, hotels and sports where they provide 'tiered' customer levels ranging from the 'deluxe

Table 7.1 Information requirements to shape customer service strategy

- Frequency of browsing visits
- Frequency of purchasing visits
- Average transaction per visit
- Items purchased
- Range purchased
- Product/services purchased/used
- Satisfaction levels
- Customer services/facilities used
- Use of different retail channels
- Comparison with other retailers visited

approach' down to the basic approach. It is also possible to reward loyal customers by offering discounts on certain transactions or enhancing the customer experience. For instance, it is common practice in elite sports such as football, rugby and baseball for clubs to provide better-quality food and beverage facilities for season-ticket holders.

7.7 Dimensions of customer service

Before we consider the key elements of customer service, we should recognize that there are two categories of service provision. The first category refers to those elements that are deemed to be compulsory; that is, the retailer cannot avoid service provision in such areas. Examples include issues that are laid out in law with regard to health and safety such as a minimum number of car parking spaces for physically challenged shoppers, materials used on floors and display units that comply with safety standards and so on. Such elements of customer service are mandatory and provide no opportunity for the retailer to generate a competitive advantage. These elements are often referred to as qualifying services.

The second category addresses areas where the retailer has discretion on the extent of provision and level of investment provided. As mentioned earlier, much will depend on the positioning strategy of the retailer, the level of resources available, competitive activity, location and the nature of the products being sold. These areas are often referred to as determining services and it is in this category that a retailer can use customer service to influence the shopper's overall experience and perceptions. Let us explore these dimensions in greater detail.

We can view the elements of determining customer services as falling into two dimensions: 'soft' and 'hard' elements.

The hard elements refer to tangible factors that the shopper can observe and assess. These include: car parking, crèche facilities, changing rooms, toilet provision, merchandise display, physical appearance of staff, ease of access and egress, queuing at checkouts, process for dealing with defective or damaged goods, dealing with complaints, overall cleanliness of the retail outlet and in-store visibility and communications. It can be argued that these dimensions are, relatively speaking, easier for the shopper to measure as they are physical in nature.

By contrast, soft dimensions are more difficult for the shopper to assess. These include: performance of the retail salesperson in areas such as product knowledge, interaction skills, ability empathizing with the shopper and inspiring confidence and trust.

These hard and soft elements combine to shape the shopper's perception of service quality. Research by numerous authors such as Gronroos (2001), Mels, Boshof and Deon (1997) and Lehtinen and Lehtinen (1991) demonstrate that the quality of the service provided has a technical or outcome dimension that relates to the hard physical dimensions. This research also identifies a functional dimension that essentially addresses the soft dimensions. Both elements play a critical role in shaping the quality of the service as perceived by the shoppers.

Parasuraman et al. (1985) developed the SERVQUAL model that has been used in many areas of services marketing including the retail sector to assess service quality. It identified five dimensions of quality. We discuss these dimensions in the context of retailing. They are as follows:

1 reliability (consistently delivering the services promises at the stated level)

2 responsiveness (providing prompt service)

3 assurance (ability to inspire trust and confidence in the retailer)

4 empathy (willingness to give some form of personalized attention to the shopper)

5 tangibles (appearance of a retailer's store layout and design, communications material and so on).

Since this pioneering work, many authors have challenged its validity and generic applicability (different sectors of industry may have different dimensions). It is not our intention here to go into too much detail on the value of the model itself. However, it is still used by many researchers (with some amendments to some of the questions in the questionnaire) as a basis for assessing customers' attitudes and perceptions of service quality.

For instance, Parasuraman et al. (2005) modified the original SERVQUAL model to take into account the emergence of online channels. This new framework incorporated two multiple-item scales for measuring service quality in online stores. The standard scale is made up of four factors: efficiency, fulfilment, system availability and privacy. The second scale only comes into play if a consumer has used recovery services. This scale featured three factors: responsiveness, compensation and contact.

Using a slightly modified version of the Parasuraman model, Turk et al. (2012) conducted research in co-operation with Hugo Boss, the German luxury fashion retailer. They found that for luxury retailers opening an online store, the critical issues in terms of perceived service quality are efficiency and design. Dimensions such as speed, navigation structure and layout of the online shop require proper testing and 'debugging' before the online store goes 'live'.

As stated earlier, the strategic value of investing in customer service also focuses on customer retention. This raises the importance of loyalty as a key consideration. Research by Iacobucci and Ostrom (1993) identifies two elements of loyalty: person-to-person (salesperson level) and person-to-firm (store level). They note that firm relationships are more short term in focus and less influential than those from the person-to-person relationships. They are, however, interrelated: trust and confidence that is established with the salesperson spread to a similar feeling about the store as well.

Research undertaken by Yuen and Chan (2010) highlighted that personal interaction, physical aspects (of the retail store) and problem-solving of retail service quality were relatively influential in affecting customer loyalty to both store and staff. While highlighting the importance of personal interaction, they observe that there is a high level of interaction between the various variables and that it would be dangerous to consider the role of the salesperson in isolation.

Gopalani and Shick (2011: 4) advocated what they call a service-enabled customer experience (SECE) as being the most appropriate strategy. Although their model is not specifically designed for the retail sector, it still has relevance. The essence of their approach revolves around the following issues:

- Targeting services to unique customer needs across the ownership life cycle such as providing information that makes the buying process easier, enhancing the value of the product or reducing ownership hassles

- Integrating these services into the fabric of the firm's operations so that customers consistently see value at every touchpoint and throughout their ownership experience

- Positioning services in the centre of the firm's marketing messages so that customers are aware of the value companies are providing through the service programme

- Increasing the customer's perceived value of the combined product and service offerings

■ Building a direct relationship with customers while still balancing the firm's current business sold through channel partners.

They identify three significant benefits that can accrue to companies as a result of adopting this approach. We examine these benefits within the context of the retail sector.

1 *Direct customer relationship*: in the context of retailing where shoppers are engaging with different retail channel platforms, it provides a mechanism for retailers to increase knowledge of who their customers are and develop insights into their unique needs.

2 *Product repurchase*: once trust and confidence have been built up and achieved, retailers can provide an omni-retail presence: where customers can seamlessly use different channels at different points in the purchase process to engage with the retailer and achieve the same customer experience.

3 *Customer advocacy*: satisfied and happy customers can act as ambassadors for the retailer. They will engage in favourable word-of-mouth (WOM) activities and also spread positive messages via the various social media tools.

7.8 Designing effective customer service strategies

We examined the role that customer service plays in shaping effective retail marketing strategies in the preceding sections. We need to consider the ways in which retailers can create relevant and meaningful strategies in this area.

Skillsmart Retail (2011) carried out research with a number of UK-based retailers. Its main objective was to examine the practices adopted by the participants in the study. Its main findings show that:

■ Customer service is a key competitive differentiator and should be seen as a long-term commitment. It will not succeed if it is viewed only as a short-term tactic.

■ Ownership of the customer service offer and the need for continuous improvement has to be driven from the top of the organization whether the owner-manager or the board.

■ Customer knowledge has to be updated constantly as their views and behaviours change and that knowledge should be used to drive service levels forward.

■ Communicate effectively to all colleagues what they individually need to do and what the benefits will be to all.

■ Measure from a customer's perspective.

The study also noted that increasingly retailers have to rethink their approach to customer service strategy. Traditionally, they have treated this area as an 'either/or' option: high service versus low cost. Now, in a retail environment that increasingly is moving towards a multi-retail channel format, the challenge is to achieve a consistent, seamless and integrated approach to customer service across all of these platforms.

Another study by Cognito (2012), a UK-based consultancy group, which surveyed over 5,000 consumers and businesses on their perceptions of receiving and delivering customer service, asked: what are the key success factors for designing effective customer service strategies?

1 **Long-term commitment to customer service from the chief executive officer (CEO) and top management**

First, if a retailer wishes to use customer service as a mechanism for competitive differentiation, it requires long-term commitment in terms of investment and from the perspective of top management and the CEO. It takes time to imbue a customer focus and a customer service mentality among staff. This will not happen through superficial documentation and desultory training programmes. Rather, such programmes should be focused on the importance of the customer to the retailer, a honing of the required skill set necessary to develop empathy with the customer, and product knowledge.

2 Acquiring and acting on customer feedback

Information is central to any decisions regarding customer service. Sharp retailers will engage in regular research with customers using a combination of surveys, panels, focus groups, online feedback and mystery shopping to acquire feedback from shoppers on all aspects of the shopping experience. Such a data set provides the ammunition for subsequent decision-making in this area. It is not sufficient to carry out sporadic research in this area however. As we noted earlier in this chapter, customers' attitudes and opinions change over time. Regular and longitudinal studies allow retailers to benchmark themselves over time and, more importantly, to assess their performance against competitors.

3 Recruit the right staff

In a cost-driven industry, there is a temptation to recruit staff using the lowest common denominator; that is, those individuals with the lowest skill set. This is not to suggest that a common set of criteria should be used by all retailers. Clearly, retailers who operate in the discount end of the market do not necessarily require self-motivated employees with university degrees.

However, even there, such employees need to have a basic understanding of the importance of the customer in the equation. By using the lowest common denominator to recruit staff, retailers run the risk of employing salespeople who are unsuited to the demands of engaging with shoppers. Where customer expectations are high in terms of speed of response, product knowledge and advice, it is critical that the retailer employs engaging individuals who have capabilities in these areas. Focused and regular training and education will hone these skills and make them even more effective in the store selling environment.

4 Avoid becoming too prescriptive in training staff

Many retailers use a 'scripted' approach to train staff. They do so in the belief that it helps to ensure some form of consistency and standardization. In some low-touch situations, for example call centres, this may be appropriate in most of the interactions that occur between customers and staff. Even in this instance, companies such as Dell have encountered heavy criticism from customers who have experienced poor levels of service from operatives.

Patterson and Baron (2010) show that in many cases shoppers are somewhat cynical about the approach adopted by salespeople in retail interactions. They can 'see through' the approaches used by these people. In such circumstances, the use of a scripted approach may be counter-productive. They identify one such script employed as GAPACT and this is highlighted in Table 7.2.

Patterson and Baron (2010) argue that this type of script effectively puts the employee in a straitjacket. It tends to work if the customer is compliant and is willing to fall in line with the scripted approach. For those customers who are unwilling to play along, they are likely to become even more cynical.

As well as constraining the employee, such scripted approaches reduce the capability of that person to improvise and adapt interaction strategies with different categories of customer. Indeed,

Table 7.2 GAPACT Framework

Greet	(Hello)
Ask	(How can I help you?)
Provide	(Hand the product to customers for inspection)
Add-on	(Suggest accessories)
Close the sale	(Should I pack these for you?)
Thank	(Show appreciation for the customer's time)

Source: Adapted from Patterson and Baron (2010: 443)

it can be strongly argued that one of the differentiating characteristics of an effective salesperson is precisely that ability to empathize with the prospective customer and adapt the approach accordingly. In the case of a retail scenario, a customer who comes into the store well versed in the product offerings, price ranges and benefits will require a different response than in the case of an individual who is a self-confessed 'technophobe' and is essentially relying on the salesperson to steer them to the product that they need.

Research by Baron, Harris and Harris (2001: 443) suggests that retail space in stores could be used more effectively in terms of employee creativity and 'facilitate a clearly thought-through customer experience. For example each floor in a department store could offer a different type of customer experience – the IT experience, the dining experience and the living experience, rather than simply a display of merchandise'.

Stores such as Hewlett Packard and Apple have moved in this direction. Sales staff engage in a number of different activities with customers, ranging from educating, advising, demonstrating, providing information and selling. Rather than engaging overtly in aggressive selling, they have to be extremely flexible and adaptable with regard to their interactions with customers.

5 Empower staff to make decisions where appropriate and necessary

A sense of balance has to be developed by the retailer in this area. Policies and procedures are still necessary in terms of laying down ground rules for staff to follow. These should cover all the touchpoints between the shopper and the retailer. However, there should still be scope to allow employees the necessary freedom to respond quickly to situations that can occur which do not fit readily within the rules and procedures. Clear lines of command should exist that identify issues and decisions that should be referred to a senior line manager and those areas where the employee has the authority to take responsibility for that decision. Wong and Sohal (2003: 259) note that:

> ❝For retail stores with a strong customer service orientation programme in place, further improvements in customer service may come through the addition of new programmes aimed at improving specific negative incidents identified. Hence, effective human resource training programmes could be instilled to equip employees to be more responsive to customers' needs and expectations, as customers value a responsive employee that can provide relevant information that addresses their specific needs, thereby saving time and reducing effort for the customers.❞

Empowering staff requires a pragmatic and common-sense approach on behalf of management. They should be encouraged (and rewarded) for showing enterprise and initiative. A one-dimensional approach where the employee has to refer every problem to higher management or where the shopper is asked to fill out bureaucratic and time-consuming paperwork is to be avoided. In some situations, the staff member should be allowed to take action; for example, making a decision on a returned item or giving a discount on a shop-soiled piece of merchandise, even if the retailer loses money on that individual transaction. In the longer term, shoppers are more likely to revisit the store and speak (in person and online) positively about it to friends if they feel satisfied about the outcome.

6 Develop relevant and focused rewards for the employees

Retailers can adopt a diverse range of monetary and non-monetary rewards for their employees. It is not our intention here to investigate these options in detail. However, a combination of a fixed wage and commission (based on sales performance) is often a popular method for motivating and rewarding staff. The nature of bonuses and commission that is paid can vary. In some instances, it may be more appropriate to reward the sales team that is on duty on any given day. This has the merit of rewarding the 'group effort' involved in creating a positive and enjoyable sales experience for the shopper. It may be more effective also to have elements of the bonus that are paid on the basis of the individual's effort. Many successful retailers also make use of non-monetary reward mechanisms as well. Individuals may be rewarded with vouchers, holidays or tickets to sports/music events on the basis of their performance relative to other employees. Employee of the month awards can also generate a strong degree of satisfaction, confidence and loyalty on the part of the winner.

7 Use metrics to measure performance

Without proper measurement of performance, no strategy or plan is likely to have much impact. It leads to a lack of direction and focus. These measures can stretch across strategic measures such as overall market share, sales and profit through to specific weekly sales target for individual staff members. Retailers can also use data from the ongoing marketing research programmes to measure performance; for example, minimum/desired/ideal customer satisfaction scores. Retailers may also identify specific performance standards that are expected of staff. These include procedures such as greeting customers within a minute of entering the store, accompanying them to the changing rooms and suggesting an additional item to the customer. Such measures can be used to determine rewards and where necessary to take remedial action in the case of poor performance or incompetence on the part of staff members.

8 Be careful of using a standardized approach to customer service in an international context

Customer service expectations vary across different geographic regions. Much of the bases for this assumption tend to be anecdotal. For instance, US shoppers are perceived as being very demanding and critical about poor levels of service. If they encounter it, they complain loudly and directly. By contrast, UK shoppers are perceived as being rather reserved in their dealings with retailers and less likely to complain loudly and directly. In some countries, particularly in developing economies where there is less choice and disposable income available, it is often assumed that retailers can get away with lower levels of customer service. There are obvious dangers from relying on such assumptions as they are largely based on stereotypical images of people and countries. However, retailers cannot afford to ignore potential differences in customer expectations as they move into the international domain. Even small differences in culture can affect customer expectations and as a consequence affect customer satisfaction, store and brand image and ultimately the successful transfer of retail format.

9 Beware of exaggerating claims

Many retailers and indeed companies in general overstate the benefits of their value proposition. In a never-ending drive for customers, there is a danger that retailers overstate their customer service levels to customers in their marketing communications strategy. Inevitably if this happens, shoppers will be disappointed by the actual experience encountered. They will also tell their friends and are increasingly likely to blog and tweet their experience to their wider network of friends and colleagues. By now the damage is done. Retailers can employ service recovery strategies in an attempt to nullify the problem but once a first impression is formed, it is difficult to regain customers, particularly those who have visited the store for the first time. A retailer is better off to deliberately understate the customer service levels. Shoppers are more likely to visit the store or website with a lower set of expectations and are then pleasantly surprised by what they experience during their visit. Instead of the vicious cycle of negativity that occurs when the promise is exaggerated, a virtual cycle creates positivity among customers as they share their thoughts.

7.9 Case in point: John Lewis Partnership

John Lewis is a UK-based retailer. It was established in 1929 by John Speedon Lewis. He focused on setting up an organization that was an alternative to the rampant capitalism which existed in many companies at that time. He thought it was immoral for his family to take so much out of the business by way of profit. His approach was to set up a partnership where everybody, employees and management, would benefit from the profits generated. This approach is to take the overall profit, identify the capital needed for investment for the coming year and then distribute the remaining profit to its partners who total 70,000.

Its CEO, for example, does not earn anywhere near the salaries that comparable CEOs from publicly quoted companies earn. Indeed, the salary is determined by boardroom rules which stipulate that it can be no more than 75 times the average earnings of the lowest paid partners.

▶

◄ John Lewis' approach to business development is cautious and is based on a risk-averse approach.

In 2010 it was voted the UK's favourite retailer for the third year running. It is recognized by many commentators as one of the foremost retailers in the area of customer service.

The partners are central to the design and delivery of customer service. As stated earlier, they are not mere employees; they share in the profit that is generated by the company. In 2009, this amounted to 13 per cent. They also have a say in the management of the company and can hold them to account at the annual presentations to the partners.

What are the main lessons that we can learn from this retailer?

1 *Make staff part of the business*: by sharing in the profits and having a say in the management and direction of the company, partners do not just feel that they are part of a business, they own it.

2 *Teach protocol – but empower staff to make decisions themselves*: a recurring theme that runs throughout the training programme is the mantra 'show enterprise'.

3 *Make sure the front-line staff provide feedback on what the customers want*: involve the partners in coming up with ideas to improve things.

4 *Be exceptional*: in December 2009 a snow storm left customers stranded at a John Lewis store. What would you do with the customers? Staff came up with the idea of a mass sleepover, where they made use of in-store merchandise to provide beds for over 100 customers, opened up the toy section to allow children to play and provided food for them instead of sending them home in a blizzard.

5 *Maintain customer service levels online*: it is critical to make online customers feel as if they are being listened to.

7.10 Learning from Nordstrom

Nordstrom, the US-based fashion retailer, is an interesting case to consider from the perspective of how it treats its employees. This company started out as a shoe retailer and has expanded its inventory to include clothing, accessories, handbags, jewellery, cosmetics and fragrances. Its headquarters is located in Seattle and it currently operates around 245 stores in 33 states. It competes directly with other luxury retailers such as Bloomingdales, Lord & Taylor and Neiman Marcus.

Its employee handbook is brief and to the point. It contains seventy-five words!

"*Welcome to Nordstrom*

We're glad to have you with our Company. Our number one goal is to provide outstanding customer service. Set both your personal and professional goals high. We have great confidence in your ability to achieve them.

Nordstrom Rules: Rule #1: Use best judgment in all situations. There will be no additional rules.

*Please feel free to ask your department manager, store manager, or division general manager any question at any time***"** *(Nordstrom internal document)*

From this succinct statement, we gain an insight into the corporate culture that prevails at Nordstrom. While it is predicated on the basis of recruiting appropriate and motivated employees, it explicitly acknowledges that it has a full belief and confidence in their ability to deliver the appropriate level of customer service. It also eschews the need for a raft of rules, procedures and regulations; instead, it places emphasis on the need to use judgement and common sense when engaging with customers in the store.

7.11 Managing customer service online

7.11.1 Context

As we noted in Chapter 2, shoppers are increasingly making greater use of online retail channels to conduct their business. Original pioneers of online channels such as ASOS and Amazon are now joined by the traditional bricks-and-mortar retailers with many of them operating a multi-channel strategy.

While early web-enabled retail channels offered limited potential by way of functionality: they were largely of an 'information-push' nature, Web 2.0 has enabled consumers and retailers to interact with each other in a more strategic way. Social media tools such as Facebook, Twitter, YouTube and blogs create more extensive opportunities for ongoing communications between the two stakeholders.

Increasingly, shoppers are making use of mobile technologies such as smartphones, tablets and iPads to engage in shopping activities. Managing the customer experience has to embrace the opportunities and challenges surrounding these new channels. Omni retailing implies that retailers have to provide a common customer experience across a multi-channel environment.

As we discuss in Chapter 8, retailers are increasingly investing in an omni-channel strategy. This involves the use of a number of different channels to engage with shoppers at the various stages of the buying process. This is not to be confused with the concept of multiple channels where the latter operate autonomously from each other. With omni channels, the objective on the part of the retailer is to deliver a seamless and integrated experience for the shopper as they engage with a retailer. For instance, shoppers may make the initial touchpoint with the retailer by visiting its website in order to glean some information about the range of merchandise or brands that is on offer. They then may visit a particular store or outlet to get some advice from a salesperson, and subsequently may telephone a call centre to get details about warranty issues. In this hypothetical case, shoppers clearly have a number of interactions with the retailer across its portfolio of retail channels.

In terms of customer experience and customer service, the challenge for the retailer is to ensure *consistency* across the different channels in order to deliver an integrated customer experience. Clearly, this can break down. For instance, the store may carry a full range of merchandise but the online channel may not have a particular item in stock. While shoppers may feel very positive about the quality of the sales personnel in the store, they may have negative perceptions about deficiencies in the online channel. This may be further exacerbated by delays and lack of help when they ring the call centre.

In the context of developments in the area of omni channels, it can be argued that the challenges involved in managing the customer experience and delivering on specific dimensions of customer service can become very complex.

7.11.2 The online shopping experience

Shoppers while not physically visiting a store, still virtually visit the retailer's store via its website. Rose et al. (2012: 309) observe that:

> **"***online shoppers encounter incoming sensory data from a range of stimuli on the e-retailer's website such as text-based information, visual imagery, video or audio delivery. They posit that the customer interprets this from a cognitive and affective perspective creating impression formation of the e-retailer website.***"**

This is supported by earlier research by Gentile et al. (2007). The data that is presented on the retailer's website is interpreted by the shopper from both a cognitive and an affective perspective. Work by Hoffman and Novak (2009) reinforces this perspective.

Rose et al. (2012) posit the view that online customer experience impression formation is largely cumulative: the shopper builds up a perception of the retailer following repeated exposure. This mirrors the way in which shoppers build up an image of the store in a bricks-and-mortar (physical store) context. In both circumstances the shopper gradually builds up a cumulative picture of the store, its merchandise, staff, facilities, store environment, price points and so on. Either they like what they see (and will gain confidence and trust in the store's value proposition) or they will go elsewhere to seek out an alternative store that will satisfy their shopping needs and expectations. The design of the website equates to the challenges involved in creating an attractive physical selling environment. This is the subject of Chapter 5.

One of the challenges facing retailers in the area of online retailing is the potential risk of not retaining full control over the creation and development of the online customer experience. While in a physical shopping environment, the retailer controls the layout, design and atmosphere of the store location, this is not necessarily the case online. In the latter case, the shopper may be accessing the website in an office, at home or in a coffee shop. Mobile technology also allows the shopper to make contact with the website while 'on the go'. In these instances there may be external variables of which the retailer may not be aware.

Rose et al. (2012) conducted a survey with over 220 respondents. They found that perceived control had a mediating effect in that it controls influences of the customer's affective state and those three variables – connectedness, customization and ease-of-use – have a direct impact on the levels of perceived control. In particular, connectedness and customization, driven by the interactive nature of Web 2.0, appears to empower customers and provide them with confidence when using online retail channels to make purchase decisions. The findings identify ease of use as a critical factor in shaping the customer's perceptions and opinions.

What can retailers learn from this study? It is critical to design a website that is easy to navigate and provides shoppers with the necessary information to allow them to arrive at a purchasing decision. Anything that is overly complex can disrupt the emotional state of the shopper and make it less likely that they will revisit and make a repeat purchase.

The study also suggests that a website that has a capability that allows shoppers to customize their own space builds a sense of personal control. This, in effect, replicates what tends to happen in a physical store context where shoppers establish their own 'rituals and routine' in terms of specific areas they visit in that store, the product categories they purchase initially and items that they leave to the end of the shopping visit. In the online context, customization allows shoppers to build up levels of confidence and control over time.

The ability of Web 2.0 with its interactive capabilities is also a critical variable in positively enhancing the shopping experience online. In effect, this allows shoppers to do the equivalent of talking and exchanging views and opinions in a physical environment. The use of blogs, for example, clearly addresses this desire among shoppers to share opinions and preferences with other like-minded shoppers.

Two other variables – telepresence (allowing shoppers to immerse themselves in the world of online) and challenge (a shopper's skills and capabilities being tested by using the Internet) – also positively influence the online customer experience.

Rose et al. (2012) also stress the need to monitor and evaluate levels of satisfaction and trust over time. Like evaluating customer standards in a bricks-and-mortar context, this exercise should examine all of the relevant touchpoints in the process; for example, receiving the relevant information about product and price, placing the order and delivery of the order through to product returns and complaints.

The research in the area of online customer service is at a nascent stage. More detailed research is needed with specific groups of shoppers such as women, older shoppers and so on. Much work also needs to be carried out on potential cultural differences and how this may affect online shopping behaviour in different geographic regions.

In summary, the following dimensions of customer service have been identified as being important for online retailers (Suryandari and Paswan, 2014: 70):

- reliability
- access
- ease of navigation
- efficiency
- responsiveness
- assurance
- security
- aesthetics
- personalization.

Retailers, while having to address these factors, tend to focus on a couple of them to identify either a point of differentiation from their competitors or because they are of critical importance to shoppers. For instance, in the early stages of online retailing, shoppers were very concerned about the issue of security. More recently issues such as perceived value, trust and offline presence have become more important to shoppers.

Much depends on the retail sector and the nature of the product being sold. Suryandari and Paswan (2014) note that consumers demonstrably have different preferences for what they will buy online or offline. Some products are more complex and require a greater degree of personal interaction; others can be purchased remotely (for example, online) and require little or no interaction. Some items require a strong degree of after-sales elements such as delivery, warranty and returns.

7.12 Case in point: ASOS

ASOS (As Seen On Screen) has been one of the major success stories with regard to online retailing in recent years. The business was established by Nick Robertson with a £2 million loan from his brother. It is now established as one of the UK's largest fashion retailers with over 12 million unique users a month, generating over 800,000 visitors to its site daily. It has expanded its operations in the last couple of years to markets such as the USA and Australia, and has created websites that are specific to those countries.

ASOS has constantly developed innovative aspects to its business model. It launched a virtual catwalk on its site in 2006 and from its base in north London it does all of the photo shoots and videos in-house. This amounts to over 2,000 items per week on average.

In 2009, it launched its own virtual designer store and ASOS life, an online community.

In 2010, it developed ASOS marketplace: a platform where boutiques and individuals can open their own individual stores.

In 2011, it developed Fashion Finder, a portal that promotes brands that ASOS does not sell.

In 2012, it developed five local language websites, reinforcing its desire to establish a robust international presence.

Most of the staff recruited by ASOS resemble the demographics of its key target market: young, trendy and predominantly female. Everything it does is aimed at the 'imagined 22-year-old', the median age of its target market. Within this overall target market, it is subdivided into three groups. Fashion Forward (consumers who set the trends); Fashion Passenger (consumers who follow the trends) and Functional Fashion (those consumers who are less trend conscious).

Much of its success has been based on a low-tech guarantee to customers: free returns. As it moves to the international sector, it now provides free shipping (a strong feature of its launch in the Australian market).

Not surprisingly, it has attracted strong competition as other retailers see the potential in this sector. At the luxury end, Net-a-Porter is a prime player and in the mid-market division NotOnTheHighStreet.com is making its presence felt. Traditional retailers such as Superdry are now generating more sales online than they do from their bricks-and-mortar operations.

What does the future hold for ASOS? Robinson sees France, the USA, Germany and the UK as its key markets along with China. The latter poses a challenge given the size and scale of the market and possible cultural differences that might be reflected in shopping behaviour.

Questions

Visit the ASOS website at www.asos.com.

1 Make an assessment of the functionality of this site from the perspective of using it to purchase a product.
2 Are there weaknesses that you found when using this site?
3 Examine the ability of this site to encourage customization.
4 Consider the level of interaction that can be generated on this site with the retailer and fellow shoppers/visitors to this site.
5 Overall, how did you rate this site from the customer experience point of view?

7.13   Constraints to effective customer service design and implementation

Retailers globally are operating in an environment that is cost-driven: customer service is often viewed as a cost rather than an investment. Much depends on the nature of the retail service that is being provided. In cases where the product is relatively complex (consumer electronics) or where the shopper requires extensive advice and consultation (ladies high fashion), high-touch service levels may be the most appropriate.

This involves the human element; that is, sales staff. As cost considerations come into play, many retailers will compromise on the quality of the sales staff employed, reduce the intensity and focus of customer service training and education and pay them the minimum wage or going rate in that particular retail sector. This can lead to poor levels of service and the resultant damage that can emerge from such actions. If employees are poorly trained in key areas such as product knowledge this can lead to dissatisfaction on the part of shoppers. Cognito (2012) found that 82 per cent of consumers said they would tell other people about a bad experience.

Employees in many instances are poorly paid. This can lead to issues of commitment and motivation and again can result in poor levels of service.

Much of the work carried out by retail employees can be boring, repetitive and of little apparent value. Retail stores only operate near to peak capacity at limited times during the week. How does the retailer relieve the monotony and keep the employee interested?

Increasingly, retailers are making use of part-time workers; for example, students and older people who wish to re-enter the workplace. This again raises potential issues about the level of commitment and enthusiasm among the workforce.

Retailers have to grapple with issues such as in-store theft (shrinkage) by staff as well as shoppers, safety concerns for staff and the general wellbeing of shoppers in the store. As a result shoppers tend to be confronted by surveillance cameras, security guards at the entrance, threatening signs and so on. While these issues are for the most part a necessary element of the shopping experience, they can create an intimidating atmosphere for shoppers and dilute the positive customer experience aspects. Friend et al. (2010) suggest that retailers might consider removing these obvious symbols of distrust in order to lessen the potentially threatening shopping environment. While there may be some scope, it is unlikely that all of these features could be removed by retailers. Therefore, the retailer has to try to achieve a balance between retaining necessary security measures such as surveillance cameras and generating a positive shopping experience for the customer.

These factors can raise serious questions about the ability of retailers to design and implement effective customer service strategy. In an earlier section, we identified a number of critical success factors that can address these constraints.

The move towards online retailing partially reduces the reliance of 'human' input. However, retailers are now challenged with the task of providing a set of integrated and seamless customer experiences across a number of different channels.

The practitioner view
Dealing with omni channels – challenges and opportunities

Alessandro Petrelli, Director of International Sales and Travel: Radley London

Alessandro Petrelli works for Radley London. Radley was founded by Lowell Harder, an Australian architect, who had a particular interest in handbags. Her sister had sent her some handbags from India and Lowell was attracted to their designs. She originally operated a stall at Camden market in London. Interest in her designs spread to such an extent that retailers such as John Lewis placed orders with her. The Radley brand was launched in 1998.

Over the years since its launch, celebrities have become attracted to the brand. Around 20 stores have opened and Radley also appears in the department stores of John Lewis and House of Fraser. It also operates an online website.

Alessandro works closely across the different channel platforms that Radley operates. We asked him about some of the key experiences of his role.

From the perspective of the customers, he sees a number of advantages coming out of the application of omni channels.

What are the advantages of an omni-channel strategy?

Flexibility

'Radley operates a "pick and collect" facility for shoppers from its own stores and has now moved to the concept of "Collect Plus". This involves partnership with third party delivery operators and allows shoppers to pick up purchases in a variety of collection points such as petrol stations. Radley has around 5,000 collection points serviced by a consolidated warehouse.'

Price transparency and price matching

'It is more and more difficult not to apply the same price levels across the different channels. For instance large retailers such as John Lewis use their own price promotions and Radley has to follow suit in order to be transparent to the customers. Shoppers will track such offers via mobile and social media and expect the same price.'

There is a consequent need for real-time availability of information for customers across the channel platforms.

Radley applies a price-matching strategy across the stores and platforms: shoppers expect that if discounts are offered on one channel, they should also be available on the other ones as well.

Trust and level of service

Alessandro states that 'More and more brands need to get some level of feedback on their performance'.

Radley works with a company called Feefo, which specializes in providing feedback to brands on issues such as customer satisfaction. This is integrated in the website and 'allows customers to see how reliable a brand is before engaging with it'.

Advances in mobile technology and social media platforms allow the shoppers to access much richer content. 'This leads to "savvier" shoppers.'

Alessandro states that 'a study by MIT in 2014 shows that 80 per cent of shoppers check online before visiting the stores. They are informed about the features of the brand and also expect sales staff to be fully informed as well as being able to respond to the level of questions.'

What are the challenges facing retailers?

Supply chain/logistics

'There is a need to provide a more complex and higher level of service in terms of delivery and returns. A need to improve the logistics operation and the type of software that we use to manage operations in terms of integrating across the different channels.'

Consistency of content across channels

Alessandro sees this issue as being critical in terms of managing key areas such as brand positioning and brand image. 'The technology has to be there to support this – particularly in terms of providing relevant content.'

'For example Burberry uses FIE technology which, through tablets and mobile technology, provides additional information to shoppers when they are in the store.

'Beacon technology also allows the retailer to push information to customers when they are approximately 50 metres from the store.

▶

◄ 'This requires an investment in the appropriate technology, which needs to be able to deal with issues such as discounts across the different channels.'

Managing the portfolio of channels

Alessandro expresses the view that 'there is clearly migration happening as shoppers move to online from "bricks and mortar stores". The costs of operating stores tend to be fixed.

'Radley needs to be creative in terms of getting people to visit stores. Can all stores be profitable? Or do we use some as a showcase?

'There is certainly a need to keep all channels relevant and effective. This means increasing the customer experience and using tactics such as personalisation.'

Maintaining a position of trust across the channels

Shoppers like to be confident about the brands that they purchase. An omni-channel approach can create potential problems in this respect.

Alessandro states 'that some channels are not under the direct control of Radley. For instance with House of Fraser, Radley operates a concession area of between 10–25 square metres and has core staff maintaining it. In the case of John Lewis, it makes a contribution to staffing but does not directly control the sales staff. This can lead to a more generic experience for the shopper'.

Managing inventory across the channels

This poses a challenge for retailers who operate an omni-channel strategy.

Alessandro notes that 'recent events such as "Black Friday" created a backlog in terms of inventory and deliveries for Radley. It took longer than normal to fulfil the orders. It only created a shift in demand: not new demand. Events like this can create a disturbance in the supply chain.'

In summary, Radley operates an omni-channel approach to managing its relationships and connecting with its customers. Alessandro's views mirror the experiences of retailers who have been identified in this chapter. The issues of control and trust are emphasized as being critical to the successful implementation of omni-channel strategies.

7.14 Conclusions

In this chapter we have examined the role of customer service in the overall context of retail marketing strategy. Customer service for many categories of retailer still plays a critical role in differentiating operations from competition. As shoppers become more demanding, informed and critical, poor customer service levels can lead to reduced loyalty and customer defection.

Retailers need to take a long-term view of customer service. In some cases such as discount retailing, it is unlikely that it will play a central role in shaping overall retail strategy. In other situations, however, customers demand high levels of interaction with staff in terms of consultation, advice and guidance. Without proper investment in recruitment, training, education and reward patterns, retailers will struggle to meet the expectations of these customers.

We have highlighted the benefits of empowering staff. As well as giving them confidence, empowerment can speed up the process in the event of a problem that might occur between the shopper and the staff representative. In terms of service recovery, this is an important consideration.

Customer service should be designed from the perspective of the customer, not from the views of the retailer. This implies that longitudinal research is critical in identifying the specific perceptions and attitudes of the target market. Without the availability of such information, there is a danger that retailers will either underestimate or overestimate the service levels and create a misalignment between what is offered and what is needed.

More recently, retailers have to consider the customer experience within the context of other channels besides 'bricks and mortar'. As shoppers go online and use mobile technologies, retailers need to understand the need to provide consistent and integrated customer experiences across these channels.

Omni retailing presents both opportunities and threats in the context of customer service strategy. Retailers can no longer rely on the store design and layout as the framework for the customer experience. As discussed in Chapter 2, shoppers are now likely to use a range of channel platforms as they go through the journey (the buying process). They may use the retailer's website or Facebook page to ascertain information about the brand or other shoppers' experiences with merchandise. They may then visit the store to make the purchase and use mobile technology to check up on the procedure for making a complaint about some aspects of their shopping experience.

As a consequence, retailers have to take on board issues such as customization, ease of navigation, transparency and telepresence when designing web-based or mobile retail channels. It is not much use if the website is well designed, innovative and creative, if the experience at the physical store is poor.

We have identified a number of constraints that can create problems for retailers when designing an appropriate customer service strategy. These range from low wages, part-time staff and repetitive work practices. These have to be factored into the recruitment, training, motivation and reward structures for staff.

Customer service is highlighted by many shoppers as being an important consideration in influencing their shopping behaviour. A recent YouGov survey (2012) shows that:

1 consumers are 54 per cent more likely to spend extra with companies with good customer service

2 47 per cent of consumers will pay a premium for products or services where they believe they are likely to receive good service

3 44 per cent of UK consumers would pay a premium of 5 per cent or more for good service; this could lead to an increase in revenue of £350 million for a typical FTSE 100 company.

While this survey is general in its treatment of customer service and not focused on the retail sector, it indicates the need for retailers to recognize the propensity of shoppers to pay more for good service and the concurrent danger of defecting to competitors if they experience poor service.

Chapter outcomes

- Customer experience management and customer service incorporate a holistic view of the shopper's engagement with the retailer: not just the in-store interaction and experience.

- Decisions on customer service strategy will depend on the positioning approach of the store, its resources and its capabilities.

- Customer service should be viewed as an investment not a cost.

- The vision for a customer service strategy should come from the top and feed through to the corporate culture of the organization.

- Employees should be empowered to take decisions and be proactive rather than relying on a scripted approach.

- Retailers have to recognize the reality that shoppers increasingly engage with them across a number of different retail channels.

- The challenge lies in providing consistent customer experiences seamlessly across all of the relevant channel platforms.

Discussion questions

1 Assess the view that customer service is a cost and not an investment.
2 Examine the lessons that we can learn from the Nordstrom case.
3 Examine the extent to which you would agree with the assertion that managing customer service is more challenging in the context of online retail channels.
4 Some commentators argue that the only way to motivate staff is to pay them more. How accurate is this view? Use examples to support your line of argument.
5 Evaluate the proposition that developing a prescriptive approach to managing customer service is the best way forward for retailers.

References

Ballantyne, D. and Varey, R.J. (2006) Creating value-in-use through marketing interaction: the exchange logic of relating, communicating and knowing. *Marketing Theory*. 6(3): 335–348.

Baron, S., Harris, K. and Harris, R. (2001) Retail theater: the 'intended effect' of the performance. *Journal of Service Research*. 4(2): 102–117.

Bitner, M.J., Booms, B.H. and Tetreault, M.S. (1990) The service encounter: diagnosing favourable and unfavourable incidents. *Journal of Marketing*. 54(1): 71–84.

Carlzon, A. (1987) *Moments of Truth*. Cambridge, MA: Ballinger.

Cognito (2012) Annual Nationwide Service Report. September.

Friend, L.A., Costley, C.L. and Brown, C. (2010) Spirals of distrust vs spirals of trust in retail customer service: consumers as victims or allies. *Journal of Services Marketing*. 24(6): 458–467.

Gentile, C., Spiller, N. and Giuliano, N. (2007) How to sustain the customer experience: an overview of experience components that co-create value with the customer. *European Management Journal*. 25(5): 395–410

Gopalani, A. and Shick, K. (2011) The service-enabled customer experience: A jump-start to competitive advantage. *Journal of Business Strategy*. 32(3): 4–12.

Grewal, D., Levy, M. and Kumar, V. (2009) Customer experience management in retailing: an organizing framework. *Journal of Retailing*. 85(1): 1–14.

Gronroos, C. (2001) *Service Management and Marketing: A Customer Relationship Management Approach*. 2nd edn. Oxford: John Wiley & Sons.

Hoffman, D.L. and Novak, T.P. (2009) Flow online: lessons learned and future prospects. *Journal of Interactive Marketing*. 23: 23–34.

Iacobucci, D. and Ostrom, A. (1993) Gender differences in the impact of core and relational aspects of services on the evaluation of service encounters. *Journal of Consumer Psychology*. 2(3): 257–286.

Lehtinen, U. and Lehtinen, J.R. (1991) Two approaches to service quality dimensions. *The Service Industries Journal*. 11(3): 289–303.

Mels, G., Boshof, C. and Deon, N. (1997) The dimensions of service quality and the original European perspective revisited. *The Service Industries Journal*. 17(1): 173–189.

Nunwood (2014) The six pillars that underpin customer experience excellence in retail. Available online at: http://www.nunwood.com/six-pillars-underpin-customer-experience-excellence-retail/ (accessed 13 October 2014).

Parasuraman, A., Zeithaml, V.A. and Berry, L.L. (1985) A conceptual model of service quality and its implications for future research. *Journal of Marketing*. 49: 41–50.

Parasuraman, A., Zeithaml, V.A. and Malhotra. A. (2005) E-S Qual: A multiple-item scale for assessing electronic service quality. *Journal of Service Research*. 7(3): 213–233.

Patterson, A. and Baron, S. (2010) Deviant employees and dreadful service encounters: Customer tales of discord and distrust. *Journal of Services Marketing*. 24(6): 438–445.

Rintamaki, T. and Kuusela, H. (2007) Identifying competitive customer value propositions in retailing. *Managing Service Quality*. 17(6): 621–634.

Rose, S., Clark, M., Samouel, P. and Hair, N. (2012) Online customer experience in retailing: an empirical model of antecedents and outcomes. *Journal of Retailing*. 88(2): 308–322.

Shostack, L.G. (1985) Planning the service encounter. In Czepiel, J.A., Solomon, M.R. and Surprenant, C.F. (eds) *The Service Encounter*. Lexington, MA: Lexington Books.

Skillsmart Retail (2011) Available online at: http://www.customerchampions.co.uk/customer- service- a-key-differentiator-in-retailing/

Sparks, L. (1992) Customer service in retailing – the next leap forward? *The Services Industry Journal.* 12(2): 165.

Suryandari, R.T. and Paswan, A.K. (2014) Online customer service and retail type-product congruence. *Journal of Retailing and Consumer Services.* 21: 69–76.

Turk, B., Scholz, M. and Berresheim, P. (2012) Measuring service quality in online luxury goods retailing. *Journal of Electronic Commerce Research.* 13(1): 88–103.

Verhoef, P.C., Lemon, K.N., Parasuraman, A., Roggeveen, A., Tairos, M. and Schlesinger, L.A. (2009) Customer experience creation, determinants, dynamics and management strategies. *Journal of Retailing.* 85(1): 31–41.

Wong, A. and Sohal, A. (2003) A critical incident approach to the examination of customer relationship management in a retail chain: an exploratory study. *Qualitative Marketing Research: An International Journal.* 6(4): 248-262.

Yuen, E.F.T. and Chan, S.S.L. (2010) The effect of retail service quality and product quality on customer loyalty. *Database & Customer Strategy Management.* 17(3/4): 222–240.

YouGov Survey Results (2012) Fieldwork: 6–9 January.

Chapter 8

Retail location strategy

✓ Learning objectives

On completion of this chapter you should be in a position to address the following objectives:

☑ Understand the relationship between the location decision and its impact on other elements of the retail marketing mix.

▶

◀ ☑ Examine the concept of space and its relevance to retail strategy.

☑ Gain an insight into the key drivers of change that shape the approach of retailers to location analysis, strategy design and implementation.

☑ Evaluate the different approaches used by retailers in assessing new site possibilities.

☑ Evaluate the methods used to assess performance of existing sites.

☑ Assess the store location decision within the context of the move to a multi-channel approach by retailers.

☑ Understand the role of legislators (government and regional bodies) in shaping retail development.

8.1 Introduction

In this chapter we address another critical element of retail strategy: the location decision. This is an aspect of retailing that has undergone a metamorphosis over the last 10 years or so. Retailers have to grapple with the challenge of identifying suitable locations for their value proposition amid game-changing developments such as online channels and a growing move towards the use of multiple retail platforms in their quest to reach out to and connect with their target markets.

In the early sections we consider the concept of space and its relevance to location decisions. In particular, we assess the different perceptions of space and how it can affect the delivery of the retail value proposition.

We examine the various global trends and developments with regard to where retailers locate their operations and, in particular, evaluate the key drivers and factors that have shaped these decisions. We identify the various methods used by retailers to evaluate potential new locations for their outlets and stores as well as techniques that are used to assess the performance of existing locations.

In the middle part of the chapter, we examine the different forms of retail space that have been adopted by retailers; in particular we look at the concepts of shopping malls, out-of-town shopping centres and high street/central business district shopping. We consider the positive and negative aspects of each concept and how factors that are largely outside the control of retailers can impact on the ultimate success or failure of such developments. Environmental concerns, social issues (crime), business rates and rental agreements are examples of such factors.

The concept of omni channels has emerged as a strategic imperative for many retailers and we evaluate its relevance in the context of location decisions. We assess the relationship between physical and virtual space. In particular, we examine the ways in which different retail formats can reinforce the core values and brand associations of a retailer. As shoppers respond to the changing retail environment, we consider how retailers can achieve a balance between physical and virtual retail formats.

Store location decisions have implications for the major stakeholders such as retailers, shoppers, property developers, governments, regional policy groups and landlords. We examine the mechanisms by which legislation for retail developments is shaped and how planning policy is crafted.

In the latter part of this chapter we discuss the location decision and its implications for other key elements of retail strategy such as store loyalty and patronage, retail brand-building and store image.

8.2 Retail location defined

The decision on where to locate a retail outlet or store has been traditionally viewed as a central element in retail strategy design and implementation. 'Location, location, location' is a statement that is often used to highlight its importance. The implication of this statement is that if a retailer makes an inaccurate or wrong decision, it will have a significant impact on the success of its overall retail strategy. We debate the merits of this perception later in the chapter.

Levy and Weitz (2004) put forward the views that while many retail strategy decisions such as merchandising and pricing can be made in a relatively short time and with immediate impact, location decisions are more long term in nature. This is due to the considerable investment required and the need to gain planning permission, acquire the necessary real estate and satisfy legislators in order to move the development forward.

We can define location as 'the physical and/or virtual space that a retailer inhabits in order to present its value proposition and provide an opportunity for its target market(s) to access its merchandise and connect with its brand values and associations'.

A number of implications arise from this definition. The link between the retailer and the shopper is strongly emphasized. Retailers have to inhabit space (physical and/or virtual) that is relevant to their target market. They need to be where the shoppers are and more importantly where they shop. In Chapter 1 we discussed the different retail formats that are used by retailers. These can range from vending machines, 'pop-up' outlets, shopping centres, shopping malls, retail parks and themed centres to online (e-tail) sites. Traditionally, retailers have relied on a *physical* presence to connect with their target market(s). In the last 10 years, this has broadened to a virtual presence.

We can also argue that there is another dimension to the concept of physical space: temporary space. This is evidenced by the emergence of pop-up stores or mobile units in various high street and shopping centre locations. In the recessionary times that we have experienced, retail developers and landlords, rather than having empty units, may be happy to rent out such space on a short-term, temporary basis. This generates revenue for them and allows retailers to operate, albeit for a short period, at a low rental cost.

8.3 Retail space

We have referred to physical and virtual space in the preceding section. At one level, space refers to the spatial area used by the retailer to present its merchandise and provide access for shoppers. While this is an accurate view, it captures only a functional view of what retailing and shopping is all about. As discussed in Chapter 3, shoppers have a number of different motivations for shopping, largely influenced by the nature or category of the particular purchase. Some purchases are functional and relate closely to the view that space is about presenting merchandise and giving access to shoppers. However, many purchases made by shoppers and the resulting shopping behaviour lean more towards greater involvement. Instead of being a purely functional activity, such purchase situations recognize the importance of shopping as a leisure and entertainment-based exercise. The emphasis in this case is on pleasure and enjoyment. In this latter case, the utilization of space has to reflect the needs of shoppers and the location of the outlet must reflect a shopping environment that addresses such needs. The emergence of mega shopping malls, reflected in a large physical space and also containing plentiful parking facilities allied to leisure facilities, are a reflection of this trend. Table 8.1 depicts the different approaches to the use of space.

Brown (1993) refers to the concept of agglomeration as being central to an understanding of how retailers address spatial considerations. Traditionally, retailers have tended to locate or cluster close to retailers selling similar or complementary merchandise. Such clusters have the effect of attracting potential customers and over time this has led to the development of shopping centres, retail parks and malls, all of which provide the opportunity for 'one-stop' shopping.

In the context of human behaviour, 'no man is an island'. It is difficult for individuals to exist in isolation, without some form of cohabitation and collaboration. This analogy has also been traditionally applied to retailing. It has been difficult for an individual retailer to exist at a location where there are no other retailers and with no opportunity to coexist with similar or complementary retailers.

Table 8.1 Using space

Functional	Social	Leisure
Facilitating purchases	Coffee shops, restaurants	Cineplex, indoor bowls

However, it can be argued that such traditional perceptions have been challenged by the development of online channels. Operations such as Amazon are not clearly identified as having a particular location. Where does this retailer exist? Is it relevant? Shoppers visit its website, engage in a search process, decide on what to buy, place their orders, pay for them and go to the (virtual) checkout. The items arrive at their home address or office a couple of days later. At no point does the shopper have to worry about physically paying a visit to a location to engage in such activities. Nor is that individual particularly interested in where that company is located. In many cases, online retailers are anonymous in terms of location. As long as they deliver on their value proposition, their physical location is of little importance. Such retail operations appear to exist in a virtual space, which is not readily identified, has a potential global reach and does not benefit from any of the traditional merits of co-locating with similar and/or complementary retailers.

8.4 Location from a micro and macro perspective

Much of the literature on retail location focuses on micro-level decisions; that is, the implications for the individual retailer. This can be within the context of reviewing performance within existing locations or assessing potential sites for further development and retail expansion.

We also need to recognize the macro perspective. This relates to the role that government and regional authorities play in shaping retail development. Other stakeholders include retail developers and investment groups. They seek out opportunities to develop retail initiatives such as shopping centres, retail parks and shopping malls and work with legislators and planning authorities to develop such opportunities. Once planning permission has been obtained, they have to attract retailers to the specific mall or centre and market the development aggressively. We examine this macro aspect more fully later in the chapter.

8.5 Retail location: the bigger picture

Before we examine some of the specific trends and developments in the area of location, we need to place our analysis in context. The last decade or so has witnessed profound changes in the way in which consumers shop. Online channels have emerged and after some initial problems have grown dramatically. Initial fears on the part of shoppers about security issues and overall trust in the system have been largely overcome as technology has improved. Greater confidence in such e-tail channels, combined with benefits such as lower prices, quick delivery and overall convenience to shoppers are some of the drivers that have led to such a growth in popularity.

While the emergence of online retail channels has major implications for buyer behaviour, it also has a profound impact on the way in which retailers respond to such developments.

Within the context of retail location, some key questions emerge. How important are physical locations? Should we reduce our level of investment in 'bricks and mortar'? Do we need to change our value

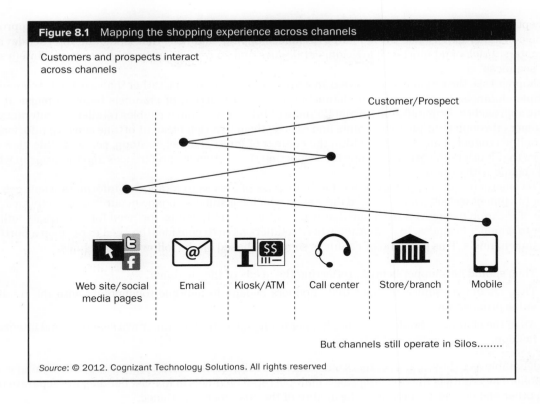

Figure 8.1 Mapping the shopping experience across channels

Customers and prospects interact across channels

Customer/Prospect

Web site/social media pages

Email

Kiosk/ATM

Call center

Store/branch

Mobile

But channels still operate in Silos........

proposition? Should we switch fully to an online retail channel? How do we get the balance right between physical and virtual retail channels? Do we understand how our target market is responding to these developments? What are the implications for our retail brand? What are the implications for customer loyalty and retention? These questions are not easy to answer. However, the way in which retailers address such issues is likely to have major significance for the very future of their business and their value proposition.

We need to link our discussion on retail location right back to the central principles of consumer buying behaviour. From recognizing that there is a problem, through the search and consultation process, the use of evaluative criteria in decision-making, the purchase of the product and post-purchase issues (warranties, complaints and so on), the shopper engages with various sources and stakeholders. In going through these iterations, the shopper encounters a number of 'touchpoints'. This can take the form of visiting retail outlets to engage in some comparative shopping activities such as brands on offer, price points and so on. It can also be reflected in visits to retail online channels or independent price comparison sites.

To further complicate matters, shoppers can weave in and out of different touchpoints at various stages in the purchasing process. Figure 8.1 depicts such a purchase situation. This highlights the increasing tendency of shoppers to seek out different platforms or channels in order to facilitate their purchases. Within the context of location decisions, we need to consider the implications that arise from this changing behaviour.

The immediate implication would appear to revolve around the observation that retailers, almost without exception, can no longer rely on one standard retail channel. As the use of virtual channels increases, the role of physical store locations needs to be redefined or in extreme cases eliminated. This has led to the emergence of what is referred to in the literature as 'omni-channel' strategies. We examine this concept in greater detail in the next section. However, for the purposes of our analysis of retail location decisions, we can define omni retail channels as 'an integrated and seamless blending of the customer shopping experience with physical and online channels'. This is similar to the concept of using multi-channel formats except that it is concentrated more on a seamless approach to the consumer experience through all available shopping channels; that is, mobile Internet devices, computers, bricks and mortar, television, catalogues and so on. The important words are 'integrated' and 'seamless'.

Shoppers see the retailer's store as a transparent and single system, rather than a set of disconnected multiple channels. In essence omni channels represent a blurring of channels between physical and online approaches. Brynjolfsson, Hu and Rahman (2013: 24) note that it enables retailers to 'interact with customers through multiple touchpoints and expose them to a rich blend of offline sensory information and online content'. Payne (2006), within the context of multi-channel strategy, supports this view and argues that it offers the greatest scope for respecting the customer's preferences and the ways in which they engage with organizations.

The emergence of technologies that facilitate ease of access to a range of information sources and order fulfilment websites has changed the way in which consumers engage in purchasing activities. The issue of location has moved from one that was unidimensional; that is, the need for a physical outlet in order to conduct business, to a situation where retailers have to consider the need to develop a portfolio of retail channels. This portfolio of channels should be based on the following guidelines.

- They should be shopper-centric, reflecting the needs of the customer.
- They should recognise the fact that shoppers engage in multiple touchpoints with the retailer's value proposition.
- All of the channels should allow the shopper to engage with the retailer in a seamless and integrated fashion.

It is debatable as to how many retailers out there have fully addressed the challenges of designing such a portfolio. The reality is that in many cases multiple retail channels may exist but they are separate from each other and deliver variations in the quality of the customer experience.

Activity

In view of the changing ways in which shoppers engage with retailers, is there a need for a physical presence for retailers any more?

8.6 Other key factors influencing the location decision

In the previous section we identified omni channels as a critical 'game-changer' in the context of location decisions. Before we assess the different retail location formats, we also consider other factors that have shaped the direction in which retailers have moved with regard to locating their operations.

Birkin, Clarke and Clarke (2002) pinpointed a number of trends that have affected the location decision. Since their publication further trends can also be identified.

1 **Greater consumer mobility**: this is reflected in the patterns of behaviour with regard to work, travel and leisure activities. The 1990s was the decade where people spent more time travelling to work and also was characterized by greater car ownership. The first decade of this century also witnessed greater numbers of people travelling internationally (bolstered by the emergence of low-cost flights). In Europe, the opening up of Eastern European countries has encouraged greater travel to and from these regions. The growth of out-of-town shopping centres, malls and retail parks mirrored these trends.

2 **Online developments**: as discussed in the previous section, online retail channels have grown dramatically as people, increasingly 'time-poor', use such options as a convenient alternative to the drudgery of having to make visits to retail outlets and stores.

3 **Mobile technology**: the last 10 years or so have witnessed major developments in the use of mobile technologies, largely built around the emergence of 3G and 4G. Twenty years ago, mobile phones were heavy, bulky and cumbersome objects and quite limited in their overall functionality. The last few years have seen developments in this area as technologies have converged. Today's phones and tablets are multi-function tools capable of great power and flexibility. In Chapters 10 and 13, we examine the ways in which these developments can be strategically harnessed by retailers. In the context of location, we can see how retailers need to respond to the ways in which shoppers use mobile technology to 'touch base' with retail offerings.

4 **Social media platforms**: while it is not our intention to fully discuss such developments, it is important to recognize the ways in which platforms such as Twitter, Facebook and blogs have shaped the way in which consumers engage with retailers

5 **Growth in expenditure on leisure-based activities**: we noted in Chapter 1 that shopping is a key leisure activity in many countries. Shopper expectations have changed in many purchase situations and retailers have to locate their operations in such a way that they address the 'entertainment' aspect of shopping more coherently and fully.

6 **Lifestyle changes**: this covers a broad range of issues. These include increasing divorce rates, the gradual erosion of the traditional nuclear family structures, single-parent families, reduction in birth rates, the ageing population in many countries, growth in single-unit housing and multi-culturalism; all have influenced the way in which people shop.

7 **Emergence of pop-up stores**: as the title suggests, this concept reflects the popularity of temporary outlets that emerge to sell merchandise without necessarily incurring the higher costs associated with the renting/leasing of retail sites (see Kim et al., 2010). This phenomenon stretches across all aspects of the retail sector. Oceanic, a Brazilian cosmetics firm, provides a good illustration of this concept. It provided its franchisees with a number of minivans that act as both delivery vehicles as well as mobile sales outlets. The vans can target prime locations used by the company's target market, such as universities, hospitals, beaches and so on. The merchandise can be customized to reflect the mobile location; for example, sunscreen blockers and skincare items for the beaches. The concept of pop-up outlets provides flexibility for retail owners (Howard, 2007). Locations are not confined to retail outlets: churches, community halls and so on can also be utilized to gain access to target customers.

8 **Multi-format locations**: increasingly, large retailers provide a portfolio of physical and virtual formats. This reflects the changing patterns of market structures and consumer behaviour. In China, for instance, over the last decade, household income has risen in real terms; consumers are less price-sensitive and are more aware of brands. Retailers have responded by creating a range of formats to deal with the diverse range of needs. Information technology (IT) and logistics infrastructure has facilitated the ability of retailers to address different formats. Carrefour, the second largest retailer in the world, operates over 10,000 stores globally. It operates four formats: hypermarkets, supermarkets, convenience stores and cash & carry outlets.

These factors emanate from the demand side of the equation. Birkin et al. (2002) cite some research carried out by Robertet (1997) that developed a framework for identifying different categories of shoppers across Europe. While the research itself is somewhat dated, it still has some resonance for retailers in terms of how and where they shop. The typologies are captured in Table 8.2.

Birkin et al. (2002) found that all six categories of shopper are present in most European countries. Each was more prevalent in certain countries. For instance, the discount shopper is more common in Germany while the neighbourhood shopper featured very strongly in Italy.

While we have to treat such dated research with some degree of caution: the data was collected before the emergence of the Internet as a serious channel option, it none the less highlights patterns of shopping behaviour that shape the retail location decision for retailers. It may also reflect the population distributions in the various countries.

Table 8.2 Six types of European consumer

1	**Smart shopper.** Young urban people, well educated, like novelty. No preferences over type of shop, will seek good value for money. (13% of European population).
2	**Demanding shopper.** Older people, well-off and selective. Seek good standards of service and are loyal to specialist shops. (13% of European population).
3	**Mall shopper.** Suburban, well-off people who prefer to obtain everything under the one roof, either in hypermarkets or shopping malls. (12% of European population).
4	**Old neighbourhood shopper.** Older people, less well-off. Conservative, value tradition and their local roots. Fixed shopping habits, favour the 'corner shop'. (21% of European population).
5	**Materialistic bargain hunter.** Mainly blue collar (working class) are avid shoppers and will use any type of outlet, but will never pay full price for anything. (11% of European population).
6	**Discount shopper.** Tend to be lower income, of all age groups and types of locality. Prefer shops which are local and offer lowest prices.

Source: Robertet (1997) cited in Birkin et al. (2002: 25)

Activity

Allowing for the dated nature of these findings, what implications are there for international retailers assessing further opportunities to expand their operations in Europe?

8.7 Case in point: Tesco in South Korea

As part of its internationalization strategy, Tesco entered the South Korean market. It recognized the fact that it had to adjust and adapt its operations if it was to capture a meaningful slice of the market. It changed its name to Homeplus and eventually became the second biggest supermarket in South Korea. However, it operated fewer stores than the number one company: E-Mart. Without major investment it was difficult to see how it could overcome this supermarket chain. The question it faced was how it could compete more strategically with E-Market with fewer stores.

It conducted detailed marketing research on the South Korean shopper. Among the findings it discovered that the South Koreans are the second most hard-working people in the world. This focus on the work ethic, however, had implications for their shopping behaviour. Most South Koreans view supermarket shopping as a task and a chore. Tesco assessed this finding and came to the view that they should build a strategy around the philosophy that 'the store should come to the people'.

Most people use the subway to get to work. Tesco put major displays of shelves depicting merchandise (and the price points) on the walls of the major subway stations. This was virtual in that they were not real shelves but pictorial representations. The strategy revolved around the notion that people would use their smart phones to shop. The barcodes of the merchandise were scanned by the shoppers. The items automatically landed in the online basket on the phone. An app handles the payments and once confirmed the items are delivered to the registered address of the individual. The net result is that people can shop with Tesco without having to physically visit the store. This value proposition addresses a key need of the South Korean shopper.

The test campaign generated over 10,000 shoppers using their smartphones. New online registrations increased by 76 per cent. Online sales increased by 130 per cent. Homeplus (Tesco) has become number one in the online market in South Korea. It is also a very close second in the offline market.

Source: Follow the link to the following site: https://www.youtube.com/watch?v=c2-UtjTMh6M

Question

1 Examine the implications that arise from this initiative for supermarket shopping in your country/region.

8.8 How to assess potential retail locations

Retailers use a number of different methods to assess the attractiveness or potential of possible new site locations for their stores and outlets. In this section we consider the way in which such techniques have evolved over the last 20–25 years. The level of capital investment required to develop suitable locations should lead to the conclusion that a retailer has to take great care in assessing new sites. The time frame involved, allied to the costs, heightens the level of risk, particularly for retailers who require large volumes of space; for example, IKEA, B&Q, Wal-Mart and so on. This is in contrast to earlier times (1960s and 1970s) when the time horizon, planning requirements, the level of legislation and relatively straightforward contracts meant that the process was less complicated and risky.

Over the last 20–25 years a number of techniques have emerged. They range from intuitive, 'gut-feel' approaches to methods that are based on the use of information technology. Reynolds and Wood (2010: 831) note that:

> *despite the growing focus in the literature on complex models driven by technology capable of increasing degrees of data processing, research in the journal has repeatedly provided evidence of marked differences in sophistication in practice across the retail sector.*

1 **Intuition**: the intuitive approach was frequently identified by researchers as a common approach to site selection (Davies, 1997; Davies and Rogers, 1984). This largely involved a visit by the chief executive officer (CEO) and/or senior management to the proposed site, followed by some discussion on its suitability. While this appears to be rather basic and superficial, it should not be underestimated. Any decision taken is based on the experience and detailed industry knowledge of the individuals concerned. We should not make the assumption that intuition is equivalent to 'guesswork'. The latter implies that there is little or no attempt to base a decision on assimilated knowledge or an understanding of what works in the marketplace. The intuitive approach is based on 'soft' or tacit knowledge that rests in the brains of the individuals tasked with site evaluation.

2 **Checklist**: in tandem with the intuitive approach, many retailers used (and continue to use) a 'checklist' approach to the assessment exercise. This has the benefit of injecting some form of 'hard' or objective elements to the appraisal of the site. Typically, such an exercise revolves around the catchment area surrounding the site. The level of shopper traffic passing through the proposed location is another key measure. This is referred to as 'footfall'. Depending on the size and nature of the retail operation, this could focus on factors within a few miles to 100 miles of the location. For instance, in the case of IKEA, it tends to locate its premises very near to junctions of main motorways or highways. In the case of the UK, it assesses the population structures within a 100-hundred mile radius of the site. This is based on the fact that IKEA's value proposition is destination-based. In other words, shoppers are willing to travel long distances in order to visit and make purchases at their outlets.

The checklist approach typically includes a detailed breakdown of the population in the catchment area on aspects such as age, gender, social class and so on. For instance, if the target market is based on young professional, mainly male shoppers, how many of them live within a 10-mile radius of the proposed location?

Retailers will also check on the level and quality of competition that exists in the area. This is particularly relevant in cases where the site is located within a shopping centre, retail park or shopping mall.

In the last 20–25 years, as management of the overall supply chain has taken on increasing significance, it is also important to consider the proximity of the supply base, transportation and warehousing issues (as they impact on the viability of the proposed location).

3 **Analogue**: this approach focuses on an attempt to forecast potential sales from the location. Retailers will base this forecast on the degree of sales generated from similar (like-for-like) stores in its portfolio. Similar stores would, in addition to sales revenue, reflect demographic profiles, geographic similarities (urban or semi-rural) and trading characteristics (for example, level of competition). The challenge for the decision-makers is to be able to identify similar stores. Given the diversity of factors that need to be assessed, this is no easy task.

4 **Competitive activities**: this approach is based on the belief that a retailer needs to be located where its main competitors are based. In many ways it is similar to a form of pricing strategy that companies adopt. In the latter case, there are price leaders and price followers. In the case of retail location, if the dominant retailer in a particular retail sector is to be found in a shopping mall, then competitors take this as a strong indication that 'this is where they need to be'. This approach can also extend to the concept of retail positioning. For instance, if a shopping mall has tenants such as luxury brands; for example, Louis Vuitton, Cartier and so on, this reflects the profile of the centre and the type of shopper that is likely to frequent that location.

Retailers also began to make use of statistical techniques in order to apply a more sophisticated and scientific approach to the site location analysis (Clarke, 1998).

5 **Multiple regression**: in this case the analysis specifies a dependent variable; for example, store turnover, and this is correlated against a set of independent variables. Clarke (1998) points out that such an approach brings a degree of objectivity to the analysis but tends to assess the location in isolation and ignores competitive issues. It also assumes that the explanatory variables are independent of each other. This may not reflect reality: some independent variables may be strongly correlated with each other.

6 **GIs and spatial modelling**: geographical information systems became popular in the 1990s as a mechanism for shedding greater insight into the location decision. Such information could be a 'geocode; that is, placed on the computer with a spatial referencing point and visually displayed through maps and graphs' (Clarke, 1998: 291). Retailers could specify population types and demographic profiles within particular areas that could also be mapped. An estimate of potential could be made when used in tandem with surveys identifying the distances people from these profiles were prepared to travel to shop.

7 **Geodemographic systems**: to add further sophistication to the exercise, geodemographic software systems allowed retailers to carry out more detailed analysis of the available information. This presented an opportunity to profile catchment areas into specific customer segments, clearly something that would have great relevance for marketers in understanding the 'make-up' of a particular locality or region. Clarke (1998) cites the popularity of the 'Insite System' developed by CACI in the UK. This was designed for the retail sector and aimed at retailers wishing to link up catchment area profiles with those obtained from their customer bases. Such developments were not confined to the UK. Webber (1993) and Birkin (1995) discuss the launch of a pan-European version of the popular MOSAIC system.

8 **Lifestyles**: marketers require as much detail as possible about people's lifestyles. This is based on the belief that the more retailers understand people's behaviour and how it is linked to their general lifestyles, the more effective marketing decision-making will be. This is particularly the case with shopping location decisions. Such information is generally collected through surveys of households and through the census of population, although the latter only provides the data at an aggregated level.

Criticisms of GIs and geodemographic data approaches (Clarke, 1998) revolve around how a retailer defines the catchment area and how to factor in the competition in such an exercise. For instance, if the drive time from the proposed location is five minutes, such models give equal weighting whether a residence is one hundred metres or four and a half miles away. The presence of competitive stores can skew this approach further.

Since the bulk of the research in this area took place in the 'pre-Internet' era, we also have to consider the impact of online shopping on such models. For many people, the issue of distance from a particular retailer, is redundant given their ability to purchase from home, the office or the local coffee shop.

9 **Mathematical models**: the emergence of IT systems and relevant software and hardware packages in the 1990s and the first 10 years of this century also enabled retailers to make use of mathematical modelling tools to 'crunch the numbers' in their quest to optimize retail location decisions. Such approaches reflect a spatial interaction approach. While data-intensive, the challenge rests with the ability to fit such models to specific retail settings. A car dealership location analysis is not

Table 8.3 Location techniques by usage (% respondents), 1998–2010

Technique	2010 (%)	1998 (%)
Experience	98%	97%
Checklist	91%	56%
Analogue	83%	39%
Cluster	68%	41%
Gravity modelling	65%	39%
Multiple regression	63%	40%
Ratio	52%	38%
Discriminant analysis	31%	12%
Expert systems	29%	13%
Neural networks	0%	18%

Source: Reynolds and Wood (2010)

similar in terms of customer and shopping behaviour to a retailer like Boots and its store location strategy (see Kuo et al., 2002).

More recent research by Reynolds and Wood (2010) sheds more insight into the approaches used by retailers. Table 8.3 captures the findings from their study.

The results are interesting insofar as the earliest techniques: experience, checklist and analogue are still the most frequently adopted tools with significant increases in the latter two. However, there is wider usage of the more quantitative techniques as well. Retailers tend to use a combination of these techniques to help them make their location decision. The findings are based on an online survey that generated a response from 43 retailers. The earlier study by Hernandez et al. (1998) was based on a bigger survey and some caveats have to be taken on board when interpreting the results of these studies.

Reynolds and Wood (2010) note that processes are less developed in the context of other key parts of the location decision. This applies to issues such as store refurbishment and store extensions. These areas are likely to play a more strategic role in store portfolio management in the next decade (certainly in mature retail sectors where there is little scope for identifying and developing prime retail locations). In addition, the anticipated further growth in online retail channels may also result in a switch away from extensive physical expansion of retail operations.

It can be counter-argued that because of the lack of availability of retail space either on the high street, the central business district or out of town, it is even more critical that retailers make use of sophisticated and robust location techniques.

Much of the extant research and publications on store location techniques is based on the experiences of large, international retailers. This is in contrast to the reality of what exists in the marketplace. While there is no doubt that in many European countries, where there is a mature and sophisticated retail infrastructure, small, independent retailers are in decline, in other European countries, most notably southern and eastern Europe, the small retailer still plays a significant role in society and, like all small firms, such retailers suffer from lack of resources and expertise. In the case of store location analysis, this usually means a lack of access to sophisticated tools that the larger retailers make use of. It is arguable if such tools are relevant for small retailers, coping as they have to with decisions on a more micro and localized level and where general information from sources such as a census and government data may not provide the level of detail required at that level (Alexander et al., 2008).

Planning policy in the retail sector

Before we consider the different categories of retail development, we need to assess the role that planning policy plays in shaping retailing. In this respect, governments and regional policymakers are active stakeholders and participants in the retail development process. Over the last 20 years different governments have taken disparate approaches to the controversial policy of planning policy. Major retail developments involve major investment, have the potential to generate employment in key regional areas of a country, require a supporting infrastructure (such as public transport, access and parking) and can impact on the environment. As a consequence, when policymakers make their decisions they have to pay attention to the positive and negative consequences that emerge from such developments.

We need to consider the stakeholders in this process as well. In addition to the retailers and shoppers, there are retail development companies and existing retailers who will be affected by such decisions. Planners have to factor the following issues into their decision-making process:

- to provide people with a diverse and balanced choice of shopping alternatives
- to assess the impact on the environment of large shopping developments
- to regenerate areas of a city or region that has fallen into decline
- to prevent situations where there is a lack of competition or where there is a danger of a dominant market position being achieved by one or a small number of retailers
- to legislate for retail developments that provide an attractive and positive shopping environment for people and which enhance the quality of living in a particular city or region
- to legislate on issues such as opening hours that reflect the needs of the population
- to preserve the historical nature and heritage of key parts of the region and/or city; for example, town squares, listed buildings and so on
- to consider retail development proposals within the context of the overall infrastructure of the site and area. In other words, what will the impact of such a development be on issues such as public transport? Roads? Car parking? Traffic flows?

If we take a global perspective on such issues, we quickly see that different attitudes and approaches exist across countries and continents. In the UK, the last 20 years have witnessed a tightening up of legislation with regard to retail developments and a more restrictive approach on the part of successive governments. The 1970s and 1980s generated a proliferation of major retail developments, largely out-of-town and on 'greenfield' sites. This was abetted by the relative looseness of the legislation and the strategic imperative of encouraging the growth of business enterprise. The UK government introduced a Planning Policy Guidance Note 6 (PPG6) in 1993 in order to restore some equilibrium to the exponential growth of shopping developments. It specifically encouraged local authorities to turn down applications for out-of-town centres and instead encourage the regeneration of city and town centres.

Many cities in the UK had (and continue to have) major problems as traditional shops and small independent retailers closed down in the face of the more popular shopping centres located outside of the main shopping streets and central business districts. This was compounded by the growth in antisocial behaviour; for example, drugs, petty crime and assault, which made such areas dangerous and unsafe for shoppers.

Further legislation in 1995 and 1996 required local planners to identify appropriate areas for development. In addition, retail developers in their submission had to address the impact of such a development on traffic conditions, the effect on existing trade on the high street and that such developments should ideally be located in town centres or central business districts.

Initially, this approach appeared to work. The number of out-of-town shopping developments decreased. Whether this was due to the tightening of legislation or the lack of availability of suitable locations (due to the exponential growth over the last decade) is debatable. A number of city centre high streets and town centres are still in a state of decrepitude and decline. The signs of 'shops to let' are very prevalent. Antisocial behaviour still exists, making such centres unattractive for shoppers, particularly at night or at weekends. The prolonged and profound recession has also not helped. The problem has been heightened by a lack of parking availability in town and city centres linked to the administration of parking fines. Further developments such as the imposition of business rates has raised the costs for many small retailers and made it unviable for them in many cases to continue trading. The growth in online shopping has also provided a shopping alternative. We examine the high street in more detail later in this chapter.

The gradual tightening up of legislation was also mirrored in many western European countries throughout the 1990s and the first 10 years of this century. Davies (2004) provides some detailed discussion on such approaches. The legislation generally focuses on the size of proposed developments. In the case of France (1996 Loi Raffarin) it favoured smaller developments. This emerged from a tightening of the earlier legislation (1973 Loi Royer). Trading hours also feature prominently in legislative measures across different countries: this was particularly the case with Germany. In Scandinavia, municipal authorities took over control of the process from central government and clamped down strongly on out-of-town developments.

In Japan, the Large Stores Law restricted the size of developments, largely as a result of pressure by the independent retailers who feared for their long-term future. While this was introduced in the mid-1970s, it has since been relaxed and was eventually abolished in 2000. Japan has traditionally employed very long and complex supply chains with layers of wholesalers and retailers. The end result has been an unwieldy and expensive distribution system that feeds through to the shopper in terms of cost. Legislation in the first decade of this century reflected a more westernized approach to the use of land. This was prompted in part by the recession that hit the Japanese economy during this period.

The USA is typical of those countries that adopt a lenient approach to planning legislation in the context of the retail sector. Such developments are largely treated within the same category as other commercial developments. Where local authorities employ zoning plans that are not planned for retail development, retail investors challenge such legislation in the courts. In recent years, there has been criticism from local communities in many states who object to the proliferation of out-of-town malls and centres.

In eastern Europe, countries such as Poland, the Czech Republic and Hungary have rather lax legislation that is open to interpretation. This has encouraged many western European retailers such as Tesco, Aldi and Lidl to increase their footprint in these markets.

In the Gulf region, states such as the United Arab Emirates have placed retailing to the forefront of their economic development. This is particularly so in the case of Dubai, which has established itself as a hub for retailing with many state-of-the-art shopping malls containing many of the top global retailers. In the quest for quick development, planning legislation, relatively speaking, is very loose.

In China, one of the fastest growing economies in global terms in the last 15 years, retail developments have emerged quickly and explosively. Rising incomes, allied to a large professional class, have created an insatiable demand for luxury brands. East coast cities such as Shanghai have seen phenomenal growth in shopping malls and complexes. Legislation has also made it easier for joint ventures between local operators and international retailers to exploit opportunities in this vast market. As other cities develop, it is anticipated that further retail developments will mirror the scale of development experienced in the large east coast cities.

In summary, we can see that there is variation in the way in which policymakers deal with retail developments in a global context. Countries and regions that have well-developed and sophisticated retail structures have tended to introduce more restrictive legislation with regard to proposed new retail developments. By contrast those geographic areas that have emerging retail structures tend to adopt a looser approach to legislation.

8.10 High street and central business district locations

Traditionally, the central locations within towns and cities were seen as being attractive areas for retailers because they were all areas where people worked and socialized. In the early to mid-decades of the twentieth century people lived in or around the central districts. Thus, it made sense for retailers to locate close to the population and also to base their operations near to other retailers to benefit from the overall 'agglomeration' effect. The latter part of the twentieth century witnessed some major changes. As populations developed, people moved outside the central parts of the city and the growth of suburbs emerged. This led to 'city sprawl' and the phenomenon of 'suburbia'. The latter term captures the notion that people travelled into the city to work but no longer saw the central districts and high street as the main focus of their lives. Retailers, in response to these developments, 'followed their customers' and developed their operations in out-of-town locations. Retail initiatives, helped by the emergence of retail investors, became larger in terms of size, range of retailers located there and ancillary services and facilities.

The emergence of powerful retailers across different sectors and the inevitable concentration of market share held by them further exacerbated the decline of the high street and central business districts as they moved to large out-of-town centres. In many cities, especially in western Europe, the central business districts lost much of their allure, particularly after office hours. The increase in crime and antisocial-related activities also led to a decline in the number of people spending time in such areas. As mentioned earlier in this chapter, many local authorities introduced very restrictive parking systems (with hefty fines applied if these were infringed by motorists), which also discouraged shoppers from spending any significant amount of time in these locations.

8.11 Regeneration of city centres

The preceding section paints a rather negative and sad picture of the high street. However, there have been a number of positive responses to these problems and issues. There is a growing realization among legislators and local authorities that central business districts and high streets need to be revitalized and made more attractive for shoppers. In a broader sense, there is an acknowledgement that poorly maintained high streets can have an adverse impact on visitors to the city or town. Attractive and shopper-friendly city centres can have a very positive and memorable impact on tourists' first impressions and, more importantly, encourage them to revisit the city.

It is dangerous to assume that retail-led regeneration on its own will lead to more vibrancy and activity in a particular city. Undoubtedly, retail developments can act as a catalyst for change: attractive retail brands located in modern and user-friendly shopping malls or centres can engender a change in perception about a particular city centre environment. However, for the overall image and perception of a city to change, such developments should take place within a wider and more strategic framework of developments.

Colomb (2006) highlights the importance of four key themes that affect the regeneration of an urban centre or location within the context of the influence of culture. These are summarized as follows.

1 **Economic approach**: cultural and arts events and festivals can play a significant role in providing cities with an identity and empowering local communities within the area.

2 **Social approach**: can help to create a civic bond and cohesion in the process of urban regeneration and make more creative use of public space. The role of culture can also help address issues such as social inequality and social exclusion.

3 **Physical approach**: the role of heritage, in city centres as well as in neighbourhoods.

4 **Integrated approach**: the role that culture and creative activities can play in acting as a driving force for urban regeneration.

This report highlights the importance of taking a holistic view of urban regeneration. The combination of culture, creativity, heritage and reappropriation of physical space all contribute to the shaping of perceptions of a particular city. The presence of a strong retail sector also plays a significant role in this process. Modern, attractive retail malls and centres provide a strong reason for visitors to come into the city. To this may be added other activities such as sporting events and the hosting of major sports competitions.

Research by Cadell, Falk and King (2008) investigated the issue of regeneration within the context of European cities. They found that among the key success factors for effective generation, the following were critical: devolvement of power to the local city authorities, creating balanced and attractive residential neighbourhoods, valuing the role of culture in the regeneration process, working across boundaries, sectors and professions, and generating a substantial part of the necessary revenue for generation from local taxes.

Cadell et al. (2008) cite the example of Roubaix, an industrial town located in France near the Belgian border. It has a population of over 100,000 and is about 10 miles from Lille. It identified retailing as playing a central role in rejuvenating the town centre. One of its historical industries was that of textiles and it focused on building up a strong textile cluster, reflected across areas such as research, education, design, production and marketing. In tandem with these developments, it also wished to capitalize on its history of selling textile and other products through mail order and local factory outlets. It developed two major factory outlets in Roubaix: L'Usine, a large disused factory that houses over 70 sales units, and McArthur Glen that takes the format of a large street containing over 50 top-brand stores. The municipal authorities also invested in improving the public transport system and car parking. As a result the two outlets bring in over two million visitors per year and the overall town centre shops attract over five million visits annually.

In summary, we should not look at retailing as the sole reason for urban regeneration; rather, it plays a complementary role (along with the activities listed above) in shaping the long-term image and perception of a particular city or district.

Many cities in Europe have witnessed the gentrification of their central areas. People are increasingly moving back into these areas to live and work. Authorities have instigated a number of policies to improve the quality of life in city and town locations. Pedestrianized zones, better public transport and better security measures have addressed some of the earlier problems. Initiatives such as 'Christmas markets' and festival weekends also draw people to central areas.

In the UK, successive governments in the last 10 years have recognized that there are major unresolved problems with regard to the regeneration of the high street and central areas in its towns and cities. In 2011 the government asked Mary Portas, a well-known retail consultant, to conduct an independent review of the British high street. In her report, she identified a number of recommendations. Table 8.4 summarizes some of her main initiatives.

Table 8.4 Mary Portas' review: main recommendations

- Put in place a 'Town Team': a visionary, strategic and strong operational team for high streets.
- Empower successful Business Improvement Districts to take on more responsibilities and powers and become 'Super-BIDs'.
- Concessions should be given in terms of lower business rates to new local businesses.
- Town teams should focus on making high streets accessible, attractive and safe.
- Local authorities should make greater use of compulsory purchase orders to expedite the development of appropriate retail initiatives.
- Run high profile campaigns to get local people involved in Neighbourhood plans.
- Developers should make a financial contribution to ensure that the local community has a proactive role to play in the planning system.
- Large retailers should act as mentors to small independent retailers.
- Make it easier to change the uses of key properties on the high street.
- Support imaginative community use of empty properties through Community Right to Buy.
- Run a number of 'High Street Pilots' to test proof of concept.
- Adopt free controlled parking schemes for town centres

Source: Anonymous (2011)

Discussion question

Assess the extent to which you would agree with the view that regenerating the high street and central business district areas is too little too late, given the major growth in online shopping.

What would you do to address the apparent problems caused by the imposition of business rates?

The government appeared to endorse the key themes emanating from the report, particularly with regard to the importance of the high street as a generator of employment and playing a key role in the heart of local communities. It put up some funding for a small number of pilot developments (as suggested in the report). However, a year on from this initiative, the uptake was poor.

Portas argued that the government had not taken the need to address the high business rates seriously, seeing this as a key obstacle to preventing an upturn in the fortunes of the high street and leasing agreements that did not reflect the reality of the level of trading, particularly in the depths of a prolonged recession.

The business rate is a tax that is based on the rateable value of the property. This equates approximately to the annual rent. Its main purpose is to provide money for local authorities and councils to spend on local service provision. The business rates generated an overall sum of £22 billion in 2012 in the UK. The main problem rests with the relative inflexibility of the process. Every five years, the Valuation Office Agency calculates the value of all commercial property. It determines the proportion of that value which needs to be paid in the form of taxes. This is referred to as the 'multiplier'. This increases in line with inflation as measured by the retail price index. If the value of the properties falls, it can still be adjusted upwards. This ensures that the proportion of revenue generated from this source remains the same. In the UK, the next revaluation date has been put back to 2017 from 2015. This effectively means that businesses are paying rents based on property valuations that were calculated before the prolonged recession which started around 2008.

Kingfisher, one of the largest retail operators in the UK, recently decided to reduce the space of its 18 stores by 5 per cent. This was instigated in order to achieve savings of £16 million in rental costs and £7 million in rates (Shah, 2013).

The twin issues of business rates and upwards-only rental agreements have particular relevance for the high street: a location that has encountered serious problems in terms of attempts to renew and revitalize its activities has to grapple also with these additional and ever-increasing costs.

Again, we need to consider the growth in Internet retailing operations. By contrast to bricks-and-mortar retailers, they do not pay any equivalent business rates in most countries and it can be argued that they are gaining an unjustified competitive advantage over traditional retail operations. It is possible that this loophole may be closed in the coming years.

8.12 Case in point: Regeneration of Belfast

Belfast as a city has undergone significant ups and downs over the last few decades. It was subject to major political strife and terrorism throughout the 1970s, 1980s and part of the 1990s. Since then, due to political reconciliation and a peace agreement, it went through a period of relative political stability and between 1998 and 2008 it experienced economic success and growth.

The global recession of 2008 not surprisingly affected Belfast and had a major impact on it and the overall economy of Northern Ireland. Unemployment doubled in the period between 2008 and 2012.

In 2004 a Regeneration Policy Statement was developed to identify the vision for rejuvenating the city. The main objectives included the following:

- enhance the role of the city of Belfast
- support and strengthen the city centre as the premier regional shopping destination

- promote the physical renewal of Belfast city centre
- create a high-quality, sustainable and vibrant urban environment to attract inward investors and potential future residents
- build on the city's rich historical character
- promote access and linkages
- promote urban economic development at key locations and on suitable sites throughout the Belfast centre
- encourage the growth of creative industries
- establish a twenty-first century economy, well placed to compete with other European cities
- promote Belfast as a premier European city.

An Urban Regeneration Potential Study carried out in 2006 identified the following key opportunity areas:

- Belfast was underperforming as a regional retail driver
- the city image was not attracting high quality retail
- there was significant capacity for growth in the supply of high-quality office stock
- the city centre needed further enhancement as a tourism/leisure destination
- further city centre living should be encouraged
- there was capacity for growth in the cultural and creative industries
- the quality of public realm (publically owned streets, pathways, parks and so on) was poor.

Since 2006 a number of initiatives were launched and developed. In the context of tourism/leisure and conference venue, the Titanic Visitor Attraction was developed. The Metropolitan Arts Centre addressed the issue of performance space and leisure. A 'Belfast: Streets Ahead' campaign focused on improving the public realm. The Belfast Metropolitan College was located in the Titanic Quarter and various developments (hotel, residential, restaurants and offices) took place in various parts of the city.

In the context of retail, Victoria Square focused on a number of retail, residential and leisure uses.

Within Northern Ireland, Belfast is the largest retail centre, with a primary catchment population of 1.8 million and 7.1 million visitors each year. It has benefited from a lack of similar competing urban centres within close proximity: Dublin is over 100 miles away and Londonderry 70 miles. Nearby shopping centres such as the Sprucefield shopping centre, however, create some competition, being located about ten miles away in the neighbouring city of Lisburn.

The Victoria Square development is anchored by the House of Fraser store and its portfolio of over 50 stores includes: Topshop, Cruise, Reiss, H&M, AllSaints and Calvin Klein. It also features a range of eateries and a cinema complex: Odeon Belfast. (Visit: http://www.victoriasquare.com/stores/ and scan the QR code to access the TripAdvisor page.)

This centre is covered and is spread over four levels. The streets are pedestrianized and shoppers can overlook the nearby River Lagan. It has won numerous awards since its inception. For instance, it was awarded a commendation by the British Confederation of Shopping Centres in 2008 (BCSC). They made the following comment: 'This is an engaging development in an area of Belfast desperate for change. The scheme has created a unique retail and food and leisure offer, with innovative design spread over two levels. Anchored by a 18,500 sq. m House of Fraser Store, the scheme has attracted a formidable retail line up including top fashion brands housed in well-designed units. With its unique central viewing platform linking all levels, the scheme offers accessible and inviting integration.'

The success of the Victoria Square development is not without its challenges. Online and out-of-town shopping present real threats. The recession has affected general occupancy rates in the city centre of Belfast, allied to reduced rental values. Compared to other cities in the UK, there is a relative lack of department store choice and a lack of modern stock that is suitable for existing and emerging retailer requirements.

▶

◀ The relative weakness of the retail offer (notwithstanding the Victoria Square development) has potential implications for promoting the attractiveness of the city as a place to live, work and study in.

Source: Belfast Urban Regeneration Potential Study: 2012 Update (2013) Department for Social Development. June.

Questions

1 By making use of the Internet search engines in addition to the material in the case, assess the role that the Victoria Square development has played in the regeneration of Belfast city centre.

2 Assess the extent to which you would agree with the view that other issues besides retailing play a more significant role in regeneration.

8.13 Trends and developments in managing shopping malls and centres

The shopping centre or mall phenomenon emerged initially in the North American market and saw consistent and rapid growth in Europe in the last 40 years or so. The selling space of such developments typically ranges from around 50,000 square metres up to the largest at around 160,000 square metres.

Within the context of the UK, Banham (2006) predicted that 2008 would see the highest level of shopping centre floor-space opening in any one year. He pointed to major developments such as the new Bullring centre in Birmingham. However, we should be cautious about the optimistic forecasts as the analysis was carried out before the arrival of the prolonged global recession in 2008.

As central business district and high street locations have experienced a decline in the last couple of decades, shopping malls and centres have encountered growth worldwide. This is indeed a global phenomenon. As economies grow and people's disposable incomes increase, so too is demand for more sophisticated, higher-quality shopping experiences. This is very evident in countries such as China and India where a wealthy and substantive professional class has emerged with relatively high levels of income. Other cities such as Hong Kong, Singapore and Dubai are arguably retail hubs and contain numerous shopping malls, plazas and centres.

Research by Myers, Gore and Liu (2008) identifies some of the key drivers behind shopping centre developments across Europe. They reinforce the message about the extent of restrictive legislation that we discussed earlier. However, they identity a plethora of developments in countries such as Poland and Russia reflecting the rather lax legislation there.

Within the context of shopper lifestyles, they recognize the general trend towards entertainment and leisure that surround the shopping experience in many purchase situations. They note that this is a relatively common phenomenon across European markets.

The ageing population across Europe also reflects the fact that such a demographic has greater spending power than ever before and requires a shopping environment that is easy to access, safe and provides a 'one-stop' shopping experience. They also seek out friends and socialize when shopping.

Myers et al. (2008) note that the increasingly restrictive legislation forces retailers and developers to revisit potential opportunities in the city centres and urban centres. This is reflected in historical sites with heritage buildings being revamped into viable and attractive shopping areas. The importance of branding and marketing such centres is becoming more critical as a reference point for differentiation.

More recent research (Savills Research, 2012) identifies five core markets for retail shopping development in Europe. They are Germany, the UK, France, Norway and Sweden. Market size, economic stability and the level of consumer expenditure are the key differentiating factors that make these countries the most popular from the perspective of retail investment in shopping centres and malls. Savills Research identified the following countries as areas that over the coming years will generate the fastest consumer spend and expected level of sales: Poland, Hungary, Romania, the Czech Republic and Austria. The report was based on a study of 16 countries. Crucially, however, the study did not include Russia.

Another study (Cushman and Wakefield, 2013) pinpoints Russia as the country poised to become Europe's second largest shopping centre development market, taking over from the UK by the end of 2013. The shift to eastern European countries is also supported by their estimate that 70 per cent of new shopping space will occur in this region. To further emphasize the growing importance of Russia, Cushman and Wakefield calculate that 2.4 million square metres of new space will be completed there, representing around 22 per cent of the entire European pipeline. France (16.95 square metres) is the largest shopping centre market in Europe followed by the UK (16.47 square metres). Turkey is identified as being second in terms of the volume of new shopping centre space with more than 1.5 million square metres of space due to be completed by 2014. More than 50 per cent of this space is located in the city of Istanbul. Of the 215 new shopping centres to be completed by 2013, over two-thirds (68.4 per cent) of these centres are located in central and eastern Europe.

A further study (DTZ, 2012) identified the future hotspots as being those cities that offer strong economic growth and which are currently undersupplied in shopping centre stock. These include Vilnius, London, Hamburg, Birmingham and Manchester.

The issue of branding is reflected in the importance of acquiring key retailers as key tenants in shopping centres. This arguably challenges the view that shopping centre developments can retain their local and historical characteristics, possibly leading to the 'sameness' about many such retail developments across Europe. We revisit the issue of anchor tenants later in the chapter.

8.14 Key success factors in shopping centre developments

■ *Tenant mix*: this refers to the 'relationship between the percentage of shop areas occupied by different store types in a shopping mall' (Yiu and Xu, 2012: 524–541). Authors such as Teller and Reutterer (2008) and Ibrahim, Sim and Chen (2003) argue that a balanced tenant mix can pull in more shoppers and generate greater sales for retailers in the shopping mall as a consequence. Key elements such as entertainment/leisure facilities and the 'one-stop-shop' phenomenon are highlighted as being important elements when developing the tenant mix. Not surprisingly, the bigger the centre in terms of physical space, the greater the ability to create an attractive shopping environment. Bigger developments can cater for leisure-based facilities such as a Cineplex and skating rinks. They can also create a number of retailers under each tenant category; for example, foodstuffs, electronics and speciality stores. Much of the analysis underpinning the development of a tenant mix is largely based on intuition, although Yiu and Xu (2012) developed a model to help with the decision-making process.

■ *Anchor store*: such a store is one that:

> **"**increases, through its name's reputation, the traffic of shoppers at or near its location. Customers, attracted by the anchor's name, are likely to visit the location ('the mall'), and thus nearby stores' sales and profits are increased by the presence of the anchor. Planned shopping malls have one or more department stores and multiple specialised retail stores in each commodity category.**"** (Konishi and Sandfort, 2003: 413)

Generally, such anchor tenants are characterised by strong brand equity, an international/global presence (or at a minimum a very strong national operator) and may also trade successfully at a standalone location. It is analogous to a well-known, marquee footballer on a team or famous film star appearing in a film. As a consequence of the presence of an anchor store, it is more likely to attract shoppers to the store. From a marketing perspective, anchor stores play a critical role in helping to shape the image and reputation of the shopping mall or centre in the minds of the shopper. Such stores clearly position the centre and provide a mechanism for differentiation from other malls in the region. The absence of appropriate anchor stores can damage the image and reputation of the shopping mall and work in a negative way in terms of failing to address the possible expectations of shoppers.

■ *Retail demand externalities*: this refers to the overall impact that the presence of high-end retailers, or an appealing tenant mix, has on overall sales, footfall and the shopping experience. The way in which retail developers locate individual stores in the centre plays a key role in shaping the shopping experience (Howard, 2007). Research by Yeates, Charles and Jones (2001) shows that the closure of an anchor department store can reduce sales in adjacent stores by around 12 per cent. However, the arrival of a new anchor store can conversely boost sales by a similar amount (Damian et al., 2011). Their findings suggest that non-anchor stores benefit significantly from the presence of anchor stores and indeed make a greater contribution to the mall's overall income than the anchor stores. However, anchor stores, because of their cachet and brand equity, pay relatively lower rents. By contrast, smaller tenants pay relatively higher rents. Interestingly, their research found that anchor stores have less influence on sales per visitor with entertainment-related facilities playing a greater role. We have to acknowledge the limitation of their research as it did not have access to the purchasing power of shoppers in the immediate environment of the shopping centres under review. However, it sheds some insight into the impact of anchor stores on the overall performance of the shopping centre.

■ *Embracing digital technology*: as discussed earlier in the chapter, the digital era has arrived and modern shopping centres need to engage with such technology in order to enhance the customer experience and draw them back. A good example of this development is the Trinity Leeds shopping centre that opened in the early part of 2013. This centre is located in the city of Leeds in the UK. With an investment of over £350 million, it represented the only major such opening in the UK in 2013.

■ *Keeping the centre fresh and vibrant*: as well as attracting new retailers to the centre and extending the retail space, leading shopping centres are looking at the pop-up or temporary shop as a mechanism to engender excitement and unpredictability for shoppers. The operative word here is 'temporary'. It provides an opportunity for smaller operators to offer branded merchandise for a short period to customers in designated space within the centre. This type of initiative addresses the potential dangers of a shopping centre becoming at best 'stale' and at worst entering a decline phase in its life cycle.

■ *Primary locations*: the prolonged recession in Europe has had relatively little impact on the demand for shopping centres and malls that are located in prime positions. However it has had a negative effect on secondary locations (for example, suburban areas that are away from the prime sites).

■ *The life-cycle effect*: as mentioned earlier, every product offering has a life cycle. The growth of the shopping centre phenomenon may peak at some point as shoppers seek alternative channels. Krosnar (2013) makes the observation that in eastern European cities such as Prague and Warsaw, shoppers are becoming bored with shopping centres. She cites the example of key high streets such as Parizka and Na Prikope in Prague and Marszalkowska in Warsaw. Such locations are becoming more popular and this is evidenced by the opening of shopping centres linked to luxury brand stores such as Gucci, Prada, Cartier and Louis Vuitton.

■ *Role of flagship stores*: global retailers such as Nike (Niketown) sometimes use prime shopping centres and malls and indeed high street locations to showcase their brand. Such outlets are large in terms of size and tend to feature new products and concepts, make use of technology to demonstrate the merchandise and use it as a mechanism for promoting and building the brand. Shoppers are attracted to such flagship stores because they know that new trends and developments can be identified and purchased at this location. Shopping centres benefit from the added footfall.

Vignette: Land Securities

Land Securities (retail developer) claims Trinity Leeds is the most digitally enabled shopping centre in the UK and retail operations director for the North Alison Niven says retailers and shoppers alike are making use of the technology available. For instance, she says customer service staff who walk around the scheme with mini iPads to help guide the shopper through the centre are proving popular: 'We've tried to make that interaction feel natural, and have colleagues standing beside store entrances — it's working very well.'

In the customer service lounge, visitors can browse iPads, and there are TVs, couches and newspapers. 'We want it to be a place to dwell, and not feel like a rushed experience,' says Niven.

The Trinity Leeds app has been downloaded more than 9000 times and its Facebook page has more than 85,000 'likes'. Add that to the Twitter performance and it seems shoppers are responding well to the centre's digital offer. 'Some of the digital initiatives have gone off the scale,' says Niven.

Trinity Leeds offers free WiFi, which is another example of the centre trying to engage with today's digitally savvy shopper. On paper at least, Trinity Leeds is an effective example of the best of what is available in shopping centre technology.

Customers can use Google Product Search to find items on sale in the centre, while retailers can use the Trinity Leeds website to personalise communication to shoppers through its embedded CRM system. Stores can also use digital screens around the centre to target promotions at Trinity Leeds' shoppers.

The screens are a new channel for retailers, and Niven says stores are 'starting to use them more and more'. For instance, Trinity Leeds hosted a 'student takeover' that attracted 10,000 students forming queues around the block to get in, and retailers used the screens to communicate their promotions, with forty-six brands providing exclusive offers.

Source: Land Securities (2013) *AI* Magazine. July: p. 16. See also Richardson, A. (2015) Destination loyalty, Land Securities. See the 'love trinity loyalty programme' online at: http://www.landsecurities.com/media/corporate-blog?id=101 (accessed 23 February)

The practitioner view
Shopping centre trends and developments

Antony Ranger, Shopping Centre Development Manager

Antony has worked for many years as a shopping centre consultant and manager with many of the world's largest shopping centre and shopping mall developers. He has experience of working in many diverse regions such as the Gulf and eastern and western Europe.

We asked him a number of questions about how he sees the current role of shopping centres and malls within the context of the shopper's needs and requirements. We also discussed some of the changing trends and developments taking place across the different regions of the world.

What is the current status of shopping centres and shopping malls?

Antony observes that 'a simple "box of shops" is no longer a viable, commercial development, given how expensive they are to set up'. Clearly, it varies across the world: 'Much will depend on the relative maturity of the retail sector and the infrastructure.' The less-developed regions can allow retail developers to use less sophisticated retail formats and structures.

'The move to Internet shopping and enhanced e-commerce platforms, allied to the ability of retailers such as Waitrose and Amazon to address the challenge of delivery of items, has meant that retail shopping centres and malls need to offer more to shoppers.

'In the Gulf region for instance, the concept of entertainment plays an important role. This is partly due to cultural factors: shopping plays a far greater role in people's lives and by nature the inhabitants of the region are sociable people, so food and beverage feature prominently in shopping malls in this region.

'However there is still a place for dynamic shops; anything that people desire and derive pleasure from such as products and items that encourage touching and feeling. The key concept here is the shopping experience.'

What other observations can you share about shopping centres across the world?

Antony observes that 'there is a great deal of diversity across several markets:

'For instance, France is not renowned (comparatively speaking) for its shopping centres. Many of the towns and villages are well laid out and provide a nice range of shops. You don't need shopping centres.

▶

◀

'By contrast, Canada is great for shopping centres. The weather actually plays a strong role in this: the winters are so severe that an array of such centres and malls has emerged to make it easy for people to shop.

'The UK is one of the more sophisticated and developed markets for shopping centres. In fact there is little development of out-of-town centres now going ahead: this is mainly due to a change in government policy. Instead many are going under redevelopment and being located in city centres. These redeveloped ones are adding features such as cinemas.'

In response to the question as to whether the initiatives proposed by Mary Portas (a UK retail expert) for changing the face of the high street are relevant, Antony made the comment that 'issues such as pay and display have damaged the high street. Duff councils have killed the high street through this and also through higher business rates. This has driven retailers out of many high street locations.

'Ultimately it comes down to catchment. Areas like Solihull have a nice profile in terms of the demographic of people who live in the surrounding areas. By contrast, towns like Scunthorpe and Grimsby will always struggle. They will never recover. Poorer areas in particular are vulnerable.'

The changing position of supermarkets

We asked Antony for his views on the notion that supermarkets have potentially damaged their business by introducing so many different formats, thus running the risk of creating cannibalization.

He noted that 'to a degree they have had no other choice. Either cannibalize yourself or others will do this for you.

'There is a trend away from supermarkets developing large format stores. It has peaked and flat-lined and may be going into decline. They are good at home delivery and people are buying food etc., more increasingly over the Internet.

'In France centres are often anchored by supermarkets. This is rare in the UK, although with redeveloped centres, a convenience store will tend to feature more strongly'.

What about the role of shopping centres and malls in developing regions such as eastern Europe?

Antony has worked in a number of cities in this region such as Prague and Warsaw and with developers in the Ukraine. He noted that in the latter case (around 2010), developers of such centres 'focused on the development of second generation shopping centres whereas by contrast, Western Europe would be at the third generation or third-plus phase of development.

When using these terms, Antony explained that first-generation shopping developments would largely equate to the traditional 'high street' format experienced in the UK and other western European countries in the 1960s and 1970s. Second generation would refer to the early versions of shopping centres that focused less on the global retail tenants and brands and more on local brands and products. This phase of shopping development would have a more functional approach with little or no emphasis on the concept of entertainment as a feature.

Third-generation developments reflect this focus on shopping as entertainment and appealing to the 'pleasure-seeking' aspects associated with the shopping experience. 'Third plus' takes this a stage further (we referred to examples such as the ski slope in one shopping mall in Dubai).

Antony noted that 'many such second generation shopping centre developments are very cheaply built. For instance in the UK buildings are planned for 60 years; by contrast, in developing regions buildings were designed not to last for much more than eight years.'

Antony does not make this observation as a criticism of developers in these regions. Rather, he recognizes the cleverness of such an approach 'because the rate of maturity of consumers was going at a much faster pace than developers experienced in other parts of the world. Shoppers were becoming more "savvy" about international brands and international retailers were becoming more enthusiastic about gaining a presence in these emerging markets. While such second generation shopping centres were not necessarily attractive places, investors had designed them in such a way that they could be quickly upgraded and replaced in response to the rapidly changing developments. The box (original site) could be turned into a multistorey car park to support a newer development at the edge of the town or city.'

What are the current and emerging developments in shopping centre/mall design?

We asked Antony to identify recent initiatives by developers to improve the product offer via their shopping centres and malls.

He noted a further focus on the concept of entertainment, particularly in the Gulf region. He cited the development of the Yas Mall in Abu Dhabi in 2014. When it was being built, it was linked to a water-world area and Ferrari World Abu Dhabi. It is also close to the Formula One race track developed to stage Grand Prix motor racing a few years earlier.

He notes that 'food and drink units are superb and the installation of fancy fountains and so on (non-revenue generating features) enhances the quality of the shopper experience'.

Antony further notes that increasingly 'retail developers have to squeeze their assets'.

He cites the example of Westfield, an Australian retail developer who strives to generate an additional 10 per cent out of their existing building by locating mobile units or kiosks in the shopping centre. These are referred to as retail mobile units (RMUs).

'Such units often operate on one-month leases. The cost of "fitting them out" is much lower than would be the case with a more traditional type of shop.'

Antony cites the example also of retail developers to allow incubator units into their centres. 'Traditionally a shopping centre would reduce its risk by allowing people in with a good track record – provenance, for instance "mom and pop" stores. The incubator unit offers shoppers distinct and interesting offers and it helps the shopping centre to get away from "clone-town" similar centres. This phenomenon is evidenced by the fact that everything is the same no matter where you go. This provides some interesting variations for the shopper.'

8.15 Conclusions

In this chapter we addressed the role that the store location decision plays in overall retail strategy formulation and implementation. Much of the discussion and research surrounding this topic was either carried out before the advent of the Internet and the subsequent growth in e-tailing, or does not explicitly examine the impact of these new channel alternatives.

While online retail channels provide a serious alternative for shoppers and continue to grow, they will never eliminate the need for physical stores. The reality is that in many countries shopping is seen as the single most popular leisure activity and provides enjoyment, not to mention therapy for many people. This particularly applies to shopping environments that focus on the experiential and hedonistic aspects.

The location decision, as we have noted, still relies to a large extent on intuition and check-lists while more sophisticated software-based models are also used.

We have seen a shift away from high street and central business district locations to out-of-town, suburban shopping centres and mall developments across most developed economies. This has been caused by a combination of tighter legislation and the lack of availability of prime locations due to the saturation effect. High streets have declined because of lack of investment on the part of local and city authorities and poor infrastructure in terms of parking, access and security. However, many governments across Europe are legislating in favour of a return to the central city or town locations and there is tentative evidence that some cities are undergoing major renewal and regeneration.

In summary, the location decision has become more complex as a result of the changing ways in which shoppers are engaging with retailers and their merchandise. Many large retailers have to grapple with the challenge of developing omni-channel options which ensure that the consumer gains a consistent experience across all of the touchpoints. For some, physical locations will reduce in importance in terms of overall retail marketing strategy. For others, there is no justification for developing physical space as their value proposition can be delivered through online channels only. The majority, however, still require some form of physical presence.

Case study: Buchanan Galleries shopping centre, Glasgow

Buchanan Galleries is located in Glasgow, which is one of the two main cities in Scotland. In fact, it is the largest city in Scotland although Edinburgh is regarded as the capital mainly because the Scottish parliament is located there.

This shopping centre is located in the city centre and is at the junction of the three main shopping streets: Sauchiehall Street, Argyle Street and Princes Square. It is often referred to as 'the Golden Mile' by business and retail commentators although some parts of this area, particularly on Argyle Street, show clear evidence of decline with many closed outlets.

It was opened in 1999 and cost around £250 million. It was a joint venture between Land Securities and Henderson Global Investors. At the time it was one of the biggest retail shopping centres (around 56,000 square metres) in the UK and far exceeded similar developments in Scotland. It adjoins the Glasgow Royal Concert Hall that is used extensively for major musical and theatrical events during the year. It is about 250 metres from the Queen Street railway station (one of the two main rail stations in Glasgow) and about 150 metres from the Buchanan Street bus station. Both the rail and the bus stations are key links to other parts of Scotland and the rest of the UK.

It contains a range of well-known stores such as Mango, River Island, Next and H&M. Other less well-known stores are also located there such as Fred Perry, Thomas Sabo and Korres. Its main anchor store is John Lewis, which occupies all of the northern part of the complex (visit its website at: www. buchanangalleries.co.uk to get fuller details on the composition of the stores operating in the centre). It currently has approximately 90 retailers operating on its premises.

Recent analysis indicates that it attracts 91 million visitors annually. It is second only to Oxford Street in London in terms of hourly footfall: 6,138 people per hour. It has been estimated that the Glasgow catchment area has an expenditure of £2.6 billion, with clothing and footwear constituting £678 million of that figure. It has parking facilities to cater for 2,000 cars.

In May 2013, the same owners invested in another development directly opposite the main entrance to the original Buchanan Galleries. This includes nine new retail units including brands such as Forever 21, Evans Cycle Company, Vans, Fat Cat and Gap. This 115,000 square foot development also contains 49 apartments. This is referred to as 185-211 Buchanan Street.

Land Securities and Henderson Global Investors announced also in 2013 that they had acquired planning permission for a major extension to the existing Buchanan Galleries complex. This was after several years of negotiation. It will see a further increase of around 65,000 square metres of retail space (effectively doubling the size of the centre). Marks & Spencer will become an anchor tenant by taking 150,000 square foot of space. In addition to new retail stores, there are plans for 15 new restaurants and a multiplex cinema. A direct link to Queen Street railway station is planned and a new multistorey car park with approximately 1,700 spaces.

This development is part of the Scottish Government's plans to regenerate a large part of Glasgow city centre. Part of this investment has been invested in the Buchanan Galleries extension (£310 million) to revamp George Square (located in the city centre and adjacent to the shopping centre). It is due to open in 2017.

Buchanan Galleries is open Monday to Saturday 10 am to 7 pm (open until 8 pm on Thursdays). On Sundays and Bank Holidays, the centre operates shorter hours of opening, 10 am to 6 pm.

Discussion questions

1 Based on your reading of the above case material and other sites you may have visited, assess the approach adopted by the investors to develop Buchanan Galleries from its original inception in 1999.

2 Buchanan Galleries is a city centre-based location. This would appear to challenge the conventional view that large shopping centres should be located out of town. Evaluate the extent to which you would agree that it is a mistake to locate such a venture in the city.

3 Marks & Spencer is to be the new anchor tenant on the new extension to the present development. Many commentators feel that this retailer has failed to perform well in recent years and has fallen

dramatically from its position of strength in the 1980s and 1990s. In your view, is it a suitable retailer for an anchor tenancy? Why? If not, why not?

4 Assess the pros and cons of the recent opening of the 185–211 Buchanan Street initiative.

5 Using the World Wide Web, carry out a search of other shopping centres located in the Greater Glasgow area. Assess the competitors. What points of differentiation do you feel the Buchanan Galleries centre has over them?

Chapter outcomes

- Retailers increasingly have to develop an omni-channel approach to satisfy shopper needs.
- This is different from a multi-channel approach: with omni channels the objective is to develop an integrated and seamless blending of the customer shopping experience with physical and online channels.
- The nature and type of shopping situation largely determines where and how consumers decide to shop.
- Experiential and hedonistic shopping motivations require a shopping space that goes beyond the simple functionality of shopping and address such factors as entertainment and leisure.
- In most developed economies there has been a move away from the high street and central business locations to large out-of-town shopping malls and centres.
- Such shopping centres are seen as the perfect answer to the provision of 'retail therapy' for many shoppers who enjoy the socialization and entertainment aspects that fit around their lifestyle.
- In many cities, particularly in Europe, there is recognition that central locations have fallen into decline and decrepitude in some cases and there is a consequent need to regenerate such areas.
- Retail developments can act as a catalyst in regenerating city centre locations.
- Retail developments must work in tandem with other critical activities such as culture, sport, heritage and the arts.
- Leading shopping malls are making greater use of technology to engage with shoppers.
- Countries such as the United Arab Emirates, Singapore and Hong Kong have used retailing to showcase their cities and act as a tourist destination for many people.
- In Europe, Western countries such as France, the UK and Germany are core areas for shopping developments. However, eastern European countries such as Russia, Poland and the Czech Republic are increasingly becoming more important as centres for such developments. Turkey (flitting between Europe and Asia) also provides an attractive environment for investors in this area.

Discussion questions

1 Assess the view that the emergence of an omni-channel approach is likely to increase the costs for retailers and confuse customers.

2 Use your local city/town as a working example. Make an audit of the existing shops and retail outlets in the main high street or central shopping area. You can do this by using the observation technique. Assess this area in terms of its existing appeal to shoppers. What recommendations would you make to the local planning authority by way of enhancing its appeal to shoppers?

3 Make a visit to a shopping centre/mall that is close to you. Examine the extent to which you believe it provides a positive shopping experience for its customers. How might it improve its value proposition?

4 Critically evaluate the proposition that anchor stores do not necessarily generate major benefits for retail developers.

5 Some retailers such as Tesco are moving to smaller retail locations that are often based in the high street. Assess the reasons for this approach to location.

6 It would appear that secondary locations (those sites located away from primary locations) are most likely to suffer. Assess the extent to which you would agree with this view.

7 Some people argue that the use of intuition and check-lists is too simplistic and fails to address the complexity of the retail location decision. In your view, is this an accurate perception?

References

Alexander, A., Cryer, D. and Wood, S. (2008) Location planning in charity retailing. *International Journal of Retail & Distribution Management*. 36(7): 536–550.

Anonymous (2011) Portas reveals her twenty-eight recommendations to revive the high street. *Retail Week*. 13 December. 18–19.

Banham, R. (2006) The UK shopping development market. *Journal of Retail & Leisure Property*. 5(3): 239–246.

Birkin, M. (1995) Customer targeting, geodemographic and lifestyle approaches. In Longley, P.A. and Clarke, G.P. (eds) *GIS for Business and Service Planning*. Cambridge: Geoinformation.

Birkin, M., Clarke, G. and Clarke, M. (2002) *Retail Geography and Intelligent Network Planning*. Chicester: Wiley.

Brown, S. (1993) Micro-scale retail location: Cinderella or ugly sister? *International Journal of Retail & Distribution Management*. 21(7): 1–10.

Brynjolfsson, E., Hu, Y.J. and Rahman, M.S. (2013) Competing in the age of omnichannel retailing. *Sloan Management Review*. 54(4): 23–29.

Cadell, C., Falk, N. and King, F. (2008) *Regeneration in European cities: Making connections*. Joseph Rowntree Foundation.

Clarke, G. (1998) Changing methods of location planning for retail companies. *Geojournal*. 45: 289–298.

Colomb, C. (2006) *Making Connections: Transforming People and Places in Europe*. Case study of Roubaix, Lille (France). Joseph Rowntree Foundation.

Cushman and Wakefield (2013) Marketbeat, *European Shopping Centre Development Report*. May.

Damian, D.S., Curto, J.D. and Pinto, J.C. (2011) The impact of anchor stores on the performance of shopping centres: the case of Sonae Sierra. *International Journal of Retail & Distribution Management*. 39(6): 456–475.

Davies, R. (2004) Planning policy for retailing. In Reynolds, J. and Cuthbertson, C. (eds) *Retail Strategy: The View from the Bridge*. Oxford: Elsevier Butterworth-Heinemann. 78–95.

Davies, R.L. (1997) Store location and store assessment research: the integration of some new and traditional techniques. *Transactions: Institute of Geographers*. 141–157.

Davies, R.L. and Rogers, D.S. (1984) *Store Location and Store Assessment Research*. Chicester: Wiley.

DTZ (2012) *European Retail Guide Shopping Centres*. March.

Hernandez, T., Bennison, D. and Cornelius, S. (1998) The organisational context of retail location planning. *GeoJournal*. 45: 299–308.

Howard, E. (2007) New shopping centres: is leisure the answer? *International Journal of Retail & Distribution Management*. 35(8): 661–672.

Ibrahim, M.F., Sim, L.L. and Chen, F.S. (2003) Positioning of shopping centres within the retail market of Singapore. *Pacific Rim Property Research Journal*. 9(1): 61–78.

Kim, H., Fiore, A.M., Niehm, L. S. and Jeong, M. (2010) Psychographic characteristics affecting behavioural intentions towards pop-up retail. *International Journal of Retail & Management*. 38(2): 133–154.

Konishi, H. and Sandfort, W.G. (2003) Anchor stores. *Journal of Urban Economics*. 53: 413-435.

Krosnar, K. (2013) Central Europe's shopping mall boom fades. *Financial Times*. 23 April.

Kuo, R.J., Chi, S.C. and Kao, S.A. (2002) A decision support system for selecting convenience store location through integration of fuzzy AHP and artificial neural network. *Computers in Industry*. 47(2): 199–214.

Levy, M. and Weitz, B. (2004) *Retail Management*. Boston, MA: McGraw-Hill Irwin.

Myers, H., Gore, J. and Liu, K. (2008) European shopping centre developments: an industry perspective. *Journal of Place Management and Development*. 1(1): 109–114.

Payne, A. (2006) *Handbook of CRM: Achieving Excellence in Customer Management*. Oxford: Butterworth-Heinemann.

Reynolds, J. and Wood, S. (2010) Location decision-making in retail firms: evolution and change. *International Journal of Retail & Distribution Management.* 38(11/12): 828–845.

Robertet, E. (1997) How social change affects retail habits: a typology of the European population. *European Retail Digest.* Winter: 4–14.

Savills Research (2012) *European Shopping Outlets – Investment Benchmark Report.* October.

Shah, O. (2013) High street casualties. *Sunday Times, Business Section.* 15 September, p. 5.

Teller, C. and Reutterer, T. (2008) The evolving concept of retail attractiveness: what makes retail agglomeration attractive when customers shop at them. *Journal of Retailing and Customer Services.* 15(3): 127–143.

Webber, R. (1993) Building geodemographic classifications. Paper presented to the Market Research Society Census Interest Group, London, 5 November.

Yeates, M., Charles, A. and Jones, K. (2010) Anchors and externalities. *Canadian Journal of Regional Science.* XXIV(3): 465–484.

Yiu, C.Y. and Xu, S.Y.S. (2012) A tenant mix model for shopping malls. *European Journal of Marketing.* 46 (3/4): 524–541.

Chapter 9

Designing and implementing retail pricing strategy

☑ Learning objectives

On completion of this chapter you should be in a position to address the following objectives:

☑ Understand the role that pricing plays in shaping the overall retail marketing strategy.

☑ Gain an insight into the basic principles of retail pricing.

☑ Examine the dimensions of pricing within the context of the retail sector.

☑ Assess the concept of value and its role in determining price.

☑ Evaluate the different approaches used by retailers when setting price.

☑ Understand the changing trends and developments that have influenced pricing strategy formulation and implementation.

☑ Examine the relationship between pricing decisions and promotional offers and the role that technology plays in this area.

☑ Assess ways in which retailers can protect their margin through 'smart' pricing.

9.1 Introduction

Pricing decisions have a critical influence on an organization's revenue, profitability and competitive position. In the context of marketing, it is the one element of the marketing mix that generates income: product, promotion and channel decisions revolve around expenditure in an attempt to make an impression in the marketplace.

Pricing is arguably the most neglected aspect of marketing strategy. It is surprising that this is so given the need to generate revenue, profits and (in the case of non-profit organizations) break even. Much of the research in marketing tends to focus on product and promotional issues. By contrast pricing does not receive the same level of attention. This is partly because marketers do not necessarily make the final decisions on pricing: it can involve many individuals and departments from finance to the legal people and the production department.

The sheer volume of sales and customer data can also act as an inhibitor. If we factor in the various cost permutations and competitive pricing strategies, we can possibly begin to understand why pricing strategy formulation and implementation more closely resembles the view of David Ogilvy, the iconic advertising expert. Ogilvy (1983) observed that:

> **❝***pricing is guesswork. Although perhaps this is an extreme view it highlights the difficulties associated with price setting. It is usually assumed that marketers use scientific methods to determine the price of their products. Nothing could be further from the truth.***❞**

This view can be challenged on the basis that technology allows retailers to capture increasingly more detailed and relevant information about shoppers' purchases and buying preferences, thus reducing the need to rely on guesswork.

This view on pricing was expressed over 30 years ago. In this chapter we examine how relevant this perception is in today's retail marketplace and environment.

In the early part of the chapter we examine pricing within the context of retailing and some misconceptions that people may hold about the issues surrounding the pricing decision. We focus on the concept of value and how this is often misunderstood by retailers in their quest for effective price-setting. While there is an underlying assumption that customers are not willing to pay more and are always looking for lower prices, bargains and discounts, we consider how retailers can command higher prices and avoid the dangers of constant price-cutting in the mistaken belief that this will always lead to more sales.

We identify the different pricing objectives that are set by retailers. We examine how recent developments and trends in areas such as mobile technology, information technology (IT) and the Internet have changed the way in which retailers go about developing strategy. In this section we look at the opportunities and challenges to emerge as a consequence of such developments.

In later sections of the chapter we examine the characteristics of the retail sector and how it differs from other sectors with regard to the dimensions that shape pricing policy. We also assess the different approaches to pricing in terms of their appropriateness and weaknesses.

We finish this chapter by assessing whether retail pricing has become more accurate, sophisticated and effective since Ogilvy made his observation over 30 years ago.

9.2   Principles of retail pricing

Retailers are challenged with the task of generating revenue from within their physical and/or virtual store operations. In order to do so they have to address the challenge of devising a pricing strategy that allows them to optimize their competitive position and deliver value to their target markets.

Effective pricing is based around the underlying principle of understanding and interpreting the relative price sensitivity of shoppers to price. This is a central part of formulating the overall positioning strategy of the retailer and identifying the part that price plays in this exercise. Retailers such as Aldi and Lidl target shoppers who place a strong degree of importance on low prices as part of their purchase decisions. As a consequence, low prices feature extensively in the overall value proposition. By contrast, other retailers target shoppers who take a wider view of the concept of value (customer service, a wider variety of merchandise, higher quality, better facilities and so on). Across the range of merchandise that is stocked in the stores, higher prices tend to predominate although special promotions and offers still feature prominently over time.

Pricing decisions have to address the long-term aspects of the retailer's operations. Prices are a visual and powerful indicator of the way in which retailers wish to position themselves in the market. Prices play a strong role in shaping shoppers' overall perception and image of the store. This has to be balanced with the pressure of delivering results to the shareholders and other stakeholders in the short term. However, it can be argued that a long-term view is essential in building a strong position in the market (Piercy, Cravens and Lane, 2010).

Retailers carry a wide range of merchandise in their stores. This can vary from as little as 2,000 items in a discount retailer like Aldi to over 40,000 in retailers such as Carrefour and Sainsbury's. This enables retailers *to adopt a flexible approach to price-setting.* Some categories can command higher prices (and higher margins) than others. It is common practice to select a limited number of items and use them as 'loss leaders'. This means that each individual item in this selection is priced at or below cost. They act as 'bait' in order to attract shoppers to the store. It is based on the principle that shoppers will purchase items from the loss leader category but also will extend their purchases to items that are priced higher and that these will generate higher profits for the retailer.

In theory retailers would like to sell their merchandise at 'full price'; that is, at the price that is printed on the item. However, this is a challenge, particularly in sectors of retailing such as clothing and electrical goods. It is particularly the case for retailers who are not competing in the 'hard discount' segment (where low prices are central to strategy) or at the 'high end' of the market (where they are targeting shoppers who are not price-sensitive). Many retailers as a consequence will lower prices through a combination of methods ('special discounts for a limited period only'; sales; 'closing-down sales' and so on).

This may have the effect of generating sales and moving on inventory, but clearly it damages the profit margins. More worryingly, it conditions the shopper to expect lower prices and shatters the credibility of the 'quoted' or 'listed' price. In heavily competitive markets and in periods of recession retailers may have no option but to engage in such practices.

As mentioned earlier, because of the large range of items on sale, retailers may be in a position to protect margin on certain categories of merchandise and use discounting on price to attract shoppers into the store and spend money.

J.C. Penney introduced a change in approach to its pricing strategy in 2012. Its new chief executive officer (CEO) introduced a pricing strategy based on the principle of 'Everyday Fair and Square Prices'. Previously, only 1 per cent of its items were sold at full price. Typically, an item listed at $39.99 would be sold at $29.99. Shoppers knew this and through a combination of special offers, coupons and so on, it became quite a complex process to operate and communicate on the part of the retailer.

The new CEO instigated a policy of selling such an item at its listed price of $30. This would only change in the event of a clearance sale. Interestingly, shoppers reacted negatively to this strategy and overall sales dropped by 19 per cent. The CEO vowed to stay with the strategy as it would take time to educate shoppers to this new way of doing business (Edwards, 2012). This example highlights one of the basic principles of retail pricing: getting the balance right between reducing prices to attract shoppers to the store and risking the devaluation of the brand.

As we discuss later in this chapter, *retailers are increasingly making use of IT to understand more accurately the ways in which their shoppers react to price.* This is very evident in the case of special price promotions and price comparative advertising. For instance, retailers make extensive use of the latter to tempt shoppers to remain loyal to the store or competitors encourage them to switch their shopping in order to benefit from lower prices.

Morrisons, one of the 'top four' UK food retailers, launched a 'Match & More' loyalty card in late 2014 to compete with the two discount retailers, Aldi and Lidl. The latter two retailers experienced increases in market share at the expense of Tesco, Asda and Sainsbury's in the previous couple of years. The loyalty card offered by Morrisons to its customers enables them to build up points from their purchases. In return they receive vouchers that allow them to make savings. The card is swiped at the checkout and the purchases are electronically matched against the prices of Aldi and Lidl. If they would have been cheaper elsewhere, points are added to the Match & More card, with 10 points equal to 1p. So, if the shop would have been £1 cheaper elsewhere, you will get 1,000 points. When the shopper reaches 5,000 points – the equivalent of £5 – they are given a £5 money-off voucher to use the next time they shop.

The 'More' element of the card gives shoppers additional points on 'hundreds of products in store and online', as well as 10 points for every litre of fuel bought from Morrisons' petrol stations. This type of price comparison campaign is typical within the food retailing sector. It also highlights the growing potential of using technology to make more detailed and reliable price comparisons with competitors. Morrisons has joined forces with a third-party specialist IT operator to carry out the price audits and process the data collected from the loyalty cards.

 As we discuss in Chapter 13, *location-based apps increasingly allow retailers to interact with their target market in a number of different ways, one of which relates to pricing.* As shoppers come into the proximity of a particular retailer's outlet, communications about special offers and price promotions can be sent to their smartphone.

Retailers work closely with their supply base. Given the dominant position held by the larger retailers in the different sectors, they are in a strong position to use their power to negotiate effectively with suppliers over price and volume (see Chapter 4). This creates the opportunity for retailers to offer lower prices to their shoppers on a number of selected categories. Suppliers also have to pay for prime shelf positions in the store outlets. For instance the phrase 'eye level is buy level' reflects the importance of having merchandise placed in such positions on the shelves. This 'payment' usually is reflected in volume discounts on the part of the supplier, enabling the retailer to maximize selling space across their stores.

By working closely with suppliers, *retailers can engage in joint price promotions to enable them to maximize revenue.* As mentioned earlier, this is increasingly being facilitated by the use of technology to capture data on shoppers' purchasing patterns and preferences. Shoppers that are more responsive to special price promotion offers can be targeted more effectively.

When designing pricing strategies in the retail sector, *retailers have to grapple with the challenge of operating multi channels*, and more recently omni-channel strategies. Shoppers increasingly use different channels at different stages in the purchasing process. Pricing decisions have to be made within the context of the implications that arise from using different channels. What will be the impact on shoppers, particularly if the retailer varies prices between its online channel and its physical stores?

Shoppers increasingly use technology to track prices on particular items of interest. Applications such as ShopSavvy and Bakodo allow shoppers to scan barcodes of items and check in real time for sources where this item may be available at a cheaper price. This raises their ability to negotiate with a retailer when they discover that the same item may be 20 per cent cheaper in another outlet of the same retailer. As shoppers dip in and out of different channels (touchpoints) with a retailer across different channels, pricing strategies will have to be more transparent and reflect the fact that shoppers are empowered with greater levels of information than ever before.

Many retailers traditionally focus on profit margin as a benchmark to determine how well they are doing in the marketplace. In light of developments in technology and the move towards omni channels in particular, retailers may have to reconsider this metric or measurement tool. *Amazon* provides a good example of this change in thinking. It operates on average margins of around 4 per cent. This is roughly 2–3 per cent lower than traditional retail competitors. However, the speed with which it turns around its inventory, allied to the zero costs of not running physical stores, means that *its return on invested capital is more than double that of its traditional competitors.*

9.3 Retail pricing in context

We noted in our introduction to this chapter that pricing is one of the least understood and most complex areas that businesses have to address. The retail sector is no different and as we shall see in this chapter, it can be even more challenging, given the characteristics of this industry.

Smith (2012) observes that in many companies, finance, sales and marketing personnel often feature in the decision-making process with regard to pricing. This can bring both advantages and weaknesses. On a positive note it implies that a cross-functional approach to this task reflects the views of key business disciplines and takes on board different philosophies and approaches.

For instance, finance and accounting people have a clear grasp of costs and the resulting implications for pricing. Core concepts such as cash flow and breakeven analysis are critical in arriving at an appropriate price for a product or service. Without such a contribution, it can be argued that the eventual price charged may not accurately reflect the costs incurred and result in lost revenue and in the worst case, extinction.

However, it is debatable whether accounts and finance personnel are fully equipped to set the price, given their lack of knowledge and interface with customers. After all, it is not their role to liaise with customers on a regular basis.

Sales personnel on the other hand deal directly with customers on a regular basis and (should) have a clear understanding about their needs and priorities, in particular with regard to the role that price plays in their decision-making process.

Marketing personnel also have an overview of their customers' perceptions and attitudes and use such information to shape overall marketing strategy. However, in many cases both of these functions (sales in particular) are often judged and rewarded on the volume of sales that they generate. It may be easier to sell certain products if price is lower and such an occurrence can lead to bias in terms of how they relay back information about appropriate price settings and levels to the decision-makers.

Some companies are now employing pricing specialists with skills in the area of setting and implementing pricing strategies that reflect a wider and more strategic overview of price in the context of business strategy formulation and implementation. These individuals come from finance, marketing, economics or mathematics backgrounds. It is likely that we shall see further growth in the recruitment of such personnel in the coming years as developments in the areas of technology and IT can create opportunities for a more analytical and scientific approach to the task of setting prices.

This is particularly so for the retail sector where retailers are in a strong position to capture large amounts of data on their customers' shopping patterns, behaviours, preferences and attitudes to issues such as promotions. We explore such developments later in the chapter.

Nagle, Hogan and Zale (2011) put forward the view that much of the decision-making surrounding pricing is about reacting to change in the marketplace; that is, changes in customer attitudes or competitive activities. This 'reactive' approach is tactical in nature and is far removed from what we might see as the desired position of employing a 'strategic, long-term perspective' with regard to such decisions. If pricing decisions are largely reactive, they run the risk of missing out on the 'big picture'; for example, long-term growth and development in a particular market as opposed to a short-term gain at the expense of a competitor. In the latter case, such an initiative may lead to a gradual erosion of price, margin and damage to the brand.

Short-term and reactive approaches to pricing can occur for many reasons. It can be argued that the main one is due to a lack of knowledge or understanding about the customer and the tendency to base such decisions on a narrow range of factors. This is demonstrated by the findings of a study by Marn, Roegner and Zawada (2003) that found that 80–90 per cent of poor pricing decisions stemmed from under-pricing. While this may be caused by many factors, it emphasizes the lack of understanding and appreciation that companies have about the most important stakeholder in the business equation: the customer.

9.4 Common misconceptions about pricing

In this section we follow up on our initial observation that many organizations show a poor understanding of the customer's attitudes to and perceptions of price in the context of the purchase decision. We highlight some myths or misconceptions about pricing from the perspective of trying to gain a better understanding of the shopper.

1 *The shopper uses rational motives for buying*: this view stems in large part from the economist's view of a customer's response to prices. In this case the customer is often portrayed as someone who is in possession of perfect information upon which a purchase decision can be made. It is not our intention to enter into a full debate on the issue of rationality. However, it can be strongly argued that such a view imposes rigidity about decision-making that largely ignores pragmatic and behavioural influences used by shoppers when making a purchasing decision. Marketers draw upon many other disciplines to formulate an understanding of consumer behaviour. In the context of the pricing decision, psychology provides some interesting insights.

   For instance, why would anybody purchase luxury brands? If we buy into the traditional economic perspective of perfect information and utility maximization, there is no logical reason why anybody would spend £300 on a pair of Nike basketball shoes. After all, such a product is made of moulded plastic by low-cost labour for a few pounds. This, of course, ignores the marketing costs and the 'innovations' that may surround the design of such a product. It also ignores such factors as 'aspiration', 'lifestyle' and 'exclusivity' that appeal to certain shoppers in the marketplace. This is not to suggest that such purchases are irrational. Indeed, a debate could be held about what constitutes rationality. The lesson from this example is that the principles of segmentation apply in this case and lie at the heart of effective pricing. Different groups of individuals have different views, opinions and attitudes. They apply different evaluative criteria when making purchasing decisions. This has to be factored into any formulation of pricing strategy.

2 *Consumers know the price of products and services*: this view is often held by decision-makers in retailing particularly. However, this can be challenged. Even on items that are bought on a daily basis (items such as bread and milk), a simple survey of friends and classmates will show a range of prices put forward in such an exercise.

   While it can be argued that the price of milk can vary in different retail outlets, most shoppers will source such an item at their preferred, regular outlet. I conducted such a survey with over 40 students recently and when asked how much a litre of milk cost, those who lived on campus or in a flat (who actually purchased such an item) generated a response that ranged from 85 pence to £1.10.

There is a learning point here for marketers. Such an example indicates that most shoppers do not deal in 'absolutes'. In other words, few of us set out to purchase an item with a specific price in mind; for example, £1. Instead, we tend to operate in terms of price-points; for example, from £200 to £300. This also introduces the concept of a *zone of indifference*. This suggests that below and above certain price points an individual would not purchase a particular item.

Let us consider an example. Suppose you have an interview for a potential job. You naturally want to make an impression and decide to purchase a new business suit/outfit. You reckon that a suit costing less than £100 would be of poor quality, would look cheap and that the stitching might come apart after wearing it a couple of times. A suit costing more than £250 would put it outside of your budget and may be somewhat extravagant. When you go to the retail outlet, you are effectively working within a zone of indifference. A suit that is priced between these price points will not put you off in any way. A good salesperson in the store will assess your attitudes and propensity to spend and steer you to a suit that is at the upper end of your zone of indifference. Of course, a poor salesperson will not pick up on this and you will probably purchase a suit at the lower end of this zone.

The lesson for marketers and pricing is that there is more flexibility and opportunities with regard to pricing and interpreting a shopper's views on price in relation to evaluative criteria.

3 *Quality determines price*: this perception is based on the belief that a product or service that is deemed to be of high quality will command a high price and that a low-quality brand will likewise be labelled with a low price. Of course, this view is based on the assumption that the shopper/customer is in a position to know enough about the brand to make such an informed judgement. However, is this an accurate portrayal of reality? In some cases, it is. Certain brands can be assessed using 'hard' quantitative measures to enable a shopper to assess its quality. For instance, cars can be evaluated on measurable factors such as fuel consumption, speed and the quality of such features as seating and 'in-car' entertainment. Even in this example, however, shoppers may be influenced by 'softer' and less measurable factors such as aspiration and brand reputation.

It becomes even more difficult in the case of services, some of which are intangible and more difficult to assess. Some purchases are made on the basis of lack of knowledge or indeed ignorance. A good example is wine. In the UK, sales of wine began to gain momentum in the early 1980s. Prior to that it was perceived as being a relatively expensive item, which was largely consumed by the upper classes. Supermarkets began to market wine aggressively that led to an increase in demand. However, many shoppers had little or no knowledge about wine; for example, the different grapes and flavours, the different wine-growing regions and so on. In many cases the price of a bottle of wine was used as the proxy measure for quality.

Some commentators in the wine business noted that for many years the French wine producers were able to consistently 'overprice' their products based on the principle that many people assumed that French wine was better than other wine-producing countries.

This strategy changed later in the 1980s when wines from countries such as Chile and New Zealand hit the supermarket shelves and shoppers realized that they could enjoy good quality wines at lower prices.

The learning point to emerge from this misconception is that shoppers may not have the knowledge or the motivation to use quality as a measure of value.

4 *Manufacturers can control the price charged by retailers*: as we noted in Chapters 3 and 4, this assumption no longer stands up under scrutiny. The power of large retailers across many sectors within retailing means that price is often determined by them. This is becoming even more prevalent given the vast reservoir of information that retailers hold about their customers' shopping patterns and the ways in which they maximize selling space in the retail outlets.

It can be argued that even retailers might be in danger of losing control over the price of their merchandise to the customer! The advent of the Internet in general and price comparison sites in particular ensures that in many cases shoppers are 'doing their homework' on the price of a range of competitive offerings. They look for any special promotional offers by an individual retailer and when they turn up in the retail store or visit the website, they are potentially in a strong bargaining position. This may lead to the retailer offering a deal to match or beat a competitive offer to get the sale.

5 *Pricing can be based on fixed and inflexible margin policies*: this has particular relevance for retailers. As customers become more aware of comparative product offerings, retailers have to grapple with the challenge of managing margins. This is challenging because of the nature of retailing. Retailers have to forecast likely demand for their merchandise in advance. In more volatile retail areas such as fashion, any mistakes made by the buyers and procurement team can lead to overstocking of certain items. This, in turn, leads to increased costs in areas such as warehousing and logistics. Items lying on shelves or in distribution centres 'eat into' the profits and can leave retailers with no choice but to engage in heavy discounting to recoup losses and generate a stream of income. Of course, 'smart' retailers are using a range of techniques to reduce their exposure to potential margin reduction and losses. We look at this in more detail later in the chapter.

6 *Pricing based on competitor strategies is more effective*: there is some intuitive merit with such an approach. This largely revolves around the argument that it is relatively risk-free. If everyone else is coalescing around a similar pricing strategy then they cannot all be wrong. However this view fails to recognize that each retailer has a set of resources and constraints that differ. One or two are market leaders and have potential advantages that do not 'trickle down' to smaller retailers who hold small market shares and do not have the scale, scope or power to shape or influence price. It ignores market realities: in some cases small, niche retailers can command higher prices due to their targeting of a more affluent, less price-sensitive segment. Indeed, such a strategy can make a retailer more profitable in a relative sense.

Even when faced by price-cutting strategies by dominant retailers in a specific retail space, a retailer can respond by focusing on the concept of value and how certain benefits can be leveraged in such a way as to offer a robust value proposition to retain existing customers and attract new ones.

The observations, of course, are not universally accepted by everyone. This is acceptable. We have highlighted these areas to demonstrate that many companies in general and retailers in particular do not invest enough time and money to fully research customers' perceptions of pricing.

9.5 Retail pricing objectives

Retailers can employ a wide range of objectives to provide direction for their pricing strategy. They can be summarized as follows.

1 *Long-term market development and profitability*: while it may be simple to assume that this should apply to all retailers, in many cases a more short-term perspective is employed. This objective recognizes the need to engage in a range of retail marketing activities (including price) that is based on the presumption that in the longer term, profit will be determined by such activities and that there is a need to view such development as one that takes time to develop. This is reflected in building market share, developing a customer base and consequent shopper loyalty, developing and shaping the value proposition and recognizing that investment is necessary before rewards are reaped by the retailer. The pricing strategy employed will be closely linked to the positioning, branding and communications strategy.

2 *Short-term market share gain or protection*: from time to time dominant retailers in a market space will engage in pricing tactics to attack the competition (either existing or new entrants). This may take the form of price cuts which are designed to encourage shoppers to switch their allegiance in an attempt to benefit from special offers or discounts that are on offer. It may also be driven by focusing on particular areas within their merchandise offerings. For instance, the retailer may wish to engage in proactive communications about its store brands or price changes in this area. In order to protect market share, retailers may introduce a new range of store brands aimed at the lower end of the price point. Conversely, retailers may also introduce such merchandise at the higher end. In both instances this may be driven by the need to protect its present market position from existing or potential competitive activities in this area.

3 *Brand and quality-led objectives*: pricing strategy formulation and implementation does not operate in isolation. Retailers may engage periodically in a repositioning of their store and brand image. This may occur through upgrades in the quality of the merchandise sold to attract a less price-sensitive segment. Such an approach may create an opportunity to sustain higher margins. In order to create consistency and credibility, the approach to pricing must reflect this upward shift in positioning. The price charged for relevant merchandise is a very visible and strong signal of the projected brand image and one that can shape a shopper's views and perceptions about a particular retail value proposition.

4 *Sustainability-led objectives*: as we note in Chapter 11, increasingly retailers have to address the general issue of sustainability and more specific issues such as recycling, energy conservation, waste management and the provision of organic product. This may have an impact on price (usually upwards due to the increased investment in such initiatives). Such changes in pricing have to be communicated to the target market in order to address concerns about increases in price or to satisfy 'ethical shoppers' who are looking for such change in overall strategy.

5 *Equitable pricing objectives*: the nature of many retail operations is such that they are multi-site operations spread across different geographic regions. Retailers are in a position now (due to more detailed and sophisticated data analysis) to provide different price structures depending on their store locations. Upmarket, high-income locations may employ a different pricing structure to an outlet located in a poorer part of a city or region. This objective can address the issue of equity or fairness and show that retailers have some concerns about the variations in spending power and income levels. This objective may have particular resonance in the case of recessionary periods.

6 *Promotions-led objectives*: in many instances retailers – often in collaboration with suppliers – will engage in special promotions of new products, special offers, 'buy-one-get-one-free' (BOGOF) campaigns, competitions and so on. These campaigns are shaped by special price deals and structures. Periodically, usually during quiet periods, for example just after Christmas or the Eid festival, retailers will launch a sales campaign to stimulate business and generate a cash flow at a time when sales are likely to decrease.

7 *Inventory-led objectives*: as we noted earlier, it is common for many retailers to have excess stock or inventory in the system; this can occur for a number of reasons: for example, over-ordering, poor forecasting, bad weather, shop-soiled items and so on. Retailers may initiate a pricing strategy based on specific price reductions to get rid of such stock and generate a revenue stream. This tactic is often referred to as a 'markdown' and we will look at this in more detail later in the chapter.

9.6 The concept of value-based pricing

Much of the existing literature on pricing suggests that many organizations price their products largely around cost and/or competitive considerations. In the case of cost, this is often exemplified by the use of what is known as 'cost-plus' pricing.

This works on the principle of calculating the costs associated with the production and marketing of a product or service and adding on a predetermined margin (usually based on the industry average). This generates the recommended price for the product. It is based on the presumption that costs can be calculated and apportioned accurately. However, this is not as easy as it appears. Unit costs change with the volume. Much of the apportioned cost is fixed and, therefore, the challenge is to somehow allocate such cost on a per unit basis.

However, such allocations depend on volume and volume changes as price changes. The unit cost is therefore a moving target. The notion that cost-based pricing can be done by making the assumption that price can be set without affecting volume is flawed.

Despite the apparent logic of focusing on cost, it creates situations that bear little resemblance to reality. If sales increase, such logic dictates that fixed costs can be spread over more units, thus lowering price. This takes no account of the fact that if demand rises, the product or service could be expected to command a higher price.

Competitive-based pricing strategies, as discussed earlier, have some intuitive logic behind them as well. For retailers who do not hold a dominant position in the market, it makes apparent sense to follow the 'industry average' and try to compete on non-price factors. It appears to be a safe and conservative policy but again contains flaws. It does not take into account the obvious fact that competitors do not have identical resources, capabilities, cost and scale. Assuming that competitors are adopting the correct pricing strategy is dangerous. Apart from the differences mentioned above, it may be more profitable to target different segments of shoppers in the market and apply a different approach to pricing, particularly in segments that are less price-sensitive.

Both the cost-centred and competitor-centred approaches to pricing miss one vital ingredient in the equation: the *customer*. One of the central themes in marketing theory is that all activity in an organization should ultimately be driven by the end user. Nagle et al. (2011) demonstrate this in Fig. 9.1.

A focus on product and cost ensures that the starting point in the pricing process is the internal operations of the company or organization. The product/service designers develop what they consider to be a strong product that is better than the competition. Finance and accounting work out the associated costs and generate a pricing structure. This determines the value proposition that is then sold to the end-user. We can see immediately that the concept of value is largely determined in this instance by internal personnel, not the customer or the end user.

We introduced a very critical word into our discussion in the preceding paragraphs and figure: value. This is a phrase that unfortunately has generated many definitions largely built around some of the following concepts:

- something a company does that is better than the competition
- delivering something that exceeds the customer's expectations
- creating a desire in the mind of the customer resulting in a purchase.

While each of these definitions has some relevance, it does not capture the essence of what we mean by value. Cram (2006) defines value as follows:

> **"***Value = perceived product benefits + perceived emotional associations – perceived price***"**

The right price is that tipping point where the benefits outweigh the customer's desire to keep the money in their pockets.

Macdivitt and Wilkinson (2011) identify 'value drivers' as being the tangible and intangible factors that when acted upon by the organization lead to an enhancement of competitive advantage. In the context of retailing, shoppers are likely to respond to those factors or cues that are relevant to their evaluative criteria. The key word here is 'relevant'. It is in this context that we need to understand their perceptions on price and how this criterion shapes their shopping behaviour in general and purchase decision-making in particular.

The concept of value means different things to different people. What might appear to be modern and trendy to one person might be perceived as being 'old-fashioned' or dowdy to another. It reinforces the need for retailers to apply the basic principles of segmentation and consumer behaviour when attempting

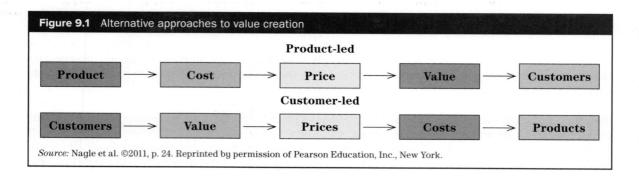

Figure 9.1   Alternative approaches to value creation

Product-led

Product → Cost → Price → Value → Customers

Customer-led

Customers → Value → Prices → Costs → Products

Source: Nagle et al. ©2011, p. 24. Reprinted by permission of Pearson Education, Inc., New York.

to develop an appropriate pricing strategy. One-dimensional cost or competition-based approaches are far too narrow and inflexible and fail in many cases to come up with pricing that is relevant for the target market.

An understanding of the value drivers allows a retailer to focus on the benefits that people seek when purchasing products. In too many cases manufacturers confuse features with benefits. This is evidenced in the area of electrical retailing. A shopper who is contemplating the purchase of a digital camera and who either visits an electrical retailer like Dixons or visits a similar online retail operation, is faced by a bewildering array of cameras with hundreds of features. For many shoppers this situation confuses them, particularly if they are not technically literate. Do they really need such a degree of choice? Do these features provide any material benefit to them? Value-based pricing puts the emphasis on the benefits that people seek and how much they are willing to pay for such gains.

9.7 The challenges of pricing in the retail context

In this section we consider the specific challenges and opportunities associated with developing a pricing strategy in the context of retailing. This sector exhibits a number of characteristics that make it different from other business sectors.

9.7.1 Multi-product and multi-site

Retailing in the case of large retail operations involves multi-site operations selling a very wide and diverse range of products and services. For instance, IKEA carries around 12,000 items in its product range and all of its stores will carry a range of these products (depending on the size of the individual store). IKEA has more than 1,350 suppliers in 50 countries. All products have the label 'Design & Quality'. Its global sourcing policy involves the purchase of items from Europe (64 per cent), followed by Asia (33 per cent) and North America (3 per cent). It operates over 300 stores worldwide and has stores in over 40 different countries. This gives us an insight into the scale of operations of a large, global retail operation. It also demonstrates the potential complexity of setting prices for such a range of merchandise that is spread over such a number of different sites and locations.

9.7.2 The service dimension

Betancourt (2004) notes that much of the retail value proposition is service-based. In addition to the process of stocking and selling physical merchandise, retailers provide services such as location, information, assortment, delivery and store atmospherics to make the shopping experience more positive and relevant for shoppers. The provision of such services has to be factored into the cost structures and the eventual pricing systems.

9.7.3 Different retail formats and channels

As we noted in Chapter 8, large retailers operate different retail formats in order to provide a full service to their respective target markets. This means that store formats carry less stock than others. Certain channels may not appeal to some shoppers. This allows the retailer to offer some form of price discrimination across the different formats and channels. This can take the form of special offers, sales promotions or deals that can only be obtained in a specific retail format or channel.

9.7.4 Varying margins across the portfolio of merchandise

Depending on the store size and format, Tesco carries up to 40,000 items. The portfolio of merchandise carried by supermarkets such as Tesco covers a diverse range of product categories and provides many opportunities to vary pricing and margins (Pulter, 2012). Retailers carry out deep analysis and appraisal of the contribution of these items to overall sales and profitability. Such items will be categorized into different groupings. For instance, a retailer may set up three or four categories or zones based on features such as volume (those items that generate around 50 per cent of overall sales), prestige (generating around 5–10 per cent), promotions (where margins and prices are reduced in order to stimulate sales (generating around 15–25 per cent) and loss leaders (items that are sold at or below cost in order to stimulate sales and attract more shoppers to the store, generating around 5 per cent).

9.7.5 Price auditing and competitive checking

Retailers constantly engage in daily monitoring of their competitors' pricing. Such analysis allows a retailer to factor this into the pricing strategy. A good example of this can be found on the website of Currys: a UK electrical retailer. It offers a price promise to shoppers. It states on its website that if a shopper finds the same product and offer for less, it will match the price and beat it by 10 per cent of the difference. It builds in a number of conditions that have to be met before it will honour the quoted price. These are summarized as follows.

1 The product offered by the competitor's website is exactly the same as the one we sell, and is offered on the same terms.
2 The product on their website must be in stock and available for delivery immediately.
3 Currys must have the product in stock.
4 Currys representatives are able to confirm the details on the competitor's website.
5 Our price promise applies to the product only, not delivery or other services.
6 Our price promise even applies up to seven days after purchase.

> **❝Our in store price promise**
> *In the unlikely event that you find a cheaper price, for the same product and offer,*
> *we'll not only match the price but also beat it by 10% of the difference*.*
> *Our price promise even applies up to seven days after purchase.*
> *Simply pop into your nearest store to speak to a colleague.*
> **Single unit purchases only. The competitor must be a retail store within 30 miles and have*
> *stock ready for delivery.*❞
>
> *Source*: http://www.currys.co.uk/gbuk/price-promise-1023-theme.html

This type of pricing is not based on guesswork or a desperate attempt to generate increased sales. Instead, it works on the principle that personnel at Currys carry out rigorous auditing of competitors' pricing strategies on a daily basis and that its prices are adjusted accordingly. A number of conditions are built into the promise to make it more difficult for a shopper to find a lower price elsewhere. It also works on the basis that few shoppers have sufficient time, energy or inclination to engage in such a detailed search process to find a lower price elsewhere.

9.7.6 Constant price adjustment

In many areas within retailing, it is common practice to adjust prices on a regular basis. In the previous section we considered the specific aspect of price auditing. In this section we consider one of the basic features of retailing: trying to balance supply and demand. As we noted earlier, retailers have to grapple with the challenge of forecasting likely demand for their merchandise portfolio. We also have to recognize that the issue of seasonality can play an important role in retailing. For instance, most retailers generate a high proportion of their revenue during key periods in the year. In Europe and the Gulf this might often be reflected in the periods leading up to Christmas or during the Eid festival. However, retailers have discovered that shoppers are becoming more aware of the benefits of waiting for special deals, sales or special discounts outside of these periods.

Retailers as a consequence have become more active in starting sales during the lead-up to Christmas in order to tempt shoppers into the store during this critical period.

The analogy of the game of poker can be used here. On the one hand, retailers need shoppers to visit their stores and spend money. However, shoppers are holding back in order to wait for the special deals. Who blinks first? Who is holding a good set of cards? Are they bluffing? Many retailers actually 'blink first' and engage in special promotions and price discounts to attract shoppers. This has the potential benefit of generating sales revenue. However, it can damage margin as prices are heavily reduced. Constant price adjustment can lead to increased traffic to the store and increased sales revenue. The danger of this approach lies in its ability to damage the integrity of the brand through constant price discounts and deals.

Kopalle et al. (2009) present an overall framework that highlights the key factors that shape the direction of retailer pricing strategies (see Fig. 9.2).

We can identify seven factors that are highlighted in Fig. 9.2.

1 *In-channel competition* refers to price competition within a particular store or across a number of stores within a retailer's operation. It also covers the impact of loss-leader price campaigns on store traffic (the number of people visiting stores).

2 *Cross-channel competition* refers to the retailer's overall positioning strategy and the extent and range of formats that it adopts.

3 *Integration with other marketing mix variables* refers to the extent of price and product customization together with promotional activities.

4 *Customer factors* that lead to demand uncertainty and the corresponding joint optimization of price, promotion and product assortment.

5 *Product type* refers to the nature of the retail offering; for example, whether the retailer operates in the fashion or staple retail sectors (for example, perishables and packaged goods) and the level of complementarity across the product ranges.

6 *Manufacturer interaction* refers to the interaction between suppliers and retailers in areas such as promotions and store brand.

7 *Medium* that recognizes that many retailers operate multi-channel strategies and the different approaches which may exist in terms of online and offline pricing strategies.

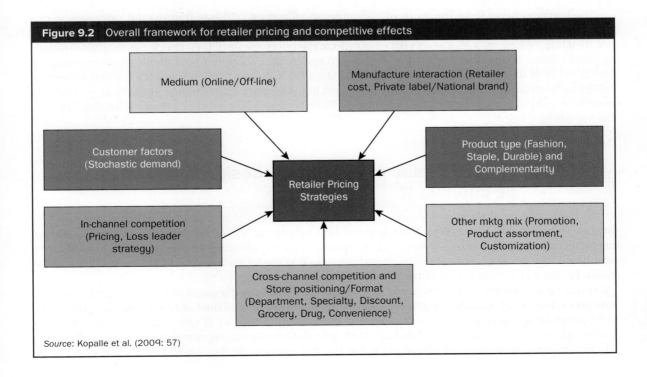

Figure 9.2 Overall framework for retailer pricing and competitive effects

Source: Kopalle et al. (2009: 57)

This framework provides a useful mechanism for gaining an understanding of the key areas that shape overall retail pricing strategy. It also recognizes the specific interactions that must be taken into account when pricing retail products, particularly in the case of in-channel and cross-channel activities. We examine specific issues that emerge from this model in later sections of this chapter.

9.8 Price image and its impact on shopping behaviour

When assessing the issue of designing and implementing retail price strategies, we need to consider the issue of price image and how it influences shopping behaviour. The issue of price image is important in the overall context of retail marketing strategy because it reflects the shopper's overall evaluation of a store or retailer. In many ways it is similar to the concept of brand image. However, the latter (as we noted in Chapter 3) reflects a multidimensional view comprising a range of price and non-price factors. Price image is unidimensional insofar as it considers the overall role of price perceptions.

Hamilton and Chernev (2013: 3) define price image as 'a function of two types of factors: retailer-based factors, which managers can directly influence, and consumer-based factors, which are particular to the individual buyers and which managers cannot directly influence'.

The price-related drivers include (1) the average price, which reflects how a retailer's prices compare with competitors; (2) the dispersion of prices, reflecting how low and high prices are distributed within a store; (3) price dynamics, which reflect the extent to which prices change within a store over a period of time; (4) price-related policies such as price promises (revisit the price promise example in an earlier section); and price-related communications such as price-based advertising.

Non-price drivers also act in tandem and these refer to the store design, layout and ambiance of the retail store, its website appearance and design, the contribution of sales staff on the floor and overall customer service policy.

Hamilton and Chernev (2013) also pinpoint consumer-specific factors that influence price image. First, individual factors that are relatively consistent over time; for example, price sensitivity and familiarity with market prices. Second, situational factors such as time pressure and the financial consequences of the purchase decision.

The learning point from the work of Hamilton and Chernev (2013) is that overall price image can influence the shopping behaviour and patronage of shoppers. It can play an important role in whether or not they buy an item on a shopping visit or postpone the purchase until they check out available options at other stores. It also influences the overall perception that shoppers hold about the attractiveness and fairness of the prices that they encounter on the store's shelves. This framework for understanding price image strongly suggests that shoppers adopt a holistic view of price image: the influencing factors should be viewed in their entirety and recognize the interdependent nature of the relationship between the variables.

9.9 How can retail price strategy design and formulation be improved?

In the early part of this chapter we suggested that pricing is one of the least understood and most neglected aspects of marketing strategy. In this section we identify the key areas that need to be addressed, the developments and trends that impact on price formulation and implementation and the enablers that can improve its accuracy and relevance.

 It can be argued that retailers are in a strong position to introduce and implement pricing policies and procedures that address the challenge of being value-based and customer-focused. As we discuss in Chapter 13, retailers were and continue to be at the leading edge of IT utilization. The use of loyalty cards and programmes allied to proactive customer relationship management policies means that they are in a potentially strong position to use the information captured to develop more targeted, customized and relevant pricing programmes for their target markets. The problems tend to occur through the sheer volume of data that is actually captured. It needs to be translated into relevant and useful information that can be used for such focused activities in the area of pricing.

Shankar and Bolton (2004) recognized that there was little research carried out on how pricing strategies could be customized for brands, categories, stores and overall within the supply chain. We assess the validity of this view by looking at more recent developments in a later section of this chapter.

9.10 Trends and developments

Grewal et al. (2012) identify a number of developments that have occurred over the last 10 years that have direct implications for retailers. Although their observations are mainly based on the North American experience, these trends can also be evidenced across many geographic regions. They note the impact of the economic environment on shoppers and the resulting implications for retailers. A deep and long-lasting recession globally has forced some shoppers to reassess their shopping patterns and behaviour. A drop in real income means that shoppers in many cases redefine their concept of value, and use store formats and options that they previously would not have considered (Ma et al., 2011). This is evidenced by the growth of food retailers such as Aldi and Lidl in the UK market as they make inroads in terms of market share on traditionally dominant retailers such as Tesco and Sainsbury's.

The use of coupons and special offers needs to be considered more strategically by retailers in light of shoppers reappraising their views on price. If strategic pricing is to occur, then retailers need to be more proactive and sophisticated in their approach to analysing data and trends in areas such as coupon/deal proneness and use of price comparison websites. In this respect, research by Murthi and Rao (2012) showed that nearly one half of purchases by customers are made on the expectation of prices rather than the ones posted in the store or on the website. They also emphasize the importance of proactive communication of such deals and offers to their target markets.

The other critical area that we need to consider takes us to the many technological developments and the impact that they have had on two key areas: the shopper and the retailer.

Two critical developments have occurred in the last 10 years or so that have profoundly affected the way in which shoppers engage with retailers and how retailers respond to such changes in behaviour. These developments are grounded in the areas of social media platforms and mobile technology. We assess both in Chapters 10 and 13 on a more general and strategic level. We consider them in this chapter from the perspective of their relevance to the design and implementation of retail pricing strategies.

9.10.1 Social media platforms and the Internet: impact on retail pricing

The growth of online channels and the more recent phenomenon of omni channels has altered the way in which many shoppers engage with retailers; seek and acquire information on a broad range of areas including pricing; form attitudes and opinions; and share information.

Websites such as Priceline.com (US-based facilitator) have emerged and provide a value proposition where shoppers (particularly in the travel and hotel sectors) can visit it and name their price for a hotel room on a certain date(s) in a particular city. Hotels can respond and meet the price quoted by the shopper. Priceline.com gets paid on the difference between what the shopper quoted and what was offered and agreed by the hotel operator. This business model has been refined and, more recently, service providers can also put up offers that the shopper can peruse and decide whether or not to avail of that opportunity.

Activity

Visit the website of Priceline: www.priceline.com. Assess the business model employed by this company.

Developments such as that of Priceline follow a 'Name Your Own Price' (NYOP) strategy and are increasingly becoming popular as alternatives to the more conventional approach to pricing where the seller – not the buyer – sets the price and the ground rules. This is a reversal of the traditional view about pricing: it explicitly recognizes that the shopper is no longer necessarily a passive recipient of decisions, communications and rules that are set by the seller and passed on to the buyer. Instead, we see (like many aspects of social media and the Internet) the buyer engaging in a 'two-way' and proactive fashion with the seller (in this case a retailer).

We should also recognize that retailers can use the developments in social media and the Internet to refine their pricing strategies. Many retailers have set up their own Facebook pages and attract vast numbers of members. They can use such sites to capture specific and valuable information (price-related) to track search and evaluation activities by shoppers. Smarter retailers will combine such information with data collected from loyalty programmes to gain a clearer picture of shoppers' perceptions surrounding the area of price; for example, reactions to special offers and promotions. When combined with more sophisticated software, retailers can 'drill' deeply into such data and arguably be in a strong position to glean some focused and relevant information in order to develop customer-centric pricing strategies.

9.10.2 Developments in mobile technology: impact on retail pricing

One of the most interesting and relevant developments over the last 10 years or so resides in the broad area of mobile technology. We examine the wider and more strategic issues on this topic in Chapter 13. Here, we consider the implications for retail pricing.

The advent of 3G and latterly 4G smartphones, along with developments in tablets and iPads, has allowed shoppers in particular to use such technology across many different aspects of the shopping process. The key word here is 'mobility'. Whereas in the early part of this century, people generally needed a fixed point and connection to access the Internet, this is no longer the case. Given the prevalence of WiFi (usually free in many locations – shopping malls, restaurants, bars and so on) across the globe, the individual no longer has to worry about having a fixed connection point or even a paid subscription to a service provider. The speed of data transmission and download on these devices has also increased dramatically, allowing consumers to capture information more quickly and in a more 'readable' manner than was the case previously.

The retail sector also is beginning to capitalize on the opportunities provided by such developments. Imagine you are walking through a major shopping mall. Your smartphone bleeps. You take it out and see that you have received a message from Zara. The message runs along these lines.

> **66** *Hi Maria, we would like to invite you into our store today. We have special offers running on our new collection of blouses that came into our store yesterday. We see that you purchased a similar item when you were last in our store and we want to flag up this offer which lasts until tonight. You can save up to 20 per cent on these items. Why don't you call in and see for yourself?* **99**

As you close the message you look up and realize that you are opposite the main entrance to the Zara store. You think to yourself: 'I might as well call in. Ten minutes won't take too much out of my schedule and I might get a bargain.'

This scenario is increasingly becoming commonplace in many retail environments and we can see how retailers can use technology to direct individual and personalized messages to the shopper as opposed to the more generic, unfocused promotions that traditionally have existed in the past.

We can, of course, raise questions of whether the approach outlined in the above hypothetical scenario represents an intrusion into the shopper's life and whether it puts undue influence on whether or not that individual will make a purchase. The reality, however, suggests that this will become a regular element of designing and implementing price promotions.

This is brought about by the developments in mobile technology and the ability to link data held by the retailer on an individual's shopping patterns and behaviour to trigger a message to the smartphone. The likelihood of getting a shopper to make a purchase in such a scenario is far higher than might be the case with a conventional print advertisement in the local newspaper identifying special deals or printing specific coupons.

The other lesson that we can learn from this example is that it occurs in real time. Let us think about the implications of this for a moment. The individual in this case is walking through a shopping mall; therefore, there is every expectation that this individual has shopping considerations at the forefront of her mind.

A trigger such as the one outlined, when she walks past the Zara store, will certainly capture her attention and because she is outside the store is likely to encourage her to step inside and visit the area where the blouses are on display. It is also likely that she might purchase two blouses in order to benefit from the special limited offer (it finishes that night). She may also purchase complementary items.

This happens in real time and takes advantage of the fact that the individual is mentally thinking about shopping and visiting certain outlets or stores in the shopping mall. The end result is a happy customer and a happy retailer!

As software develops, we can see also that retailers can link up information captured at various customer touchpoints in relation to their engagement across different channels, social media platforms and visits to physical stores.

Retailers are also making more proactive and strategic use of mobile apps to target customers with information. This allows for daily communications with shoppers who have downloaded such apps and special offers and discounts can be communicated again in real time to such shoppers.

Grewal et al. (2012) cite the example of Amazon that created an app called Price Check. This allows shoppers to check prices at physical stores. If they then make a purchase of the product that they checked out via this app, Amazon gives them an extra 5 per cent off their purchases (up to a maximum of $5). The use of such apps, pioneered initially by Apple and its iPad, has led to an explosion of usage among shoppers. Brynjolfsson et al. (2013: 24) note that 74 per cent of US smartphone users used their phones to obtain location-based information in 2012. They also use the following examples to highlight how retailers are taking advantage of opportunities created by location-based applications.

> **66** *Walgreens, for example, has teamed up with Foursquare, a location-based social networking website, to offer customers electronic coupons on their phones the moment they enter a Walgreens store. Saks Fifth Avenue has also worked with Foursquare to steer consumers toward physical locations by offering goodies (such as high-end brand Nars lipstick). Macy's offers free Wi-Fi in its stores; consumers can scan QR codes on products to see online product reviews, prices and exclusive video content on fashion trends, advice and tips.* **99**

These examples highlight the possibilities of retailers collaborating with relevant third-party facilitators. This can create even more focused price promotion strategies that can be aimed at specific stores or locations.

9.10.3 Retailer-based technology enablers

Mobile technology opens up opportunities for retailers to engage in a 'two-way' process with shoppers. This takes place largely outside the physical stores and outlets. Other technology enablers that can be located within stores can also enhance the shopper experience and generate price-oriented strategies as well.

Grewal et al. (2011) highlight numerous examples, some of which we look at here. For instance, retailers like Staples and CVS have made extensive use of interactive, stand-alone kiosks within the store. In this instance, shoppers can use the kiosks to print off loyalty programme reward coupons. They can also connect customers with the retailer's online website in the event of items in the physical store being out of stock.

Electronic shelf labels (ESLs) make it much easier and efficient for retailers to implement frequent and 'real-time' price changes so that shoppers can clearly see the changes and take up any offers or discounts. This is particularly relevant for dynamic pricing – a technique that we look at more closely in a later section in this chapter.

Ever more sophisticated technologies such as eye-tracking technology can allow retailers to track eye movements and reactions to certain stimuli. In the context of price-related activities, retailers can check shoppers' reactions to the placement of price signals on shelves. It can also be used to potentially great effect with regard to the item placement on planograms; that is, the position of special offers/discounts on the shelves (top, bottom or middle).

This section has examined some of the critical trends and developments and how they have (or are likely to) impact on shopper behaviour with particular reference to pricing. Some of these developments, mainly in technology, are either in their infancy or are capable of more sophisticated and more detailed levels of implementation. They undoubtedly provide retailers with challenges and opportunities in their quest to generate more sales and profit. In the next section we consider some of the approaches to pricing that can be found in the retail sector.

9.10.4 Impact of the Internet on retail pricing strategy

As we noted earlier in this chapter, retailers are gradually embracing the concept of omni channels. This is a step up from the use of multi channels. The latter implies that a retailer operates a number of channels; for example, physical stores, online channel and call centre. However, each operates autonomously from each other. Omni channels, however, recognize that shoppers engage with the retailer across a number of different touchpoints (channels) during the course of the purchasing process. There is a need, therefore, to ensure that the shopper receives a consistent and seamless experience across the touchpoints. For instance, it is not acceptable to find that a shopper visits a store and sees an item that they wish to purchase at a later date only to discover when going to the online channel that the item is out of stock.

In the context of pricing, retailers have to make decisions about the approach they adopt towards price-setting (Kaufman et al., 2009). Do they charge the same price across the different channels in a uniform way? Do they vary price across individual stores and online? How are customers likely to react? Does it damage profitability? What implications does it have for existing stores? Are as many of them needed as before?

Many retailers follow the principle of *price discrimination*; that is, charging different prices for the same product to different segments of customers across the different retail channels. This is based on the presumption that some shoppers prefer to pay a little more for the product in a physical store setting, in return for the advice and expertise proffered by the salesperson. This reassures them and the perceived risk (especially with expensive or technological products) is reduced. Others prefer to purchase online and benefit from a lower price in return for less service and expertise.

As noted earlier, shoppers tend to dip in and out of channels throughout the buying process. One effect of this phenomenon is that in many situations shoppers are using the physical store to learn about the products from demonstrations and advice. They then seek out the cheaper price at the retailer's online site. More worryingly, they may purchase the item from a competitor as they use their smartphone applications to help them identify a cheaper price. This suggests that retailers have to adopt a flexible and transparent approach to pricing as opposed to one that is based on rigidity and designed to protect an existing channel. This may mean that in the longer term, for instance, a retailer may have to carry out an audit of the viability of its existing physical store portfolio and engage in some rationalization.

The issue is complicated by the fact that the online and physical channels have different cost structures. The former avoids the costs associated with operating a number of physical stores (rent, staffing, heating, lighting and so on). By contrast, online channels require investment in the management of inventory, transportation and delivery. Retailers have some flexibility in factoring these costs into the ultimate price that is charged to the shopper. For instance, delivery may be free or tiered. In the latter case, shoppers may be asked to pay for delivery within a specified time period from the placement and payment of the order; for example, four hours, as opposed to next day delivery that might be free.

Employing a unified pricing strategy across the different channels is likely to prove very difficult in practice. Issues such as geographic distance between stores, different cost structures, availability of inventory and different tax systems inevitably means that some differences are likely.

Retailers have to manage their reputation also and this can be challenging as they may vary their prices across the different channels. This can create confusion in the minds of shoppers and act as a source of irritation if they see a lower price on the online channel than they actually paid when they bought the item in the store (see Luo and Chung, 2010; Yan, 2008).

The increasing use of technology, by both retailers and shoppers, leads to more interactive shopping. This phenomenon is characterized by shoppers playing a more proactive role in determining the eventual selling price of the item or service. Early examples of this include retailers like Priceline.com and the European charter airline LTU. The latter operator offers a 'bid and fly' system.

Retailers are also making use of online auctions to generate business. While this is used more extensively in business-to-business markets, retailers see the benefits of such an approach because it affords the shopper the opportunity to interact with others in determining the ultimate value of an item of merchandise (Kashef et al. 2014).

Spann et al. (2012: 141) engaged in some interesting research in this area. They concluded that:

> **"**bidders tend to view a bid-elicitation mechanism not merely as a means of expressing their bids, but also as a source of information about both the offered product (e.g., its quality or market value) and the retailer (e.g., what bid amounts might be acceptable).**"**

We are likely to see more of this type of interactive shopping over the coming years.

Online retailers offer the perennial '365/24/7' value proposition. Online shoppers are not restricted to opening and closing hours and can interact and engage whenever and wherever they choose to do so. The ability of retailers to offer real time, dynamic price promotions that can be altered almost immediately, also creates opportunities for shoppers to benefit from lower prices. This is likely to be negated somewhat, however, as retailers increasingly adopt digital technology and electronic shelf labels in store. As a consequence, such offers and promotions can also be proffered in the physical stores as well.

In summary, there is no simple answer to the impact of online channels on retail pricing strategy. The increasing move towards omni channels and the propensity of shoppers to flit between different channels means that retailers have to substantially revise their overall thinking with regard to retail strategy in general and pricing in particular. If there is too much of a difference between prices online and offline, then the long-term viability of many of the physical stores may be threatened. Many of these premises in the 'worst case scenario' would effectively become showrooms where shoppers learn about the brands and then purchase elsewhere. The value proposition has to be revised in this case or store rationalization is inevitable in many sectors of retailing. However, many shoppers enjoy the social aspect of shopping and it would be too simplistic to suggest that 'bricks-and-mortar' outlets will disappear. This allows retailers to generate some price discrimination across the channels to take account of the different cost structures.

9.11 Case in point: Dixons and electronic shelf labels

Dixon Retail plc, a UK-based multi-channel electrical goods retailer, began working with a third-party specialist on electronic shelf labels in a number of their stores in late 2013. This is a departure from the traditional printed shelf-edge labels that have been a feature of many retail stores over the years. Electronic shelf labels have a number of potential advantages. First, they eliminate printing costs and staff time (in terms of placing the labels on the shelves, updating them and taking them down when the promotion finishes). Special offers such as price deals, price matching and promotions can be updated automatically and in real time. This contrasts with the time needed to roll out a price promotion using traditional printed material.

'The trial is taking place across 10 categories at the Dixons 2,100sqm Currys & PC World store in Aylesbury, with the project being managed by the Herbert Group, who are a leading productivity solutions provider to retailers, and the UK partner for Pricer. The Pricer labels that have been deployed comprise of the new family of High Definition Pricer SmartTAGs (SmartTAG HD), which offer fine resolution for text and graphics rendering, along with 170 degree wide viewing angle, and industry leading low reflection in all lighting conditions. Utilising enhanced diffuse infrared technology for wireless label updates, Pricer SmartTAG technology is fast to update information and does not suffer from interference from in-store radio frequency, which is particularly important in a mixed electrical product store environment.

'Raj Sangha, Business Development Manager at Herbert, commented: "Until now, in-store merchandising has been limited in its responsiveness to changes in the market place and consumer dynamics, and is generally reactive rather than adaptive. An ESL solution, such as the Pricer SmartTAGs that we installed for Dixons Retail, provides the ability to implement an adaptive and engaging merchandising strategy, adding real value to bricks and mortar stores."

'Simon Swanborough, Project Manager at Dixons Retail, commented: "We're excited to be trialling ESLs in our Aylesbury store. We hope this new generation of shelf edge labels will drive even greater ▶

◀ customer confidence in our pricing, as well as provide further information at the point of purchase to help customers make informed choices. As the new technology is used more widely, we hope to see customers interacting with these through their smartphones and QR codes, or by using social media to 'like' particular products. The technology provided through Herbert gives us the chance to look at how ESLs can work across the store for both customers and colleagues, and we look forward to hearing what our customers think."'

Source: Dixons Retail deploys cutting-edge Pricer electronic shelf labels. *Retail Technology Review*. 27 November, 2013.

9.12 Approaches to pricing in the retail sector

We consider in this section some popular approaches to pricing that are used by retailers. We also look at newer techniques that have emerged in recent years, mainly due to the developments in the areas of technology and data collection and integration that we discussed in earlier sections.

9.12.1 Everyday low pricing (EDLP)

This approach to pricing is based on the presumption that the price of every product in the store will be as low as possible on a daily basis. This takes account of competitors' pricing and the objective is to match if not beat them across the various categories of merchandise in the store. Wal-Mart is often credited as the 'father' of this approach.

Variations on this approach often occur. For instance, some retailers do not try to keep low prices on all products in the store. Instead, retailers may instigate this policy for a selected range of items and aggressively match or beat the competition on these items.

This approach rules out the notion of using regular sales as a ploy to attract customers into the store. One positive outcome from this approach is that it steers shoppers away from the notion of 'predictable discounting'. This happens where shoppers become conditioned to the view that if they wait a bit longer before making a purchase, the retailer will have a sale where the item will cost less. If EDLP is implemented and communicated clearly, there is a strong possibility that the shopper will not be so certain about potential sales and price reductions. However, if it is applied aggressively, it can create an ever-downward spiral of price decreases, especially if competitors reduce their prices and the retailer (in order to deliver on its promise of EDLP) reduces its prices as well. In the worst case scenario, this actually damages the integrity of the brands and the overall reputation of the retailer.

9.12.2 Hi-Lo

This approach advocates the use of sales periods to stimulate and boost store traffic and turnover. The retailer in this case will alternate prices on specific levels between regular 'high' levels and 'low' sales levels. This is in contrast to the EDLP approach that keeps away from price promotions on the basis that prices are consistently low. Smith (2012) makes the observation that EDLP shoppers tend to have a stronger expectation about prices. This may be explained by the fact that they routinely see the same prices on the shelves.

Hi-Lo operators tend to attract shoppers with a higher willingness to pay. This, in part, might be explained by their relative lack of conditioning about the likely prices. By contrast, EDLP shoppers tend to buy more items (a bigger shopping basket).

Much will depend on the nature of the product being sold. Relatively complex items that require more input from the salesperson in the physical store and thus require higher levels of personal interaction with the potential buyer may be less suited to the EDLP approach.

9.12.3 Markdowns

Markdowns are a constant feature across all retail formats and operations. They are effectively reductions in the price of items that reflect their present market position. They are inevitable because it is impossible to be 100 per cent accurate in forecasting likely demand for an item or particular product category. Some retail sectors are very volatile and unpredictable (for example, fashion). There are some factors that we cannot control (for example, the weather). In the latter case, particularly in countries that have varied weather patterns, a wet summer means that people may not buy summer clothes. The end result for the retailer is unsold stock. Markdowns are a method of clearing such stock out of the system and generating a revenue stream, albeit less than what was planned originally.

Some markdowns are acceptable, particularly if they are caused by factors outside the control of the company. Some, however, are not acceptable. These may occur because of poor forecasting and inventory management, items ordered due to the personal preferences of the owner or buyer and not supported by any hard evidence that there is a demand for such items, careless presentation and handling of items in the store resulting in shop-soiled items that have to be reduced in price. They can also occur due to poor pricing: overestimating the price that people are willing to pay or pricing too low and creating suspicion about the quality or worth of the item in the mind of the shopper.

In order to avoid a situation where shoppers become conditioned to markdowns and price reductions, retailers need to communicate clearly why the price has been reduced, otherwise they are perceived as regular and predictable discounts. Such items should be placed at the back of the store in an attempt to encourage shoppers to buy extra or complementary items during their visit.

More efficient forecasting and inventory management can reduce the extent of markdowns. Fast-fashion retailers such as Zara are good examples of retailers who do not make the mistake of carrying large volumes of merchandise, thus running the risk of being left with them on the shelves.

9.12.4 Dynamic pricing models

This approach to pricing is gaining greater currency and importance within the retail sector in recent years. This is a direct result of technology and software enablers that allow retailers to capture much more accurate and 'live' information on demand patterns. Retailers use information captured from company enterprise resource planning systems and Internet purchasing patterns to set the price. This allows for frequent updates on pricing and adjustments that reflect demand in real time. Airlines and hotels (operating in service sectors that are perishable and not capable of being stored) have been at the forefront in the use of dynamic pricing tools.

Companies such as SAP and Oracle have developed software that allows organizations to carry out detailed analysis of data to track purchase patterns and estimate price elasticities (the relative sensitivity to price changes). The use of bar scanners, online purchases and other point-of-sales data capture tools and, more importantly, the integration of such data allows retailers to project demand through the use of price analytic software. Nagle et al. (2011) further note that the online channels used by many retailers are the ideal vehicle for conducting price experiments and special offers. Sales patterns from such sites are captured automatically and can be analysed immediately, allowing for price adjustments to be made quickly and transparently on the website.

Generally, commentators are positive about the likely improvements that retailers can generate in terms of more accurate and relevant pricing structures. However Nagle et al. (2011) inject a note of caution by stating that dynamic pricing models are based on historical data and may not necessarily take account of changes in the future patterns of demand.

9.12.5 Subscription-based promotions

Grewal et al. (2011) cite the example of online retailers such as Gilt, RueLaLa and Hautelook who offer a limited set of fashion products for limited time periods to select groups of customers who must subscribe to that site. There are variations on this approach. For instance, some allow subscriptions only after they have been proposed and invited by another subscriber. This heightens the sense of exclusivity and the offers may only be available for a very limited period; for example, one day or less. Other variations include rewards for existing subscribers if they introduce another potential subscriber.

9.12.6 Markup pricing

This refers to the difference between the cost of an item and its selling price. The markup added to the cost price makes up the retail price. For instance, a retailer may purchase a bar of soap for £1. It seeks a 50 per cent markup. This is calculated by multiplying the cost price (£1) by the markup. This gives us a figure of 50p. Add this to the cost price and the selling price is £1.50. The margin, however, is different. In this case in order to get a margin of 50 per cent the retailer would need to sell the bar of soap at £2. This is because half of the selling price gives the margin. Margin is defined as the percentage of the selling price that is profit. The markup is the amount over the cost of the goods that you add to give the selling price. Some commentators refer to this approach as cost-plus pricing.

9.13 Case in point: IKEA

IKEA, the global household furniture retailer, provides an interesting example of how a retailer can address the issue of providing lower prices than the competition to its customers. It adopts a holistic view of its business operations and constantly seeks out areas where greater efficiencies can be achieved. This is not necessarily based on making the ready-to-assemble furniture cheaper. Let us examine how they achieve the overall effect of lower prices.

IKEA was one of the pioneering retailers to focus on the challenge of recycling merchandise. Each store has an 'AS-IS' section. The Recovery Department plays a strong role here. Careful examination of items both in the store and in various distribution points and depots allows IKEA to place such merchandise in this section. It affords shoppers the opportunity to pick up bargains that are serviceable and are available at a lower cost than non-damaged items.

Customers also place unwanted items in various collection bins in the stores. These items are examined and various parts are salvaged and sold as 'spares'.

IKEA's designers and engineers strive to reduce the amount of material used and wasted in production. Additionally, many waste products are then used to make new products. This helps to reduce the overall cost and makes a potentially significant contribution to the environmental challenge.

IKEA places (relatively speaking) less emphasis on the role of personal selling and customer advice within its stores. It takes the view that customers do not need too much 'hand-holding' and relies instead on the 'self-service' concept that the shopper will take the initiative. It works on the assumption that shoppers also 'do their homework' before coming to the store. This generates savings in terms of reduced wages. This also extends to the provision of customer services. While generating the potential risk of higher complaints and accusations of customer service, it has a potentially positive and significant impact on the cost structure.

The corporate culture of IKEA revolves around the concept of thriftiness. This is driven by the values of its founder, Ingvar Kamprad, who always flies in economy class and insists on his senior management team doing likewise. This thrifty concept permeates through to all management personnel across the company: they are encouraged to turn off lights and be on the alert to identify areas where energy savings can be generated.

IKEA addresses the issue of design entirely from its in-house personnel. It has been widely acclaimed for offering affordable and trendy furniture items. By relying on its in-house designers, it avoids the large costs associated with outsourcing the task to third-party agencies.

Because of the sheer scale of its global operations, IKEA can enter into advantageous relationships with its supply base. In return for offering long-term, large contracts, it can extract beneficial price arrangements. This leaves IKEA in a strong position when developing its overall retail pricing strategy.

As might be expected, transportation contributes in a major way to the cost structure of most retailers, particularly given the multi-site nature of their operations. IKEA eschews expensive modes of transportation such as air. Instead, it focuses on the use of container cargo and the use of tractor trailers to move products around its distribution centres and stores. IKEA also uses sophisticated software to help it to make decisions about the locations of distribution centres and stores in order to maximize efficiencies and keep costs to the minimum.

The issue of location of its stores in particular addresses the cost structure. Nearly all of its stores are located in high-density areas of population and just off junctions to motorways. This allows IKEA to benefit from very high levels of store traffic or 'footfall'. This is further helped by the fact that in most countries shoppers are prepared to travel long distances to an IKEA store, hence the benefit of locating just off the motorway. Warehouses are located quite close to stores. This also reduces the potential exposure to higher costs.

The standard use of plain brown cardboard as packaging is also a clear indicator of IKEA's desire to keep costs to the minimum. Such packaging is cheap, easy to use and can be wrapped around any form of its ready-to-assemble furniture items.

IKEA uses wordless instruction materials. This generates considerable savings as it eliminates the need to translate the written word to the native languages of the many nations in which IKEA operates.

Source: based on: http://www.ikeafans.com/ikea/ikea-why-ikea/10-keys-to-ikeas-low-prices.html. This link is no longer available as it was taken down by IKEA. The retailer felt that the owners of this site had breached the proper use of trademarks associated with IKEA. See http://arstechnica.com/tech-policy/2014/07/ikea-lawyers-stay-busy-policing-the-web-as-they-take-on-ikeafans-com/ for a fuller explanation for this move.

Discussion question

1 Examine the extent to which you agree with the view that the influence of the founder has profound implications for the subsequent approach to pricing. What happens when he dies?

9.14 Conclusions

In this chapter we have examined the role that retail pricing formulation and implementation plays in shaping overall retail marketing strategy. We noted that we cannot treat pricing decisions, structures and policies in isolation from the other aspects of the retail marketing mix. Pricing has profound implications for retail positioning, brand image and segmentation.

The challenges facing retailers on the issue of pricing are large and complex. Many commentators note that it is one of the least understood elements of marketing and that organizations consistently employ techniques that do not necessarily reflect the realities of the marketplace and, as a consequence, show a lack of understanding of the consumer's perceptions, attitudes and opinions on price and the role that it plays in their purchasing behaviour.

The nature of retailing, particularly in the context of large retailers, produces its own set of challenges and opportunities. Large retailers operate in multi-site locations and through different retail formats (both physical and online). They carry very large volumes of merchandise and operate in diverse economic and geographic locations. Charging uniform prices may not be the appropriate way to structure pricing policies and we noted the increasing tendency of some retailers, particularly in the supermarket category to introduce pricing based on equity or fairness in order to account for low-income versus high-income areas.

We recognized that retailers also are in a relatively strong position to take advantage of the recent trends and developments in the general marketplace. Social media platforms, the Internet and mobile technology, allied to technology enablers and the ability to capture and analyse vast quantities of information, potentially place 'smart' retailers in a strong position to design focused, personalized value-based and customer-centred pricing strategies. The challenge lies in 'making sense' of the data and communicating promotions and deals clearly and transparently, using relevant platforms to the target market on a customized basis.

Suppliers can also become involved in this exercise through various collaborative ventures. For instance, data collected by the retailer can determine price elasticities of shoppers and quantify their proneness to deals or sales promotions. Such information can be shared with manufacturers in order to maximize such campaigns.

In the introduction we quoted the views of Ogilvy (1983) and stated that we would revisit the relevance of that statement at the end of this chapter. In the intervening years, it is reasonable to conclude that the trends and developments in areas such as technology, software and data analysis have created the opportunity for retailers to become more strategic and proactive in their ability to develop customer-centric pricing strategies. The question is: are they doing it?

Chapter outcomes

- The retail sector faces specific challenges with regard to pricing due to the multi-site, multi-format nature of its operations.
- Too many retailers focus on unidimensional issues such as cost or competitive-based pricing and do not take sufficient account of the most important stakeholder of all: the end user.
- Retailers need to fully understand the concept of value and embed it into their value proposition.
- Pricing should start with the customer, not the internal operations of the retailer.
- Developments in social media, the Internet and mobile technology have altered the way in which the shopper engages with retailers. This extends to their perceptions, opinions and attitudes to price.
- Smart retailers are making proactive use of technology enablers to capture more customized, focused and relevant data on their target market's demand and purchasing patterns.
- This potentially allows retailers to become more flexible and proactive in setting prices.
- This potentially can reduce the level of predictability that often exists with price promotions, markdowns and sales.
- Such developments can help retailers manage their inventory more efficiently and establish more effective collaborative relationships with their suppliers.

Discussion questions

1 Assess the appropriateness of a cost-focused approach to pricing for a small, independent retailer running a jewellery shop in a prime shopping street in your city.

2 Examine the extent to which you would agree with the view that developments in social media platforms and price comparison sites mean that the shopper now is in a stronger position to negotiate price with the retailer. Use examples to support your point of view.

3 Should retailers be concerned about the need to introduce markdowns as part of their pricing strategies? Share your views on this issue.

4 Critically assess the proposition that retailers will increasingly intrude into the lives of shoppers by sending them unwanted price promotions through smartphones and apps.

5 Some people argue that intuition can still play an important part in shaping pricing policies. Indicate the extent to which you would agree with this perception.

6 Select a retailer of your choice. Visit its online channel. Make an assessment of the way in which it communicates price promotions and special offers to its target market. How might they improve this aspect of the online channel?

7 Assess the advantages and disadvantages of utilizing dynamic pricing in a retail context. Use a detailed example to support your point of view.

References

Betancourt, R. (2004) *The Economics of Retailing and Distribution*. Cheltenham: Elgar Publishing Ltd.

Brynjolfsson, E., Hu, J. and Rahman, M.S. (2013) Competing in the age of omnichannel retailing. *Sloan Management Review*. Summer: 23–29.

Cram, T. (2006) *Smarter Pricing: How to Capture More Value in your Market*. Harlow: Prentice Hall/Financial Times.

Edwards, H. (2012) Opinion. *Marketing*. 13 June.

Grewal, D., Ailawadi, K.L., Gauri, D., Hall, K., Kopalle, P. and Robertson, J.R. (2011) Innovations in retail pricing and promotions. *Journal of Retailing*. 87(S): 43–52.

Grewal, D., Roggeveen, A.L., Compeau, L.D. and Levy, M. (2012) Retail value-based strategies: new times, new technologies, new consumers. *Journal of Retailing*. 88(1): 1–6.

Hamilton, R. and Chernev, A. (2013) Low prices are just the beginning: price image in retail management. *Journal of Marketing*. 77 (November): 1–20.

Kashef, A.M., Bryant, A. and Rau, P.A. (2014) 'Name your price' – online auctions and reference prices. *Journal of Product & Brand Management*. 23(6): 420–428.

Kaufman, R.J., Lee, D., Lee, J. and Yoo, B. (2009) A hybrid firm's pricing strategic in electronic commerce under channel migration. *International Journal of Electronic Commerce*. 14(1): 11–54.

Kopalle, P., Biswas, D., Chintagunta, P.K., Fan, J., Pauwels, K., Ratchford, B.T. and Sills, J.A. (2009) Retailer pricing and competitive effects. *Journal of Retailing*. 85(1): 56–70.

Luo, W. and Chung, Q.B. (2010) Retailer reputation and online pricing strategy. *Journal of Computer Information Systems*. 50(4): 50–56.

Ma, Y., Ailawadi, K.L., Gauri, D. and Grewal, D. (2011) An empirical investigation of the impact of gasoline prices on grocery shopping behavior. *Journal of Marketing*. 75 (March): 18–35.

Macdivitt, H. and Wilkinson, M. (2011) *Value-based Pricing: Drive Sales and Boost Your Bottom Line by Creating, Communicating and Capturing Customer Value*. Boston, MA: McGraw-Hill Education.

Marn, M.V., Roegner, E.V. and Zawada, C.C. (2003) Pricing new products. *McKinsey Quarterly*. August.

Murthi, B.P.S. and Rao, R.C. (2012) Price awareness and consumers: use of deals in brand choice. *Journal of Retailing*. 88(1): 34–48.

Nagle, T., Hogan, J.E. and Zale, J. (2011) *The Strategy and Tactics of Pricing: A Guide to Growing More Profitably*. 5th edn. Boston, MA: Pearson.

Ogilvy, D. (1983) *Ogilvie on Advertising*. London: Pan.

Piercy, N.F., Cravens, D.W. and Lane, N. (2010) Thinking strategically about pricing decisions. *Journal of Business Strategy*. 31(5): 38–48.

Pulter, S. (2012) Tailor-made Tescos! Stores will adapt product range and deals to suit affluence of the area. Available online at: http://www.dailymail.co.uk/news/article-2090377/Tesco-shake-Firm-adapt-product-range-deals-suit-affluence-area.html#ixzz2xXniXS2c 23 January (accessed March 2015).

Shankar, V. and Bolton, R.N. (2004) An empirical analysis of determinants of retailer pricing strategy. *Management Science*. 23(1): 28–49.

Smith, T.J. (2012) *Pricing Strategy: Setting Price Levels, Managing Price Discounts, and Establishing Price Structures*. Boston, MA: South-Western/Cengage Learning.

Spann, M., Haubl, G., Skiera, B. and Bernhardt, M. (2012) Bid elicitation interfaces and bidding behaviour in rational interactive pricing. *Journal of Retailing*. 88(1): 131–144.

Yan, R. (2008) Pricing strategy for companies with mixed online and traditional retailing distribution markets. *Journal of Product & Brand Management*. 17(1): 48–56.

Chapter 10

Designing and implementing effective marketing communications strategies

☑ Learning objectives

On completion of this chapter you should be able to address the following objectives:

☑ Understand the different retail marketing communications objectives that are employed by retailers.

☑ Examine the main components of the marketing communications mix.

☑ Assess the relevance and impact of the 'new' communications tools.

☑ Evaluate the use of celebrities in endorsing the retailer's image and product range.

☑ Examine the role of online advertising.

☑ Assess the role of personal selling.

☑ Examine the concept of co-operative advertising and promotion.

☑ Assess the role of online communities and their role in building relationships between customers and retailers.

10.1 Introduction

Marketing communications is a critical part of the overall retail marketing mix. No matter how strong the value proposition put forward by the retailer, it will fail to register in the mind of its targeted audience unless it is clearly communicated to them via relevant media channels.

In this chapter we examine the key elements of the retail communications mix. Like many aspects of retail marketing, developments in the areas of technology in general and social media in particular have forced retailers to reappraise the way in which they interact with shoppers. As we shall see later in this chapter, a range of alternative new media options have opened up both opportunities and challenges for retailers. In particular, some of the traditional communications channels such as TV, radio and print advertising are undergoing forensic analysis in terms of their continuing usefulness and relevance in the broader context of retailers 'getting their message across to their target market(s)'.

In an increasingly changing environment where shoppers are changing the way in which they engage with television, communicate with family, friends and wider members of their social network and pursue leisure and entertainment, retailers still have to grapple with the challenge of attracting and retaining customers. While the overall objectives may remain the same, changing social and lifestyle trends mean that they have to set out to achieve the objectives with a different approach and mindset to that which may have worked effectively in a previous era. We examine these changing trends and developments with respect to their implications for communication strategy in this chapter.

Traditional communications models were based on the supposition that the relationship between organizations and consumers was 'one-way': they generated a message that was then directed at the intended audience via various communications channels. Consumers then decoded the message and (hopefully) responded in an appropriate manner; that is, they made a purchase or became aware of a particular brand or value proposition.

Developments in the area of social media however have turned this model on its head. Instead of the communications being one-way, consumers can actively choose to engage with the organization through expressing their views and opinions on particular social media platforms. This has led to organizations in general recognizing the need to 'hold conversations' with and listen to the views of their target markets. We examine the implications of this shift in the nature of the relationship between customers and organizations.

We can no longer assume, particularly in a dynamic business sector such as retailing, that consumers are passive in nature and are the mere recipients of various communications messages and cues that are sent from the organization.

In an era of global retailing where the emphasis is on cost efficiencies and reduction across the supply chain while at the same time improving the quality of the value proposition, retailers are increasingly questioning the appropriateness and validity of the various dimensions of the retail marketing communications mix. This is most evident in the context of setting communications budgets and allocating resources in the most effective way across the communications channels. These developments provide the background for our analysis and investigation of retail marketing communications in this chapter.

This chapter focuses on communications as it relates to initiatives that are external to the store. In Chapter 5 (Managing the selling environment), we considered the challenges of managing in-store communications.

10.2 Retail marketing communications objectives

As is the case with any aspect of strategy development and formulation, we need to assess the various marketing communications objectives that set the scene and direction of the message. When we consider the various categories of objectives, we should link our analysis to issues raised in earlier chapters on positioning and brand-building and development.

10.2.1 Image-related objectives

1 **Positioning**: the way in which retailers wish to be positioned in the mind of their target market(s) sets the overall agenda for their various marketing communications messages. In order to build a brand identity, they need a simple and transparent proposition to bring to the marketplace. For example, Hugo Boss, the global fashion retailer, positions its brand as an upmarket clothing retailer. This sets the tone for its subsequent range of brand designs and its marketing communications (www. investis.com/boss/pdf/en/f_hugobossgroup). As we noted in Chapter 2, in order to establish and reinforce this desired position, it has to achieve a strong level of consistency in its retail communications activities.

2 **Lifestyle**: some retailers, particularly in the upmarket and luxury end of the market, try to align their brand values with a particular lifestyle exhibited by their target market. Retailers such as Gucci, Cartier and Louis Vuitton cultivate an image for their intended target market that is designed to make them feel part of a high-value, exclusive club. This can be achieved by purchasing merchandise that signifies such membership by the prominent appearance of the logo/label on the product.

3 **Low-cost**: low-priced products sold on the basis of high volume and low margins form the cornerstone of marketing communications messages for many retailers. Primark constantly reinforces this message through its communications activities. Although it engages in relatively little formal advertising, the slogan 'look good pay less' features prominently in its messages. These four words encapsulate the brand essence of Primark: it sells attractive-looking merchandise at low prices. This theme is reinforced by the styles and range of merchandise sold: Primark does not claim to sell high-quality items.

Image-related objectives such as those identified earlier, address the longer-term strategy of the retailer and its operations. As well as setting the agenda, it provides a boundary for all of its marketing communications activities. Any initiative that steps outside of the overall image of the retailer is likely to send 'mixed messages' to the target market. At best, it will confuse them and at worst it can alienate them. It could be argued that Marks & Spencer has fallen into this trap in recent years. The question as to who is its target market is difficult to answer if we consider some of its recent promotional campaigns.

Vignette: Marks & Spencer

In late 2013 Marks & Spencer developed an advertising campaign based on the use of a number of so-called 'iconic' ladies such as actresses, sportswomen and models. Featured ladies included: the actress Helen Mirren, Olympic gold winner medallist Nicola Adams, the artist Tracey Emin and the ballet dancer Darcy Bussell. It spent over £5 million on the campaign, mainly based on TV and print advertising. Two years previously it ran a similar type of campaign featuring Myleene Klass, Twiggy, Dannii Minogue, the singer VV Brown and the Brazilian model, Ana Beatrix Barros. Neither approach appears to have worked.

The use of such a diverse range of women sent mixed messages to the typical Marks & Spencer female shoppers. They tend to be middle-aged and middle-class and somewhat conservative. Controversial figures such as Tracey Emin did not necessarily resonate with such an audience.

The retailer has struggled in the women's clothing area. Part of its problems would appear to rest with the identification of its target market. It has attempted over the years, through a new fashion line (Per Una range), upgrades and store redesigns and the development of its online retail channel, to appeal to a younger market. Yet many of its advertising campaigns would appear to be aimed at the middle-aged, middle-income woman.

Source: Craven, N. (2013) 'Make or break' M&S ad blitz is a £5 million flop as middle class women turn against Tracey Emin. Available online at: http://www.dailymail.co.uk/femail/article-2456916/Make-break-M-amp-S-ad-blitz-5-million-flop-middle-class-women-turn-Tracey-Emin.html#ixzz2yrRxrmJe)

Question

1 Using Internet sources, assess the following statement: Marks & Spencer will continue to struggle in the women's clothing range until it clearly identifies its target market as long as it continues with this type of advertising that appears to rely on celebrities only.

10.2.2 Sales-related objectives

We can consider a number of such objectives in this section.

1 **Building sales volume**: many retailers develop specific communications strategies in order to build sales volume. This can be achieved by focusing on sales promotions and can take a number of different forms. Some promotions focus on price and are built around a limited number of items. We referred to the concept of loss leaders in our chapter on pricing. Good examples of this approach can be found in the food retailing and electrical retailing sectors. Such promotional campaigns can be run by the retailer operating alone or as part of a co-operative promotional approach (working with one or a selected number of suppliers).

2 **Building customer traffic**: a key element in building sales revolves around attracting or pulling visitors to the store website. This can be achieved through a number of communications techniques. The launch of new product lines or the summer collection (in the case of fashion retailers) can form the basis of an advertising campaign or a social media strategy in order to generate traffic. The use of a celebrity can also feature in an advertising strategy to attract customers.

3 **Increasing sales through loyal customers**: as we noted in Chapter 6, customer loyalty programmes can identify shoppers by different categories of expenditure. Direct and customized marketing communications can be directed at such customers offering various incentives to purchase extra items or 'trade up' to more expensive merchandise.

10.2.3 Corporate social responsibility-related objectives

1 **Good citizenship**: in an effort to be seen as good corporate citizens, retailers may engage in initiatives designed to portray them in a positive light in the communities within which they serve and

operate. This can range from providing computers to schools located in socially deprived areas in a city to more strategic activities. For instance, IKEA is a key partner in UNICEF's global activities, particularly with regard to the rights of children. It is active in India and works with UNICEF on various child protection initiatives. Much of the communications activities in these instances revolve around public relations. If implemented properly, such campaigns can generate an abundance of 'good news stories' and project a retailer in a positive light. It can be argued that it may be necessary in order to counteract negative publicity that a retailer may generate about its activities.

2 **Ethics**: retailers are often criticized for their approach to global sourcing and in particular for abusing their power by using suppliers who have questionable practices with regard to using child labour or operating in unsafe working conditions. Many large retailers publish a code of ethics with regard to their policies in dealing with suppliers and signing contracts.

3 **Climate change**: retailers address this issue and many take proactive action in order to comply with government agencies. An example of this is taken from a recent study. Woolworths (South Africa) is meeting the growing pressure from customers to address climate change. The company uses its website, social media, magazines and in-store marketing campaigns to communicate its efforts to stakeholders. It has embarked on a new relationship with the environmentally focused TV programme 50/50, and was behind an expedition up Mount Kilimanjaro in January 2011 to create awareness around the impact of climate change on coffee farmers in Tanzania (Sustainalytics, 2012).

4 **Social issues**: retailers can focus on social issues and include them as part of their marketing communications strategies. Perhaps the best exponent of this has been Benetton, the Italian fashion retailer (Sanderson, 2012). It became famous (or infamous!) throughout the 1980s and 1990s for its controversial and hard-hitting print and billboard advertising campaigns. These ranged from featuring prisoners on 'death row' in the USA to a mercenary holding the thigh bone of a war victim in his hands to a man in a suit walking through a flood in India holding a briefcase and a picture of a man on the point of dying of AIDS in his hospital bed. Such controversial messages enraged some elements of society. Benetton remained unapologetic, arguing that it saw one of its functions being to highlight social inequity and victimization of the poor and deprived.

10.3 Components of retail integrated marketing communications

In this section we consider the makeup of the various elements of the retail communications mix.

Schultz et al. (2012) identify the broad range of communications channels that are available to organizations in their quest to design an integrated strategy. It is important that we recognize the relevance of the word 'integrated' when we refer to retail communications strategies. First, it recognizes that retailers are likely to use a combination of tools at various times to get across their message to their target market. One method alone is unlikely to achieve the necessary effect. Second, it recognizes the need to achieve consistency and coherence across the various communications initiatives.

Figure 10.1 identifies three interlocking elements that constitute the communications mix. We consider each briefly and examine them in greater detail throughout the course of the chapter.

10.3.1 Traditional media channels

These channels refer to the typical channels that organizations including retailers have used for decades to communicate their message to a target audience. Many of them allow for one-way communication; that is, the sender of the message pushes out the communication via the channel to the recipient. There is little opportunity for the receiver of the message to interact with the sender. The assumption is that the message is received and decoded by the recipient. However, this is debatable as it assumes that the message has been received, encoded and interpreted by the receiver. In an increasingly complex world, it

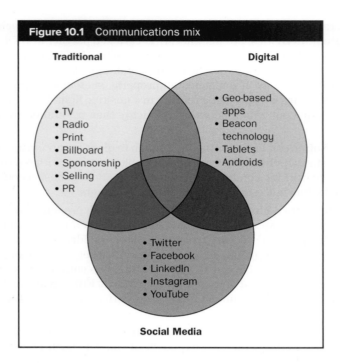

Figure 10.1 Communications mix

seems to be a big assumption that this will happen on a regular basis. The average consumer is exposed to so many forms of communication on a daily basis that the end result is often one of confusion, misinterpretation and a failure to register in the mind of the shopper.

The other common feature with many traditional media channels is the lack of focus and customization with regard to the message. It cost $4 million to book a 30-second advertising slot during Superbowl (the major US football final in the USA) in 2014. This would have exposed the brand to over 112 million TV viewers in the USA. In terms of reach and coverage, it covers a large number of individuals. However, it is a typical form of mass advertising and does not present much opportunity to customize or target any single individual.

10.3.2 Digital media channels

These channels essentially facilitate information to be stored and transmitted electronically and encoded digitally. Such technologies allow retailers to capture data on shoppers, track purchase patterns and use such information to develop customized messages that can be tailored to each individual. Developments in mobile technology such as smartphones and tablets facilitate two-way communication. This is in sharp contrast to the 'information-push' approach of the traditional media channels such as radio and print advertising.

The most commonly used digital media by shoppers are email and Internet search. Further developments such as Internet Protocol TV (IPTV) create opportunities for greater engagement and interaction. We can see this in the context of the way in which people are beginning to change their habits in relation to consuming sport: subscription channels like Sky and ESPN are increasingly adding larger content and data for download and interaction.

10.3.3 Social media channels

Typically, such channels involve third-party operators who have created and operate platforms such as Facebook, Twitter and LinkedIn. Schultz et al. (2012) note that such platforms were not set up originally to facilitate commercial activities and communications. Instead, they were designed for use as social interaction tools among friends and small social networks. The attractions for commercial organizations such as retailers became obvious, one aspect being the ability to engage with customers and monitor various views, opinions and experiences through the postings and contributions to such platforms.

We assess the benefits and dangers of using such platforms as part of the retail marketing communications mix in greater detail later in the chapter.

The framework developed by Schultz et al. (2012) does not include a specific reference to communications tools such as sponsorship, sales promotions and public relations. We should also include tools such as WOM advertising and viral/buzz marketing. Such methods typically involve using social media platforms to generate awareness, interest and excitement in a brand by using video clips, a narrative (story) or interactive games. Like the analogy of a virus, the message spreads across the social network sites among friends, work colleagues and so on. The end result of a successful viral marketing campaign is heightened awareness and interest in the brand at little or no cost (when compared to paid advertising) to the retailer.

Vignette: Edeka

Germany's largest supermarket chain, Edeka, created a YouTube video featuring a song in which its private brands are being referred to as 'supergeil' – which can mean both super-cool, or super-horny. German electro-pop musician and actor Friedrich Liechtenstein performed the song. The video quickly went viral, reaching over 8 million views so far, and even attracting an international fan base. Buzzfeed in the US called it 'The Most Gloriously Entertaining Commercial You'll See Today'.

Unsurprisingly, the campaign was most successful in reaching younger people. Almost half of all German 18–30 year olds who were aware of the Edeka brand, were aware of the Edeka advertising after 'supergeil' took off. This is an all-time high since the beginning of 2013 and during the course of the campaign this age group registered a higher level of awareness with Edeka than competitor Rewe or German discounters like Lidl or Aldi. Twentysomethings' perception of Edeka also beat out the other German food retailers since the video started to take off, so successfully, about a month ago.

Source: http://www.brandindex.com/article/german-food-retailer-edeka-lands-viral-marketing-hit-0, 1 April 2014.

Question

   1 Do you believe that such a viral marketing campaign has any value in terms of the longer term?

The relevance and contribution of the social media platforms

Perhaps the most significant development in business over the last 10 years or so has been the exponential growth in the use of social media platforms by consumers and organizations. This permeates through all aspects of engagement between the two parties. In this section we consider the contribution of social media platforms to retail marketing communications.

Mangold and Faulds (2009: 358) define social media:

> **❝** *Social media encompasses a wide range of online, word-of-mouth forums including blogs, company sponsored discussion boards and chat rooms, consumer-to-consumer e-mail, consumer product or service ratings websites and forums, Internet discussion boards and forums, moblogs (sites containing digital audio, images, movies, or photographs), and social networking websites, to name a few.* **❞**

The most commonly used social media platforms used by marketers are identified in Table 10.1. We should inject a note of caution when reviewing these figures. First, a US consultancy group undertook this research and it reflects a snapshot of the position as it stood in 2014. As we know, the usage of social media platforms is likely to vary across different geographic regions. Second, they reflect usage by both Business-to-Business (B2B) and Business-to-Consumer (B2C) companies. This report suggests that B2C-focused marketers (this would include the retail sector) are more likely to use platforms such as Facebook, YouTube, Pinterest and Instagram. Twitter, of course, features very prominently with B2C marketers.

Interestingly, B2C marketers expressed the desire in this survey to learn more about Facebook, Pinternest and Instagram. This suggests that there are more opportunities to exploit with such platforms in the context of interacting with their respective target markets (see Kunz and Hackworth, 2011). It is likely that since 2014 other platforms may emerge to act as attractive alternatives to the existing options.

The list of social media platforms in Table 10.1 contains a diverse range including ones that are created and generated by companies, created and developed by third-party organizations and ones that are designed to allow for networking between individuals. Due to the dynamic and constantly changing nature of social media, by the time you read this chapter it is entirely possible that many of the platforms listed here will have disappeared and been replaced by newer and more innovative channels.

Schmidt and Ralph (2011) identify four different categories of social media.

1 **Social network or online communities**: Facebook, YouTube and MySpace are the most prominent of such platforms. They allow individuals to create their own accounts and subsequently share information, music, videos and so on with friends or followers (people who have joined their group). Companies have also moved into this space and many have set up their own Facebook page to engage and connect with individuals who are interested in or loyal to their particular value proposition.

2 **Blogs**: this form of social network has permeated across many aspects of life from politics, music and entertainment through to brands and retail. Within the context of the retail sector, many people

Table 10.1 The retail marketing communications mix

Facebook	94%
Twitter	83%
LinkedIn	71%
YouTube	57%
Blogging	55%
Google+	54%
Pinterest	47%
Instagram	28%
Social review sites (e.g. Yelp)	17%
Forums	13%
Geo-location (e.g. Foursquare)	12%
Social bookmarking (e.g. Reddit)	11%
Short-form video (i.e. Vine)	9%
Podcasting	6%
Snapchat	1%

Source: Social Media Examiner (2014: 23)

create their own online space to share their thoughts, views and experience on a particular retailer or a particular service encounter that they have had in a particular store. Like-minded individuals can read these blogs and post their views and comments. From the perspective of the shopper, it can create an environment where, as a result of reading and participating in such blogs, the individual can feel more informed about issues that pertain to the retailer or to a particular purchase decision.

3 **Microblogs**: this variant of more traditional blogs recognizes that people do not necessarily want to or have the time to read long articles or text messages. Twitter is the most popular platform as it restricts the individual to a specific number of words in any one message. It allows for constant and more frequent engagement between people.

4 **Really simple syndication (RSS)**: this tool is increasingly gaining in popularity and acts as an alert to people who subscribe to it about key information or developments from certain websites that the individual is particularly interested in. It means that there is no need for the individual to have to continuously visit a range of sites and scroll through the various web pages to get to that point of interest. A good example in the retail context would be where a retailer periodically puts up special offers and promotions on its website. An RSS alerts the shopper.

Since the emergence of social media platforms (see Table 10.2), a number of developments have occurred in parallel. As the platforms have developed and attracted more and more followers and participants and grown globally, they have become an attractive vehicle for advertising. Such activity is referred to as search (engine) advertising. It allows advertisers to monitor specific statistics such as the number of people that visited the site, clicked on the various features and went further and sought further information or actually completed a sale. This analysis provides far more detail and rigour than the general data that can be captured from traditional advertising campaigns (TV, radio and so on).

While much of the information and communication is generated by users and customers, companies in general and retailers in particular have also created social media platforms or have become active participants in established ones in order to send messages to their target audience. More importantly, retailers can now interact and engage with customers. By establishing Facebook pages and generating a vast number of fans/followers, they can fulfil a number of objectives that are not necessarily possible with traditional communications channels. These are summarized as follows:

- linking to and engaging with consumers who share common interests
- responding to common concerns, perceptions and opinions
- tracking shoppers' search, evaluation and purchase patterns
- monitoring the shopper's experiences with the retailer (both positive and negative)
- generating instant and continuous data (marketing research)
- building confidence and trust among shoppers
- using social media to communicate sales promotions at slow periods of the year
- encouraging shoppers to come up with new ideas for products

Table 10.2 Monthly active users (Globally)

Facebook	1.15 billion
Google	359 million
Twitter	215 million
Instagram	150 million
Pinternet	20 million
Reddit	2 million

Source: Morrison (2014)

- reinforcing and strengthening brand values by connecting with shoppers
- shaping and influencing shoppers' purchases (based on the information captured)
- identifying shoppers' proneness to special offers and sales promotions (level of price or bargain sensitivity)
- creating and sending individualized messages to the shopper (in contrast to traditional media platforms)
- stimulating interest, desire and excitement among shoppers (for example, competitions, 'teaser' campaigns and submissions by shoppers).

Kunz et al. (2011) cite some examples of retailers who have made effective use of social media platforms. For instance, Dell, the computer technology company, has made extensive use of Twitter for a number of years to connect with its customers. In addition to building its brand, it has also generated sales. This is exemplified by its periodic 'Twitter Only' special offers where thousands of its followers get an exclusive offer on various Dell products and services.

10.4.1 Benefits of social media platforms for shoppers

Shoppers can benefit from participating on social media channels in the following ways:

- access information about specific retailers, brands and special offers
- contribute views and opinions about shopping experiences
- learn from other like-minded shoppers
- engage in comparison pricing and information on retailers and brands
- develop a personalized relationship with fellow shoppers and the retailer
- save time and benefit from the convenience of being able to 'visit' the retail store in a virtual sense
- get some preferential treatment from retailers by virtue of being a follower or fan in the form of special offers or previews of upcoming product launches
- feel more confident about making purchases (particularly high-involvement, high-value ones) either online or when visiting a physical store
- feel a sense of belonging and being part of a community.

10.4.2 Potential dangers of using social media channels as part of the retail communication mix

We have highlighted the main features and benefits associated with social media channels from the perspective of the retailer and the shopper. Our focus in this chapter is on the way that retailers can utilize such channels for the purposes of marketing communications. We also need to consider the potential limitations and dangers associated with using such platforms as part of the communications process.

One of the distinguishing features of many social media platforms is that they have open access in various forms. This can range from fully open; that is, anyone can participate or read material, to sites where people have to subscribe (no charge or payment). This issue of openness also raises the question of control. With many traditional communications channels, the retailer has control over the design, format and content of the message that is being sent. This is not necessarily the case if social media platforms are used. The message can be altered or altered in such a way that may lead to the brand itself being damaged. This raises serious questions for retailers.

Communications via social media can lead to criticism from members or followers. This can generate a large amount of negative comments and posts and in some cases such content can be offensive in nature. How can retailers control such a situation? For instance, should a Facebook page that is created by the retailer be moderated? Should negative criticism be removed? Should it be used as a learning experience or a form of marketing research?

Fournier and Avery (2011: 206) provide some interesting discussion and analysis of the problems associated with social media. In particular, they highlight the changing environment where 'we've moved from a world where the brand set the agenda, to a world where consumers decide if – and when – brands are invited in'.

This raises a fundamental issue for both retailers and consumers. While social media platforms appear to be designed for retailers to communicate their brand values and their value proposition in a focused and individualized manner, they were created in the first instance for people and for interaction between friends and the wider social network.

It could be argued that companies in general, including retailers, have forced or manoeuvred their way into such platforms and have tried to manipulate the relationship to suit their particular agenda. Hence, the title of Fournier and Avery's book, *The Uninvited Brand*.

It could be further argued that this invasion is not alone unwanted but also threatens the privacy and personal space of consumers. By subscribing to Facebook for instance, an individual allows organizations (in most cases unknowingly) to monitor and track their contributions and search behaviour. Such activities by retailers draw criticism from various consumer groups and may in some cases work against them.

Retailers have to be careful about dealing with the negative aspects of social media platforms. Due to their open and largely unregulated nature, it is important to have a strategy in place to deal with such crises and emergencies.

There is no 'one-size-fits-all' approach. However, adopting a policy of transparency and honesty can help to overcome negative publicity or comment on social media platforms. Any attempt to obfuscate or mislead shoppers is likely in the longer term to cost a retailer customers and business. Shoppers are more informed and proactive in their dealings with retailers and are not as prepared as previous generations to put up with such behaviour.

In cases where the negative comments or views expressed are offensive or inflammatory, retailers have to take action and remove such contributions. On a more positive note, retailers can adopt a proactive approach to negative communication from customers on social media platforms and use it to reshape various aspects of their strategy. Ignoring it or pretending that it has not happened only exacerbates the problem and will lead to ever-greater longer-term damage. By offering a solution to the problems or issues raised by followers, the retailer can address the crisis. Clear communication of offers and products that are of real value to the shopper enhance the relationship between the two parties. On the other hand, confusing and potentially misleading communications can sour the relationship and lead to increased levels of cynicism and dissatisfaction.

Activity

A well-known discount retailer in the furniture sector is encountering numerous critical comments on its Facebook page about its sourcing policy. The sheer volume of such posts has built up over the past month and the chief executive officer (CEO) feels that it has come about because of a TV programme about its sourcing policies. The negative comments centre on allegations that it has used suppliers in southern Asia who have been accused of using children to manufacture the products. You have been asked to advise the CEO as to how his company can implement a social media communications strategy to prevent any further damage. Detail the advice that you would provide.

10.4.3 Summary

In the preceding section we considered the advantages and disadvantages of social media in the context of retail marketing communications.

Research by Schultz et al. (2012) suggests that while there is strong evidence to support the level of consumer interest in social media, the actual impact of the use of such platforms is problematic. More worryingly from the perspective of retailers, their research suggests that shoppers are potentially becoming less loyal to a specific store or outlet. The abundance of digital technologies allows people to access information and make comparisons between retailers on issues such as price, range and quality of merchandise and customer service policies. Arguably, this will increase as digital technologies widen their appeal and usage globally.

Vignette: Hugo Boss

Hugo Boss, the German apparel and accessories retailer, was one of the earliest fashion retailers to actively use social media platforms to connect and interact with its target markets. It has done so in an imaginative and creative manner. For instance, in 2012 it made use of 3D technology in the launch of its Fall/Winter collection, Boss Black Fall/Winter 2012, from Beijing via a live stream video. The video and all of the promoted merchandise contained in the launch were also in 3D.

The subsequent launch of the video was available on Hugo Boss's website in the 'Fashion Show' section and all of the images, video and text were in 3D. Customers could also engage with additional material that did not feature at the fashion show. Hugo Boss also included competitions on the site with various prizes on offer to participants.

Hugo Boss also made the Boss Black 3D campaign social-oriented with tie-ins across multiple social media channels. On Facebook, Hugo Boss took advantage of the new Facebook Timeline to inform visitors about the live stream fashion show. Images on the Hugo Boss Facebook page were in 3D, helping to add additional fun and excitement to the campaign.

Hugo Boss continued its promotion for the 3D fashion show with its Facebook posts. It posted links to the 3D hub on its website, and its posts engaged and conversed with visitors about the event. It created a storyline for the event, developing 3D videos teasing viewers about different elements taking part in the fashion show. The videos were hosted on YouTube, playing within a Hugo Boss branded YouTube player and linked to from Facebook.

Hugo Boss tied in these social media elements to its 3D fashion show campaign. Typically, most brands would separate each media outlet (web, Facebook, YouTube) and either develop a separate content for each or post the same content for each. Hugo Boss, however, created a true integrated campaign and used each outlet based on how its consumers were using them. Consumers used YouTube simply to see videos, so any video content for the campaign lives within YouTube. Consumers used Facebook to see what their friends and favourite brands were up to, so Hugo Boss posted links that directed consumers to their website hub while making the content engaging and shareable. Finally, consumers were using the Hugo Boss fashion show website hub to see rich content, flash animations, models and the latest fashions – something they were not doing in other media outlets at the time.

Sources: Adapted from bryannagy.com, Hugo Boss uses an Integrated 3D Social Media Campaign, 28 April 2012 and Lamb, J. (2011) Why Hugo Boss is a social media king. *Luxury Daily*, 14 January

10.5   Word-of-mouth (WOM), buzz and viral marketing

This section considers how retailers can make use of relatively inexpensive, informal and interactive tools in order to get across the message to its target market. Word-of-mouth is a tool that presents both challenges and opportunities for retailers. While other elements of the marketing communications mix have a relatively high level of control (the retailer determines the content and structure of a TV advertisement), WOM by contrast cannot be fully controlled and in the worst case scenario can run totally out of control (bad publicity over unethical sourcing). As we noted from our discussion in Chapter 2 shoppers, particularly with high-involvement purchases, use their family, friends and colleagues as sources of advice and guidance. Positive WOM about a particular retailer and its merchandise, customer service, price levels and so on, can play a significant part in influencing the subsequent purchase decision. Advice, recommendations and guidance from such a personal and intimate source is often much more effective than traditional forms of advertising (TV, print, radio and so on).

Retailers can use creativity to stimulate WOM in a number of different ways. For instance, viral marketing allows retailers to generate interest, curiosity, excitement, discussion or visits to websites. People share their views, 'spread the word' and generally become wrapped up in the excitement. Within a short period of time and like a virus, the message spreads and can play a significant role in the communications mix.

Vignette: Topshop

Topshop, the UK fashion retailer, attracted more than two million people to its live streamed fashion show at London Fashion Week on Sunday, with the retailer claiming to sell out of some lines during the broadcast. The show, streamed live on Facebook, allowed users to share their favourite looks with friends using the social network. Viewers used 'open graph' technology allowing them to post messages about the Topshop show, called 'Unique', automatically on Facebook and Twitter. The retailer trended globally on the latter social networking site. Topshop reported that some items, including a printed panel dress, sold out within an hour and that traffic to Topshop.com from the USA, where it has just opened boutiques in Nordstrom department stores, reached a record level.

Source: http://www.digitalstrategyconsulting.com/intelligence/2012/11/viral_video_marketing_case_studies_the_best_virals_of_2012

Campaigns such as the one highlighted by the example of Topshop are often referred to as buzz or viral marketing campaigns. They bring customers and branders together, revolving around a particular activity or theme. In the case of Topshop, this retailer made effective use of social media platforms to drive the message and generate buzz globally among its target market.

Buzz or viral marketing is a good example of how a retailer can integrate the message with other elements of the marketing communications mix. The costs associated with viral marketing campaigns are much lower than some of the more conventional communications tools.

10.6 Role of personal selling

For many organizations personal selling plays a critical role in the marketing communications mix. Retailing is no different. The Internet and the growth of online channels may be seen as a threat to physical (bricks-and-mortar) stores and, by implication, the personal selling function. For high-involvement products (fashion, electrical, IT, luxury brands and so on), the retail salesperson can still influence and shape the purchase experience. In such situations, the online channel may be used by shoppers to gain some information about the merchandise, price points and so on before they go to the retail store to make the actual purchase. It can also work in reverse: shoppers may seek the advice and expertise of retail salespeople about product options, demonstrations of different models or product warranties and then visit the website to make the actual purchase.

In Chapter 7 we considered the issue of customer service, and product knowledge and customer empathy are fundamental aspects. They also impinge on the sales function in a retail store. Arguably, the growth in multiple or omni channels has changed the nature of the relationship between shopper and salesperson.

Vanheems, Kelly and Stevenson (2013) note that this change may be exhibited in situations where the salesperson is no longer 'the sole keeper of knowledge': the customer has done the homework on the Internet prior to a visit to the store. Far from being a passive player in the engagement with the retail salesperson, the customer demonstrates some knowledge and understanding of the respective competitive offerings. It is possible that in many cases the function of selling may differ. Likewise, the role of the salesperson may change in the context of the engagement or interaction with the shopper. They need to be adept at using technology such as tablets and augmented reality to engage with shoppers and provide the necessary advice and expertise.

It can also be argued that salespeople may become disillusioned by the advent of online channels where the shopper purchases the items and threatens the very existence of the sales function.

The role that the salesperson plays in reinforcing the retailer's brand image cannot be underestimated. When the shopper visits the retailer's online channel, they expect a similar level of consistency when they subsequently visit the store and engage with a salesperson. Any variation in the experience can create dissatisfaction in the mind of the shopper.

Salespeople within the store need to become more adaptable in their engagements with customers. Vanheems et al. (2013) found that they increasingly engage with the website and customer in the store and accompany the shopper through various parts of the website. This may help in jogging the shopper's memory about issues that they may have considered earlier when visiting the website. It can also be used effectively by the salesperson to verify information about a particular item, its price point, warranty details and so on. The combination of the salesperson, the customer and the website can create a reassuring atmosphere. It can also help salespeople if they want to highlight items that may not be available in that particular store.

The role of the salesperson as mentor, coach and adviser increases in light of the changing nature of the engagement. A visit to an Apple store demonstrates this point. The Apple in-store personnel are available to visitors to the store if needed. They do not engage in the central act of selling. In many cases they sit down with the shopper and steer them through a demonstration of a particular model. They act clearly as advisers or coaches, particularly in extending the knowledge of a shopper or highlighting features that are not all that clear on the Apple online channel.

In summary, personal selling still plays a significant role for many retailers in the overall marketing communications process. While the sales function may be undergoing some changes, the activities and responsibilities are critical in:

- reinforcing the overall retail brand image and positioning
- reassuring the shopper and ensuring consistency in the overall purchase experience
- steering the shopper to specific items in the store or promotional offers.

10.7   Retailers and sponsorship

Sponsorship is another element of the marketing communications mix that presents opportunities for retailers to get across their message to their target markets. Sponsorship is about a retailer investing in a particular event or organization to support and communicate its overall marketing objectives, its marketing and promotional goals. Most of the sponsorship takes place in the areas of sports, the arts and community-based activities, with sport attracting the largest proportion of investment.

Sponsorship allows a retailer to align its brand values and attributes with a similar entity or brand. Retailers can also use the particular sponsorship to engage with their target market through a range of activities such as competitions, entertainment and participation in order to maximize the marketing opportunity and create a positive experience for the customers.

The type of sponsorship a retailer will engage in is largely dependent on its overall objectives. Spar International represents a partnership of independent retailers and wholesalers that operates in over 35 stores worldwide with over 13,000 stores. It commenced operation in the Netherlands in 1935 and operates a number of different formats throughout the various countries, ranging from convenience stores to hypermarkets and mid-range supermarkets. It also uses a number of sub-brands such as Eurospar and Superspar. It has successfully expanded into major markets such as China, Russia and India.

Spar's core values revolve around freshness, quality and customer service. Since 1996 it has been a sponsor of European athletics. It sees the sport of athletics as being synonymous with health, fitness and overall wellbeing. This provides a strategic fit with Spar's own emphasis on providing nutritious products to its customers. It has sponsored many of the European Athletics Cross-Country championships. In 2014 this event was staged in Samokov, Bulgaria.

In order to leverage the maximum amount of benefit and exposure from sponsoring such events, Spar (2014), as principal sponsor of European athletics:

> **❝***aims to always be visibly present onsite during each international event. To do this we have developed the SPAR Nutrition Zone concept whereby visitors can join in the fun with games*

and creative activities with us. Through sharing fun food facts, the SPAR Nutrition Zone aims to provide a thorough understanding of nutrition so that both current and future generations learn how healthy eating can contribute to growth and development.

A cornerstone of athletics is the running element, ranging from 60-metre sprints to marathons of 42 kilometres. Many Spar (2014) partners offer opportunities for running clubs to meet at their stores, making this very accessible to all consumers.

The European Athletics events of which SPAR is principal sponsor comprise three elements – indoor/outdoor and cross-country, spanning the entire year of competition. We work with the national partner in each country to develop maximum awareness of the sponsorship and the critical link with individual athletes who are also consumers of independent retailers. We are proud to be involved with European Athletics, an organization which strives to bring passion and enthusiasm for their sport to viewers, spectators and participants.

We can see from this example how a retailer can use sponsorship to good effect. For instance, it associates its brand values with a sport that also has similar associations and attributes. This creates many opportunities for 'good news stories' that can be built around the retailer's involvement with the event. In the case of Spar, individual stores can sponsor local, community-based athletics events. This allows the retailer to establish its community-based credentials and involvement. With the growing emphasis being placed on corporate social responsibility, such activities can project the image of the retailer as a good 'corporate citizen' to good effect.

10.8 Sales promotions

Sales promotions are used by retailers to stimulate a response from shoppers within the in-store or online retail environment. In both cases the shopper tends to be in a 'purchasing mode of behaviour'. Whether walking through the physical store or navigating around the web page, the shopper is either actively looking for information to help with the purchase decision or is in a frame of mind to purchase merchandise.

Promotions can fulfil the objective of attracting shoppers into the store and explore various parts of it to learn more about what is on offer. Likewise on websites, retailers will also use such initiatives to tempt shoppers to make purchases and benefit from either price or non-price deals.

Within the physical store environment, retailers make use of banners, shelf labels, 'bus-stop' signs (print material in the shape of a bus-stop sign) and 'Toblerones' (stands in the shape of the Toblerone chocolate brand) to highlight to shoppers special offers and deals and to direct them to the relevant part of the shelf or aisle. Sales promotions can be split into price and non-price promotions.

Lee (2002: 104) notes that 'price-oriented promotions include price discounts, coupons and rebates. Non-price-oriented promotions include free samples, sweepstakes, contests and premium user programmes.'

From a retail perspective, retailers can use sales promotions to push sales of selected product categories. They can also use promotions to shift stock that is not moving off the shelves as quickly as they would like.

Suppliers also work closely with retailers in this area. For instance, when a supplier is launching a new product, it will liaise with the retailer and set up a promotional strategy based on price or non-price factors. The retailer provides the 'platform' or environment for the supplier to advertise and promote the new product. Suppliers may also focus on seasonal products; that is, items related to Christmas, Eid, Halloween or Easter.

As we discussed in Chapter 4, the relationship between retailers and suppliers revolves around such promotional initiatives. Retailers are keen to participate in promotions; they help to attract interest and attention on the part of shoppers and provide extra reasons as to why shoppers should patronize their store.

Increasingly, retailers are looking for 'differentiated promotions'. In our interview with Kevin McNally from P&G in Chapter 4, we see the importance of trying to get away from constant and incessant price promotions and instead seek out more innovative and creative promotions. By building a promotion around a particular event such as the World Cup, Olympics or Commonwealth Games, both suppliers and retailers can heighten the level of excitement and interest among shoppers.

While the recession has forced retailers to use price-focused promotions, the challenge of making the promotion stand out from the competition has encouraged retailers and suppliers to seek non-price-dominated promotions.

We noted in Chapter 4 that retailers and manufacturers are key players in the supply chain. This can cause conflict and co-operation between the two parties. In the case of marketing communications, there are opportunities for retailers and manufacturers to co-operate and benefit from such initiatives.

Roslow, Laskey and Nicholls (1993) note that the challenge for manufacturers is to develop and build the brand whereas for retailers there is a strong need to increase traffic through the stores. Dominant retailers, because of the power that they wield in the supply chain, can put pressure on certain categories of suppliers (challenger brands) to participate in promotions and advertising. Suppliers similarly in a dominant position can also leverage pressure on retailers to engage in similar activities.

The increase in the ability of retailers to capture data on shoppers' expenditure patterns, brand preferences and propensity to respond to special offers makes the notion of co-operative promotions and advertising more attractive. Such co-operative initiatives work on the principle that the manufacturer pays for some or all of the costs of local advertising. It benefits from potentially increased sales and greater brand awareness while the retailer uses the advertising campaign to attract more traffic to the store. Similarly, a manufacturer may be launching a new product and involve a retailer in a joint sales promotion campaign; for example, a special price offer for a limited period only or a 'buy one get one free' strategy, again for a limited time. If there is a true sense of trust and co-operation, both parties can gain mutual benefits from such campaigns. However, in some cases distrust and suspicion are more common features of the relationship. Fears over sharing information about customers may militate against focused sales promotions for example. Manufacturers may feel that they have been pressurized into such initiatives and may not get much benefit.

10.9   Public relations

All organizations are tasked with the challenge of managing relationships with their key 'publics'. By this term, we mean the various stakeholders that directly or indirectly can shape, influence or affect the image and perception of the organization. Retailers are no different.

Phillips (2006: 212) cites a definition from a well-known practitioner in the field on the scope and remit of public relations. 'Public relations is the management, through communication, of perceptions and strategic relationships between an organisation and its internal and external stakeholders for mutual benefit and a greater social order' (Valin, 2004). The key words in this definition are 'perception' and 'relationships'. Public relations (PR) is fundamentally about managing the perceptions that people and organizations hold about the retailer. It is also about assiduously developing and maintaining relationships with stakeholders so that the retailer projects a positive image.

Retailers in particular often generate negative publicity among the various publics. For instance, Tesco and Wal-Mart have been heavily criticized for various activities such as perceived worker exploitation and low wages in the case of the latter and a dominant market position that has 'killed off' small retailers in the case of the former.

Other retailers such as Primark have been accused of implementing unethical and exploitative sourcing strategies. McDonald's has had to ward off allegations of foisting unhealthy food on society in general and young people in particular.

As we observed earlier in this chapter, the era of corporate social responsibility has well and truly become established. This ensures that retailers have to be very careful in terms of managing publicity, particularly negative issues that emerge in the media.

Managing public relationships revolves around projecting the business in the best possible light and minimizing any negative publicity that may arise from the retailer's activities.

Starbucks is a good example of a retailer who has engendered criticism in the media. In recent years in the UK, Starbucks has received adverse publicity for not apparently paying appropriate taxes and employing a scheme that allows the company to circumvent paying too much in tax. In 2013 it introduced an initiative called 'suspended coffee'. If a customer buys this product, Starbucks will contribute the value of the purchase to its charity partner, Oasis, who, in turn, will distribute it through its community hubs in the UK. It was originally introduced in its outlets in the Italian market.

This is an example of an initiative that generates some positive comments and a degree of warmth about the brand. It is a relatively low-cost strategy that can help to negate potential adverse publicity.

Arguably, the role of public relations takes on even greater significance in an environment that is increasingly being driven by social media platforms. In situations where negative comments and experiences are posted by consumers, retailers have to be vigilant about handling such situations.

10.10 The effectiveness of traditional communications media

While retailers are increasingly widening their marketing communications budget to include expenditure on the so-called 'new media tools' such as social media, they also continue to be major users of traditional marketing communications media such as TV, print and radio. In this section we consider the effectiveness of such tools in a changing environment.

Danaher and Dagger (2013) note that CEOs are indicating a shift in focus from traditional media tools to increased use of social media and online advertising. While it is difficult in every case to fully assess the effectiveness of a particular marketing communications initiative, such a shift indicates at the very least that organizations are reappraising their approach to the use of traditional media communications in light of developments that we discussed in the previous section.

The issue of assessing the effectiveness of marketing communications is made more complex by the fact that many organizations do not rely on a single method; instead, they utilize a number of different tools to get their message across to their respective target markets.

Danaher and Dagger made extensive use of data captured from a retailer's customer database and loyalty programme to compare the effectiveness of multiple media. Although based on one detailed case study, the extent and detail of the data allowed for some interesting and detailed analysis of customers' responses to various communications initiatives (spread over 10 different media, both traditional and new, and run as a blitz campaign over one month). They found that seven of the ten media used generated retail purchase incidence and outcomes (increased sales and increased profits) during the course of the one-month campaign. Interestingly, the most effective communications channels all came from the so-called 'traditional' area: catalogues, TV and direct mail. The radio channel also proved to be successful.

Clearly, we have to be careful in interpreting the findings from this research. First, it was based on only one (albeit detailed) case study. As a consequence, some of the findings are likely to be specific to that retailer, given the nature of its business, the scale of its operations and its location (Australia). Second, in this particular case, shoppers could not make a purchase via an online channel, thus weakening the likely impact of online advertising.

Although the new media channels did not prove to be that effective in terms of generating purchases and increased sales, the authors acknowledged that the medium of sponsored search (for example, Google) is effective, particularly in terms of the low costs associated with this medium.

Further research in this area is necessary before more accurate judgements can be made about the relative effectiveness (or otherwise) of the various media. This can be helped by the increasing availability of detailed customer information that can be gleaned from various sources such as loyalty programmes, online surveys and point-of-sale data capture.

Tuli, Mukherjee and Dekimpe (2012) note that advertising expenditure can often act as an important signal for investors. This is because it provides a proxy indication of the ability of the retailer to attract new customers or reinforce their value proposition to existing loyal shoppers. Their findings indicate that advertising expenditure has a significant positive impact only in situations where there is a presence of a large unanticipated increase in earnings. Otherwise, retailers can find it difficult to justify such expenditure when the retailer is experiencing a downturn in performance. This reinforces the often-held view that marketing budgets in general – and advertising budgets in particular – are the first area to experience cuts when companies are struggling.

Despite the increasing use of mobile and digital media, retailers still recognize that traditional tools such as TV, press and radio can address the issues of reach and coverage. This can be particularly relevant in instances where the retailer has marketing communication objectives such as reinforcement of the value proposition, promotion offers and increasing brand awareness.

Television as a medium is undergoing significant change. On a general level, we are witnessing the convergence of technology. For instance, is it accurate to describe our Android or iPhones as 'phones'? It can be strongly argued that this is a very narrow and inaccurate description of such products. A typical smartphone is an amalgamation of an entertainment centre, a repository of data, a word processor, a music centre, an interactive communications device and a phone. Similarly, the modern TV is also adopting many of these characteristics.

Internet Protocol Television (IPTV) has emerged as a viable technology that is slowly gaining traction in terms of popularity among consumers across geographic regions. Since 2014, the level of adoption varies considerably with the highest levels of penetration in France, Russia and China. In the UK, the adoption rate is around 5 per cent. It is not unrealistic to assume that TVs with instant access to the Internet allow for advertisers to engage in more interactive forms of communications with their respective target markets.

Radio advertising plays a significant role in keeping the name of the retailer at the forefront of shoppers' minds. Advertising on commercial radio channels also succeeds in getting the message to people as they travel to work and in many cases have to battle through the tedium of traffic jams. Retailers can also use the medium of radio to link the message to a particular promotional campaign that it is running. In some ways it can be seen as a useful medium for reinforcing the brand values of the retailer and complementing other campaigns in an integrated way.

Direct marketing tools such as flyers or leafleting are used by food retailers to let people know about a particular campaign. Leafleting to households plays an informational and reinforcement role about a campaign. When combined with in-store promotional material and signposting, it can work in an effective manner. The emergence of location-based apps and smartphone technology may lead to a reduction in the use of traditional direct marketing in the coming years. However, the basic principle of directly targeting shoppers with specific messages will continue.

10.11 Case in point: TV's reign over?

TV's reign over: ad spending to end after three decades

Television's hold on advertising budgets is beginning to falter, with forecasts indicating its share of global advertising is to peak after three decades of growth.

Television is expected to capture 40.2 per cent of the $532bn global ad market in 2013 before falling to 39.3 per cent of the total market in 2016, according to Publicis' ZenithOptimedia. WPP's GroupM is also predicting that TV's share of the global advertising market will decrease slightly in the coming year.

The transition is the result of digital media chipping away at television's dominance amid broader upheaval in the industry.

ZenithOptimedia forecasts that the Internet will boost its share of the ad market from 20.6 per cent in 2013 to 26.6 per cent in 2016. Within that category, mobile advertising will grow by an average of 50 per cent a year between 2013 and 2016, contributing 36 per cent of extra ad spending.

TV will account for 34 per cent of new ad spending, with newspapers and magazines declining by an average of 1 per cent and 2 per cent a year.

In recent years, marketers poured money into digital ads largely at the expense of print media. TV not only held its ground but grew as marketers sought to reach mass audiences.

That scale is tipping. While TV will still deliver growth in ad spending, digital media and the rise of online video are the real competitors for ad dollars, said Jonathan Barnard, ZenithOptimedia's head of forecasting. 'After television ad spending has grown pretty consistently for at least the last 35 years … there will be quite a lot of disruption to come over the next 10 years.'

Overall, mobile ads account for just 2.7 per cent of global ad spend in 2013 but are likely to rise to 7.7 per cent of the market by 2016, overtaking radio, magazines and outdoor ads.

Automated ad buying technologies are also forecast to gain traction. Interpublic's MagnaGlobal thinks ad spending funnelled via such systems will increase to $32bn in 2017, up from $12bn this year.

Forecasts for global ad spending vary, as lingering economic uncertainty clouds the outlook. ZenithOptimedia estimates global spending will increase 5.3 per cent in 2014 to $532bn, while GroupM has cut its growth estimate back to 4.6 per cent, from 5.1 per cent previously, to $531bn.

Source: Steel, E. (2013) TV's reign over ad spending to end after three decades. *Financial Times*. 8 December 2013

Question

1 Do you think that the overall picture presented in the above discussion case is applicable to the retail sector? Using the various search engines on the Internet, identify the main trends in media expenditure by the large global retailers.

10.12 Celebrities and endorsement in retailing

The use of celebrities drawn from the fields of sport, music, films and fashion is a common feature of many marketing communications initiatives developed by retailers. In this section we consider the pros and cons of using such individuals in promoting the retailer's message to its target market.

Celebrities are individuals who are well known to the general public for their achievements and performance in a particular field of activity. While many cultures and regions in today's global environment appear to be fixated and immersed in the concept of celebrity, the phenomenon is not a new creation of the twenty-first century (McCracken, 1989). As far back as the eighteenth century, an individual named Josiah Wedgewood worked as a potter in the UK and was a supplier to Her Majesty Queen Charlotte. He promoted his business as 'potter to Her Majesty' (Dukcevich, 2004). Since then a plethora of companies has used celebrities as a mechanism for endorsing their products (Erdogan, Baker and Tagg, 2001). The retail sector is probably one of the most extensive users of celebrities. The logic for designing a marketing communications initiative around such individuals revolves around three reasons:

■ **Credibility**: the belief that the celebrity has similar values and attributes that are closely associated with the brand values and attributes of the retailer. The target market also positively identifies with these values and attributes.

■ **Recognition**: the target market has a very high level of recognition when they see images of the celebrity.

■ **Popularity**: the celebrity generates high levels of positive opinions and perceptions.

As a consequence of using celebrities to endorse the retailer's value proposition, it is assumed that shoppers will be strongly influenced and exhibit a stronger tendency to patronize that retailer and be more disposed to purchasing merchandise.

The challenge for retailers revolves around making the correct selection of an appropriate celebrity endorser to build the advertising campaign around. The concept of source credibility plays a central role in shaping this decision. This concept revolves around two dimensions: expertness and trustworthiness. The former refers to the individual's knowledge, skill and expertise in a particular area (for example, Rory McIlroy and golf). The latter relates to the confidence levels of the shopper that the individual provides information about the product in an objective and honest fashion.

We have to be careful in interpreting the importance of source credibility. The earlier research in this area implicitly suggests that a celebrity can successfully endorse any product as long as they are credible and well liked by the target market. Silvera and Austad (2004) put forward the view that consumers are more positive about an advert or message if the celebrity is believed to truly relate to the product.

The concept of source attractiveness is also influential in shaping the selection decision. This revolves around three dimensions: familiarity (the extent of recognizability associated with the celebrity, likeability (the degree of affection generated by the celebrity in the mind of the consumer) and similarity (the extent to which the individual sees the celebrity as a mirror of themself). This also introduces the issue of the physical attractiveness of the celebrity and the way in which this can influence the behaviour and perceptions of the shopper.

Stallen et al. (2010) concluded from their research that positive feelings towards a celebrity are transferred to positive feelings about the brand. The ability to generate sales from the use of celebrities is the main reason why retailers engage in this form of marketing communication.

Critics of the source credibility and source attractiveness models argue that they do not place sufficient emphasis on the need for a strong relationship between the celebrity and the product or brand that is being endorsed. This leads to an alternative view that is referred to as the 'match-up' theory. Such a hypothesis argues that there should be a strong 'strategic fit' between the demographics and personality of the endorser with those of the brand. The issue of alignment is critical in this case. As well as the overt popularity and success of the celebrity, they must be perceived as empathizing strongly with the brand values and associations. The net result is a very positive perception in the mind of the shopper.

The net effect of a strong alignment between the endorser and the brand can also overcome negative or cynical perceptions that the celebrity is only engaging in the exercise to generate extra income. This can weaken the overall impact of the communications initiative. When selecting a potential endorser for a product, there is a danger that the brander will be influenced by the level of success of the celebrity. For instance, in the Indian market over the last 20 or so years, one sports celebrity has dominated the scene. His name is Sachin Tendulkar and is regarded by many as one of the best cricketers ever to play the game. At one point during the height of his popularity, it was estimated that he was endorsing over 300 brands. We would have to question the potential effectiveness of such endorsements in light of our comments in the preceding paragraph.

Another danger with the use of celebrity endorsement relates to the assumption that the celebrity will remain popular and successful over a prolonged period of time. In particular, sports athletes have a life cycle of success and performance. A dip in form, ageing and bad publicity or behaviour can clearly have an adverse impact on the perceptions that people may hold about that individual. In recent years, celebrities such as Tiger Woods and Lance Armstrong, iconic figures in their respective sports and indeed within society in general, experienced negative publicity that had a major impact on their image. This resulted in many branders dropping them from their advertising campaigns as they did not wish to be associated with such behaviour and negative publicity.

Research conducted by White, Goddard and Wilbur (2009) tentatively supports the view that the demise or decline in the image of the celebrity can engender negative perceptions about the particular brand that is being endorsed by that individual.

Some retailers are going beyond the basic practice of simply using celebrities to endorse their brand in an advertising campaign. In order to link the values and image of the endorser more closely to the merchandise sold by the retailer, some are using celebrities in a more strategic and potentially more proactive manner. For instance, River Island, the fashion retailer, has recently used Rihanna (singer) to design a range of merchandise. By involving her more fully in the retail strategy, it can be argued that they can generate greater awareness and popularity with their target market. It could, of course, be counter-argued that such an approach deflects attention away from the real challenge of coming up with designs and clothing that customers actually want.

In summary, the use of celebrities is a common practice by retailers. Generally, such an approach can work well in situations where there is a perceived high level of credibility and trustworthiness of the celebrity within the target market. The retailer has to be careful, when selecting a celebrity, that there is a strong alignment between the values and personality of the individual and the brand associations. This is likely to generate stronger and more positive perceptions.

10.13 Online retail channels as a marketing communications tool

We have already noted the growing importance of the Internet as an overall mechanism of doing business and engaging with customers. In this section we consider the Internet as an advertising medium and how retailers can make effective use of it to get their message across to existing and potential customers.

Based on the number of visits shoppers make to the website, the number of clicks they make and purchase patterns, companies can develop targeted and focused messages based on these behavioural characteristics.

In the context of retailing, we have noted that retailers increasingly use an online channel as part of their omni-channel strategy to attract shoppers, and provide a positive shopping experience that will attract shoppers back to that site. The online channel provides a logical mechanism for retailers to advertise their merchandise, direct shoppers to specific promotions and special offers, alert them to new product lines and generally provide a virtual environment for sharing information and interacting with their customers.

Because of the information about customers that is captured online by the retailer, the various marketing communications are more focused and relevant to the target market. Research by Sanje and Senol (2012) shows that online shoppers are receptive to online advertising and highlight the importance of this channel in the marketing communications mix. However, online channels provide a far wider range of opportunities for retailers to communicate and engage with shoppers. Earlier in this chapter we stressed the importance of the social aspect of shopper behaviour. We considered the role of tools such as Facebook and Twitter. Online channels can also be used to develop communities of like-minded shoppers who engage with each other on the site, sharing experiences and posting blogs. The benefits of developing virtual communities are well developed in the literature. Hagel and Armstrong (1998) were two of the earlier researchers to highlight the concept.

While such communities may have limited value for retailers who concentrate on selling merchandise that is largely functional and low-involvement in nature, it can be argued that high-involvement, hedonic and experiential areas retailing would have greater significance for shoppers. Kim and Jin (2006) suggest that such communities can be stimulated by the retailers. For instance, suggested topics and issues can be posted on the site (based on the retailer's understanding of issues and trends in that particular sector). Alternatively, shoppers can use areas of the site to start discussion threads, share experiences and views and generally use the facility to build relationships with each other and with the retailer. Since then technology allows for more sophisticated and visual use of the site through videos and vidpods, to name but a couple of such features.

The practitioner view
Managing marketing social media and marketing communications

Sam McLean, Social Media Manager, Peter Vardy CarStore (www.petervardycarstore.com)

Sam manages the social media platforms and other aspects of marketing communications for Peter Vardy CarStore in Glasgow. The original Peter Vardy Group was established in 2006. The Peter Vardy CarStore opened in December 2013 and focuses on the used car market. It uses innovative methods to sell cars. Scan the QR code to discover how Peter Vardy CarStore operates in terms of overall business strategy and its approach to design and layout in its outlet.

We spoke to Sam to get an insight into how the company addresses the area of marketing communications with a particular focus on social media platforms and mobile technology.

Where does social media fit in to the overall communications strategy at Peter Vardy CarStore?
'Peter Vardy are one of the dealerships that are more at the forefront of using digital. ▶

◀ 'Every year everyone from each of the dealerships goes to a conference in Perth – the central area of the company: the managers and directors meet to discuss overall strategy and identify specific themes for the coming year. The theme for 2015 was established as "digital disruption".

'For 2015 the main theme for the group is the concept of digital disruption. The CarStore is a bit of a test-bed in that respect.

'I was the first person in the group to start in a role where we actually brought social media in-house: rather than somebody at Head Office handling it.'

What are the main elements to your role in this area?
Sam noted that in addition to the social media role, his task is to 'manage the advertising online. In the case of each and every car in stock, making sure that they are online – on the website, with accurate details: making sure that price and specifications are correct. And also Autotrader which is our biggest portal to the market. The challenge is to enhance the click-through ratios for each advert and so on.'

What is the role of Facebook in terms of communications strategy?
Sam stated that this plays a very important role and that it is being used more strategically.

'The CarStore has its own Facebook site and the others work on the overall Peter Vardy site. We have petervardybmw.com and that will take you to the BMW part of the business. We also have a Vauxhall site.'

Every Wednesday the team have a conference call and review performance from the previous week in the social media area. The company focuses on the issue of engagement rather than the number of 'likes'.

In terms of evaluation and measurement, Sam noted that Facebook helps companies in that respect, within its insights section. 'It tells you your engagement per page and it breaks it down into how many clicks, how many shares, how many comments and how many likes. Also the amount of negatives – how many people have "unfollowed" the company.'

How do you deal with negative postings or comments?
Sam makes the following observation. 'We will always respond in the first instance by acknowledging it as an issue. Then try to encourage them to send us a message. So we can take a phone number and a contact name and then can pass it on to our sales manager and I will work with him to try and resolve the matter. Nine times out of ten we will get a resolution.

'There are two sides to it. Firstly making sure that you have a happy guest. We don't want people to have a bad experience. Also encouraging them to post a message later, saying that the matter was resolved satisfactorily.'

We asked Sam if social media is taking on a greater proportion of the allocation of the marketing communications budget.
'Yes, definitely with the general trend towards online and mobile these days. Going back maybe 10 years, in the motor trade ... the average consumer would visit an average of four different sites before purchasing a car. Now, it is below two, around 1.6 sites. This is because they will do a lot of research online and, especially the way Facebook works, they will do research on the social media page as well, to see reactions.

'The average buyer nowadays is so much clued up. There are so many outlets: and social media is just one of them. Friends will mention that they are thinking of buying a car and will mention it on their own Facebook page and invite people to comment as to whether or not it is a good buy or bad or whether it is good value.'

Sam feels that the light-hearted and 'fun' approach tends to work well. He cited the use of Hamish as an example. Hamish is the highland cow that features in the CarStore and is in fact a car (mini). Sam uses Hamish in the social media campaigns and he is dressed up to reflect certain times during the year.

'Hamish has a set of bunny ears on him during the Easter holiday period and at Halloween he appears as a ghost. This is not necessarily doing anything to encourage a purchase, but it contributes to the brand identity.'

Besides Facebook and Twitter, are there any other social media platforms that you use?
Sam mentioned Instagram and YouTube as being very relevant mainly because they are both image-based.

'Because you can see the car on Instagram ... the visual aspect. It also goes with the aspirational side of things. Instagram, being image-based, is very good for that.

'YouTube and any sort of video formats are also relevant. That's why we always try to send a personal video to a potential customer, when we receive an email or a personal enquiry about a particular car, with a personal description on it. This provides a "visual walk-through" for the guest. It also provides a personal touch. We have a person who makes the videos. Instead of a couple of fixed photos, they get to see a bit more of the car.'

Sam feels that consumers will still continue to buy the car in a physical location. This is because they want to experience the car; its interior, features and so on. However, social media plays a critical role in the search and evaluation process.

10.14 Conclusions

In this chapter we have considered the developments, challenges and opportunities with respect to retail marketing communications. This is clearly a central element of overall retail strategy: getting the message across to the target market is central to all business activities and retailers are no different.

We examined the major growth in the areas of digital and mobile communications and their respective impact on communication design and implementation. The exponential growth in the use of social media by consumers has major implications for all aspects of retail strategy and in particular how retailers engage and communicate with existing and potential customers.

These changes have meant that retailers have to reappraise the way in which they allocate resources to their promotion and communications budget. Traditional media platforms such as TV, radio and print advertising still play a significant role in establishing geographic reach and coverage. In terms of building brand image or reinforcing the brand values of the retailers, such media platforms still offer a range of benefits.

However, traditional media tools are largely based on the principle of one-way communication where the retailer pushes out a message to its intended target market. Questions can be asked whether such messages register with the intended recipient. The advent of TV zappers often means that people switch to other channels when the advertisement appears on screen, for example.

The use of social media platforms allows retailers to engage in two-way conversations with their target market. As well as providing a mechanism for marketing research, retailers can stimulate discussion, encourage like-minded members of the community to share their opinions and experiences and also engage in buzz or viral marketing campaigns.

The danger of using social media platforms lies in the potential loss of control of the medium by the retailers. Bad publicity or poor performance in areas such as customer service can lead to many negative comments and opinions on platforms such as Facebook and Twitter. Whereas good stories can result in successful viral marketing (a virtuous circle), negative publicity and comments can spiral into a vicious circle.

Criticisms have also been made of the intrusive nature of social media and the danger of retailers using the information in a manipulative way that can damage the consumer.

Retailers need to develop an *integrated* approach to marketing communications. Many retailers use a combination of traditional, digital and social platforms (see Fig. 10.1) in their attempt to successfully engage with their target markets. By contrast retailers such as Zara engage in relatively little formal paid-for forms of advertising and base their strategy instead on WOM and social media platforms. There is no-one-size-fits-all approach to designing and implementing marketing communications strategies.

We can conclude, however, by stating that from now on, retailers will focus more on customized, personalized and individualized forms of communications with their target market. Advances in IT allow for the capture of relevant, 'real-time' information on a plethora of shopping patterns, behaviours and preferences. This can be used proactively by retailers to stimulate, encourage and tease customers into purchases. We see this clearly in the case of Amazon. Based on purchases, preferences and opinions, Amazon can proactively send messages to shoppers identifying similar products that they may be interested in buying. They can also highlight upcoming, new products that might interest shoppers based on previous purchases.

Case study: John Lewis and its Christmas advertising campaign

John Lewis, the UK department store, has traditionally focused on Christmas as a mechanism for projecting its brand image and values. This is in line with the approach of many retailers in different sectors who see this period as critical in terms of maximizing revenue.

For instance, it is estimated that many of the top retailers such as Waitrose, Debenhams and Marks & Spencer (see our earlier case at the beginning of this chapter) spend an estimated £390 million on advertising over the last three months of the year (http.www.wallblog/2013/11/12/are-retailers-wasting-money-with-their-big-budget-christmas-tv-campaigns/).

While there is a danger that shoppers become fed up with the plethora of TV adverts, John Lewis has attempted to develop an annual Christmas TV advert that tries to position itself as the 'top of the Christmas campaigns'. Typically, this involves the use of a well-known song, delivered by an up and coming singer. The 2014 campaign featured one that was written by John Lennon and is called 'Real Love'. The singer is Tom Odell and both he and the song play on a number of different emotions.

See https://www.youtube.com/watch?v=iccscUFY860

It also features much of what Christmas portrays and contains typical aspects such as snow and a child waiting expectantly and patiently for the 'big day' so that he can receive his presents. The snow of course is fake (the advert was filmed during the summer of 2014). The family as portrayed in the advert reflects a typical middle-class family from east London (a lot of the film was shot in Victoria Park, Hackney – a suburb of London).

The advert contains a penguin who is called Monty. He is a friend of Sam (the boy in the advert). They play together and in the film both of them are playing Lego in the local park and use a trampoline. Sam realizes that his friend is lonely as he gazes tearfully at other couples walking in the park.

Saddened by this observation, Sam gets his friend, Monty, the one thing that he feels will cheer him up, a fellow penguin. The ad cuts to Christmas morning and under the tree is Mabel, a lady penguin.

Of course, Monty is an imaginary friend. This becomes evident when Sam picks up the two penguins from under the tree and we can clearly see that they are not real.

John Lewis had denied that the ad is based on a best-selling children's book entitled *Lost and Found*, written by Oliver Jeffers. This coincidently also features a boy, a lonely penguin and a search for a friend.

John Lewis only started to advertise on television in 2007 and in recent years has gone for this 'blockbuster' type of advert: a strong ballad, a popular singer, a nostalgic theme, family, love and, of course, toys. The 2014 Christmas TV campaign generated a lot of interest on Twitter and achieved over 13 million views on YouTube.

Source: Adapted from Wallop, H. and Ruddick, G. (2014) Watch: John Lewis's 2014 Christmas advert. *Daily Telegraph*. 12 November. © Telegraph Media Group Limited 2014.

Questions

1 Assess the rationale for John Lewis pursuing this type of TV advertising strategy.

2 Examine the extent to which you would agree with the view that the messages contained in this advert have little or nothing to do with promoting the brand values of a department store.

3 Many commentators argue that social media platforms will eventually lead to the demise of traditional media channels such as TV. How accurate is this view? What implications does it have for a retailer like John Lewis?

Chapter outcomes

- The communications landscape has been transformed by developments in the digital, mobile and social areas.
- Retailers have to reappraise their approach to marketing communications budget allocation.
- New media provide the opportunity for dialogue: traditional media work on the principle of a monologue.

- Social media platforms offer opportunities and threats for retailers.
- There is a danger of intruding into people's lives and becoming an unwelcome 'party pooper'.
- Viral marketing in tandem with the use of social media can offer creative and relatively low cost options in the marketing communications framework.
- The use of celebrities can enhance the retailer's brand and register it more effectively in the mind of the shopper.

Discussion questions

1 Examine the extent to which you would agree with the assertion that traditional advertising platforms such as TV and print advertising are in irreversible decline.

2 Assess the dangers associated with using celebrities as a central part of a retailer's marketing communications strategy.

3 Evaluate the view that retailers are placing too much trust and confidence in using social media platforms as part of their marketing communications campaign.

4 Identify the main steps involved in creating a successful viral marketing campaign.

5 Many commentators argue that the role of personal selling will decline as retailers increasingly use online channels to promote and sell their merchandise. Examine the extent to which you would agree with this view.

6 Why should a supplier become involved in a co-operative promotional programme with a retailer?

References

Danaher, P.J. and Dagger, T.S. (2013) Comparing the relative effectiveness of advertising channels: a case study of a multimedia blitz campaign. *Journal of Marketing Research*. 50 (August): 517–534.

Dukcevich, D. (2004) Forbes most influential businessmen: Josiah Wedgwood. Available online at: www.forbes.com

Erdogan, B.Z., Baker, M.J. and Tagg, S. (2001) Selecting celebrity endorsers: the practitioner's perspective. *Journal of Advertising Research*. 41(3): 39–49.

Fournier, S. and Avery, J. (2011) *The Uninvited Brand*. Boston, MA: Boston University School of Management.

Hagel, J. III and Armstrong, A.G. (1998) *Net Gain: Expanding Markets Through Virtual Communities Technologies*. Boston, MA: Harvard Business School Press.

Kim, H. and Jin, B. (2006) Exploratory study of virtual communities of apparel shoppers. *Journal of Fashion Marketing and Management*. 10(1): 41–55.

Kunz, M.B. and Hackworth, B.A. (2011) Are consumers following retailers to social networks? *Academy of Marketing Studies Journal*. 15(2): 1–22.

Kunz, M.B., Hackworth, B., Osborne, P. and High, J.D. (2011) Fans, friends and followers: social media in the retailer's marketing mix. *Journal of Applied Business and Economics*. 12(3): 61–68.

Lee, C.W. (2002) Sales promotions as strategic communication: the case of Singapore. *Journal of Product & Brand Management*. 11(2): 103–114.

Mangold, D.J. and Faulds, D.J. (2009) Social media: the new hybrid element of the promotion mix. *Business Horizons*. 52(4): 357–365.

McCracken, G. (1989) Who is the celebrity endorser? Cultural foundations of the endorsement process. *Journal of Consumer Research*. 16(3): 310–21.

Morrison, K. (2014) The growth of social media: from passing trend to international obsession. *Infographics*. 27 January.

Phillips, D. (2006) Towards relationship management: public relations at the core of organisational development. *Journal of Communication Management*. 10(2): 211–226.

Roslow, S., Laskey, H.A. and Nicholls, J.A.F. (1993) The enigma of cooperative advertising. *The Journal of Business and Industrial Marketing.* 8(2): 70–79.

Sanderson, R. (2012) Benetton puts faith in family. *Financial Times.* 23 March.

Sanje, G. and Senol, I. (2012) The importance of online behavioral advertising for online advertisers. *International Journal of Business and Social Science.* 3(18): 114–121.

Schultz, D.E., Block, M.P. and Labrecque, L.I. (2012) Consumer retailer preference and Facebook: friends or foes? *International Journal of Integrated Marketing Communications.* Spring: 7–18.

Schmidt, S.M.P. and Ralph, D.L. (2011) Social media: more available marketing tools. *The Business Review.* 18(2): 37–43.

Silvera, D.A. and Austad, B. (2004) Factors predicting the effectiveness of celebrity endorsement advertisements. *European Journal of Marketing.* 38(11/12): 1509–1526.

Social Media Examiner (2014) Social media marketing report: how marketers are using social media to grow their businesses. Available online at: www.SocialMediaExminer.com

Spar (2014) Annual Report.

Stallen, M., Smidts, A., Rijpkema, M., Smit, G., Klucharev, V. and Fernández, G. (2010) Celebrities and shoes on the female brain: the neural correlates of product evaluation in the context of fame. *Journal of Economic Psychology.* 31: 802–811

Sustainalytics (2012) Building a sustainable South African Food retail sector: issues for responsible investors. August.

Geißler, H. (2014) German food retailer Edeka lands a viral marketing hit http://www.brandindex.com/article/german-food-retailer-edeka-lands-viral-marketing-hit 1 April (accessed March 2015).

Tuli, K.R., Mukherjee, A. and Dekimpe, M.G. (2012) On the value relevance of retailer advertising spending and same-store sales growth. *Journal of Retailing.* 88(4): 447–461.

Valin, J. (2004) Overview of public relations around the world and principles of modern practice. Remarks made by Jean Valin, APR, Fellow CPRS Chair of the Global Alliance at the CONFERP conference, Brasilia.

Vanheems, R., Kelly, S.J. and Stevenson, K. (2013) The Internet and the modern death of a salesman: multichannel retailing's impact on the salesperson's role. *International Journal of Integrated Marketing Communications.* Fall: 91–100.

Wallop, H. and Ruddick, G. (2014) Watch: John Lewis's 2014 Christmas advert. *Daily Telegraph.* 12 November.

White, D.W., Goddard, L. and Wilbur, N. (2009) The effects of negative information transference in the celebrity endorsement relationship. *International Journal of Retail & Distribution Management.* 37(4): 322–335.

Digital Strategy Consulting (2012) Viral video marketing case studies – the best virals of 2012. Available online at: www.digitalstrategyconsulting.com/intelligence/2012/11/viral_video_marketing_case_studies_the_best_virals_of_2012.php (accessed March 2015).

Chapter 11

Retailing and sustainability

✓ Learning objectives

On completion of this chapter you should be in a position to address the following objectives:

- ✓ To understand the concept of sustainability and the associated themes.
- ✓ To assess the way in which sustainability has evolved and its implications for the supply chain in general and retailers in particular.
- ✓ To evaluate the approach of government agencies and policymakers to the sustainability agenda.
- ✓ To examine the role of the retailer within the context of society.
- ✓ To examine the initiatives taken by retailers to move the sustainability agenda forward in areas such as the environment, employees, sourcing, production and recycling.
- ✓ To examine key performance indicators used by retailers to measure the impact of sustainability initiatives.
- ✓ To assess the growth in ethical or 'green shoppers'.

11.1 Introduction

Supply chain management has evolved over the last 40 years from a functional and operational concept to one that has become a strategic imperative for any organization that wishes to compete in an effective manner in its respective product/service sector. Retailers are often central and powerful players in a supply chain and we address the role of retailers within the context of the supply chain throughout this chapter.

Influential articles by Porter and Kramer (2011) and Pfitzer, Bockstedde and Stamp (2013) have articulated a strong argument for organizations developing strategies that create shared value. They argue that many companies define the creation of value too narrowly: focusing on short-term financial gains but failing to see the longer-term issues such as the wellbeing of customers and the society in which they operate. This approach places overall business success alongside social progress. It is different to some extent from the concept of social responsibility as it puts societal issues at the centre (rather than at the periphery) of business strategy.

Over the past 10 years or so, another critical development has emerged that has forced organizations to take a more extended view of supply chain strategy. Environmental concerns have emerged from a wide spectrum of sources that have forced governments, policymakers and industrial leaders to assess the implications for their business operations.

Resource depletion issues and damage to the planet have been critical in this respect. This has also led to companies having to consider the wider social responsibilities that they hold with regard to their involvement in local and national communities. The concept of the 'ethically driven' organization has gained greater currency in the last 20–25 years.

The pressures to address these issues by governments, environmental pressure groups and scientists mean that companies can no longer ignore or evade the topic. Many of the activities that take place within the supply chain are directly affected by the question of sustainability. This is particularly so in the case of inventory management, procurement, product design, transportation and facilities management.

In this chapter we assess the issues of sustainability, the environment and social responsibility for retailers, the customer-interfacing participants in the supply chain. As we noted in earlier chapters, retailers are increasingly the dominant and most influential member of the supply chain in many sectors. As a consequence, they can play a critical role in shaping the overall approach of other members in the chain to address these issues. Their influence is reinforced by the degree of retail concentration that exists across many developed economies and the subsequent power which they wield within their respective supply chains.

We begin by examining the concept of sustainability and how it has evolved in recent years. In the early sections we consider the issues within the context of the supply chain. Then we focus on the specific case of retailing and assess the key drivers that have led retailers to embed sustainability issues in their strategies. We consider the overall impact of sustainability on the various dimensions of the supply chain and focus our analysis on the retailing function. Supply chain considerations are important because retailers' source material from suppliers, set quality standards, are driven by issues such as cost and competitiveness and as a consequence have to work and collaborate with a number of partners and organizations in the supply chain. For instance, decisions on where to source have major implications for sustainability and its role in retail strategy formulation and implementation.

We evaluate the potential benefits that can emerge for retailers who take a proactive approach to the issue of sustainability. We also consider some of the mistakes made by some retailers in this area.

We examine the response of retailers to the sustainable or 'green challenge' and assess whether these initiatives are just a cosmetic gesture or part of a serious attempt to embed the concept into their overall retail strategy. If sustainability is placed at the centre of a retailer's strategy, can it generate a potential competitive advantage? What does the future hold for the issue of sustainability? We consider some short case studies of how retailers are addressing the topic.

We assess the impact of sustainability on shoppers. How are they responding to specific issues such as environmental protection, ethical considerations and consumption?

11.2 Sustainability and retailing: the key issues for marketing

Retailers lie in the middle between the manufacturers and the final consumer. As we have noted throughout this book, larger retailers in particular have gained a great deal of power over the last few decades. In many cases they set the agenda for their supply base in the context of price, quality, delivery of product and so on. Therefore, they control much of what goes on in the supply chain.

As we shall see in later sections of this chapter, the issue of sustainability touches all aspects of the operations of a retailer.

In terms of dealing with its supply base, retailers have to address the issue of ethical sourcing. There have been many cases cited where retailers have not paid enough attention to the conditions that pertain in many of their suppliers' operations. Child labour, unsafe working conditions and low pay typify the allegations and evidence that has been brought to bear on the retailers. In response, the more socially conscious ones have introduced codes of behaviour and quality, factory and labour standards in an attempt to eradicate the problems.

Within the context of managing a retailer's operations, issues such as energy efficiency, carbon footprint and recycling are now high on the agenda. In the main, such issues have been forced upon retailers by policymakers. By the very nature of the business, retailers are major consumers of energy: multi-site locations, distribution centres, transportation of merchandise up and down motorways and so on. As we discuss later in the chapter, retailers have been introducing a range of initiatives in these areas to both drive efficiencies in their operations and address some of the environmental considerations.

The consumer also lies at the heart of the issue of sustainability. Increasingly, we are witnessing the growth of the 'green-minded' shopper. This segment exhibits concerns about the way in which products are developed (for example, using natural resources, not using animals to test and develop the product and so on). They also take into consideration the provenance of the products. Where were the items manufactured? Did it involve exploitation of workers? Child labour?

Retailers and the constituent members of their supply chain do not work and operate in isolation. They set up their operations and stores in living communities. The ethos of corporate social responsibility argues strongly that they behave as good 'corporate citizens'. This is particularly relevant for retailers, many of whom have caused problems in communities and attracted much criticism. In the UK, for instance, Tesco has been heavily criticized for its apparent attempt to 'Tescotize' many towns and villages through its multi-format strategy: large supermarkets, middle-range supermarkets and convenience stores. This has led to the demise of many small independent retailers.

McDonald's has attracted criticism for its range of food products that are deemed to be unhealthy and a large contributor to the obese nature of many people. In fairness, it has responded over the last 20–25 years by addressing the challenge of creating healthier foods on its menu.

In one of the early sections of this chapter, we explore the purpose of business in general and retailers in particular. Is the sole objective that of profit maximization? While in many cases this is at the forefront of business strategy, we consider the concept of 'shared value' and its relevance for the key stakeholders.

Retailers, because of their ubiquitous nature, have to address the issue of sustainability. It can no longer be considered as an 'optional extra'. In many sectors, enlightened retailers are implementing a range of initiatives to drive the sustainability agenda forward. While some may gain a temporary competitive advantage, this is unlikely to remain the case as we 'fast forward' a decade or so ahead. Governments are increasingly setting standards and legislation that has to be addressed. We examine the critical issues in the next sections of the chapter. Because of the importance of the retailer within the context of its supply chain, we take a holistic approach to the analysis and assessment of the issue of sustainability.

In order to create, develop and deliver value to its final customers, retailers increasingly have to place sustainability at the forefront of their marketing strategy. A failure to adequately address the issues outlined in the preceding paragraphs will hinder the ability of the retailer to satisfy the needs of its target markets.

Vignette: Woolworths in South Africa

Woolworths operates in the South African market and sells a wide range of merchandise including food and clothing. It has over 400 stores (in different formats and in some cases franchised operations) in this market and employs 220,000 people. It operates two main distribution centres and deals with a wide range of suppliers and agricultural producers.

The philosophy of the company goes beyond basic environmental considerations to address issues of economic growth and social development. This has major relevance for a country like South Africa where many businesses and stakeholders take the view that such issues are a cost to the business.

The company captures its philosophy and core values in its 'Good Business Journey' project, which it established in 2010. This document sets out a number of project targets across three major categories: ecological, social and economic. It is strongly championed by senior management and the key strategists in the company. A brief summary of the key areas is outlined here.

Ecological: energy items, carbon footprint items, water items, food packaging items.

Social: customer tracking study, number of permanent employees, training and skills development, employment equity, health and safety, corporate social investment.

Economic: revenue, return on equity, share price applications, food market share indicators.

Dos Santos, Svensson and Padin (2013: 107) note some of the benefits that Woolworths has derived from this strategic exercise. They include 'understanding product provenance and ensuring that products are safe, healthy, sourced ethically and without harm to the environment'.

It has also had the effect of increasing its corporate reputation among the stakeholders and further enhanced its relationships with suppliers, non-governmental organizations (NGOs) and other companies. It has also made significant savings as a result of implementing this strategy.

Dos Santos et al. (2013) also point out the importance of this approach, given the nature of the South African economy that could be described as 'developing' and where there are large variations in terms of employment and poverty.

Sustainability in context

The evolution of sustainability as a strategic issue for business is difficult to place within a particular era or decade. It is based on the general principle that any activity by an organization must take into account the greater good of society and the planet. If we take such a broad view of sustainability, it takes us into areas such as social responsibility, environmental concerns (pollution, waste, carbon footprint and so on), working conditions, protection of consumer's rights, globalization, ethics and concern for the future wellbeing of society as well as the present.

This strongly suggests that any organization within a supply chain can no longer make decisions without taking into account the greater good of society and the planet. It also explicitly identifies the concept of equity and fairness as being central to such business decisions. Actions that infringe on this basic principle have the effect of creating negative consequences for individuals or organizations or society in general.

It is difficult to provide a precise definition of sustainability as different disciplines take different interpretations of what it means. Some of the physical sciences focus on the need to protect and nurture the ecological systems and structures that make up the Planet Earth. In the context of business, the same principles of protection apply within the overall context of supply and demand.

Bonn and Fisher (2011) review some of the definitions that have been put forward in the literature to explain this phenomenon. They quote from the World Commission on Environment and Development (1987: 8) who defined sustainable development as meeting 'the needs of the present without compromising the ability of future generations to meet their own needs'. This is central to understanding the essence of sustainability: organizations have to take on board not just the impact of their strategies on the current generations, but they also have serious obligations to future generations as well, particularly in terms of how they interact with and make use of the Planet's resources and the overall environment.

Landmark events have taken place in the last 20 years that have focused the minds of all of the stakeholders on the issue of sustainability. These include the Earth Summit (1992), the World Summit on Sustainable Development (2002), the UN World Summit (2005) and the Copenhagen Summit (2009). Although differences exist between policymakers and governments regarding the correct approach, there can be no doubt that the combined effect of these meetings is to create an environment where there will be increasingly stringent and robust legislation put in place to address issues such as the disposal of waste, carbon emissions and so on.

These developments require a change in practice for many organizations, particularly those that operate in the 'for profit' sectors. Whereas previously such corporations have been answerable to their shareholders and have been judged by the financial and business media in terms of performance, now, they are also to be judged by a wider range of stakeholders such as governments, consumer groups, environmentalist groups and so on. Decisions that are made within the context of the supply chain are central to this development; we now explore this more fully.

The notion of social responsibility has attracted many adherents for a number of previous decades. Influential authors such as Friedman, Drucker and (within the marketing context) Kotler have long advocated the need for businesses to take account of societal needs and requirements when developing and implementing strategy. However, Friedman adopted a view that did not place a great deal of emphasis on society, arguing that the primary role of business is to generate as much profit as possible for its shareholders. This contrasts with the view that activities by corporations should not be made in isolation and certainly not to the detriment of the greater good of society.

It may be more accurate to view sustainable development as the 'umbrella' or overarching term that covers a number of related themes. These can be identified as corporate social responsibility, environmentalism, 'green marketing', the 'ethical consumer', the 'ethical business' and more specific issues such as employee working conditions, sourcing policies, recycling strategies, waste management, price transparency and 'green logistics'. We consider these issues later in this chapter.

11.4 Supply chain management and corporate social responsibility

In broad terms, all organizations have had to grapple with the issue of corporate social responsibility. The basic principle of corporate social responsibility is that companies should not follow blindly along the mantra of achieving profits at any cost whatsoever. Instead, they should pursue a strategy that recognizes that any actions or activities performed by the organization concerned should be carried out with the broader concern of the community and society in general at the forefront of their strategy development. This covers a spectrum of issues ranging from designing dangerous products to damaging the environment to purchasing from companies that take advantage of child labour to the disposal of waste material. Arguably, all of these issues impact directly on the management of the supply chain.

Willard (2002) was one of the first authors to make explicit reference to the concept of the *triple bottom line (3BL)*. This has been adopted widely by many organizations in the intervening years. It is also used synonymously with corporate social responsibility.

Markley and Davis (2007: 763–774) note that:

> **❝**the idea behind the 3BL paradigm is that a corporation's ultimate success or health can and should be measured not just by the traditional financial bottom line, but also by its social/ ethical and environmental performance (hence the term 'triple bottom line').**❞**

This links closely to the corporate social responsibility paradigm which suggests that organizations can be held socially and ethically accountable by a much wider range of stakeholders than the traditional ones such as the employees, shareholders and customers. This is an important consideration when trying to gain an understanding of the changes that organizations need to make to their strategies. The decisions taken with regard to business strategy in general and the supply chain strategy in particular will affect: the local community within which the organization operates; the wider regional and national community; and may have a direct and/or indirect impact on the social and economic wellbeing of existing and future generations.

Retailers typically produce reports on their activities in the area of sustainable development. This includes statements on how they manage environmental and social risks. A typical example of the former would be the approach that they use to design new retail stores/outlets/developments, focusing on environmental concerns with regard to such issues as energy efficiency, materials used and so on. While the primary audience for retailers is their shareholders (in the case of a publicly quoted company) the 3BL frameworks widen the audience to other key stakeholders such as shoppers, local communities, the media and financial publications.

As well as the economic, social and environmental criteria, corporate governance is also becoming an important consideration, particularly for potential investors, as they assess the relative attractiveness of the organization. The way that the company is run, and the background of the owners, are critical concerns with regard to governance.

Many of the initiatives by retailers are characterized by self-regulation; that is, the criteria and measures used are determined by the retailers. They tend to lack any robustness from the perspective of external and independent sanctions if they do not achieve the targets or key performance indicators.

11.5 The key drivers of sustainable supply chain management

A number of key drivers have led to the concept of sustainable supply chain management (Mann et al., 2010). They can be summarized as follows:

- **Legislation**: this may manifest itself in the form of general environmental laws introduced by individual governments. Typically, such measures emerge because of public opinion, lobbying by special interest groups, and research evidence provided by academics from the science community and industry groups. Increasingly, legislators are instigating policies with regard to energy efficiencies and carbonization that companies have to address in their strategies.

- **Environmental drivers**: some companies are not motivated to address sustainable issues because of legislation alone. Those that pursue a more socially responsible approach may do so because of genuine concern over the protection of the environment. Disposal of waste, reverse logistics issues and building products that facilitate recovery are examples.

- **Financial drivers**: companies may act in these matters because they sense an opportunity to make cost savings. This improved performance may evolve from better operational performance, recapture of value from recovered products, reduction in costs, newer markets or improved profitability and reduction in liability risks.

- **Internal business process drivers**: such issues as warranties, claims and recalls, periodical replacement of installed capacity and so on, can emerge because of the need to achieve greater efficiencies and effectiveness in the supply chain.

- **Customers**: greater sophistication and higher expectations from customers can force companies to improve the defect rate or more proactively address the 'green' agenda. This is particularly important in many sectors where there is evidence that this segment is on the increase. Retailers such as Tesco and Carrefour are increasingly introducing products that are potentially attractive to this group of customers.

- **Social**: a growing recognition that there are other stakeholders besides the primary ones such as customers, employees, suppliers and regulators. Secondary stakeholders include local communities, activist groups, religious organizations, trade associations, social advocates and so on.

There are internal and external dimensions to corporate social responsibility. In the case of internal considerations, we refer to initiatives and policies that operate within the confines of the organization. For instance, many retailers instigate policies and procedures with internal staff to make them more aware of the need for social responsibility concerns when dealing with customers. For instance, this can be reflected in the sales techniques employed in retail outlets where staff are instructed to be open and honest with shoppers in terms of recommending appropriate and relevant merchandise to them and forsaking the temptation to encourage them to buy a more expensive or profitable item. Human resource issues such as social inclusion, gender equality and career development are also examples of socially responsible internal practice.

The external dimension refers to practices that move outside the 'four walls' of the retailer and have an impact on the wider stakeholders. For instance, some retailers employ rigorous policies with regard to managing their suppliers. For retailers who source from developing economies, this is often reflected

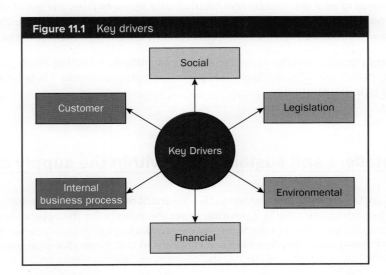

Figure 11.1 Key drivers

in the standards that local suppliers have to observe with regard to working conditions, non-use of child labour and appropriate wages.

11.6 Sustainable and green supply chains defined

We have already examined the concept of supply chain management and the key components of the supply chain process in Chapter 3. We now need to examine how the basic definition of supply chain management has changed as a consequence of the emergence of the green and sustainable agendas.

Before providing a definition of green/sustainable supply chain management, we should briefly revisit our earlier discussion on the 3BL. Any such definition should make explicit recognition that such a sustainable supply chain should perform well on financial (profit and loss) measures as well as performance indicators in both the social and environmental areas. Pagell and Wu (2007) argue that when we use the term 'sustainable supply chains', we are referring to the broad managerial decisions and behaviours.

In this chapter the generic term 'sustainable' is adopted to encompass all of the issues that impact on the supply chain. In the literature the terms 'green' and 'sustainable' are used interchangeably. Srivastava (2007) conducted a major review of the literature and observes that earlier studies and publications tended to adopt a narrow focus and perspective, addressing specific issues such as industrial ecology. These studies have looked at specific concerns such as green purchasing, product design, green manufacturing, environmental safety and so on.

Srivastava (2007: 54–55) adopts the following definition of GrSCM as 'integrating environmental thinking into supply-chain management, including product design, material sourcing and selection, manufacturing processes, delivery of the final product to the consumers as well as end-of-life management of the product after its useful life'.

Emmett and Sood (2010: 9) also employ the term 'green' and note that green supply chains 'consider the environmental effects of all processes of supply chain from the extraction of raw materials to the final disposal of goods'. They inject a cautionary note however by observing that 'in many organizations, there is limited collaboration and visibility...' (p. 9). As a consequence, partners in the supply chain have limited information regarding the carbon footprint and greenhouse gas emission of other partners in the supply chain. This implies that in addition to sharing information on the customer base, companies have to be more open with other parties in the supply chain about information on specific sustainability-related issues.

The following definition encapsulates the views of researchers and supply chain strategists in the relevant literature streams. Sustainable supply chain management is:

> 66 *the management of raw materials, information and services from the point of origin to the point of consumption and back, focusing on the delivery of value while explicitly addressing social, ethical and environment concerns in the supply chain process.* 99

This definition recognizes the broader concerns that we identified earlier but emphasizes that it is more than simply recognition: it must explicitly include performance measures and benchmarks that are built around sustainability in the strategy.

11.7 Retailers and sustainability within the supply chain

Retailers, as noted earlier, are in many instances the dominant organization in the supply chain. Because of the power that they wield, they are in a position to set the agenda for the approach to sustainability.

Retailers traditionally have been to the forefront in introducing innovative practices and procedures. We discuss some of these developments in other chapters in this book (for example, initiatives, store layout, design and location). In this section we consider some of the developments they have undertaken with regard to sustainability.

11.7.1 Sourcing policy

Cost and competitive pressures, allied to the trend towards globalization, have led retailers to increasingly source material and product from developing countries. The benefits initially are self-evident: lower labour costs alone can offer large savings to retailers. However, some leading retailers such as Nike and Primark have faced considerable criticism for their sourcing policy. They have been accused of sourcing from suppliers who employ child labour, operate in dangerous and unhealthy factories (sweatshops), exploit people and generally infringe some of the basic principles of human behaviour. Nike and Primark, along with many retailers, have developed a code of behaviour for their dealings with suppliers from developing economies in order to address these issues.

11.7.2 Case in point: Fastflo

The chief executive officer (CEO) of Fastflo (not the real name), a leading low-cost, fast-fashion retailer, is facing a potentially damaging problem. A journalist from a newspaper has contacted her and is looking for a comment on some evidence that he has discovered about its sourcing policies. The journalist has spent a month in Cambodia and has visited a number of suppliers to this retailer. He has discovered that these suppliers are subcontracting some of the work to other smaller suppliers to keep the cost down and ensuring that the quick turnaround times demanded by the retailer can be met. The journalist is planning to publish a detailed exposé of his findings in a major newspaper article at the weekend.

The CEO is thumbing through the stated policy of the retailer with regard to its code of standards. She has a critical decision to make. Should she respond to the journalist? If so, what should she say? How can she overcome the potential damage that might occur as a result of the article? What are the issues that she needs to address? Can she make any positive spin on the story?

The code of behaviour covers the following issues:

- Fastflo is fully committed to monitoring the production, labour and work conditions arrangements with all of its suppliers.
- Fastflo carries out regular inspections of each supplier's facilities.
- Fastflo employs local and independent auditors to carry out such inspections. They compile an annual, certified report on the standards witnessed during the inspections.
- Fastflo expressly forbids the use of any child labour.
- Fastflo only approves suppliers that pay a living wage in the respective regions and countries where the suppliers are located.
- Fastflo only deals with suppliers that meet its high standards of production and the capability to meet its stringent delivery schedules.

The CEO has cause to be concerned. Fastflo has built its reputation and its success on its ability to produce very cheap clothing at low prices that cater for shoppers looking for affordable, yet fashionable and trendy merchandise. It has enjoyed considerable success in the UK, France and Germany and is planning to expand its operations in other European countries over the next two to three years.

She is angry because she feels that there is jealousy in the trade and the media about the success of Fastflo and that they are being used as a mechanism to address wider and bigger issues about poverty in the third world. She is also aware that cost pressures in the industry, allied to an apparently insatiable demand for cheaper and cheaper merchandise on the part of shoppers, has led to Fastflo having to take a hard line with suppliers on key performance indicators such as delivery times and adherence to cost issues.

Of even greater concern is the fact that recently she received a letter from a member of a child protection organization based in Pakistan requesting a meeting to discuss potential issues about child exploitation by Fastflo.

She is somewhat reassured by the fact that Fastflo is a member of the Ethical Standards Commission, an umbrella organization that has developed a code of standards on ethical sourcing.

▶

◀ She is also confident that the large demand for Fastflo's merchandise can provide a robust reminder that the retailer will continue to remain a strong player in a very competitive fashion sector.

Question

1 If you were in the CEO's position what would you do to specifically address the issues raised by the journalist?

Activity

Visit the websites of the following retailers: Zara, Next and Primark. Assess the published information (if any exists) on the policies and procedures used by these retailers when sourcing material. How robust are these approaches? How might they be improved or made stronger?

11.7.3 Reducing the carbon footprint

Increasingly, legislators underline the need for everyone to reduce the 'carbon footprint'. This term is used to describe the total amount of CO_2 emissions for which an individual or organization is responsible (Thompson, 2007). Thompson estimates that UK retailers account for around 7 per cent of total UK carbon emissions.

Retailers use space to develop retail outlets and shopping malls. They are one of the heaviest users of the road and rail infrastructures to move their products to distribution centres and outlets. In order to use road transport, they are inevitably one of the biggest users of fuel. They burn up energy and generate gas emissions. They are major users of packaging and generators of waste. Likewise, shoppers establish a carbon footprint as they make their shopping trips to physical retail outlets. In the case of online shopping, carbon emissions also occur as retailers have to deliver the orders from the store or distribution centre to people's homes or offices.

Up to the beginning of this century, the carbon emission issue was not at the top of the legislative agenda in many countries. When retailers developed retail space, there was little comparative pressure placed on them to address 'green issues'. Likewise, little attention was paid to the other factors identified in the preceding chapter.

In recent years, retailers have had to respond to the growing importance of carbon footprint in the context of more demanding government and legislative policy. Within a particular store there are three main constituents that make up the consumption of energy, and they are as follows:

- lighting
- heating/cooling
- equipment.

The onus is on retailers to control energy rather than generate it. Marks & Spencer has been one of the pioneers in the area of carbon emission reduction. Since 2003 it has reduced carbon emissions by 30 per cent per square foot in its UK retail operations and it aims to reduce it by a further 25 per cent in the coming five years (Thompson, 2007). Thompson highlights two particular retail developments: a refit of a 1930s building in Bournemouth that achieved energy savings of 25 per cent and a reduction in CO_2 output of 92 per cent; and a new store in Glasgow that created 55 per cent of energy savings and an 85 per cent reduction in CO_2.

Similarly, in the case of a critical issue for many retailers, home delivery, there is evidence that retailers are introducing effective initiatives. Sainsbury's announced in 2007 that it was converting 20 per cent of its fleet to electric power.

Edwards, McKinnon and Cullinane (2010) carried out one of the first studies to compare conventional shopping trips and home delivery in the context of CO_2 emissions. They identified a number of factors that affect carbon emissions. They include: 'on average, when a customer buys fewer than 24 items per shopping trip (or fewer than seven items for bus users) it is likely that the home delivery will emit less CO_2 per item purchased'. They highlight some potential limitations with their findings however. For instance, it assumed that the car journey was specifically for shopping and a product which was ordered via an online channel was delivered first time. However, the findings provide some initial recommendations for retailers regarding how they can measure the effectiveness of their delivery strategies and the ways in which consumers shop (see also Fieldson and Rai, 2010).

Initiatives such as the use of natural lighting and rainwater harvesting are also aspects of policy that retailers are using to address the carbon footprint issue. Many of these initiatives, however, have to be considered in the light of the lack of knowledge or awareness on the part of shoppers. There is little evidence to suggest that they recognize the relevance or importance of these initiatives by retailers. This requires policymakers and companies to invest some time in raising the importance of these initiatives, particularly in terms of how they can improve the quality of life for society and protect the environment and planet. How likely is it that shoppers will try to combine a shopping trip with another activity, such as visiting the library or dropping children off at school, to reduce carbon emission? This may be a somewhat fanciful view, given that shopping is seen as a key leisure activity for many and forms the basis of a discrete trip for many people. We develop this issue in greater detail later in the chapter.

11.7.4 Waste management and recycling

The issue of waste has become a critical matter for many countries. The cost of waste disposal to retailers has increased inexorably, particularly in countries such as the UK where landfill taxes are applied. Companies in general and retailers in particular have to grapple with the challenge of either paying the costs of waste disposal or implementing recycling initiatives in order to become more efficient and thereby reduce costs. Many countries have also got a problem because of a lack of availability of suitable landfill sites. The retail sector, because of the nature of its business, is one of the biggest generators of waste. Recycling, therefore, presents opportunities to reduce costs and at the same time adopt a more socially responsible approach to environmental concerns. The cost attached to waste management provides a healthy spur for retailers to address this issue (see Baharum and Pitt, 2010).

The Dixons Group, the UK-based European retailer specializing in consumer electronics products, has been proactive and to the forefront in developing measures to use sustainable and recyclable materials (Jones, Comfort and Hillier, 2005a).

11.8 Retailer sustainability strategies: the evidence

In the context of the retail sector, there is a paucity of research on the specific approaches used by retailers to develop sustainability strategies. Earlier studies provide evidence that the large European retailers recognize the importance of CSR within their framework, particularly in the context of generating long-term growth, improving the environment and being able to contribute to the communities where they are located. Many of the loftier objectives such as reducing energy use and ambitious reduction in carbon emissions are counterbalanced by more pragmatic objectives such as achieving greater efficiencies and cost reductions across the supply chain (Jones et al., 2005b).

Retailers have addressed the issue of ethical sourcing in a number of different ways. A code of behaviour document is the most commonly used mechanism. This identifies a number of aspects of sourcing that retailers explicitly take a position on. It guides the way in which they identify, evaluate, select and draw up contracts with suppliers.

The weakness of such an approach, however, lies in the voluntary nature of the arrangements. Whether it is retailer-specific or sector-specific, it lacks robustness and relevance if there is no legal requirement to comply with the statements and aspirations (Preuss, 2009).

The level of robustness and detail associated with codes of conduct varies greatly across the retail sector. It can be further complicated by the length of the supply chain within which the retailer operates. For instance, how many tiers or levels of suppliers are involved in the process? Are there sub-suppliers involved? Can these companies be tracked or audited successfully by retailers? Some retailers build in specific clauses in the contract with suppliers that force them to comply with a range of ethical issues such as working conditions, wages, health and safety and so on.

More recent published research assessed the sustainability strategies employed by five leading European retailers: Tesco, Sainsbury's, Carrefour, Groupe Casino and Ahold. The researchers collected data from the numerous sustainability and annual general reports published by these retailers over a period of five to six years. They assessed the performance of the retailers based on guidelines that were developed in the Global Reporting Initiative (GRI) that was launched in 1997 by the Coalition for Environmentally Responsible Economics (CERES) in partnership with the United Nations Environmental Programme (UNEP). The subsequent guidelines were published in 2000.

The findings reveal variations in approach to strategy development by the retailers. Each company has its own agenda for sustainability that it pursues. Tesco formally addressed the sustainability issue in 2002 when it started to publish environmental reports. Specific indicators such as lorry fleet carbon dioxide emissions and plastic recycling targets appeared in the earlier reports. In some years, fewer indicators were mentioned in the reports. By contrast, Sainsbury's followed a more predictable approach. As well as setting targets, it identified initiatives to tackle climate change that required engagement with other key stakeholders in the chain such as suppliers. Its activities in 2008 and 2009 centred on energy efficiency in its stores.

Carrefour set a key priority of improving the energy efficiency of its stores by 20 per cent by 2020. For unsold food across the different countries within which it operates, Carrefour works closely with local charities to organize redistribution. It has also moved from using wooden boxes and crates to reusable plastic containers.

Groupe Casino (a French retailer with a range of branded operations such as Leader Price, Spar, Petit Casino, Supermarchés and Franprix) has also focused on reducing energy consumption as well as optimizing the refrigeration systems and reducing the environmental impact of goods transport. Its warehouses make use of 'intelligent' battery-charged forklift trucks that can be programmed to use the optimal charge for providing the precise energy required to operate.

Ahold (a Dutch supermarket group covering a range of operations such as Giant-Carlisle, Albert Heijn, Albert/Hypernova and Stop&Shop) moved to a more demanding approach to sustainability around 2008. It began to collect data to define its carbon footprint, including fuel, gas and electricity consumption together with emissions of refrigerator leakage. It also collected third-party data from distribution centres. Its managers also began to identify and benchmark energy consumption and make investments in appropriate energy-efficient equipment. The retailer works closely with its suppliers and shares best practice across its retail formats (Bobe and Dragomir, 2010).

11.9   Sustainable retailing: a source of competitive advantage?

The emergence of environmental and energy–climate issues has forced companies to incorporate them into their overall business strategy development. In the last decade, we have seen a raft of legislation across many countries and regions which means that organizations cannot evade the issues. A key to successful strategy development and implementation is the concept of differentiation. Organizations constantly strive to identify one area where it can make its product or service stand out from that of the competition. Consider any industry sector and see how companies address this issue. Some focus on low prices; others on superior product quality or higher levels of customer service. We can see where organizations seek to gain 'first-mover' advantage by instigating initiatives in the area of sustainability in order to differentiate themselves from the competition and gain some 'kudos' in the process. It is an immutable law of business that no competitive advantage can last forever. Even the most unique and innovative product or service will be superseded at some point by a superior product or process. In the case of sustainability, our preceding discussion suggests that it is no longer a new or unique concept: it has been on the agenda for most companies for the last 20 years. Some retailers have sought to be innovators in this area and have attempted to proactively introduce robust policies across their business operations to gain first-mover advantage. Others have sought to 'jump on the bandwagon' by introducing cosmetic changes to their strategies. Some have adopted a 'wait and see' policy and have only acted when they have been compelled to do so by legislation. It can be argued that short-term competitive benefits can accrue to retailers, particularly if they are proactive and take action ahead of impending legislative action on the part of the governments.

The overall results show that leading retailers are engaged in a diverse range of initiatives to address the overall issue of sustainability. There is a move towards a more robust approach where targets and key performance indicators are used to measure the effectiveness of the activities. We have to inject some caution, however, as the analysis is based largely on published reports and statements from the retailers and does not necessarily provide an insight into the internal thinking that prevails within senior management in the respective retail operations. While the segment containing green, socially aware shoppers is likely to grow in future years, it still represents a relatively small percentage of the overall population. This is exacerbated by the general level of cynicism that pertains in many countries about the merits of investing in green energy and technology. Are people willing to pay more for their clothing or food products to support a more environmentally friendly approach to sourcing by retailers? The evidence is mixed in this respect.

As we discuss later in the chapter, there are still large variations in terms of the consumer's understanding of and attitude to sustainability globally. As the 'green consumer segment' grows apace, it is likely that companies cannot evade the challenges of encompassing sustainability within their business and supply chain strategies.

Activity

Conduct a brief search of the Italian retailer, Benetton, using standard electronic library services at your college and/or Google and other websites. Assess the strategy employed by this retailer over the last few decades in the specific area of sustainability. What are your conclusions? Did it gain any differential advantage? How did its competitors react? Would you deem the strategy employed to be a success?

As with many approaches to gain a potential differential advantage, initiatives in this area can lead to some short-term benefits for the organization concerned. Longer-term benefits can accrue but only if senior management take actions that have a lasting impact on the supply chain strategy.

11.10 Limitations of adopting sustainable retail supply chains

The preceding section strongly suggested that this is a topic that cannot be ignored in the context of supply chain management development and implementation. If organizations continue to ignore such issues, it is likely that they will be usurped by their competitors or ultimately be rejected by their customer base. The term 'greenwashing' has entered into the business lexicon in recent years. It can be defined as situations where companies misrepresent what they do with regard to green initiatives. In essence, they use public relations to put a positive spin on such activities and, in the worst case scenario, lie about what they do.

TerraChoice (2009), an environmental marketing and consulting firm, notes on its website that in its experience, many companies pursue a strategy that at face value appears to be addressing the issue of sustainability, but on closer examination, contains some disingenuous practices. It refers to this as the 'seven sins of greenwashing'. They are summarized as follows.

1 **Sin of the hidden trade-off**: a claim suggesting that a product is green based on a narrow set of attributes without attention to other important environmental issues. Paper, for example, is not

necessarily environmentally preferable just because it comes from a sustainably harvested forest. Other important environmental issues in the paper-making process, such as greenhouse gas emissions or chlorine use in bleaching, may be equally important.

2 **Sin of no proof**: an environmental claim that cannot be substantiated by easily accessible supporting information or by a reliable third-party certification. Common examples are facial tissues or toilet tissue products that claim various percentages of post-consumer recycled content without providing evidence.

3 **Sin of vagueness**: a claim that is so poorly defined or broad that its real meaning is likely to be misunderstood by the consumer. 'All natural' is an example. Arsenic, uranium, mercury and formaldehyde are all naturally occurring, and poisonous. 'All natural' isn't necessarily 'green'.

4 **Sin of worshipping false labels**: a product that, through either words or images, gives the impression of third-party endorsement where no such endorsement exists; fake labels, in other words.

5 **Sin of irrelevance**: an environmental claim that may be truthful but is unimportant or unhelpful for consumers seeking environmentally preferable products. 'CFC-free' is a common example because it is a frequent claim despite the fact that CFCs are banned by law.

6 **Sin of lesser of two evils**: a claim that may be true within the product category, but that risks distracting the consumer from the greater environmental impacts of the category as a whole. Organic cigarettes could be an example of this sin, as might the fuel-efficient sport-utility vehicle.

7 **Sin of fibbing**: environmental claims that are simply false. The most common examples were products falsely claiming to be Energy Star certified or registered. © 2015 UL LLC. Reprinted with permission.

Almost all of these so-called sins can be explained by the fact that they play on the lack of interest, knowledge or on lethargy that exists on the part of many consumers globally. We examine this in greater detail in Chapter 12. Undoubtedly, as the segment that is identified with the environmentally and socially concerned consumer grows, and as the level of interest and concern increases, it will become more difficult to 'play games' with the end user.

In some cases shoppers are willing to pay a premium price for products and services that claim to be green. This can provide a strong motivation for retailers to be 'extravagant about the truth' and make some questionable claims about their value proposition.

A number of sceptics, largely in the form of opinion formers, journalists and some scientists, have cast some doubt on the extent of the damage that is being done to the environment. This has induced some healthy cynicism in the minds of a number of companies and consumers globally. It has played a role in slowing down the acceptance level that consumers and organizations may have to radically alter their lifestyles and product designs, respectively. This has not been helped by the perceived costs of complying with some of the recommendations that have been made by various government 'think-tanks' and opinion formers. It is most evidenced in the aviation sector where many lobby groups are campaigning determinedly to pressure governments into introducing a range of taxes to address the issue of carbon footprint. Many consumers are not prepared to accept such recommendations because they perceive that they will be priced out of flying, particularly to long-haul destinations. Governments are also introducing levies and taxes to subsidize green energy and have also drawn criticism from sceptical members of the public.

A superficial examination of many product and service sectors suggests that if governments introduce more rigorous and overarching sustainability legislation across the spectrum of business activities, a number of central questions will have to be addressed. Are consumers willing to change their lifestyles radically to accommodate such change? For instance, will people stop visiting long-haul destinations to take vacations? Are consumers willing to pay more for sustainable initiatives? For instance, will they pay extra taxes to address the damage to the environment? Are retailers proactively working on alternative technologies and designs that will cause less damage to the environment? For instance, are car manufacturers developing an alternative to the existing 'oil-based' products? As noted earlier, will shoppers be prepared to pay more for environmentally friendly merchandise that has been produced in safe and fair surroundings? At this stage, there are no obvious answers to these questions. However, the inconclusive evidence that exists at present suggests that consumers, legislators and organizations will have to take hard decisions in these areas over the coming years.

11.11 Benefits of adopting a sustainable retail supply chain strategy

We have highlighted the possible criticisms that have been made of organizations that would appear to pay 'lip service' at best, or are disingenuous with the truth at worst, when claiming to engage in a strategy that projects the image of being socially and environmentally responsible in the context of supply chain management. The big question facing senior management, however, revolves around the potential benefits that can accrue from pursuing a coherent and planned approach to incorporating sustainability into the supply chain.

Emmett and Sood (2010: 8) identify a number of benefits and group them into five broad categories.

Environmental
- Integrated environmental considerations and supply chain management process reduces emission of greenhouse gases
- Reduction in waste, pollution and environmental degradation.

Technological
- Creates a platform for further technological advancement by identifying areas where they would have maximum impact on reducing environmental degradation
- Provides a systematic process whereby greening opportunities can be identified throughout the supply chain
- Dedicated technologies can be developed for the processes having greening opportunity
- Enables more efficient use of resources
- Increased visibility of the financial and operational benefits.

Economic
- Increased organisational profitability due to positive net financial impact of Green Supply Chain projects
- Reduced procurement costs from more efficient energy and material use
- Reduced compliance and disposal costs from decreased waste generation and use of hazardous materials
- Significant new organisation because of customer-related environmental initiatives
- Increased benefits by merging supply chain optimisation efforts and environmental management efforts.

Regulatory
- Keeps the organisation well ahead of the regulatory wave, creating an impetus for innovation, organisational learning and change
- Addresses the issue of global warming which is one of the most important concerns of environment experts and policymakers across the world
- Addresses public and regulatory hostility towards environmentally harmful organisations.

Social
- Positive word-of-mouth, viral marketing opportunities, and recognition as one of the leaders
- Increased sales for environmentally preferable products result in a clean neighbourhood
- Safer workplace and clean working environment
- Better health, reduced occupational health and safety costs, and manpower costs.

Ultimately, the benefits that we identified earlier, will, depending on the nature of the product/services category, become established practice as customer preferences and legislation force retailers to take a proactive approach to managing sustainability across their respective supply chains. It is certainly possible that some organizations, by seizing the initiative, can obtain a competitive advantage in the short to medium term. This will depend, however, on the willingness of senior management to embrace fully the principles of sustainability across all of its internal business functions and also across all of its upstream and downstream partners. This ultimately will deliver an integrated approach to sustainable supply chain management in a strategic and proactive manner as opposed to 'cherry-picking' the easier elements of the supply chain and making 'cosmetic' gestures to the notion of 'greenness and sustainability'.

11.12 Case in point: Inditex – sustainable retail supply chains in action

Inditex and the Pro-Kyoto project

Inditex is a large Spanish retail organization that has developed eight brands worldwide (Zara, Pull and Bear, Massimo Dutti, Bershka, Stradivarius, Oysho, Zara Home and Kiddy's Class) and 3,914 stores in 70 countries. In the mid-2000s, the Spanish government and the European Commission increased the fines for companies that exceeded the agreed CO_2 emissions. Inditex was far in excess of the approved levels and harboured concerns about the effect that this would have on its corporate image. As part of its overall strategic environmental plan to cover the period 2007–2010, it identified five specific projects that address a number of critical areas where its supply chain operations and structures impact on the environment and the Planet's resources.

One of these initiatives was labelled the Pro-Kyoto project. This initiative focuses on the logistics operations of the group. It specifically sets an objective of achieving a 20 per cent reduction of greenhouse gases generated by transportation.

The following strategy was established:

1 *A bio-diesel programme*: Zara's entire fleet of transportation vehicles to be run on bio-diesel. The vehicles concerned will be operated by third-party logistics providers.

- Fleet driver training programmes on fuel-efficient driving to be run in conjunction with the logistics suppliers. All vehicles to comply with the European Commission's EURO 5 NOx vehicle standard, two years ahead of its enforcement.
- Zero-emissions electric vehicles to be used in factories and logistics centres.

2 *Eco-efficient store model*: working with a local university to design an ecological energy management model for retail outlets in areas such as lighting, to drive efficiencies in consumption.

- Eco-certification for all plastic and paper bags used by the group
- Training for store personnel to raise awareness of environmental impacts.

3 *Integration of environmental and energy actions in the production facilities*: this covers its headquarters, its logistics centres and 11 textile factories.

- Investments include a 5,000 kW cogeneration plant, a 1,500 sq ft. solar installation and an 850 kW wind turbine.

4 *Carbon footprint project*: it will measure the carbon footprint of each of its manufacturing processes and adopt strategies to reduce it.

- The Terra project involves tree planting as an effective way of closing the energy/CO_2 loop.

Inditex, at the outset of this strategy, was faced with the problem that no biofuels were readily available in Spain. It also had to address a high degree of scepticism among senior managers, combined with a fear of technology change.

Inditex expects that the group and its various brands will be enhanced by the evidence of good practice in the area of sustainability. Clear environmental benefits will accrue as CO_2 emissions will be reduced by 850 tonnes per year due to the use of bio-fuels. They also expect to see benefits from creating more socially aware drivers.

Source: Adapted from Cetinkaya, B. et al. (eds) (2011) *Sustainable Supply Chain Management: Practical Ideas for Moving Towards Best Practice*. Berlin: Springer Verlag, pp. 191–195.

Question

1 To what extent do you believe that Inditex will gain a competitive advantage from pursuing this approach to supply chain management?

11.13   Why bother? Evidence so far

McKinnon et al. (2010) report on three influential studies that were administered in 2007 and 2008. The main findings are summarized in Table 11.1.

It is interesting to compare the findings from these studies. Most of the motivations highlighted suggest that companies see business benefits either from pursuing a sustainability agenda with regard to supply chain issues or from a need to comply with existing or pending legislation. The benefits tend to coalesce around public and customer relations or from a cost reduction perspective. None of the respondents identify altruistic benefits such as saving the environment or making more effective use of the planet's resources. We should not be entirely surprised as companies engaging in business are largely driven by profit motives and are answerable to their shareholders.

Zhu et al. (2010) studied green supply chain practices among Japanese manufacturers. Based on interviews with 10 large corporations, they found that they had implemented internal environmental management practices at a high level. Such internal practices involved: the commitment to green supply chain management from senior managers and mid-level managers, cross-functional co-operation for environmental improvements, total quality environmental management, environmental compliance and auditing programmes, ISO 14001 certification and evidence of environmental management systems. When compared with results from an earlier study on Chinese counterparts, the Japanese companies had implemented these practices at a far higher level. Both studies showed that Chinese and Japanese companies implemented external practices at similar levels. While the higher levels can be partially

TABLE 11.1 Key motivation for the greening of supply chains

Eye for Transport (2007)	Aberdeen Group (2008)	Insight (2008)
Improving public relations (70%)	Desire to be leader in sustainability (51%)	Optimise logistics flow (18%)
Improving customer relations (70%)	Rising cost of energy / fuel (49%)	Improve corporate image (16%)
Part of CSR agenda (60%)	Gaining competitive advantage (48%)	Reduce logistics costs (15%)
Financial ROI (60%)	Compliance with legislation (31%)	Achieve compliance (15%)
Government compliance (60%)	Rising cost of transportation (24%)	Satisfy customers (14%)
Decreasing fuel bills (60%)		Differentiation (11%)
Increasing SC efficiency (55%)		Develop alternative networks (10%)
Decreasing risk (50%)		
Improving investor relations (38%)		

Source: Adapted from McKinnon et al. (2010: 18)

explained by more robust and tougher legislation in Japan, the findings indicate that it is important to get 'buy-in' and ongoing commitment from senior and mid-level managers before a company can hope to convince external partners of the benefits of a strategic approach to sustainability in the context of supply chain management.

Activity

UK food retailing, as is the case in many countries, is dominated by four large retailers: Tesco, Asda, Sainsbury's and Morrisons. Together and through all of their respective retail formats, they are responsible for over 75 per cent all food sales.

The Sustainable Development Commission (SDC) (2008) published a report that reviewed various government and retailer initiatives to support a sustainable food system. This report identified the retailers as being in a very strong position to influence and develop 'a greener, healthier, fairer food system through their influence on supply chains, consumer behaviour and their own operations' (p. 8).

While the retailers have been active in introducing initiatives to reduce the carbon footprint and emissions across their respective supply chains, there has been criticism of their efforts, particularly that they have done so for public relations marketing benefits and cost reduction rather than for any real concern over the environment and the Planet's resources.

Task

Visit the website of the Sustainable Development Commission: www.sd-commission.org.uk/publications/downloads/GreenHealthyAndFair.pdf

Select *one* of the four main food retailers. Conduct a web search of its activities and initiatives with regard to the management of its supply chain.

Assess its approach to sustainability. Is it 'cosmetic' or is it a proactive approach to address the issues of concern with regard to the environment and social concerns? How successfully does it address the concerns of the Sustainable Development Commission report?

11.14 The voice of the shopper

So far in this chapter we have considered the issue of sustainability from the perspective of the retailer and its role in the supply chain. We now assess the voice of the shopper with regard to issues such as the environment, green marketing, corporate social responsibility and ethical standards.

In Chapter 2 we considered the factors that shape the shopper's perceived image of a retail store. For some shoppers, ethical issues in general and the approach of the retailer to this factor can play an important role in deciding whether or not to patronize that store. Many studies have portrayed the ethically concerned shopper as someone who is generally young, well educated and falling within a middle to upper-class background. Some studies also highlight the fact that this category of shopper tends to be predominantly female (Prothero, 1990; Roberts, 1996). Shoppers who express such concerns also have a tendency to become involved in activities that are relevant to the community and to the protection of the environment.

A more recent study of US shoppers reinforces the results from earlier research that the ethical shoppers tends to be young and well educated (Wei, Planchon and James, 2013).

Research by Memery, Megicks and Williams (2005) developed a preliminary typology to identify some of the key factors in the environment and social responsibility when shaping shoppers' buying behaviour in the context of retailing. The seven core categories they identified are summarized as follows:

- *Food, drink and product safety*: GM foods, additives, BSE in cattle, pesticides on foods.
- *Animal welfare*: organically reared, animal testing, feeding antibiotics.

- *Honest labelling*: nutritional content, small-print legibility, allergy warnings, country of origin.
- *Advertising and promotions*: unethical targeting of children, false representation of products, intrusive advertising.
- *Ethical trading*: traceability of supply chain, parent-friendly layout, fair pricing policies, fair prices for suppliers, selling local produce.
- *Human rights*: fair trade/working conditions, power of retailers, child labour and employee welfare.
- *The environment*: sustainable forests, organically produced, overpackaging, recycling facilities, greenhouse effect.

These findings present a useful initial attempt to pinpoint the range of factors that come under the general heading of environmental and social responsibility concerns that influence the buying behaviour of the ethical shopper. We should avoid treating this research as being conclusive. Since 2005 various governments have developed a more proactive approach to deal with environmental issues. Retailers (as discussed in this chapter) have become more proactive in developing initiatives to address this category of shopper and to comply with the increasing legislation in the area of waste management, recycling and carbon footprint.

The growth of social media platforms has also opened up opportunities for retailers to engage with their target markets in a more customized and focused manner. Further research is needed on the impact of such platforms on the ways in which retailers communicate their approach to the environment and socially responsible initiatives. We address this in greater detail in our chapter on retail marketing communication.

Figure 11.2 Barriers to and enablers of the consumer adoption of sustainability-oriented offerings

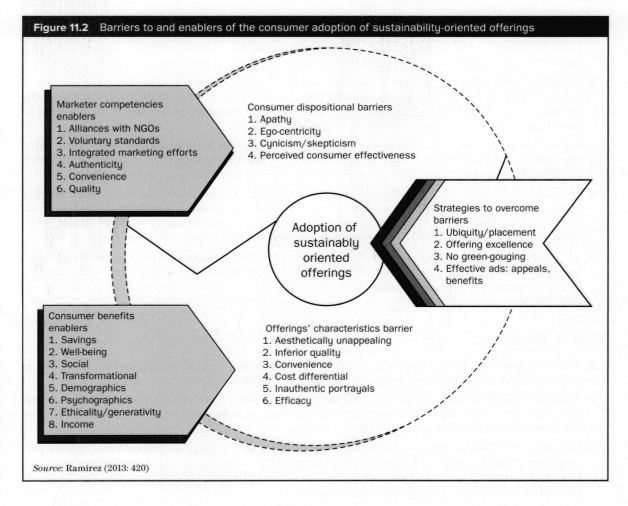

Marketer competencies enablers
1. Alliances with NGOs
2. Voluntary standards
3. Integrated marketing efforts
4. Authenticity
5. Convenience
6. Quality

Consumer dispositional barriers
1. Apathy
2. Ego-centricity
3. Cynicism/skepticism
4. Perceived consumer effectiveness

Adoption of sustainably oriented offerings

Strategies to overcome barriers
1. Ubiquity/placement
2. Offering excellence
3. No green-gouging
4. Effective ads: appeals, benefits

Consumer benefits enablers
1. Savings
2. Well-being
3. Social
4. Transformational
5. Demographics
6. Psychographics
7. Ethicality/generativity
8. Income

Offerings' characteristics barrier
1. Aesthetically unappealing
2. Inferior quality
3. Convenience
4. Cost differential
5. Inauthentic portrayals
6. Efficacy

Source: Ramirez (2013: 420)

The profiles of ethical shoppers vary across different geographic regions. A study of shoppers in the Gulf region identified three clusters of shoppers. The first category was labelled as *principled purchasers*. These shoppers are characterized by the emphasis they place on ethical behaviour in their day-to-day activities. They are scrupulous in matters such as not taking advantage of mistakes made by retail assistants; for example, undercharging for an item or giving too much change back. *Suspicious shoppers* are categorized as individuals who are mistrustful of other people. This is reflected in their dealings with retailers where they feel they may be taken advantage of in certain buying situations. They tend to be idealistic and do not wish to do anything that might hurt others. The final category, *the corrupt consumer*, is someone that is similar to suspicious shoppers but is less idealistic and is predisposed to take advantage of any situation that presents an opportunity for personal gain (Al-Khatib, Stanton and Rawwas, 2005). While this study is region-specific, it provides some insight into behavioural characteristics that impinge on shopping behaviour.

The scepticism of many shoppers is a theme picked up by Ramirez (2013). Combined with general apathy across many segments and allied to levels of cynicism, this presents the greatest challenge for companies and retailers to address in their move towards sustainable strategies. Figure 11.2 provides a framework by which a number of enablers and barriers to sustainability are identified. Although the research is exploratory in nature, it provides us with some indicators of the perceptions of consumers about environmental and social responsibility issues and how retailers may respond.

Based on the evidence from research in this area, we can identify some implications for the various stakeholders.

11.14.1 Shoppers

- Generally so-called 'ethical shoppers' are still in a minority, although this segment is likely to grow over the next decade due to increased awareness levels, legislation set by policymakers that forces them to recognize the consequences of doing damage to the environment, for example recycling personal waste, and the marketing efforts of both retailers and manufacturers.

- Scepticism and cynicism still prevails in the minds of many shoppers about the general issue of sustainability. This is reinforced by the perception that they have to pay more for 'environmentally friendly' merchandise. They also equate higher prices with the belief that retailers are 'cashing in' and charging more than is necessary for such items.

- A perception that there is nothing extra to be gained (benefits or added value) from purchasing environmentally friendly merchandise or adopting an 'ethical' approach when making a purchasing decision. The issue of 'what's in it for me?' is perhaps an apt phrase to encompass this view.

- In some retail sectors such as fast-fashion, certain shoppers are driven to shop in such stores by the cheap prices. It is clearly questionable whether such prices can be offered to shoppers without compromising on ethical issues such as 'sweatshop' production, exploitation of workers in less-developed economies and even more contentious areas such as child labour (see Phau and Ong, 2007).

- At a more general level, there is a 'built-in' resentment in the attitudes of some shoppers cultivated by the fact that many governments and legislators are pushing through legislation to address green or environmental issues. The rapidly increasing costs of energy in Europe encapsulate the perception that society is paying a high price for no perceived benefits.

11.14.2 Retailers

- Retailers need to be more transparent and up-front with their sustainability initiatives. It can be argued that much of the green marketing initiatives is more about style than substance.

- Retailers need to educate shoppers. They can possibly do this more effectively by engaging in collaborative initiatives with other key stakeholders such as policymakers, consumer associations, environmental organizations and so on.

- Retailers should be cognizant of the need to provide some incentive or reward for shoppers who purchase 'ethical' products. While the production and/or sourcing of such merchandise may cost more to the retailer, it is still important in the short term to incentivize shoppers. This can be implemented as part of a parallel educational campaign.

- Retailers should recognize that the only way to combat scepticism and cynicism is to market ethical products that are demonstrably better in terms of value to the shoppers. This is a long-term challenge.

- Developing community-based activities that bring tangible benefits is one way to develop a more positive perception among shoppers. This addresses the concept of being a 'good corporate citizen' and can lead to a demonstrable sense of goodwill to the retailer in the local communities.

11.15 A framework for developing sustainable retail supply chain strategies

As we come to the end of this chapter, we need to consider a framework that provides a guideline for developing a sustainable supply chain. In this section we consider one approach that can help us gain a better understanding of the processes and challenges involved in designing and implementing a supply chain strategy that encompasses the sustainability issues discussed earlier in this chapter.

The bestLog project was initiated in 2005 as a direct response to the European Union's (EU) policy of supporting research initiatives into the relationships between the logistics and supply chain decisions of individual European companies and the very high level of traffic volumes that has occurred in Europe over the last 20 years.

Nine partner countries (Belgium, the Czech Republic, France, Germany, Poland, Spain, Sweden, Switzerland and the UK) continue to participate in this project. Their key contribution is to promote

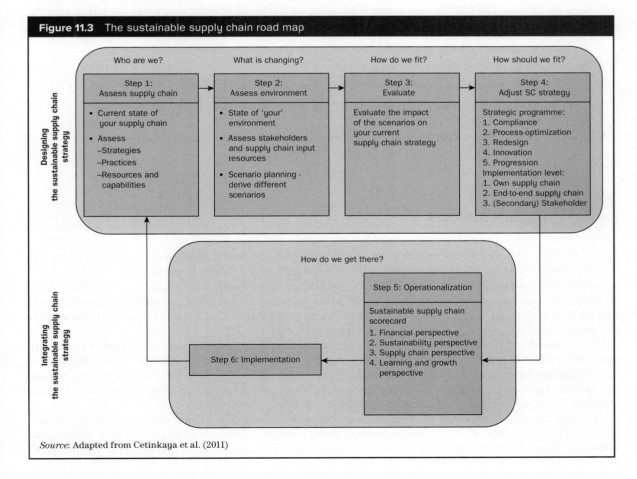

Figure 11.3 The sustainable supply chain road map

Source: Adapted from Cetinkaya et al. (2011)

and disseminate best practice to the supply chain professionals in an attempt to improve supply chain management practice across the European business environment. They have put forward a framework for organizations to use when developing a sustainable supply chain strategy.

This framework recognizes that the exercise is not about implementing some popular practices that can gain short-term favourable publicity. It is an iterative exercise that has to be developed over time and refined to integrate long-term sustainability principles as a central plank of the supply chain strategy. The framework is shaped by a focused analysis of five major questions:

1 Who are we (assessing the current position of our organization)?

2 What is changing (assessing the environment: current and future)?

3 How do we fit (evaluating the risks and opportunities)?

4 How should we fit (applying this analysis to existing strategy and identifying strategy changes)?

5 How do we get there (focusing on implementation issues and balancing social, economic and environmental objectives)?

The final step in the process is to focus on the key ingredients that are necessary to successfully implement the strategy.

If applied properly, this framework encourages organizations to adopt a systemic approach to the incorporation of sustainability into the supply chain strategy. It applies the basic principles of strategic planning such as the SWOT analysis and the balanced scorecard to allow for a coherent and robust supply chain strategy that takes account of the specific characteristics of that organization's market and competitive environment.

We can also gain an insight into the key factors that need to be addressed if a retailer wishes to seriously address the challenges involved in establishing corporate responsibility and sustainability into their strategies. The UN Global Compact-Accenture CEO Study (2010) pinpointed the following key attributes for embedding sustainability:

1 Such issues should be fully embedded into the strategy and operations of a company.

2 Boards should discuss and act on these issues.

3 Companies should embed these issues through their global supply chain.

4 Companies should engage in industry collaborations and multi-stakeholder partnerships to address development goals.

5 Companies should incorporate these issues into discussions with financial analysts.

11.16 Conclusions

In this chapter we have considered the issue of sustainability and how it impacts on a retailer's strategy. We have considered the implications across the retail supply chain. While large retailers generally hold a considerable amount of power and influence, any initiatives in the areas of social responsibility, environmentalism and green marketing can only be achieved with co-operation and collaboration between key players in the supply chain such as suppliers. Shareholders and other key stakeholders also need to be convinced of the merits of pursuing such a strategy.

We assessed the benefits and potential drawbacks of pursuing sustainability strategies. There is an inexorable move in many countries to address major issues such as climate change. If we project forward over the next couple of decades, it is unlikely that this trend will be reversed; indeed, it is more than likely to increase in pace. Therefore, retailers cannot ignore the implications of existing and potential legislation and should embed sustainability issues in their retail strategies.

We also noted that consumers in general and shoppers in particular exhibit varying degrees of commitment to the concept of ethical shopping and 'green retailing'. This would appear to be a global phenomenon. There is still a substantive group of consumers who display apathy and ignorance about such issues. Consequently, challenges lie ahead for legislators, government and organizations to educate society about environmental issues. From a marketing perspective, it can be a 'hard sell' if people do not see any obvious or immediate benefits from adopting an ethical stance with regard to their purchasing habits.

This problem is exacerbated by a level of scepticism and cynicism that exists in society. This is often reflected in the perception that any initiative to do with the environment is seen as an added cost for shoppers. It is not helped by the tendency of some retailers to engage in 'greenwashing': where false or exaggerated claims are made about products and which lack any substance to show that they are genuine initiatives that support the protection of the environment.

The onus is on retailers to come up with initiatives that demonstrably highlight value and benefits to shoppers. This is not an easy task and it may take a generation (10–15 years) before sustainability becomes a central part of a shopper's evaluative criteria when engaging in the act of purchasing.

We have considered areas of good practice in the area of sustainability by retailers (Marks & Spencer and Inditex). Their respective approaches to sustainable strategy development and implementation highlight the importance of engaging proactively and longitudinally with key stakeholders such as other members of the supply chain, internal staff, customers, media and environmental groups. Such approaches need strong leadership and vision from the CEO and the board of directors. A proactive and strategic approach to sustainability requires the organization and its external partners to embrace change and all of the issues and challenges associated with change management.

Case study: Marks & Spencer

Marks & Spencer, the UK retailer, has over 700 stores in the UK and operates in over 40 countries globally. It specializes in selling clothing and food products aimed at the middle to high-end of the market. It has been in existence since 1884 and in 1998, at the height of its performance, it was the first British retailer to declare pre-tax profits of over £1 billion.

Within the context of sustainability, Marks & Spencer was to the forefront in setting an agenda for social responsibility. After fighting off a hostile bid in 2004, it set about reshaping its overall commitment to the area of social responsibility. In 2007 it launched what it called 'Plan A'. This ambitious plan set over 100 targets to be met by 2012 and revolved around a number of central platforms. In particular, it addressed issues in the following areas: climate, waste, sustainable materials, fair partnership and health.

The launch of Plan A was characterized by a very strong level of leadership from senior management in general and the CEO at the time, Sir Stuart Rose. When he handed over to Marc Bolland in 2010, he ensured that the new CEO would also carry on the developments outlined in Plan A. The level of visibility associated with the involvement of senior personnel was reflected in the appointment of a senior executive to oversee the initiatives of other senior managers across its operations; that is, food packaging and formulation, development of green factories with clothing suppliers and living wage initiatives in areas such as Bangladesh.

The oversight of Plan A is led by 'the how we do business committee', led by the chairman with input from senior executives from across the company. It meets on a monthly basis and also meets regularly with the executive board to ensure that the initiatives identified in Plan A are aligned with overall group strategy.

Marks & Spencer was cognizant of the need to engage with the wider stakeholders. It started with staff and institutional investors and branched out to customers and civil society shareholders. In recognition of the growing evidence of climate change from the scientific fraternity, it decided that it needed to increase its efforts further in the area of sustainability. The retailer had already generated savings from its sustainability initiatives. It set itself the target of becoming the world's most sustainable retailer by 2015.

The main change in focus meant that whereas previously social responsibility and environmental commitments were add-ons to business operations, run by a specialist CSR function, it now builds in these issues into business purpose and strategy. It explicitly requires each part of its business operations to change the way they do business. Senior management see the revamped Plan A as a change of management brand. For instance, in the area of procurement, purchasing executives have to address many of the original targets as they impact on suppliers' practices.

▶

A key factor in the implementation of Plan A was the need to engage proactively with the other members of the supply chain. Over 1,500 suppliers participated in a Knowledge Exchange programme. This involves ongoing workshops and conferences on various sustainability issues.

They also began some formal engagement with customers. They segmented customers into three categories: disinterested; 'light greens' (those who might engage if Marks & Spencer made it easy for them to do so); and 'deep greens' (those committed to changing their shopping behaviour). For instance, the retailer took the decision to charge 5p for disposable carrier bags, with all proceeds going to an environmental charity called Groundwork.

Another key platform in Plan A is the employees. Each of its stores in the UK has a Plan A champion who takes responsibility for involving co-workers in initiatives and activities. Regional networks also meet on a regular basis to discuss experiences and good practice.

In order to drive Plan A forward, Marks & Spencer works with a range of external stakeholders and organizations such as universities, charities, Greenpeace and Compassion in World Farming. An interesting initiative is its long-standing relationship with Oxfam (a large development charity organization). Oxfam give out £5 redeemable vouchers for use in Marks & Spencer outlets when people donate old Marks & Spencer clothing to them.

Marks & Spencer uses Ernst & Young as an independent auditor to assess performance with regard to whether or not targets have been met and, if not, what needs to be done to achieve success. It sees great value in having such a third-party overseer applying comprehensive auditing procedures that would also be applied to standard profit and loss accounts.

Source: Material for this case was developed from Grayson, D. (2010) Embedding corporate social responsibility and sustainability: Marks & Spencer. *Journal of Management Development*. 30(10): 1017–1026.

Questions

1 To what extent do you believe that Marks & Spencer are the leaders in the field of sustainable retailing? From your reading of this topic, put forward another retailer who might also be described as a leader.

2 As a marketer, do you believe that such initiatives are relevant for shoppers? How might Marks & Spencer improve their communications strategy to shoppers?

3 Do you see Plan A as a cost or an investment for Marks & Spencer?

Chapter outcomes

■ The issue of sustainability has increased in importance over the last 20 years.

■ The term 'sustainability' is an umbrella phrase that covers issues such as ethical shopping, environmental protection, corporate social responsibility, green consumers and green marketing.

■ Retailers have to be cognizant of the fact that it is no longer accurate or acceptable to focus exclusively on profit as the only reason for their existence. They are also answerable to a wider set of stakeholders such as society in general and the local communities where they operate their outlets and stores.

■ The triple bottom line concept is often used to reflect the wider social responsibility objectives of retailers.

■ Increasingly, retailers are recognizing that sustainability strategies are not a cost but an investment. For instance, real cost savings can be generated from initiatives in areas such as recycling, waste management and designing eco stores.

- From the consumer perspective there is still a strong degree of apathy and ignorance about ethical shopping.
- From a marketing communications perspective, retailers have to demonstrate that there are benefits and 'wins' for shoppers who adopt an ethical stance. Some shoppers are not prepared to pay for such merchandise if they do not see any tangible benefits from having to pay 'slightly more' or 'a lot more' for a particular item.
- This is exacerbated by the focus of many retailers on cost reduction and competing on the basis of low prices.
- Retailers who wish to implement effective sustainability strategies should recognize the importance of 'leading from the top'. Without strong leadership and vision, it is unlikely that long-term, strategic initiatives can be implemented.
- Retailers cannot drive forward the sustainability agenda without commitment and buy-in from other members of their supply chain; for example, suppliers.

Discussion questions

1 Assess the view that employing sustainable retail marketing strategies will increase the cost of merchandise for shoppers.
2 To what extent do you agree with the view that retailers have not helped the cause of sustainability by engaging in greenwashing tactics?
3 Some retailers believe that they can gain a competitive advantage by investing in sustainability strategies. Is this an accurate perception in your view?
4 If you were asked to provide some advice to a small independent retailer who wants to engage in sustainability initiatives, what recommendations would you make to that individual?
5 Retailers who compete in the low price and affordable fashion sector have been accused of exploiting working conditions in developing economies. How can they take a more responsible position with such suppliers if it means that prices will rise for shoppers?
6 You are employed by a large food retailer to work in the area of corporate social responsibility. You have been asked to meet with customers and engage with them on the topic of ethical shopping and how it might benefit them. Detail the issues that you would cover with them.

References

Al-Khatib, J.A., Stanton, A. and Rawwas, M.A. (2005) Ethical segmentation of consumers in developing countries: a comparative analysis. *International Marketing Review.* 22(2): 225–246.

Baharum, M.R. and Pitt, M. (2010) Retail shopping centre recycling initiatives. *Journal of Retail & Leisure Property.* 9(3): 201–10.

Bobe, C. and Dragomir, V. (2010) The sustainability policy of five leading European retailers. *Accounting and Management Information Systems.* 9(2): 268–283.

Bonn, I. and Fisher, J. (2011) Sustainability: the missing ingredient in strategy. *Journal of Business Strategy.* 32(1): 5–14.

Cetinkaya, B., Cuthbertson, R., Ewer, G. et al. (eds) (2011) *Sustainable Supply Chain Management: Practical Ideas for Moving Towards Best Practice.* Berlin: Springer Verlag, pp. 191–195.

Dos Santos, M.A.O., Svensson, G. and Padin, C. (2013) Indicators of sustainable business practices: Woolworths in South Africa. *Supply Chain Management: An International Journal.* 18(1): 104–108.

Edwards, J.B., McKinnon, A.C. and Cullinane, S.L. (2010) Comparative analysis of the carbon footprints of conventional and online retailing: a 'last mile' perspective. *International Journal of Physical Distribution and Logistics Management.* 40(1): 103–123.

Emmett, S. and Sood, V. (2010) *Green Supply Chains: An Action Manifesto*. Oxford: Wiley.

Fieldson, R.and Rai, D. (2010) An assessment of carbon emissions from retail fit-out in the United Kingdom. *Journal of Retail and Leisure Property*. 8(4): 243–58.

Jones, P., Comfort, D. and Hillier, D. (2005a) Concentration and corporate social responsibility: a case study of European food retailers. *Management Research News*. 28(6): 42–54.

Jones, P., Hillier, D., Comfort, D. and Eastwood, I. (2005b) Sustainable retailing and consumerism. *Management Research News*. 28(1): 34–42.

Mann, H., Kumar, U., Kumar, V. and Singh, M.I. (2010) *Drivers of Sustainable Supply Chain Management. The IUP Journal of Operations Management*. IX(4): 52–63.

Markley, M. and Davis, L. (2007) Exploring future competitive advantage through sustainable supply chains. *International Journal of Physical Distribution and Logistics Management*. 37(9): 763–774.

McKinnon, A., Brown, M., Whiteing, A. and Cullinane, S. (2010) *Green Logistics: Improving the Environmental Sustainability of Logistics*. London: Kogan Page, p. 18.

Memery, J., Megicks, P. and Williams, J. (2005) Ethical and social responsibility issues in grocery shopping: a preliminary typology. *Qualitative Market Research: An international Journal*. 8(4): 399–412.

Pagell, M. and Wu, Z. (2007) Building a more complete theory of sustainable supply chain management using case studies of 10 exemplars. *Journal of Supply Chain Management*. 45(2): 37–56.

Pfitzer, M., Bockstedde, V. and Stamp, M. (2013) Innovating for shared value: companies that deliver both social benefit and business value rely on five mutually reinforcing elements. *Harvard Business Review*. September: 101–107.

Phau, I. and Ong, D. (2007) An investigation of the effects of environmental claims in promotional messages for clothing brands. *Marketing Intelligence Planning*. 25(7): 772–788.

Porter, M.E. and Kramer, M.R. (2011) Creating shared value: how to reinvent capitalism and unleash a wave of innovation and growth. *Harvard Business Review*. January–February: 1–17.

Preuss, E. (2009) Ethical sourcing codes of large UK-based corporations: prevalence, content, limitations. *Journal of Business Ethics*. 88: 735–747.

Prothero, A. (1990) Green consumerism and the societal marketing concept: strategies for the 1990's. *Journal of Marketing Management*. 6(2): 87–103.

Ramirez, E. (2013) The consumer adoption of sustainability-oriented offerings: toward a middle-range theory. *Journal of Marketing Theory and Practice*. 21(4): 415–428.

Roberts, J.A. (1996) Green consumers in the 1990's: profile and implications for advertising. *Journal of Business Research*. 36: 217–231.

Srivastava, S.K. (2007) Green supply chain management: a state-of-the-art literature review. *International Journal of Management Reviews*. 9(1): 3–80.

TerraChoice (2009) The Seven Sins of Greenwashing. Available online at: http://sinsofgreenwashing.org/findings/the-seven-sins/ (accessed March 2015).

Thompson, B. (2007) Green retail: retailer strategies for surviving the sustainability storm. *Journal of Retail & Leisure Property*. 6(4): 281–286.

UN Global Compact-Accenture CEO Study (2010) A new era of sustainability.

Wei, S., Planchon, J.M. and James, W.L. (2013) Who will go green? A preliminary study of US consumer segmentation demographics. *International Journal of Business Strategy*. 13(4): 157–164.

Willard, B. (2002) *The Sustainability Advantage: Seven Business Case Benefits of a Triple Bottom Line*. Gabriola Island: New Society Publishers.

World Commission on Environment and Development (1987) Our common future.

Zhu, Q., Geng, Y., Fujita, T. and Hashimoto, S. (2010) Green supply chain management in leading manufacturers: case studies in Japanese large companies. *Management Science Review*. 33(4): 380–392.

4

Retail Internationalization

Part contents

Chapter 12

Retailing and internationalization strategy: development and implementation

✅ Learning objectives

On completion of this chapter you should be able to address the following objectives:

- ☑ Understand the underlying motivations for internationalizing retail operations.
- ☑ Appraise the various theories of internationalization and their relevance to retailing.
- ☑ Examine the selection criteria for evaluating international markets.
- ☑ Assess the various modes of entry that are available to retailers.
- ☑ Examine the implications for the retail supply chain as a consequence of internationalization.
- ☑ Understand the challenges involved in transferring a retail format from a domestic setting to an international environment.
- ☑ Evaluate the standardization versus adaptation dilemma.
- ☑ Appraise the reasons for retail divestment.

12.1 Introduction

For many retailers the challenge of internationalization lies at the heart of their overall business strategy development. Opportunities in domestic markets are often finite and once a retailer achieves a certain degree of size, scale and scope, it has no alternative but to seek opportunities outside of its domestic market if it wishes to expand its operation and grow its business.

It can be argued that due to the Internet, increasing mobility of consumers, fragmentation of the media and constant exposure to global trends and developments, there is a trend towards convergence of taste, attitudes and behaviour among consumers globally. The global market is increasingly more open to access for retailers. In certain sectors such as fashion, music and entertainment, it is perhaps more pronounced than others. This is not to suggest that the task is becoming easier for retailers. As we shall see in this chapter, many retailers fail (sometimes dismally) to transfer their retail formats and concepts successfully to international markets. It can also be argued that differences in culture, shopping behaviour, legislation and infrastructure collectively and individually create barriers and challenges for retailers as they seek success in international markets.

The Internet and the subsequent development of online retail challenges often mean that a retailer can achieve international sales and penetration almost overnight. This phenomenon challenges the conventional view that internationalization is in many instances a slow and incremental process. Although there is some merit in the concept of 'instant' internationalization, the pressure on other areas of the retail supply chain often means that without a proper retail infrastructure – information technology (IT), logistics, warehousing, customer service support and so on – it becomes almost impossible to sustain a 'global' presence.

In the early part of this chapter, we consider the underlying motivations for seeking international expansion and the various criteria that retailers use in order to evaluate the attractiveness of such opportunities. We then consider the various theories of internationalization and their relevance in today's business environment.

The middle section of this chapter considers the various approaches that are available to retailers as they consider expanding their retail concepts and formats to new markets outside of their domestic settings. Three critical factors impinge on this decision: cost, risk and control. The various modes of entry ultimately revolve around these issues. These factors needed to be benchmarked against the

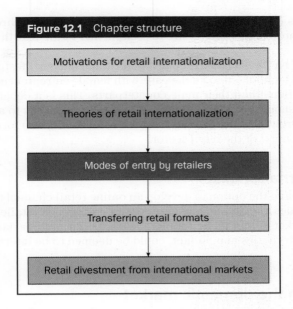

Figure 12.1   Chapter structure

- Motivations for retail internationalization
- Theories of retail internationalization
- Modes of entry by retailers
- Transferring retail formats
- Retail divestment from international markets

existing (and potential) capabilities, competences and resources of the individual retailer. We examine this aspect of retail internationalization in some detail.

Transferring a successful retail format and concept to an international market is not easy. Retailers have to grapple with the issue of a different culture, different facets of shopping behaviour and shopper attitudes. A lack of understanding or knowledge of such local considerations can often scupper the chances of success. We consider these issues and look at some examples of successful and unsuccessful international retail expansion strategies.

We consider the concept of retail divestment: a situation where the retailer has decided to strategically withdraw from a particular international market and assess the underlying reasons for such a decision. We look at the impact of divestment on overall retail strategy.

12.2   Why internationalize? Underlying motivations

We begin our investigation of retail internationalization by positing the following question. Why bother seeking international opportunities? For many retailers this issue may be obvious: we have to in order to further increase our sales, profitability and scale of operations.

12.2.1 Reasons for not internationalizing the retail operation

While this view has great appeal, we should recognize that some retailers have no desire to seek such opportunities. Many small retailers operate in a local environment where their existence and operations are embedded in the local village or community. They have neither the resources, capability or desire to grow beyond this fixed geographic boundary. Further expansion would place too much strain and emphasis on investing in a more complex retail infrastructure: IT, logistics and personnel to name but a few considerations.

Some owners, as identified in the literature on small business enterprises (SMEs), wish to achieve a certain type of lifestyle that bears the fruit of their investment in the business. The founder of a small niche retailer, for example an antiquarian bookshop, may desire a lifestyle that provides a nice house, a couple of foreign holidays, the ability to cover schooling and university for children and the ability to indulge in leisure activities (for example, sailing). If this can be achieved through the present scale of operations then it can counterbalance any desire to seek further retail growth opportunities in national or international markets.

Studies such as the one by Weeks (2009) suggest that establishing a 'lifestyle' business has negative connotations. This is often highlighted to be the case with female entrepreneurs. It is argued that many females have lower aspirations than their male counterparts. This is a debatable issue and is outside the scope of this text. We should recognize, however, that it is dangerous to automatically assume the importance of continued growth as the driving force for establishing any form of business enterprise, including one within the context of the retail sector.

12.2.2 Instant 'internationalists'

The advent of the Internet and the option to develop an online retail channel that can be used for sales and order fulfilment provides a relatively low-cost possibility for such retailers to generate sales from a wider international market. Many niche retailers, such as our antiquarian bookseller, add such a channel to their business activities and, in fact, could be deemed to be international in terms of their operations.

12.2.3 Saturation in the domestic market

For many retailers, however, retail internationalization is at the heart of their business operations and strategic development. Without the presence of such initiatives, the reality for many is that opportunities for further growth in the domestic market may be non-existent. The market may be saturated or the scale of operations of the retailer in that market may be restricted by legislation due to its dominant market position. The domestic market may also be mature, often evidenced by the existence of a small number of dominant competitors who have 'snapped up' the best retail locations. As a result, a retailer has to consider the international environment if it wishes to seek further growth.

12.2.4 Scaling up the retail business

For many retailers, the ability to grow the business operations to a certain scale has major competitive advantages. Increasing the number of store outlets leads to increased sales. Increased sales enhance the bargaining position with suppliers. As a consequence, better deals and discounts. This, in turn, can create a scenario of lower prices and greater cost competitiveness. If the opportunity to grow domestically is severely reduced or eliminated then internationalization becomes an imperative for that retailer.

Writers such as Wrigley et al. (2005) describe such motivations as largely *reactive* in nature. This implies that the decision to internationalize is not based on long-term, proactive and strategic decision-making. Rather, it is the result of the recognition that there are no further opportunities in the domestic market and that the retailer is forced into a position of internationalization. It also implies that international initiatives were almost seen as a 'last resort' for retailers and only to be undertaken when domestic opportunities had evaporated.

12.2.5 Proactive reasons

Evans et al. (2008) put forward the view that such a reactive approach has largely been replaced by a more proactive focus by retailers on internationalization. They cite a number of reasons for this occurrence. Some provide opportunities; others act as potential impediments. These include:

- the greater expansion of the EU to 28 member states (as of 2014)
- China's membership of the World Trade Organization (WTO) and its economic growth, largely fuelled by more 'open' business practices
- a more turbulent economic climate following the Southeast Asian financial crisis at the end of the 1990s
- the threat of terrorism: post-9/11
- significant advances in communications technology.

12.2.6 Emergence of major 'new' geographic markets and growing liberalization of economies

Since Evans et al.'s article was published in 2008, the world generally has faced a significant global recession. India has experienced significant economic growth due to its more liberal policies with regard to business investment.

We have also witnessed the emergence of eastern European economies and other countries such as Brazil. The exponential growth in online retail business has also had an impact on the attitudes of retailers to internationalization. This has also been exacerbated by a tendency towards conformity in tastes and attitudes (for example, fashion).

Myers and Alexander (2007) also highlight the overall reduction in political barriers globally as a significant stimulator of business growth in general and for the retail sector in particular.

12.2.7 Economic integration

Myers and Alexander (2007) further argue that in the context of Europe, there is an ever-increasing trend towards economic integration. Retailers from Germany and France are in the vanguard when it comes to retail development in countries such as Austria, Italy, Spain and Switzerland that account for over 60 per cent of such retail activity. They are responsible for over 40 per cent in other European countries such as Andorra, Belgium, Greece, the Netherlands, Luxembourg, Portugal and the UK. The Netherlands, the UK and Sweden are peripheral regions.

12.2.8 Building the global retail brand

The emphasis placed by retailers on building the brand has also had a significant impact on internationalization. We discussed the concept of brand-building more fully in Chapter 6. Moore and Doyle (2010) point to the emergence of 'brand-led' fashion retailers such as Gap, Abercrombie and Fitch and Victoria's Secret in the USA and subsequently in European and Asian markets as a good example of the power of the brand in establishing a strong position in these markets.

Moore and Doyle (2010) also note that in this sector and at the luxury end, retailers such as Gucci and Burberry have taken on the responsibility for brand creation, development and distribution. This allows them a stronger degree of control over all aspects of the value proposition and value delivery in areas such as communications, pricing and so on.

We should not underestimate the importance of this issue of control. It is critical in terms of achieving a level of consistency when attempting to position the brand in different markets. Some modes of entry reduce the ability to control the value proposition, resulting in inconsistency and mixed communication signals across international markets. We develop more detailed discussion on this issue when we assess the different ways in which retailers can establish a presence internationally.

12.3 Theories of retail internationalization

Numerous authors and researchers have developed a range of theories and frameworks to explain the concept of retail internationalization. It is not our intention in this chapter to systematically review all of them (a full assessment can be found in Alexander and Doherty, 2009: 55–84). Instead, we consider the main frameworks and the key themes to emerge from this body of research in order to help us more fully understand the behaviours and decision-making of retailers.

The genesis of this work began to emerge in the mid-1970s. Researchers in Scandinavia (Johanson and Wiedersheim-Paul, 1975) argued that the process of business internationalization is gradual and incremental. As companies entered into new geographic markets, they did so initially in a cautious and conservative manner, cognizant of the dangers of moving too quickly without fully understanding the nature and structure of this new retail market. As they established a degree of knowledge and confidence, they gradually expanded further into wider geographic markets. While their research was not specifically on the retail sector, the concept of incremental and gradual international expansion featured prominently in subsequent and more focused studies on retail internationalization.

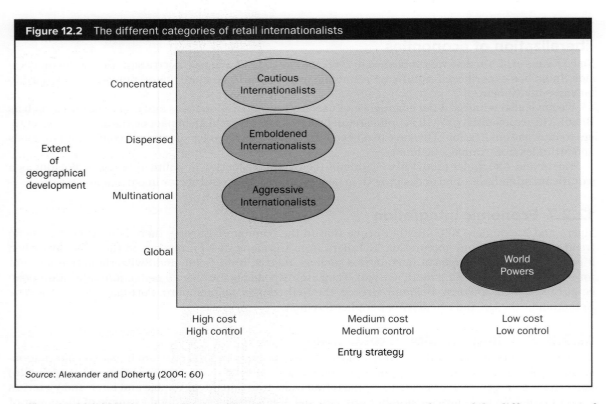

Figure 12.2 The different categories of retail internationalists

Source: Alexander and Doherty (2009: 60)

Treadgold (1988) developed a classification system in an attempt to understand the different types of international retail operators. This framework is displayed in Fig. 12.2.

The framework is somewhat dated. However, it provides a useful initial conceptualization of the process of internationalization. It also recognizes the importance of the cost and control dimensions associated with expanding the retail operation to new geographic markets. It failed to recognize fully that retailers actually used many different mechanisms for entering specific markets. In some cases retailers would go for acquisition or a merger with a local retailer in the area. In other cases, the same retailer might use franchising as a mechanism for market entry. We consider the various entry modes later.

Dunning (1981) within the context of general business internationalization put forward what is referred to as the eclectic theory. This is based on the view that international organizations build up significant advantages which can form the basis for development and exploitation in international markets. They largely revolve around ownership-specific, location-specific and internalization advantages.

Another major source for understanding the process of internationalization is based on the concept of network theory. This argues strongly that the internationalization process is based on and facilitated by social interaction and relationships that evolve and develop over time. While grounded initially in the context of manufacturing, it has also been applied to the retail sector.

Within the context of retail internationalization, Bianchi (2011) puts forward the view that the international retailer establishes a competitive advantage through a combination of its internal organizational and managerial capabilities as well as the necessary resources to allow it to expand its operations internationally. The former refer to aspects of its offering such as merchandise assortment, pricing, sourcing or relative uniqueness of the retail concept. The latter covers the experience, attitudes and leadership of management within that organization.

For retailers, in contrast to manufacturing firms, the real challenge lies in transferring a retail format, which has proved to be successful in a domestic setting, to a new environment which has a (relatively) different set of norms, culture and shopping behaviours. In the case of manufacturing companies, it could be argued that the process of internationalization is often based on cost considerations covering issues such as labour and production. It does not have to grapple with the challenge of engaging and selling either directly or indirectly to customers. There is less emphasis on the need to understand fully the social dynamics and culture of the country where the production facility is located.

For instance, if Dell decides to locate its production in an emerging South American country, it does not have to address the same degree of complexity as would be the case if it was establishing a retail structure. In fact, when it moved into the Chinese market in the late 1990s and tried to apply its direct model of selling, it discovered that the Chinese shopper valued the concept of 'high touch'; that is, personal interaction, and was uncomfortable with the notion of purchasing a laptop or PC over the Internet. It struggled to make any significant impact in the Chinese market as a result. Dell had to adapt its model and set up sales demonstration areas in shopping malls in the key areas of the larger cities. It was not possible to directly transfer a hitherto successful retail format to this part of the world and adaptation had to be introduced if it was to have any hope of competing successfully.

This example introduces an important consideration within the context of retail internationalization (Palmer, 2005): retail learning. Palmer and Quinn (2005) argue that in order for a retailer to make a significant impression in the international setting, it must address the following questions.

- What do retail internationalists identify as the most important lessons learned from their experience of internationalizing retail operations?
- To what degree has this knowledge been absorbed by the internationalizing retail company?
- What is the locus of international retail learning diffusion or transfer?
- What are the outcomes from the lessons learned and how do these shape the future decision-making and learning behaviour of the retailer?

This is encapsulated in Fig. 12.3.

This is a useful contribution to our understanding of the process of retail internationalization. First, it recognizes the iterative nature of internationalization: you learn from experience and feed that back into your internal domain, reflect and dissect and make adjustments accordingly. From this process, it can be argued that the retailer is in a stronger position to anticipate and address potential impediments that may exist in a particular market more successfully.

Second, it forces us to move away from the rather simplistic 'stages of growth' frameworks that have been advanced in many of the models. As a consequence of retail learning, a retailer may suddenly decide to reduce its activities in this area, retrench its operations and focus on its core markets. By contrast, a retailer may adopt a more aggressive approach to internationalization due to developments in a particular market. This challenges the notion that internationalization is both incremental and inevitable.

Jonsson and Foss (2011: 1082) capture the essence of this approach in the following statement:

> **"***Experiential knowledge is vital to the internationalization process, because it not only yields a reduction of the risks involved in going abroad, but also provides a vehicle for acquiring knowledge of internal and external resources and of opportunities for combining them.***"**

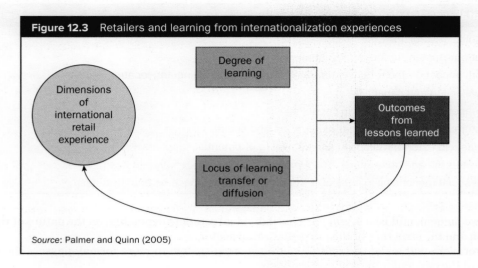

Figure 12.3   Retailers and learning from internationalization experiences

Source: Palmer and Quinn (2005)

12.4   Selection criteria for evaluating international markets

While retail opportunities internationally may exist for many retailers, they may not be appropriate or feasible in terms of developing a market entry strategy. Fundamental questions have to be addressed. They include the following: What factors should we consider when assessing the potential of an international market? How do we measure these criteria? Should we treat them equally or should we weight them in order of importance? Have we the capability and resources to tackle this market?

The answers to these questions require retailers to engage in some in-depth primary research (both quantitative and qualitative) as well as making extensive use of secondary data in order to take an informed decision.

The exercise involves an assessment of the external considerations and factors relevant to the potential market and an internal appraisal of the retailer's internal capabilities and resources. Clearly there has to be a close fit between these two dimensions. This is a critical consideration: there is no point in pursuing an attractive market unless the company has the ability to address the challenges of getting access and making an impression. We explore these issues more fully in this section.

Measurable criteria
Per capita GDP/GNP
Population trends/demographics
Percentage of middle-class/income groups
Urbanization versus rurification
Number of households and composition
Education standards
Access to Internet
Transportation measures (number of cars, public transport, rail links and so on)
Retail sector as a contributor to the overall economy
Extent of international retailers operating in the region/country
Fiscal issues (level of personal and corporate taxation, business rates, local taxes)
Levels of consumption and retail expenditure

The above list is indicative and is not listed in order of importance or weighting.

Judgemental considerations
Level of political stability
Attitude of government to foreign investment/ownership
Legislation: impact on the retail sector, retail ownership, planning and location issues
Labour availability and capability
Local management availability and capability
Infrastructure: IT, logistics, Internet penetration and speed
Sourcing issues: extent, availability and capability of potential suppliers
Shopping patterns and behaviours
Corporate social responsibility/ethical/environmental/green concerns and attitudes

Again, these judgemental issues will vary for individual retailers depending on the nature of their value proposition and the structure of the particular retail sector.

Many retailers will make use of a weighting/scoring system to more formally assess the merits or otherwise of the particular market under review.

Figure 12.4 2012 ORDI country attractiveness

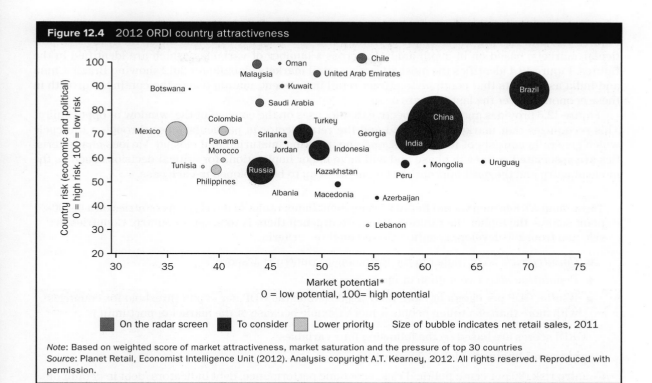

Note: Based on weighted score of market attractiveness, market saturation and the pressure of top 30 countries
Source: Planet Retail, Economist Intelligence Unit (2012). Analysis copyright A.T. Kearney, 2012. All rights reserved. Reproduced with permission.

Figure 12.5 The GRDI window-of-opportunity analysis

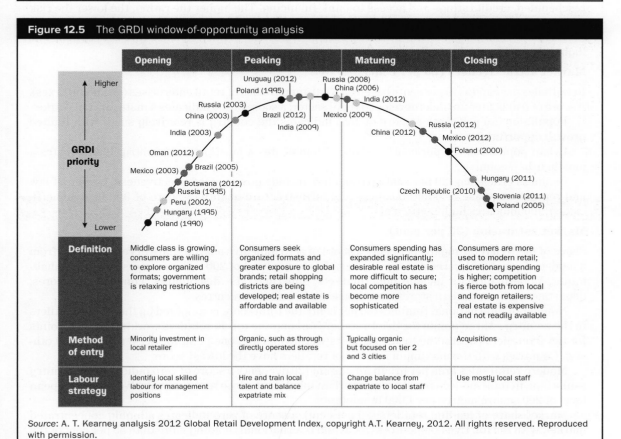

Source: A. T. Kearney analysis 2012 Global Retail Development Index, copyright A.T. Kearney, 2012. All rights reserved. Reproduced with permission.

AT Kearney (2012) develops an annual report that presents a Global Retail Development Index (GRDI). Figures 12.4 and 12.5 present a couple of frameworks that they use to assess the attractiveness of particular markets, based on in-depth analysis across a number of variables, which are identified in the figures. Figure 12.4 identifies the most attractive retail markets globally for 2012 showing Brazil, China and India as markets that continue to attract retail investment, mainly due to the continued growth in these economies over the last 10 years or so.

Figure 12.5 provides another perspective that focuses on the concept of the 'window of opportunity'. This recognizes that markets in general and the retail sector in particular goes through a life cycle which generally consists of four phases: opening, peaking, maturing and closing. Various characteristics are associated with each phase and will have major implications for critical decisions such as the mode of entry and the most appropriate labour strategy to be employed in each case.

The annual AT Kearney Global Retail Development Index ranks 30 developing countries on a 0–100-point scale – the higher the ranking, the more urgency there is to enter a country. Countries are selected from 200 developing nations based on three criteria:

- *Country risk*: 35 or higher in the Euromoney country-risk score
- *Population size*: two million or more
- *Wealth*: GDP per capita of more than $3,000 (Note: the GDP per capita threshold for countries with more than 35 million people is more flexible because of the market opportunity.)

GRDI scores are based on the following four variables:

Country and business risk (25 per cent)

Country risk (80 per cent): political risk, economic performance, debt indicators, debt in default or rescheduled, credit ratings and access to bank financing. The higher the rating, the lower the risk of failure.

Business risk (20 per cent): business cost of terrorism, crime, violence and corruption. The higher the rating, the lower the risk of doing business.

Market attractiveness (25 per cent)

Retail sales per capita (40 per cent): based on total annual sales of retail enterprises (excluding taxes). A score of 0 indicates an underdeveloped retail sector; a score of 100 indicates a mature retail market.

Population (20 per cent): a score of zero indicates the country is relatively small with limited growth opportunities.

Urban population (20 per cent): a score of 0 indicates a mostly rural country; 100 indicates a mostly urban country.

Business efficiency (20 per cent): parameters include government effectiveness, burden of law and regulations, ease of doing business and infrastructure quality. A score of 0 indicates inefficiency; 100 indicates highly efficient.

Market saturation (25 per cent)

Share of modern retailing (30 per cent): a score of zero indicates a large share of retail sales is from a modern format within the average western European level of 200 square metres per 1,000 inhabitants. Modern formats include hypermarkets, supermarkets, discounters, convenience stores, department stores, variety stores, warehouse clubs and supercentres.

Number of international retailers (30 per cent): the total score is weighted by the size of retailers in the country – three points for tier 1 retailers (among the top 10 retailers worldwide), two points for tier 2 retailers (within the top 20 retailers worldwide) and one point for tier 3 retailers (all others). Countries with the maximum number of retailers have the lowest score.

Modern retail sales area per urban inhabitant (20 per cent): a score of zero indicates the country ranks high in total modern retail area per urban inhabitant, close to the average Western European level of 200 square metres per 1,000 inhabitants.

Market share of leading retailers (20 per cent): a score of zero indicates a highly concentrated market, with the top five competitors (local and international) holding more than 55 per cent of the retail food market; 100 indicates a fragmented market.

Time pressure (25 per cent)

The time factor is based on 2007–2011 data, measured by the compound annual growth rate of modern retail sales weighted by the general economic development of the country (CAGR of GDP and consumer spending) and CAGR (2006–2011) of the retail sales area weighted by newly created modern retail sales areas. A score of 0 indicates a rapidly advancing retail sector, thus representing a short-term opportunity.

Data and analysis are based on the United Nations Population Division database, the World Economic Forum's Global Competitiveness Report 2010–2011, national statistics, Euromoney and World Bank reports, and Euromonitor and Planet Retail databases.

Source: http://www.atkearney.com/en_GB/consumer-products-retail/global-retail-development-index/past-report/-/asset_publisher/r888rybcQxoK/content/2012-global-retail-development-index/10192#sthash.usA6gbZz.dpuf

The approaches used by Kearney are only one way of addressing the question of how to assess the attractiveness of particular markets and are not necessarily the best or most comprehensive frameworks available. They do, however, highlight some critical issues in this important decision area in retail internationalization.

12.5 Case in point: HEMA comes to the UK

HEMA is a Dutch department store chain that was established as far back as 1926. It was founded by two entrepreneurs, Arthur Issac and Leo Meyer. Spurred on by the severe economic depression around that time in the Netherlands and in the rest of Europe, they established a store primarily aimed at catering for people with low incomes who were struggling to survive the harsh economic climate. They set out to offer shoppers a wide range of household items at affordable prices. The company was established as Hollandsche Eenheidsprizen Maatschappij Amsterdam – the 'Dutch Unit Price Company of Amsterdam'.

HEMA enjoyed a major growth period during the post-war prosperity in the Netherlands as shoppers' disposable incomes grew. The company widened its range of merchandise and introduced a franchise system to meet its expansion targets.

Currently, it supplies own-brand products across 14 categories: these include apparel, personal care and food products. It operates in neighbouring countries such as Belgium, Germany, Luxembourg and France. It has also introduced an online channel to complement its traditional department store channels.

HEMA's core value proposition is captured in the following paragraph.

'The HEMA style can be summarised in two words: "exceptional simplicity", by which we mean that products are both simple and exceptional. Long before the term "home brand" was invented, we were creating and manufacturing our own products ranging from towels to lamps and from underwear to bicycle lamps – day-to-day items with HEMA's special signature, suited for any budget. The process of turning day-to-day items into something exceptional is not limited to the drawing board: it also involves the commitment of the employees in our stores and at our head office, at our distribution centre and in our bakery' (adapted from The HEMA story, p. 2).

This concept of exceptional simplicity is exemplified in its design of a pink frying pan to their Jip and Janneke fizzy drinks. The company also runs an annual HEMA design competition, which was where the award-winning Le Lapin (the original, classic tea kettle) emerged from.

Every item that appears in their stores is designed and branded by HEMA.

Its first store opened in the UK in June 2014. The 2,700 square feet store was located in Victoria, central London. This initial store stocked products across the beauty, toys, stationery and confectionery categories. It also opened larger stores later in 2014 and those outlets planned to expand the range of merchandise to include home and garden categories.

Some retail experts suggested that the HEMA value proposition approximated closely to the Poundland concept, which has proved to be successful in the UK as a result mainly of the deep recession since 2008.

HEMA's chief executive officer (CEO), Ronald Van Zetten, however, disputed this comparison. He felt that a closer and more accurate comparison would be with Woolworth's (long since gone from the UK retail scene).

▶

◀ In 2014 the average price of an item in its UK stores was £3. It initially planned to carry around 6,000 stock-keeping units (skus), although its larger stores in other countries carry around 17,000 skus.

In addition to HEMA's first store opening in Victoria, London, it opened another store in Kingston, London with a selling space of 4,300 square feet and trading over two floors. In August it opened a third store, again in the London area (Bromley), with a trading area of 4,800 square feet. HEMA felt that by introducing stores of different sizes, it would in effect act as a market test to see which one would be more appropriate in the longer term. The preoccupation with the London area was revealed in its plan to develop a further seven stores in the greater London area over a two-year period.

A retail analyst made the following observation prior to the launch of the HEMA brand in the UK.

'Ahead of its arrival, HEMA has been mistakenly compared to UK discounters. However, its prices are somewhat higher, although it backs that up with quality that is generally well regarded in its homeland. The business is also well-known for its quirky and well-designed products and it is perhaps no coincidence that its first UK stores will be in relatively affluent locations.'

Source: http://www.retail-week.com/property/in-pictures-dutch-giant-hema-unveils-first-uk-store/5061053.article

Questions

1 Assess the view that HEMA's entry to the UK market is opportunistic, given the deep and prolonged recession in that market, and that it has little prospect of making a long-term impression in this market.

2 To what extent would you agree with the view that HEMA's value proposition is too similar to other retail offerings in the UK market?

12.6 Standardization versus adaptation dilemma

When developing an internationalization strategy, retailers have to make a critical decision on the nature of the retail format that is going to be transferred to that particular region or country. The following questions have to be addressed. Is it possible to fully replicate all aspects of our retail value proposition in this new market? Can we work on the assumption that what has worked well in our domestic market will continue to be successful? If not, what adaptations or adjustments have to be made? Are these adaptations likely to be major or minor?

Park and Sternquist (2008) make a distinction between international retailers and global retailers. They suggest that retailers such as Wal-Mart are characterized by their tendency to adapt their value proposition and its elements and could be described as a 'multinational retailer'. By contrast, global retailers are more likely to make superficial adaptations. With a proven formula already established in their domestic setting, such retailers roll out and largely replicate their existing model. We should note that it can be dangerous to adopt a very rigid approach in distinguishing between a standardization versus an adaptation approach to retail internationalization.

Evans and Bridson (2005) argue that we should view both approaches as the two extremes in a continuum.

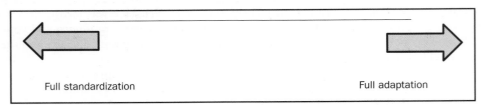

Full standardization   Full adaptation

It is unrealistic to expect that a successful and winning retail formula can be fully transferred to an international market without some form of adaptation. As we have noted in previous chapters, culture shapes the way in which societies behave and interact. This is very influential in the area of shopping behaviour and heavily influences tastes, preferences, attitudes and opinions. In our chapter on customer service, for instance, we noted that shoppers' expectations about this issue can vary worldwide. In countries such as the USA, shoppers tend to be very demanding and complain if they receive what they perceive to be 'poor service' at a retail outlet. In other regions, shoppers may be more tolerant of similar service levels. It could be partially explained by the fact that the level of choice and competition may not be as high as other geographic regions or a relative lack of sophistication on the part of shoppers in a particular region.

This introduces us to the concept of *psychic distance*. Evans and Bridson (2005: 70) define this as 'the distance between the home market and a foreign market resulting from the perception and understanding of cultural and business differences'. In essence, it refers to the likely similarity or closeness versus likely difference in the gap between these two points. It does *not* equate to geographic distance. For instance, although Australia and the UK are very far apart from a geographic location perspective, it can be argued that due to the historical relationship between the two countries, there is a cultural similarity between them in terms of culture.

The issue of adaptation can be driven by similarities or differences in the overall retail infrastructure, legislation, extent and level of competition, national sentiment and so on. If a potential new retail market has a similar retail infrastructure (IT, transport, telecommunications and supply capability), there may be less need to adapt the retail value proposition. In situations where there are significant differences, the retailer will have to make some adjustments to its existing business model. Many retailers who entered the Indian market over the last 10 years or so have had to take account of the challenges of logistics and physical distribution of merchandise in that country to operate in an effective manner.

Adaptation may be necessary across the various dimensions of retail strategy (pricing, quality and depth of merchandise offered, location, customer service, store design and layout, marketing communication and relationships with suppliers).

Vignette: IKEA and its internationalization strategy

IKEA is one of the most successful international retailers over the last 30 years or so. When it entered the Chinese market, it found that some of its core beliefs and principles about the nature of its value proposition did not stand up in this large and challenging market.

For instance, IKEA has based its strategy on offering relatively fashionable household items at low and affordable prices. This concept works well in many countries. The core segment is individuals in the 25–30 age bracket, mainly female, who are furnishing their first flat/home and do not have the disposable income to afford more expensive household items.

In the large Chinese cities, retail stores are located close to or in the cities. This is in contrast to other countries where large shopping malls are based well outside the city limits. Home delivery is also a significant influence in the purchase decision and IKEA has had to link up with local entrepreneurs who provide such a service to customers. As many Chinese people live in flats with balconies, IKEA has included model sets and special balcony sections in its stores.

There is an absence of a 'do-it-yourself' culture in China. IKEA makes use of local operators who help customers assemble their purchase.

The catalogue is central to IKEA's marketing communications strategy in many countries. Due to the distances and costs involved in distributing this item, much of the promotional work is done within the stores.

Store design and layout has to take account of the way in which Chinese society lives and operates at home. The concept of size is different: people live in smaller spaces and, as a result, designs of items such as beds and sofas have to take account of this (smaller items).

In summary, IKEA has made significant adaptations to its traditional business model in order to develop its operations within the Chinese market.

Source: Adapted from Johannson, U. and Thelander, A. (2009) A standardised approach to the world? IKEA in China. *International Journal of Quality and Service Sciences*. 1(5): 199–219

▶

◀

> ## Question
>
> 1 Assess the extent to which you would agree with the view that IKEA may have compromised too many of its core business principles in its attempt to make an impact in the Chinese market.

In summary, the standardization versus adaptation issue is perhaps the wrong way to view the decisions that have to be made by retailers over this question. Some form of adaptation is necessary. The question is to what extent the retailer has to reshape its overall strategy. Jonsson and Foss (2011) introduce the concept of *flexible replication* as a way of explaining the most pragmatic approach to this issue.

This recognizes that full replication (standardization) is not feasible or indeed desirable as it ignores obvious areas where differences occur across different international retail markets. Instead, a combination of standardization and adaptation is the most appropriate strategy for retailers. However, flexibility should be at the heart of this approach. Retailers learn from their internationalization activities in specific markets and as we discussed earlier in this chapter, experiential knowledge and learning are crucial inputs into this approach. This accepts that mistakes can be made. However, retailers should respond to and reflect on such experiences and incorporate adaptations to the business model as a result.

12.7 Retail internationalization entry options

The mode(s) of entry to a particular geographic region represent a critical decision for retailers. Such a decision is influenced by a number of critical factors. These include the following: control, cost, risk, flexibility, speed of coverage, critical mass and regulations. We consider each issue in detail.

- **Control**: different modes of entry provide differing levels of control from the perspective of the retailer. By control, we mean the extent to which the retailer retains control over various aspects of its strategy. At one extreme, full control would occur where the retailer does not have to rely on any external or independent individual or organization to establish a presence in a particular country or region. By contrast, the more a retailer has to depend on the services and contribution of independent operators, the possibility exists that it will lose certain elements of control over its operations.

- **Cost**: by using middlemen or intermediaries, the retailer has to provide a range of support mechanisms to ensure that the value proposition is consistent with its domestic offering. Such support revolves around areas such as marketing, human resource development, advice on location and acquiring appropriate locations, financial training and so on. If a retailer wishes to establish a physical presence by formally acquiring properties or existing local retail operations, it will also encounter high levels of investment.

- **Level of risk**: international expansion entails some form of exposure to risk. As retailers invest in new partnerships, acquisition and/or merger and physical retail development of locations, the degree of risk will vary. This is particularly the case in environments that exhibit a high degree of difference in terms of cultural and societal shopping behaviour.

- **Flexibility**: retailers may need to adapt their operations in a particular country in order to resonate with the needs and requirements of a different culture or society. By making a major investment commitment to acquire and/or build retail locations, it reduces the ability to be flexible or adaptable in the event that the initial entry strategy does not succeed. By contrast, a greater reliance on partnerships with local operators can prove to be easier and less costly to become detached from.

- **Speed of geographic coverage**: for large retailers, in particular, speed of entry and expansion may be a driving imperative. Modes of entry that can be established quickly; for example, franchises, can allow a retailer to achieve a position of having numerous outlets or stores within a year to 18 months.

- **Critical mass**: in tandem with speed of entry is the issue of the need to establish a sufficient number of outlets to enable the retailer to benefit from issues such as economies of scale. A bigger operation means that a retailer can gain access to a wider geographic range of shoppers and benefit from cost savings and reductions, particularly in terms of negotiating with local suppliers. By contrast, some retailers do not seek growth based on the quantity of stores. Retailers targeting the exclusive end of the market may work on the opposite principle and focus their efforts on establishing a limited number of outlets in exclusive shopping areas of the major cities.

- **Regulations**: we refer here mainly to legal issues that are imposed on foreign businesses by the government of the particular country. For instance, in the Gulf region, many of the states insist on a foreign company having a local partner. This is a legal requirement and means that in essence that partner becomes involved in the establishment of the operation. The partner is also a part-owner of the business operation in that particular region or country.

The nature of the market, the extent and depth of competition, the size and resources of the retailer and the quality of connections and networks that it has with key stakeholders in the proposed geographic area will also shape the specific type of entry mode that it pursues (Waarts and van Everdingen, 2006).

In the next section we consider the different entry modes that are available to retailers.

12.8 Modes of entry

12.8.1 Context

Table 12.1 attempts to assess the alternative modes of entry (discussed in this section) as against the criteria that we have identified above.

A recent study (Barclays, 2013) indicates how UK retailers have set about developing international expansion. It provides a contextual backdrop for our subsequent investigation of the entry mode options. Tables 12.2 and 12.3 present the main results from Barclays' survey of retailers with less than £2 million annual turnover and retailers with greater than £2 million annual turnover.

These findings suggest that many UK retailers seek a balance between the issues of cost, control and coverage. Entry modes such as wholesaling and franchising are typical examples of this. They recognize the important role that local representatives play in establishing a coherent presence in a particular geographic region. This necessitates some dilution or relinquishing of control in recognition of

Table 12.1 The GRDI window-of-opportunity analysis

Criteria	Control	Cost	Level of risk	Flexibility	Gaining critical mass	Regulations
Modes of entry						
Acquisition	✓✓✓	✓✓✓	✓✓	✓	✓	✓✓✓
Mergers/joint ventures	✓✓	✓✓	✓✓	✓	✓	✓✓
Organic growth	✓✓✓	✓✓✓	✓✓✓	✓✓	✓	✓✓✓
Franchising	✓✓	✓	✓	✓✓	✓✓✓	✓
Flagship stores	✓✓	✓✓	✓	✓✓	✓	✓✓
Wholesalling	✓✓	✓	✓		✓	✓✓

✓ = Low   ✓✓ = High   ✓✓✓ = Very high

Note: The evaluations used in this diagram are indicative only and are likely to vary from region to region

Table 12.2 UK retailers <£2 million

Mode	%
Online	81%
Franchising	13%
Physical stores	13%
Joint ventures	10%
Wholesaling	6%
Licensing	0%

Source: Barclays (2013: 24)

Table 12.3 UK retailers >£2 million

Mode	%
Online	50%
Wholesaling	38%
Franchising	25%
Physical stores	25%
Joint ventures	19%
Licensing	6%

Source: Barclays (2013: 24)

the fact that such parties have an understanding and knowledge of local business culture and traditions. Franchising also provides an opportunity to share the risk with potential investors in the franchise system and it also achieves the benefit of gaining relatively quick coverage of a region, thus providing the retailer with a 'critical mass' of retail outlets.

12.8.2 Organic growth

This approach provides an opportunity for the retailer to retain full control over its operations and its existing retail strategy. It means that it does not have to rely on local intermediaries to create and deliver the value proposition in a particular country. It also means that the retailer can exit the market more quickly if projected targets are not achieved; for instance, it has not committed to complex contracts with other parties that could slow down the process of exit. It is also possible to experiment with different formats and adapt operations as the business develops.

However, it does not offer the opportunity of growing quickly and achieving a critical mass of outlets or stores. This may not apply to certain retailers: some opt for an exclusive or semi-exclusive approach and are more concerned about achieving visibility in a select and exclusive number of key locations (such as prominent shopping malls). By opting for establishing its own stores, the retailer will have to engage in a full location analysis exercise. This can be difficult due to the lack of local knowledge, particularly in the case of legal barriers. By effectively going it alone, the retailer is in danger of exacerbating the problem of the lack of local knowledge. A form of partnering can overcome this issue.

In summary, organic growth (or growing internally) allows the company to have very high levels of control over its operations. The costs of pursuing this approach are also high and the degree of risk is also relatively high compared with other entry mode options.

12.8.3 Acquisition

Acquisitions represent a mechanism whereby a retailer can take over an existing local retailer and establish a presence in a country or region relatively quickly. In theory, this entry mode appears to have the benefit of allowing a retailer to acquire the assets, capabilities and support mechanisms of an established retailer. Cash flow from the existing stores is immediate and relatively seamless (allowing for some time to convert and 'badge' the outlets). This is in contrast to trying to establish a presence through organic growth where the retailer purchases or leases properties in appropriate locations. The length of time and cost required to achieve such organic growth would be far longer in gestation and implementation than the acquisition of established retail outlets belonging to an existing retailer. What theory proposes, however, does not necessarily translate into practice. In many cases it can be difficult to simply acquire and take over an existing retailer and expect a perfect match in terms of strategic fit. The retailer who is being acquired inevitably is encountering problems (hence the possible reason for it to be in the market for acquisition). It may have a number of unproductive and unprofitable outlets, it may simply be offering a 'tired' format that shoppers no longer find appealing or it may be struggling in areas such as branding and marketing.

The length of time needed to 'turn around' such an organization, remove poor management structures and personnel, change the branding and close down unprofitable outlets may take far longer than originally anticipated. The issue of rebranding should not be underestimated. Even though the new logos and brand identifiers can be placed externally and internally within stores, local shoppers may still take some time to associate with the 'new' retailer's value proposition and merchandise.

Alexander and Doherty (2009) point out the example of Wal-Mart when it entered the German market in the late 1990s by acquiring 21 stores from Wertkauf and a further acquisition of 74 stores from Interspar. Over eight years later it announced its divestment from operations in Germany and sold these stores to Metro. One of the reasons advanced for this divestment was a failure to understand the German customer and a lack of appeal to the tastes of these shoppers.

By contrast, Alexander and Doherty (2009) point out the success of the luxury fashion group, Louis Vuitton Moet Hennessey (LVMH), which has consistently pursued an acquisition strategy and has built up a strong and varied portfolio of retail brands in addition to its three original offerings.

Acquisitions may work better when the retailer expands via this mode in countries that are relatively close in terms of culture and shopping behaviour and where management structures and capabilities are similar (low psychic distance).

Acquisitions, when they do not work out, can take some time to exit from. We look at divestment in more detail later in this chapter. The level of risk associated with this mode of entry is considerable. It requires significant financial resources to execute the strategy and there is clearly a danger of overvaluing and, as a consequence, paying too much for the acquired retailer. Many retailers underestimate the amount of resources needed to align management structures, IT systems and supply chain processes. This is particularly relevant in situations where the retailer is moving to economies that are less developed than the domestic markets.

In summary, acquisitions can provide a retailer with a reasonably quick way of establishing a presence in the chosen international market. However, it is also associated with high levels of risk. In addition to the costs involved in acquiring local retail operations, such a strategy is usually well publicized and, if it goes wrong, can also attract much critical and negative comment in the financial press.

12.8.4 Mergers

Mergers are similar to acquisitions in terms of the perceived benefits and problems. Mergers, by contrast to acquisitions, involve a sharing of resources. It is based on the presumption that if two retailers come together and identify each other's strengths and weaknesses, the resulting synergy can result in a stronger and more competitive entity. The two companies involved generally form a single company. Such an approach often encounters difficulties in trying to overcome different management and corporate cultures. Essential issues such as the type of management style that should prevail in the new entity can create major problems. Key strengths that may have existed in the individual organizations can be eradicated when the new structure commences operations. Essentially, two companies become one and the management and corporate ethos of one or both will disappear.

12.8.5 Joint ventures

Joint ventures are another variation of the principle that by two companies coming together, benefits can accrue to both parties in the pursuit of business development and expansion. In the context of retail joint ventures Robinson, Clarke-Hill and Bailey (1998) highlight the reduction of risk and local knowledge as being prime motivators for this approach.

When compared with the acquisition and merger modes, it does not require the same degree of 'upfront' investment. It presents an opportunity for a retailer to work with and gain access to the local knowledge and capabilities of the partner in the arrangement, thereby increasing the possibility of success in achieving the objectives behind the project. It also helps the retailer to climb the learning curve in terms of familiarization with local shopping patterns, culture and business operations.

Owens and Quinn (2007) assess the literature on international joint venture research and conclude that the management initiatives involved in directing and implementing joint ventures are often challenging and can create relatively high levels of instability across the participating partners. Motivations for pursuing such a strategy may differ and change between the partners as the process evolves. While the joint ventures may have clear and strategic goals at the outset, there is a danger that one of the partners may behave in an opportunistic manner and damage the overall objectives. The concept of a joint venture is based on the principle of mutual dependence between the partners. Anything (such as opportunistic behaviour) can threaten this basic condition and lead to less than optimal results.

As is the case with mergers and acquisitions, joint partners have to grapple with the challenges of dealing with different management cultures. The ultimate challenge is to achieve a 'strategic fit' resulting in synergies from co-operation between the two retailers. For instance, in the later 1990s, Zara entered into a joint venture arrangement with the German firm Otto Versand, and as a consequence benefited from the latter's expertise in the distribution sector in the large German market (Lopez and Fan, 2009). Similarly, the Italian market presented difficulties for Zara due to the practice of local traders deciding whether an international brand can operate in a particular city and on the amounts of money required for the transfer of stores. As a consequence, Zara entered into a joint venture with Gruppo Percassi, a successful firm in the property sector in Italy in 2001.

Research conducted by Owens and Quinn (2007: 766) with a number of retailers who engaged in joint venture initiatives identified the following problems areas:

- disagreement over strategy
- disagreement over operating process
- poor senior management relationships
- partner and/or company resources weakness
- partner inefficiency
- poor performance.

They also put forward the view that the adjustment period for generating and implementing the areas of co-operation and overcoming corporate and management culture differences is shorter than is the case for manufacturing companies that enter into a similar joint venture arrangement. This makes it even more challenging and requires an intensive period of investment in resources, mainly management, to drive the necessary changes.

As mentioned earlier, legal requirements in certain regions such as some of the Gulf States stipulate a local partner. This means that some form of joint venture is essential if potential opportunities are to be pursued.

Joint ventures can run into trouble for a number of reasons besides the incompatibility of the two partners. Auchan, the large French retailer, has over 2,400 supermarkets and under 650 hypermarkets in over 14 countries. In 2012 it signed a licence agreement with Landmark, a retail group in India, who operated over a dozen hypermarkets in that country. The plan was to turn the licence arrangement into a full joint venture. However, some confusion over the lack of clarity with which the Indian government views foreign direct investment, allied to varying practices in different Indian states, has led to a breakdown in the relationship. Mandatory local sourcing requirements also complicated the nature and process of the relationship between the two parties. Of the global retailers operating in the Indian market, Tesco is the only group to have entered a formal joint venture agreement (they instigated a deal with Tata Group's Star Bazaar and have committed around £150 million to the investment).

In summary, joint ventures create an opportunity for a stronger degree of control over the operations. However, we should not underestimate the challenges involved in aligning the respective corporate cultures of both parties in the arrangement.

12.8.6 Case in point: South African retailers and opportunities in the African market

The continent of Africa represents one of the last frontiers to be conquered by the large retailers. It is large in every sense, both in terms of population and land mass, and is made up of 53 countries.

In many respects it resembles the analogy of 'the sleeping giant'. While some of the countries are wealthy in terms of minerals and oil, the continent has arguably been riddled over the years with corrupt governments and conditions that make it difficult for companies to gain a foothold in such markets. This is often characterized by protectionism, lax regulations and that word again, corruption.

It differs from other continents in terms of infrastructure in general and retail infrastructure in particular. Areas that retailers take for granted in other markets can pose huge obstacles in Africa, roads and transportation modes being two cases in point. Delays in moving products from ports can also add to the headache for retailers, causing difficulties in making inventory available in stores and outlets.

South African retailers nonetheless see opportunities in the African markets. For one thing, they are geographically close to many markets. For instance, outlets in Zambia can be reached by truck in a day from a city such as Johannesburg.

South African retailers can also gain a potential advantage by having access to manufacturing operations in their own country that are not easily available in other countries on the African continent. Costs and efficiencies can be addressed by 'back-hauling' of items to South Africa; for instance, strawberries from Zimbabwe and fish from Mozambique.

The structure of retailing in African markets differs from that of other continents. On average 90 per cent of consumer sales come from what might be labelled 'traditional' retailers (How we made it into Africa, 2015). Such retailers are typically found on the side of roads or on streets and are represented by stalls, kiosks, table tops and grocers. In South Africa, this percentage drops to around 40 per cent, perhaps reflecting the more developed retail environment in that country.

Shoprite, a large South African retailer, was one of the first retailers to develop opportunities in other countries in Africa. Others such as Pick n Pay and Woolworths have followed with similar initiatives. For instance, Zambia has shown strong signs of economic growth in recent years, bolstered no doubt by Chinese demand for copper.

Interestingly, of the 10 fastest-growing economies globally in recent years, six are located in Africa – highlighting the growing attractiveness of this region for retailers who are intent on international expansion. This is particularly the case for South African retailers seeking some form of escape from the local and relatively stagnant domestic economy.

South African retailers have to grapple with obstacles that many commentators would take for granted in other parts of the world. For instance, when Shoprite decided on a particular location for one of its stores in Nigeria, it found that three other people had claims on that plot of land, each of them holding deeds to demonstrate the authenticity of their claims!

Many traditional stores do not have basic features such as air conditioning and tiled floors.

Shoprite, because of its pioneering ventures into other African countries such as Nigeria and Zambia, potentially holds the benefit of 'first-mover' advantage. This may sustain it from competitive pressures from other South African retailers. However, the way in which large cities are developing across Africa is not happening necessarily in a planned and coherent way: it is haphazard and unplanned in fact.

African shoppers tend to be rather conservative in terms of their willingness to try out new brands and merchandise. While the population of many African countries is large, and growing, there is still a wide preponderance of what might be described as 'poor' consumers. Their requirements are relatively basic and unsophisticated. The local, traditional retailers know their customers and are in a strong position to decide on the correct price and quantity for many items, particularly in the food categories. This is in contrast to established and well-developed retail markets on other continents where the branders work closely with the retailers to develop effective in-store and online retail marketing strategies.

While South African retailers might appear to have a couple of inherent competitive advantages, they will not have it all to themselves: Wal-Mart, the world's largest retailer, has been eyeing these opportunities as well. It bought a majority stake in a company called Massmart in 2011. This organization is made up of four divisions that provide high-volume, low-margin and low-cost distribution of mainly branded products across 381 stores in 12 countries in sub-Saharan Africa.

Similarly, Carrefour, another major global retailer, has recently entered into a joint venture with CFAO, a distributor of cars, drugs and sportswear. It is anticipated that other global retailers such as Tesco are doing their homework in vast continents as well.

In summary, Africa represents a challenging, yet attractive continent for retailers. For South African operators in particular, it potentially allows them to expand their operations from their domestic market that has shown signs of stagnation in the last few years. It is debatable whether they have any competitive advantage that can be sustained in the longer term. Already, the sharks (in the form of global retailers) are circling around this large land mass with its high levels of population.

Source: Based on: http://www.howwemadeitinafrica.com/gdp-and-population-data-not-enough-to-predict-brand-success-in-africa/47206/
http://www.economist.com/news/business/21586551-sluggish-home-market-pushing-south-africas-big-retail-chains-northward-grocers-great

▶

◀ **Questions**

1 Assess the challenges of entering the African market from the perspective of a large UK supermarket group.
2 How relevant is the joint venture approach to this challenge?

12.8.7 Wholesaling

This option is perhaps the least costly one to instigate as it does not require a physical presence in the particular targeted country. This approach simply means that a retailer's merchandise is distributed and sold by a local retailer. A good illustration of this is Waitrose, the UK supermarket group. Since 2005 over 500 of its product lines have been stocked in Hong Kong by the local supermarket group, ParknShop. This has worked well and has given the Waitrose brand a physical presence in this market that still has a large expatriate population of UK people.

The costs are lower because there is no need to establish physical stores or an online presence. The only serious costs that are incurred surround supply chain activities such as ensuring that inventory is available to the local retailer. There are no long-term legal contracts to sign: each party in the relationship can terminate it with almost immediate effect.

This entry mode also has the added benefit of allowing a retailer to 'test' shoppers' reactions to its merchandise in the short term. If the response is favourable, it can then contemplate the prospect of other entry modes in an attempt to build on the initial brand awareness and acceptability.

There are 'downsides' however. A ceding of control over the way in which the merchandise is presented and positioned in the local retailers' stores is inevitable. Because it is a wholesaling arrangement, it is almost certain that the local operator will demand strong margins from the sale of the merchandise, resulting in potentially low returns for the retailer. This, of course, has to be counterbalanced against the exposure that its brand will receive in that particular country or region.

It is not always easy to identify a potential local operator that fits strategically with the brand values and overall positioning of the retailer. A poor decision in this area can damage the integrity and credibility of the brand. The UK retail group, Arcadia, entered into an arrangement with Nordstrom, a successful US retail chain, and sold its brands in 14 of the latter's stores in North America. This worked well and ensured that Arcadia's brands were represented in a retail chain that was compatible with its positioning strategy.

12.8.8 Franchising

Franchising has proved to be one of the most popular mechanisms for retailers to develop their internationalization strategies. It is rooted in the concept of a contractual arrangement between the owner of the brand/product /service (the franchisor) and the various parties who agree to buy into the concept (the franchisees). In addition to providing the right to the franchisee to use the brand name and trademark, the franchisor provides a range of support activities, ranging from financial advice, site location guidance, training staff and marketing-related support to the franchisee (Coughlan et al., 2001).

It is not, however, just an economic arrangement between the parties involved. There is a strong social component to the relationship. Franchisees have to be identified, selected and contractually signed up to the deal. The process of subsequently managing this relationship involves a high degree of social interaction (Tikoo, 2005).

Franchising offers a number of strong benefits for the franchisor. First, it allows the retailer to gain penetration and geographic coverage relatively quickly in a particular region. More importantly, it can do so without a major element of cost or risk. It also generates revenue immediately. In the context of cost and risk, the franchisee essentially takes on the risks associated with locating and opening the outlet in a particular city or town, not the franchisor. Therefore, the latter does not incur the typical costs associated with renting, leasing or purchasing a property (Rondan-Cataluna et al., 2012).

The franchisee also pays the franchisor an up-front fee for the right to buy into the franchise arrangement. The amount of money to be paid will depend on how well established the concept is. McDonald's, for example, would clearly be one of the world's iconic brands. In order to acquire a McDonald's franchise for an outlet, the average fee could be anywhere from £500,000 to £1 million depending on the location. The retail franchisor receives a flow of income directly the contracts are signed.

Second, the franchisee typically pays an annual percentage of sales to the franchisor. This can vary from 2 per cent to 5 per cent depending on the figure that is specified in the contract. Thus, the retail franchisor receives an 'ongoing' annual source of revenue, again without incurring any significant degree of risk. In return, the franchisees receive a range of support mechanisms such as marketing support and budget, financial advice and guidance on store layout and design. Again, the extent and depth of support can vary from one franchise arrangement to another.

In theory, there should be mutual benefits for each party in the contractual arrangement. From the retailer's perspective, it gets relatively quick growth at a relatively low cost and risk. For the franchisee, it is buying into an established and proven value proposition, thus reducing the risk that would normally be associated with starting a new business venture. The retailer can also take advantage of the expertise of the franchisor's marketing, finance and human resources personnel to help it to exploit the business opportunities to the full. In practice, however, it may not necessarily be as accurate as the theory suggests.

First, there is the presumption that the support mechanisms provided by the franchisor are appropriate and to the level necessary for the franchisee to benefit from. Doherty (2007) sheds some interesting insight into this issue. She identifies two categories of support: strategic franchise management support and operational franchise management support.

1 Strategic franchise management support

These activities refer to the overall running of the business and include the franchise manual, the development plans and the monitoring of financial data. They are deemed to be strategic because they affect the long-term viability of the business operation.

- **The franchise manual**: the manual is critical as it specifies (normally in great detail) the 'way to run the business'. Any deviation from the practices outlined in this document can lead to ultimate termination of the contract. From the franchisor's perspective, this helps to address the issue of consistency of delivery across the various franchisees participating in the system. The dangers of inconsistency threaten the viability of the overall operations. For example, an individual expects to encounter the same level of service, décor, and quality of the food (allowing for some regional variations) in a McDonald's outlet in Glasgow as would be the case in Zurich. Any variations threaten the credibility of the brand and send confusing messages to consumers. The manual is the DNA of the business model.

- **The development plans**: these plans identify the expectations in terms of sales and profitability for the particular outlet. The key word here is 'expectations'. It is important in theory for the franchisor to help the franchisee with realistic and achievable targets. If this does not happen, it will generate dissatisfaction among franchisees. It will also make it more difficult for the franchisor to attract new franchisees. The plan can be formally or informally reviewed. Doherty's research suggests that a range of approaches can be identified.

- **Monitoring financial data**: many franchisees lack essential skills in the area of finance. Franchisors see this issue as being critical to the long-term viability of both the relationship and the value proposition. This can generate some areas of tension between the parties involved. Some franchisees see this as an intrusion into their business operations. However, from the franchisor's perspective, it is important to have a clear picture of how the various franchisees are performing relative to each other and relative to set sales targets. Successful franchisors can very quickly identify 'problem cases' and intervene to provide assistance and guidance.

2 Operational franchise support

These initiatives are designed to help with the day-to-day running of the franchise outlets and cover a number of areas.

- **Support for initial store opening**: for many retailers store design and layout are critical factors to generate sales. From the franchisor's perspective, all of the outlets should have a strong element of conformity and consistency in terms of presenting the brand values through its merchandise. The professional expertise of the franchisor should alleviate some of the problems if it works closely with franchisees on various aspects of store design, layout and identification of suitable locations.

- **Visits**: by making regular visits to each of the franchised outlets, the franchisor can identify likely problems or issues that may arise. For international operations this can add a significant cost to the running of franchise systems. In the case of large international operations, the franchisor will make use of what is often referred to as 'Master Franchisors'. These are individuals or organizations that have local knowledge and expertise and are tasked with the challenge of recruiting and training potential franchisees. In addition to these tasks, the Master Franchisors may take responsibility for carrying out such visits.

- **Product/merchandise range reviews**: this aspect is relevant for fashion and clothing retailers. Fashion shows at the retailer's headquarters enable franchisees to view the projected new lines for the coming season or year, allowing them to make decisions about which items are likely to sell in their home markets.

- **Advertising and marketing support**: practice in this area tends to vary. Some retailers provide extensive support from head office by way of advertising and point-of-sale materials. Other retailers insist on franchisees committing a certain percentage of annual sales to marketing and advertising activities. The importance of monitoring activity in this area should not be underestimated: any deviation from the overall marketing communications on the part of individual franchisees can lead to confusion and a blurring of the standard message.

- **Training**: ensuring that management and employees across the franchise system meet the expectations set out in the franchise manual is central to a successful franchise. This becomes even more critical in an international context where language differences and variations in the capabilities of indigenous workforces can occur. Some retailers conduct the training at head office; others address this task in the specific country.

In summary, the level and depth of support that is provided to franchisees plays a critical role in determining its ultimate success. The essence of any successful franchise system rests with the ability of the franchisor to control the process. There is little room for autonomy to be given to franchisees. It can be argued that such a process is not suitable for entrepreneurial individuals. They tend to thrive on challenges, spotting opportunities, doing things differently and changing the business model. They can become very frustrated if they enter into a franchise agreement and are faced with the manual that specifies in detail how everything has to be done. There is little or no room for trying out new ideas or innovations.

Franchising has a great appeal for individuals who wish to be self-employed and have some capital to invest in a suitable proposition. It is less risky than a start-up venture because the concept has already been tested and proven.

12.8.9 Case in point: Parfois

This Portuguese company was established in 1994 and specializes in fashion accessories. It covers a number of categories including shoes, hats, jewellery, handbags and purses. It opened its first store in the city of Porto and focused its growth in shopping centres throughout the main cities of Portugal. Its value proposition revolves around offering high-quality merchandise at low prices. It used franchising as a growth mechanism in Portugal before looking at international opportunities. Forte and Carvalho (2013) note that this early introduction to franchising provided Parfois with the necessary experience of recruiting suitable franchisees and developing a management system before it looked at other markets.

In 2003 it moved into the international arena and used two modes of entry: franchising and own stores. It chose Spain and Saudi Arabia for its first ventures. The latter opportunity arose from an approach to Parfois by the Azadea Group. Saudi Arabia was deemed to be attractive because it had a large population who exhibited a keen desire to purchase brands from western Europe with the standards of quality associated with such products.

Because of its limited financial resources, management felt that it made sense to enter into an agreement with the Azadea Group because the latter organization would be taking the risk and the investment necessary to build up a franchise system in Saudi Arabia. Parfois opened its own stores in Spain. It felt that this was less risky given the geographic and cultural closeness of this market.

Since 2003 Parfois has expanded its operations into other Middle-Eastern countries (United Arab Emirates and Kuwait). It sought further growth in Kazakhstan, Latvia, Romania, Russia, Ukraine, Jordan, Oman and Angola. In 2009 it entered the following markets: Croatia, Bahrain, Egypt and Poland. In 2010 further expansion saw it entering Bulgaria and Philippines. The use of own stores and franchising mirrors the strategy adopted by another well-known fashion retailer, Zara.

The eastern European markets, from the perspective of the retail sector, witnessed major growth with the development of the shopping centre/mall concept. This fitted well with the original Parfois approach of locating stores in such locations. In the case of Kazakhstan, Parfois was a pioneer in terms of being one of the first European fashion retailers to enter this market. Likewise, in the case of the African market, it was one of the early European entrants to Angola (a former Portuguese colony).

It encountered some problems with Russian franchisees. Disputes arose over agreed expansion plans and over payment issues. Contracts were cancelled and the subsequent closure of stores in this country. It has since re-entered this market.

In the context of opening its own stores, Parfois did just that in 2005 in the case of the French market. Senior management felt that if it was to have credibility as an international fashion retailer then it should be represented in one of the most iconic 'fashion' cities in the world, Paris.

It also opened its own store in Poland (2009). It based this decision on the basis that this country had one of the largest populations in Europe, was a member of the EU and had relatively strong levels of political and economic stability.

Source: Developed from material covered in the following article: Forte, R. and Carvalho, J. (2013) Internationalization through franchising: the Parfois case study. *International Journal of Retail & Distribution Management*. 41(5): 380–395

Questions

1 Assess the approach to internationalization that was used by Parfois. To what extent do you agree with the proposition that it appears to be unstructured and unplanned?

2 Opening its own stores in Poland would appear to more risky than using a franchising system. Examine the extent to which you would agree with this view.

12.8.10 Flagship stores

This is a variation on the option of growing internally and involves the establishment of a store in a particular country. Varley (2007: 176) defines a flagship store as 'the pinnacle in a retail chain, usually large and located in a high footfall prestigious location, with a full range of merchandise but an emphasis on the more expensive high quality and high fashion lines'. In some cases retailers such as Nike use the flagship to unveil new merchandise or product launches. This helps to increase the anticipation and excitement among shoppers and generates favourable publicity within the general and social media.

Nobbs, Moore and Sheridan (2012) note that the flagship store concept is not new: it has evolved from lifestyle stores to online/digital stores in its most recent guise.

Flagship stores (as we discussed in Chapter 5) can also be used to encourage shoppers to interact with merchandise. The broader objective of entertaining shoppers often features. Nobbs et al. (2012) cite the example of the Armani store in Milan. This covers a space of 129,000 square feet and goes beyond a simple stocking of merchandise to include a confectionery counter, a Japanese restaurant, a bar and a Sony electronics gallery.

Flagship stores act as a 'beacon' for the brand. They tend to be larger than the conventional stores or formats. They feature the latest design/merchandise and are often located in iconic buildings or shopping malls. In addition to attracting actual shoppers, they can be used very effectively as a public relations vehicle to target key opinion formers and influencers such as fashion or technology journalists. While the cost of locating and developing such a store at first glance can appear to be very high, the additional benefits of using it as a mechanism for promoting the brand and its values cannot be underestimated. The flagship store concept is particularly helpful within the context of internationalization as it allows the retailer to 'showcase' its brand essence to a new audience and focus on key elements such as new designs.

12.8.11 Online

This entry mode is perhaps the most intriguing of all of the options facing a retailer within the context of internationalizing its operations. Over the last 10 years or so, we have witnessed many retailers, irrespective of size, embrace online channels in an attempt to connect with customers. Many have developed the Internet further to include an online fulfilment channel where shoppers can make purchases online (see Sinkovics, Sinkovics and Ruey-Jer, 2013).

This challenges the conventional thinking behind internationalization: namely, that expansion into international markets is incremental and is built up gradually over time. Online channels mean that a retailer can become an 'instant global' operator. Once the website is designed and placed on the web, it can attract shoppers from literally all over the world who can visit its different areas, assess the merchandise on offer and make a purchase.

For small or niche retailers the attractions of developing an online channel are high. Typically, small retailers do not have the required financial resources or capability to develop an international presence quickly. A website that has order placement and fulfilment capabilities presents an opportunity to drive sales from customers that do not have to physically visit a store.

There are significant challenges and barriers that have to be addressed, however, if such a channel can meet the requirements and needs of the international shopper. First, the retailer must have in place an appropriate supply chain strategy to meet customer service expectations, particularly in the areas of delivery, dealing with complaints, damaged merchandise, meeting warranty guarantees, processing payment, inventory availability and third-party logistics. Any failure or deficiency in these areas will inevitably lead to customer dissatisfaction. Legal/fiscal issues also need to be addressed, particularly in the context of paying tax on items and complying with local regulations that may vary from region to region.

As we discussed in Chapter 8, many of the larger retailers develop omni channels or multi-channel platforms to connect with their customers worldwide. An online channel in the case of an omni-channel strategy attempts to provide the same level of consistency and customer experience as that experienced through other channels throughout the buying process. A multi-channel approach simply means that the retailer operates a portfolio of channels to deal with different categories of customer. Companies such as ASOS only operate through the medium of an online channel. Its ability to grow and develop its business is largely dependent on employing a supply chain strategy that can meet the requirements of its worldwide customer base. It is more likely that an online channel will play a complementary role to other channel formats. It also recognizes that some customers prefer to do their shopping online without the inconvenience of having to physically visit a store.

12.9 International retail divestment

Alexander, Quinn and Cairns (2005) recognize that retail internationalization is not all about growth and expansion. At certain junctures in the process, retailers have to address the potentially unpalatable option of withdrawing from a particular country or region. Such divestments may not necessarily lead to a full withdrawal however. It may lead to a significant downsizing or reduction of operations while at the same time maintaining a presence in the particular market or country. Alexander et al.'s research suggests that adverse economic or trading conditions may lead to the possibility of divestment. However, larger retailers may decide to stay in such markets because of management commitment to that area or due to relationships with local partners. They also note that divestment does not necessarily mean failure. Divestment may occur due to financial restructuring and tighter management of assets as opposed to a failure to reach sales or market share targets.

There is no doubt that divestment decisions can lead to negative publicity, particularly within the financial community who may perceive such a strategy as a signal of failure. Divestment may occur because of an objective reassessment by senior management of a retailer's presence in a market. It may well be that the retailer will revisit that market with a different entry mode at a later point in time.

12.10 Challenges involved in transferring a retail format

Failure to make an impact in an international market is not uncommon for retailers who have successfully developed a proven format in their domestic market. This can occur for a number of reasons such as:

- a failure to research shopping patterns, tastes and preferences properly
- difficulties in identifying suitable suppliers who have the capability to meet acceptable quality and delivery expectations
- legal problems arising over contract development and approval
- weaknesses in IT, telecommunications, transport and road infrastructure
- lack of availability of appropriate managers with the requisite experience and capabilities
- lack of availability of suitable shop floor salespeople and operatives
- provision of relevant and depth of support to local partners.

These challenges suggest that it is perhaps more complicated for retailers than traditional manufacturers when internationalizing their operations. The service dimension of retailing in particular places great importance on the ability of retailers to deliver the value proposition through its sales-floor operatives and its management. Given the diversity of cultures that are reflected in shopping behaviour, it can be challenging in terms of interacting with shoppers and delivering value.

12.11 Case in point: Tim Horton and the Gulf market

Tim Horton is a Canadian restaurant business that started operations in Hamilton, Ontario in 1964. The founder was a professional ice hockey player. Its core value proposition is built around the concept of fresh produce of a high quality, backed up by exceptional customer service and with a strong community focus.

Over the decades it has become the largest quick service restaurant operation in Canada and its brand has achieved iconic status in that country. It has recognized the need to adapt to changing customer needs and demands. The current menu spans a broad range of categories that appeal to guests throughout the day, such as flavoured cappuccinos, specialty and steeped teas, home-style soups, fresh sandwiches and freshly baked goods including donuts, muffins, bagels, cookies, croissants and pastries.

The focal point of its proposition is the freshness of its coffee. It practises a policy of serving the coffee within 20 minutes of brewing it, otherwise it is thrown out. It also makes its coffee available in cans so that customers can drink it at home or in the office as well as at one of its restaurants.

As of 31 March 2013, Tim Horton had 4,288 system-wide restaurants, including 3,453 in Canada, 808 in the USA and 27 in the Gulf Cooperation Council (Tim Horton Annual Report, 2013). Pressure in its local market from competitors such as Starbucks and McDonald's encouraged the senior management team to consider internationalizing its operations. Its first port of call was the Gulf region.

In 2011 Tim Horton opened its first outlet in the Gulf region. It initially targeted Dubai and started its operations on the Sheikh Zayed Road, a prominent part of the city.

It decided to enter this geographic region by entering into a Master Licensing Agreement (MLA) with the Apparel Group that is based in Dubai. This allows the latter to develop and operate Tim Horton outlets in the region.

A Master Licencing Agreement requires the holder to have the capabilities to adopt a franchise system and adapt it to fit the requirements and demands of a specific market. The holder pays a Master Franchise fee to the franchisor and incurs all of the costs associated with the setting-up of the system in the particular country. ▶

The Apparel Group is a global fashion and lifestyle company and manages a number of major brands in the region. It operates over 600 stores in over 14 countries. These include: Tommy Hilfiger, Cold Stone Creamery, Aldo, Aeropostale, Kenneth Cole and Nine West.

Since 2011 it has established over 19 outlets in the United Arab Emirates. It opened its first outlet in Oman in 2012. The agreement with the Apparel Group is based on a five-year strategic plan. This plan foresees over 120 multi-format restaurants in operation across the United Arab Emirates, Oman, Bahrain, Qatar and Kuwait.

Tim Horton's CEO, Marc Caira, expressed the strategy of the company in this statement. 'This is not about plastering the Tim Hortons brand everywhere, this is about taking the brand where it makes sense and where we can further build' (http://globalnews.ca/news/952063/tim-hortons-looks-at-global-expansion/).

In September 2013 Tim Horton opened its first outlet in Kuwait (located in the Avenues Mall in Kuwait City).

In late-2013 it opened its first 'drive-thru' outlet in Abu Dhabi (United Arab Emirates).

In May 2013 it announced further plans to expand into Saudi Arabia. This strategy hopes to have 100 restaurants opened in this major state by 2018. It entered into another partnership with the Apparel Group. Its main focus in Saudi Arabia will be in the large urbanized areas (http://www.arabianbusiness.com/tim-hortons-plans-100-saudi-outlets-by-2018-501417.html).

Questions

1 Why did Tim Horton choose to enter the Gulf region as the first part of its internationalization process?

2 Assess the merits and problems associated with the market entry mode. Do you think that the Apparel Group was a good choice?

The practitioner view
Developing a brand in international markets

Russell Donaldson, Director of Marketing at Dawnfresh Seafoods Limited

Russell Donaldson has worked with Dawnfresh Seafoods Limited in his capacity as Director of Marketing. We spoke to Russell about the challenges of developing and managing own labels and branded products and dealing with the major supermarket groups.

The company is a family-owned business and its origins can be traced back to over three centuries. It is the largest trout producer in the UK and the largest supplier of loch trout in the world. It sells chilled, frozen and finished fish products to a wide range of customers, in both the branded and own label categories. Its customers include Tesco, Sainsbury's, Asda, Morrisons, Marks & Spencer, Selfridges and a range of restaurants, farm shops and distributors. You can find out more about the company by visiting its website at the following link:

http://www.dawnfresh.co.uk/

In Chapter 6, Russell gave us an insight into how he manages the challenge of dealing with own brands and branded product. We ended that part of the interview by getting his views on the RR Spink brand. In this interview he shares his views and experiences with us on the challenges of developing such a branded product in the international retail environment.

What are the motivations for developing a branded product in international markets?

Retailers such as Caviar House and Prunier operate in numerous airports globally. For instance, Prunier features in over 20 airports in Europe and the gulf region.

Russell notes that 'while there is a micro-niche market for RR Spink in the United Kingdom, it is at the high-end of the market and would not give Dawnfresh sufficient scale to make it viable in the longer term. Europe provides a niche but on a bigger scale.'

How have you gone about developing an international strategy?

Russell is conscious that expansion in Europe needs to be measured and phased in terms of its approach. 'A key question is which retailer would we fit best with? So we have done a lot of research in Belgium – we see that as an entry market into Europe because by going into a market like France for example, you are taking on some very big players in a massive market. If we got a listing (with a major French supermarket) at this time, our factory could well fall over because there is so much demand we might not be able to cope. Whereas if we got a listing in a Belgian supermarket, we have the capacity.'

Why Belgium?

Russell noted that Belgium is a relatively small country from a population perspective. More importantly the food retail sector is very clearly defined.

'We know that Delhaize are right up at the premium end. Then you have Carrefour who are in the middle. And Colruyat, they are at the bottom tier. So there is a very clear tiered structure. The route to market there is easy, relatively speaking. If we got a listing in a Belgian supermarket, we have the capacity. There, we can test and prove the concept and expand the capacity behind that demand.

'We think that if we go into Delhaise and offer them a smoked fish from Scotland, which is Freedom Food accredited, there is real sustainability surrounding it. That is one of the sustainability marks with food in the UK. It is an RSPCA kind of mark that says the animal that is in this foodstuff has been well treated in every way, from birth to slaughter.

'The RR Spink brand is super-premium.

'Supermarkets see trout as not being one of the top five species. It's not salmon. That is good for us. Everyone is selling smoked salmon in Europe. We are selling smoked trout and we can point out why it is superior to smoked salmon. We can go and do taste sessions and sample our customers and we will bring buyers from some of the big European retailers to the lough where the fish is grown and show them the story. We can really sell that magic, that emotion.

'In the UK buyers see it as salmon is what sells, trout doesn't sell, if you don't give us the right price, we will just take trout off the shelf. They have that power in the UK. They have that power as well in Europe, but if we widen our scope, if it doesn't work in Belgium, we can try it in Luxembourg. We can test and adapt and move market. Hopefully we won't have to spend huge amounts of money doing that. The EU legislation allows you to smoke it in Scotland. This is in contrast to the American market where there are various health and safety regulations which would require the smoking of the fish to be carried out in that market.'

How does Dawnfresh gain access to the Belgian market?

Russell comments that 'we are working with a local marketing/sales agency who specialise in taking foreign brands and helping them understand the Belgian market. They also establish introductions to buyers in that market. They are already working with the likes of Walkers shortbread. They have looked at our brand and see a market for it. They will map out for us what is selling and who is selling what. Where do we fit? What products within our range would work for us?

'They are information brokers and will help us build the story that will get us in there to see the buyer. After that it is between us and the buyer.

'We don't have anyone on the ground in Belgium. So if the buyer needs something at short notice, they can contact this agency. If the business grows, we can put a sales office in there eventually. So it is about route to market.'

Russell has considered other potential markets such as Switzerland. However, the company does not have any contacts there and as the Belgian experience suggests, it is important to work with contacts in the local market. As Russell observes, 'sometimes international development occurs opportunistically'.

In the longer term, international brand development will play a critical role in the future of Dawnfresh Seafoods Ltd. A substantial proportion of its business is in the own label sector. The more rewarding area potentially lies in branded products.

As Russell notes, 'Strategically we are over exposed to UK retail.'

12.12   Conclusions

In this chapter we have assessed the issue of retail internationalization and the critical decisions that impact on retailers as a consequence of seeking expansion and growth in this area. Motivations for internationalization can range from a lack of opportunities for further growth in the domestic market, approaches from prospective international partners to the strategic identification of potential opportunities in a particular country or region.

We assessed the critical issue of whether to standardize or adapt retail operations and formats in order to succeed internationally. Given the diversity of conditions, cultures and shopping patterns across different regions, it is almost impossible to fully replicate an existing format in its entirety.

We noted the importance of learning from mistakes. Reflective learning is key to successful internationalization. This recognizes that mistakes are made. The real issue is whether retailers can learn from such mistakes and how this can be addressed in any subsequent revised strategy.

We also considered the key criteria that retailers use for evaluating potential countries or regions in terms of attractiveness. Such criteria include: economic performance indicators, level of political stability in the country, availability of labour, level of infrastructure surrounding areas such as IT, transport and telecommunications, and availability of appropriate suppliers.

We extensively examined the various entry mode options that are available to retailers. Key factors shape the approach. Issues such as control, cost, risk and coverage lie at the heart of such decisions. Entry modes that offer high levels of relative control of the operations (organic growth or acquisition) also exhibit high levels of costs (acquiring the local retailer or purchasing/leasing suitable premises). By contrast, entry modes such as franchising are less costly and risky but inevitably lead to a dilution of control and power and more roles and responsibilities are performed by the local partner.

We looked at the issue of divestment; that is, where a retailer makes a decision to exit from a particular country or region. We noted that such a strategy does not always fully equate to the concept of failure. A retailer may downsize operations or exit but revisit that market at a later date. Financial restructuring decisions may also influence such decisions.

Chapter outcomes

- Retailers face greater challenges and complexities than purely manufacturing corporations when they pursue an internationalization strategy.

- Traditional retail internationalization strategies have tended to be incremental and locations that are 'close' geographically and culturally have been the preferred choices.

- Adaptation of the existing retail format is essential if a retailer is to make inroads into a particular region.

- Learning, reflecting and readjustment have been identified as being critical aspects in the journey of internationalization. This recognizes that mistakes can be made but the experiences that derive from internationalization can be fed back into the management system and addressed in the revised strategy.

- Various entry modes exist for retailers. Key influencing factors in the decision-making process largely revolve around issues such as control, cost, risk and coverage.

- By establishing an online channel, retailers can circumvent the need for any intermediaries or partners. They can also become 'instant globals' and, therefore, challenge the conventional belief that international growth can only be approached in a sequential and incremental manner.

- Online channels, however, need a strong supply chain infrastructure to allow them to deliver value to the customer to the service expectations level that are appropriate to that market.

- Developments in the areas of omni and multi channels mean that the supply chain structure and strategy takes on even greater importance.

Discussion questions

1 Examine the extent to which you would agree with the view that the best approach to retail internationalization is to start with countries that are geographically and culturally close to the retailer.

2 Assess the perception that franchising is too prescriptive and directional and gives the franchisees little or no opportunity to try out new ideas.

3 Examine the key challenges involved in setting up an online channel for the global market.

4 Evaluate the following statement: 'Reflective learning is at the heart of successful retail internationalization.' Use examples to support your point of view.

5 Assess the validity of the various theories of internationalization that exist in the retail literature.

6 Critically assess the perception that joint ventures promise a lot but deliver very little to the retail partners.

References

Alexander, N. and Doherty, A.M. (2009) *International Retailing*. Oxford: Oxford University Press.

Alexander, N., Quinn, B. and Cairns, P. (2005) International retail divestment activity. *International Journal of Retail & Distribution Management*. 33(1): 5–22.

Kearney, A.T. (2012) *Global Retail Development Index*. London: AT Kearney.

Barclays (2013) *The Global High Street: Opportunities for Retail*. London: Barclays Bank plc.

Bianchi, C. (2011) The growth and international expansion of an emerging market retailer in Latin America. *Journal of Global Marketing*. 24: 357–379.

Coughlan, A.T., Anderson, E., Stern, L.W. and El-Ansary, A.I. (2001) *Marketing Channels*, 6th ed. Englewood Cliffs, NJ: Prentice-Hall.

Doherty, A.M. (2007) Support mechanisms in international retail franchise networks. *International Journal of Retail & Distribution Management*. 35(10): 781–802.

Dunning, J. (1981) *International Production and the Multinational Enterprise*. London: Allen & Unwin.

Evans, J. and Bridson, K. (2005) Explaining retail offer adaptation through psychic distance. *International Journal of Retail & Distribution Management*. 33(1): 69–78.

Evans, J., Bridson, K., Byrom, J. and Medway, D. (2008) Revisiting retail internationalization: drivers, impediments and business strategy. *International Journal of Retail & Distribution Management*. 36(6): 260–280.

Forte, R. and Carvalho, J. (2013) Internationalization through franchising: the Parfois case study. *International Journal of Retail & Distribution Management*. 41(5): 380–395.

Johanson, J. and Wiedersheim-Paul, F. (1975) The internationalization of the firm: four Swedish case studies. *Journal of Management Studies*. 12: 306–322.

Jonsson, A. and Foss, N.J. (2011) International expansion through flexible replication: learning from the internationalization experience of IKEA. *Journal of International Business Studies*. 42: 1079–1102.

Lopez, C. and Fan, Y. (2009) Internationalization of the fashion brand Zara. *Journal of Fashion Marketing and Management*. 13(2): 279–296.

Moore, C.M. and Doyle, S.A. (2010) The evolution of a luxury brand: the case of Prada. *International Journal of Retail & Distribution Management*. 38 (11/12): 915–927.

Myers, H. and Alexander, N. (2007) The role of retail internationalization in the establishment of a European retail structure. *International Journal of Retail & Distribution Management*. 35(1): 6–19.

Nobbs, K., Moore, C.M. and Sheridan, M. (2012) The flagship format within the luxury fashion market. *European Journal of Marketing*. 44(1/2): 139–161.

Owens, M. and Quinn, B. (2007) Problems encountered within international retail joint ventures: UK retailer case study evidence. *International Journal of Retail & Distribution Management*. 35(10): 758–780.

Palmer, M. (2005) Retail multinational learning: a case study of Tesco. *International Journal of Retail & Distribution Management*. 33(1): 23–48.

Palmer, M. and Quinn, B. (2005) An exploratory framework of analysing international retail learning. *International Review of Retail, Distribution and Consumer Research*. 15(1): 27–55.

Park, Y. and Sternquist, B. (2008) The global retailer's strategic proposition and choice of market entry. *International Journal of Retail & Distribution Management*. 36(4): 281–299.

Planet Retail, Economist Intelligence Unit (2012) *AT Kearney Analysis*. London: Planet Retail.

Robinson, T., Clarke-Hill, C.M. and Bailey, J. (1998) Skill and competence transfers in European retail alliances: a comparison between alliances and joint ventures. *European Business Review*. 98(6): 300–310.

Rondan-Cataluna, F.J., Navarro-Garcia, A., Diez-De-Castro, E.C. and Rodrigues-Rad, C.J. (2012) Reasons for the expansion in franchising: is it all said? *The Service Industries Journal*. 32(6): 861–882.

Sinkovics, N., Sinkovics, R.R. and Ruey-Jer, B.J. (2013) The Internet as an alternative path to internationalization? *International Marketing Review*. 30(2): 130–155.

Tikoo, S. (2005) Franchise use of influence and conflict in a business format franchise system. *International Journal of Retail & Distribution Management*. 33(5): 329–342.

Treadgold, A. (1988) Retailing without frontiers. *Retail and Distribution Management*. 16(6): 8-12.

Varley, R. (2007) *Retail Product Management*. Abingdon: Routledge.

Waarts, E. and van Everdingen, Y.M. (2006) Fashion retailers rolling out across multi-cultural Europe. *International Journal of Retail & Distribution Management*. 34(8): 645–657.

Weeks, J.R. (2009) Women business owners in the Middle East and North Africa: a five-country research study. *International Journal of Gender and Entrepreneurship*. 1(1): 77–85.

Wrigley, S., Moore, C. and Birtwistle, G. (2005) Product and brand: critical success factors in the internationalization of a fashion retailer. *International Journal of Retail & Distribution Management*. 33(7): 531–544.

Chapter 13

Retailing: the impacts of social and technological change

✓ Learning objectives

On completion of this chapter you should be in a position to achieve the following objectives:

- ✓ Assess the main trends and developments within the global retail sector.
- ✓ Critically review the contribution of technology to these developments.

▶

◀ ☑ Identify the implications arising from these trends for the key stakeholders.

☑ Evaluate the various potential responses from retailers to these trends and changes.

☑ Examine the implications for supply chain structure and strategy.

☑ Understand the changing nature of shoppers and how this is reflected in shopping behaviour and attitudes.

☑ Appraise new retail business models that may emerge.

13.1 Introduction

We come to the final chapter in this book. In some ways it is dangerous to engage in any attempt to project what might happen in the retail sector as we look to the future. By the time you read this chapter, it is entirely possible that it may be out of date or that many of the observations will no longer have any 'future' element to them as they may already be happening in practice.

However, at a basic level, this chapter in some ways acts as an attempt to synthesize issues that we have examined in some detail across the preceding chapters in this book. We have attempted to look at retail marketing management within the context of critical areas. These include the supply chain, the shopper, the retail environment and the marketing strategy decision areas of the retailer. We have also examined a range of cases and examples to see how, in practice, retailers address the various challenges associated with designing and delivering a credible and relevant value proposition to their target market(s).

Drawing upon the views and research of various organizations and retail commentators, we consider how the retail environment is likely to develop over the next decade or so. In broad terms, we are living in an age that has undergone and continues to undergo major changes in the way in which people live their lives and engage with each other. This has been shaped by a major transformation in the area of technology and social media. The ways in which we communicate with each other, make assessments, judgements and comparisons and share experiences is far different from 10–20 years ago. The relationship between society, government and organization has also changed irrevocably across the globe. Technology has changed the way people work. Leisure, entertainment and sport have been transformed in terms of how people consume and engage with events and destinations. In this chapter we 'drill down' further to consider how this impacts on retailing in general and retailers in particular.

We consider the impact that technology will have on the way in which the supply chain is configured and managed and how it is likely to change over the coming years. Some commentators argue that this will further tip the balance of control in favour of powerful retailers. Others argue that more power and control is likely to reside with shoppers. We consider the alternative views in the middle section of this chapter.

We revisit the perennial debate about the future of 'bricks-and-mortar' retail channels and their relationship with online channels. The trends point to an inexorable move towards the latter. However, is this phenomenon an accurate portrayal of shopping patterns and preferences? If this shift to virtual as opposed to physical retail channels is happening to the extent that research suggests, does it mean the end for the lavish shopping malls that are so prevalent in major cities worldwide? We introduce some discussion in an attempt to address this question in the later stages of this chapter.

Before we look in detail at the way in which the retail sector will look over the next decade or so, we should note that this is not about making predictions or engaging in 'wild' presumptions about the future. Instead, we will try to generate some objective discussion based on existing patterns of shopping behaviour and technological developments. The rate of change will vary across different regions and economies: we should avoid making sweeping generalizations and recognize that the rate of change will be largely dependent on the state of a particular country's economy and willingness to embrace change.

Technology and information

We begin our assessment of the future of retailing by considering the critical role that technology plays in shaping the agenda and the arena for delivering retail value propositions and its relationship with information. In many of the preceding chapters we have analysed the impact that technology has had on various aspects of the retailer's marketing strategy design and implementation. We have also examined the impact on the shopper. In this section we synthesize the main developments and specifically consider future implications.

As far back as 2011, a study by Deloitte (2011) explicitly recognized that an increasing number of technology devices are being used at an increasingly fast rate by consumers. This is evidenced by the technological developments in the areas of smartphones, WiFi, tablets and PCs. The term 'mobility' is a constant feature in all of this. Further developments are inevitable as society embraces 4G technology. Without claiming to be a 'technology' expert, it is reasonable to assume that future developments will address issues such as speed of access, wider and more sophisticated access, more focused and customized design of apps to allow consumers to communicate and access information and so on.

Such developments will also affect basic issues such as the role of cash and money in society. As I write this chapter (early 2015), there is already evidence to indicate that financial institutions are testing out technology that will eliminate the need for people to physically carry cash as they go about their everyday lives. In the context of shopping and retailing, we will make payments via our smartphones and retailers (once they have the relevant information about us on their systems) can take such payments automatically and seamlessly.

The concept of mobility means that conventional methods of communications are superseded and embellished by the ability of organizations and individuals to connect with each other in a more fluid, dynamic and sophisticated way than ever before. Retailers, in particular, are increasingly seeing the opportunities in this context. As shoppers walk past a particular store in a shopping mall or shopping centre, retailers can connect with them by sending personalized messages about specific promotions or special offers that fit into their shopping and brand preferences. Data about an individual customer (captured on the retailer's 'big data' systems) can trigger such communications. For instance, when a shopper revisits a particular store, a message can be 'pinged' to the smartphone welcoming that person back to the store and suggesting specific products that might be of interest to them.

This scenario can be expanded to technology developments in other areas. For instance, automotive manufacturers are reconfiguring the internal design of a car. Have a look at the modern dashboard of a car. The features on it are multiplying at a very quick rate. A good example of this phenomenon is the emergence of Tesla Motors. This US company specializes in designing electric cars. The interesting observation about this company is that it is not a conventional car manufacturer like Toyota and Ford. It is actually a 'technology' company from Silicon Valley. It brings a totally different perspective to the challenge of designing cars that cater for the future needs of society. This is evidenced in areas such as dashboard design where it uses a '17 inch' screen and a high level of technological capabilities.

These advancements are arguably the way of the future. As they become increasingly more widespread and adopted by traditional car companies, we are likely to see opportunities for retailers in terms of communicating with people as they drive by stores. Features such as interactive in-car billboards can provide alerts as you pass a store, for instance. Special offers, promotions and so on can flash across the dashboard screen and tempt the driver and passenger to make a stop and take advantage of these deals.

Jim Carroll (2014: 3), an American futurist, projects the following scenario:

> **❝***You are driving along and ask Siri (your electronic 'helper') in your dashboard where you can buy a dozen eggs.*
>
> *She will put up five stores on the map and you will pick one. The car's autonomous driving technology will take you there and the embedded payment technology will pay for your purchase.***❞**

Carroll (2014) suggests that this type of situation is likely to occur by 2017. While the accuracy of such a prediction might be in doubt, it is reasonable to anticipate that in future years, variations of this scenario will be a common feature for many shoppers. Retailers who fail to acknowledge the likelihood of such a situation at best will find that they run the risk of losing their competiveness.

Activity

In the context of car retailing, make a visit to a local car showroom. Carry out a visual audit of the selling space or area and assess how effectively the car retailer is making use of technology to enhance the experience for the prospective car purchaser.

13.2.1 Location-based shopping apps

We discussed this concept in Chapters 8 and 10 of this book. As shoppers move around, apps downloaded by them from retailers allow the latter to connect and communicate with them. The advent of mobile marketing is based on the notion that it is far more effective for companies to target their customers at times during the day when they are in proximity to the outlet or location. For instance, if shoppers walk through a shopping mall on a Saturday morning, pass a Starbucks coffee shop and receive a personalized message inviting them in to take advantage of a special discount on a 'skinny latte and muffin' due to their continuing loyalty, this is more likely to work than if that same message was sent generally to people who happened to download this app.

Mobile marketing, it can be argued, takes the generic and random nature of advertising and communication out of the equation. For instance, there is potentially little value in receiving a message from your local favourite Italian restaurant about a special offer if you are out of the country on business or on vacation. This latter communication is more likely to irritate customers.

Mobile marketing works on the basic principle that by downloading an app, customers are prepared to share information with that organization about their background, preferences and shopping patterns. This forms the basis for the retailer or organization to personalize any subsequent communications. This point should not be underestimated. Tuk and Golovanova (2014) cite research that indicates that 42 per cent of consumers expressed the view that none of the communications which they receive from organizations are either useful or relevant. This strongly suggests that there has to be strong elements of relevance and context to the delivery and reception of such messages. It also highlights the potential dangers of using such mobile marketing techniques. We return to this issue later in the chapter.

Technologies such as iBeacon facilitate the process of mobile marketing. This technology is essentially a variation of the Bluetooth technology and was developed by Apple. In the context of retailing, a shopping centre or individual retailer who has installed the appropriate sensors will be able to track a shopper who has downloaded their app to within a distance of around 50 metres. Tuk and Golovanova (2014) quote examples of how sports organizations such as the San Francisco Giants and many major league baseball clubs have adopted this technology to alert fans in the stadia to seat upgrades, video clips and information about food and beverage offers.

The concept of geofencing is also a variation of the preceding developments. This technology allows retailers to send messages to the general public who enter a specific geographic area such as a shopping mall or shopping precinct. For instance, tourist associations can alert people visiting a particular part of a city or district about upcoming events that are due to take place that weekend.

As these technologies evolve, we see some interesting innovations. A developer called Shopkick has established partnerships with major US retailers such as Macy's, Toys R Us and Target. Such relationships are based on the concept of rewarding customers when they visit a particular store. These rewards are referred to as 'kicks'. For instance, if a shopper visits a Macy's store and makes a purchase, they will receive a reward in the form of a certain number of 'kicks'. These can be redeemed later when a sufficient quantity has been built up by way of discounts and so on.

Perez (2012) notes that this use of technology allied to a reward can overcome the danger of physical stores simply becoming showrooms. This phenomenon is evidenced in the increasing tendency for shoppers to visit a store, get advice and a product demonstration from sales assistants and then use an online channel to get the best possible deal or price. In this case the retailer provides a valuable contribution to the shopper's decision-making process but receives no financial benefit as the sale goes to another organization. By rewarding the shopper for making the purchase directly in the store, it can be argued that both parties win: the retailer gets the sale and the shopper gets an incentive in the form of reward points.

13.2.2 Problems and challenges with mobile marketing

The examples outlined in the preceding section highlight that mobile marketing is increasingly being adopted by organizations in general and retailers in particular. Its attractions to retailers can be summed up as follows.

- It provides a greater depth of information about individual shoppers.
- It tracks shoppers' visiting patterns to shopping areas, malls and specific stores.
- Such tracking data can be linked with data the shop holds about a shoppers' spending patterns in its stores.
- Personalized, relevant and focused communications can be sent to the shopper.
- Such communications have a location-based context: they arrive on the shoppers' mobile devices when they are in the proximity of the store or geographic area (shopping mall or precinct).
- Provides the retailer with a deeper understanding of store traffic patterns.
- Messages and adverts are sent and received in real time.
- As the number of users of smartphones and associated devices continues to rise, so too will the likely sophistication of such technologies increase.
- Because mobile marketing generates the potential for such personalization and customization, investment in this area is likely to generate a greater return on investment in the longer term.
- Price promotions and special offers in particular are likely to be much more effective than the traditional, general campaigns witnessed in the past.
- Ultimately drives prices down for shoppers.

Given the array of benefits outlined above, it is not surprising that this aspect of marketing is proving to be a hot topic with so many organizations in general and retailers in particular. However, a number of issues have arisen that cast a shadow over such initiatives. The first and most fundamental question is this. How is the consumer likely to respond to such developments? Subsidiary issues revolve around the awareness of shoppers about such technologies and apps, the way in which such information is used by retailers and their attitudes and perceptions about potential invasion of privacy.

A recent survey (Mobile Payments Today, 2014) indicates that over seven out of ten shoppers are against the usage of such technologies specifically in the context of being tracked when visiting stores and malls. Over five out of ten indicated that they do not want to receive any 'push' notifications on their phones from retailers.

Such findings indicate that the increasing adoption of location-based technologies is likely to generate some form of negativity in the minds of shoppers. In a 'worst case scenario', this could eventually lead to a strong element of distrust and cynicism on the part of shoppers and may impact on the nature of their ongoing relationship with a specific retailer.

This can be counterbalanced by the argument that such practices can help shoppers to make more informed decisions about their purchases, leave them in a stronger negotiating position with a retailer and ultimately shift the boundaries of control in the relationship to the shopper and away from the retailer. It certainly reinforces the need to 'educate' shoppers to the potential benefits that might accrue to them as a consequence of downloading such apps and sharing information with retailers.

13.2.3 Managing big data

The challenge of managing data and turning it into relevant and applicable information has been a recurring theme throughout this book. We have recognized the importance of information allowing retailers to achieve a more dominant position in relationships with suppliers (Chapters 3 and 4). We have cited examples of how retailers can use information as a critical tool for building store loyalty and retaining customers in the context of the use of store loyalty cards in Chapter 6.

Big data is a term that has taken on increased usage and significance in the context of any debate about retail strategy development. Without a coherent approach to managing big data, it is likely that retailers will sink under the sheer volume of data being captured and fail to translate such data into actionable and relevant information.

The challenge of managing big data is exacerbated by the exponential growth in data that is generated from activities such as social media platforms and website browsing (discussed in Chapters 9 and 10). The increasing sophistication of hardware, software and middleware systems allows for more detailed data collection and analytics.

The challenges become even more complex as retailers move to the adoption of multichannels and omni channels in their quest to satisfy shoppers' changing needs and requirements. This is counterbalanced by the increasing power of big data stores to collect and process vast amounts of data. Savitz (2012) points to the emergence of big data companies like Hadoop who work closely with large retailers to address this issue. One particular retailer holds over more than two petabytes on shoppers – gathered from a range of sources such as websites, sales devices, tablets and smartphones. Hadoop uses its processing power to analyse data.

We have cited the example of Amazon as being one of the pioneers of big data analytics and driving increased sales through the insights it gains from information captured on its customers' shopping patterns and preferences.

Milian (2014) cites the example of how Wal-Mart has addressed big data management. In 2011 it acquired a company called Kosmix. It reconfigured this company and set up an operation called WalmartLabs. This company developed a search engine for people to find products. This initiative increased sales and perhaps more importantly formed a bridge or a link between Wal-Mart's in-store and e-commerce data.

Such examples indicate the direction which many retailers are now taking with regard to managing data and transforming it into relevant and actionable information. Over the next decade or so, such practices will become even more prevalent across the different retail sectors. As technology further develops and evolves, we will see more sophisticated practices.

13.2.4 The impact of technology in-store

In Chapter 5 we fully examined the in-store selling environment. It is not our intention to necessarily replicate material discussed there. In this chapter we synthesize some of the main trends and project forward as to what the typical physical store may look like in the next decade or so.

The role of the physical store in the overall context of shoppers' buying behaviour has been questioned by many commentators, particularly in light of the growth of online channels. Do shoppers still require the services that go along with a physical store such as salespeople providing advice and guidance? Do they need to physically touch and interact with merchandise? Do they still view the act of shopping as a pleasure or a hindrance? Variations on these issues appear regularly in the literature. The answers to these questions are not simple. Indeed, it could be argued that the issues raised in these questions take an overly simplistic view of matters. This is something that we will explore more fully in this section.

Our analysis of the selling environment in Chapter 5 strongly indicates that physical stores will continue to play a significant part in people's lives over the coming years. In many shopping situations shoppers view the activity as part of their leisure time and derive great pleasure from visiting shopping malls and centres. Retailers and retail development companies have responded to this phenomenon by creating 'cathedrals of shopping': large retail spaces containing global brands, fully supported by an array of 'entertainment-focused' initiatives and features. This provides clear and visual evidence that physical retail outlets continue to attract shoppers and address a real need. Therefore, it is relatively easy to arrive at the conclusion that we will not see the elimination of retail stores any time soon. However, this does not mean that retail developers can bask in the continued success of shopping malls, retail parks and shopping centres. The emergence of online channels as a viable alternative has become prevalent across different geographic regions. Most of the larger retailers have responded by developing multi-channel or omni-channel retail formats to connect with shoppers and address the changing patterns of purchasing behaviour.

It might be easier to address the earlier questions if we identify the critical variables that come into play in the purchasing decision-making process. First, we have to delineate the type of shopping activity. In Chapter 2 we identified a continuum ranging from purely functional shopping (supermarket or convenience store) to hedonic and experiential (fashion shopping, luxury goods).

Key variables such as price, information, price comparison, access to expertise (sales assistants), personalization and customization, product interaction and engagement, retail theatre, atmosphere and socialization (meeting friends, mixing with like-minded people) all enter the 'melting pot' across all phases of the purchasing decision-making process. The relative importance placed on these variables by the shopper will vary according to the type of shopping situation. Table 13.1 depicts an attempt to identify how the online and physical retail channel formats adxdress these variables.

Table 13.1 Ability to address criteria

Criteria	Channel format					
	Physical			Online		
	Low	Medium	High	Low	Medium	High
Price		*				*
Price comparison		*				*
Access to expertise		*	*		*	
Atmosphere			*	*		
Product interaction			*	*		
Socialization			*		*	
Support		*			*	

This basic allocation of 'ticks' to particular boxes should not be interpreted as being a scientific attempt to assess the abilities of the respective channel formats to address the criteria we have identified. However, it should prompt some thought around the central issue of the role of physical stores both now and in the future. It becomes apparent that neither formal, physical or virtual, has the capability to address *all* of the variables. It is also evident from our previous discussion on the developments in the areas of omni- and multi-channel formats that consumers use a range or portfolio of channels across the stages of the purchasing decision-making process (problem recognition, search, evaluation and comparison, purchase and post-purchase; see Baird and Kilkourse, 2011).

Our discussion in this and previous chapters indicates strongly that we will *not* see the elimination of physical stores in the coming years or indeed decades. The diverse range of channel formats used by shoppers, however, alerts us to the fact that retailers will have to engage in a major strategic appraisal of each of their channels' formats including the physical store.

13.3 The store of the future

I place a question mark over the title for this section because it is dangerous, if not impossible, to make any accurate predictions about the store of the future. All we can do is identify some of the present trends and try to project forward.

The reality for many retailers is that the nature, purpose and strategy behind the physical retail channel will change in response to changing shopper patterns and behaviour, allied to technology trends that we discussed earlier in this chapter.

Deloitte's (2011: 2) report on the future of the retail store makes the observation that:

> **❝** *Going forward, the store needs to be an embodiment of the brand and a 'destination' for consumers where they can do much more than simply browse and transact; it will no longer operate as a silo but as an integral part of the multichannel experience.* **❞**

This statement is significant because it explicitly recognizes the changing retail environment with regard to the need for multi-channel and/or omni-channel formats. We have already noted in Chapter 8 that this shift in thinking and approach has been happening across different retail sectors over the last few years: this is not new or indeed something that might happen in the future. However, we can make a reasonable assumption that further developments in this area will continue to take place in the coming years.

Deloitte's report highlights a range of changes, many of which are currently taking place, some to a limited degree and others that are likely to come into play. We have touched on some of these points already and will focus on those developments that are likely to play a significant role in the coming years. A central theme in this report revolves around the notion that the stores of the future will no longer have as their main driver the need to push sales within the outlet. Instead, they are likely to become a 'brand and product showroom that drives revenue across all channels' (Deloitte, 2011: 5).

In order to meet this challenge, stores will have to devise facilities that facilitate the experiential nature of shopping. This addresses issues such as creating a lifestyle experience that is associated with the products and product engagement and interaction. We have considered the Apple example already in Chapter 5 on the selling environment. In the future, this approach and framework will be extended by a broad range of retailers who will make use of a range of in-store technologies. As we noted earlier, the physical store (and the array of interactive tools and technologies) will not be a 'standalone' or isolated in nature. Instead, they will interact with other channels and technologies (for example, smartphones and apps; see also PWC, 2012).

Mehta (2014) identifies nine areas that will impact on the store of the future. They are summarized as follows:

1 **Personal shoppers** will become a standard accompaniment for most shoppers. This concept is a variation on the traditional apps and will perform the role of an electronic shopping partner for the individual shopper. It will log a range of detail such as the shopper's patterns, number of visits to stores, attitudes to special offers and price promotions, patterns of expenditure, level of loyalty to particular brands and so on. It will synchronize with various retail stores and allow the latter to share information with the shopper when they visit a store. It will prompt the shopper with details about product offerings that resonate with the information they have captured and shared with the personal shopper tool. IBM and its Watson Group are partnering with an e-commerce company, Fluid, to develop a personal shopper app. Initiatives such as this one are likely to be a common feature within the retail sector in the coming years.

2 **Fewer in-store 'traffic jams'** will make the process of visiting a store more seamless and convenient than before. Based on the typical items purchased and a mapping of the shopper's typical physical navigation of a store, the retailer will send an updated map of where the products are located.

3 **Juicy bait hooks passers-by**: retailers will target people who walk by their store through highly personalized offers or messages about things like new styles or reminders about items saved on a wish list. A woman passing a beauty store may be prompted to enter after receiving an alert that she is likely to be running low on moisturizer, given the date of her last purchase and previous buying behaviour. This again is based on the use of apps and the synching of the apps with sensors located in the store.

4 **Self-checkout 2.0**: shoppers will no longer queue to check out and pay for items. When they pick up items they can scan them, decide on a payment method and process them electronically. They carry no cash and the process is relatively seamless and does not generate delays.

5 **Customer service on demand**: through point-of-service applications or mobile or tablet devices, sales associates will instantly and automatically access a shopper's profile, customer preferences and buying history to provide a better and efficient experience. Predictive analytics will be leveraged to know what a customer wants before they ask for it. This generates more focused advice and guidance, maximizes the use of sales assistants and speeds up the process for the shopper.

6 **Virtual fitting rooms and aisles**: shoppers will access information and special offers through augmented reality while moving through a store or seeing how they would look wearing something without trying it on. Consumers will also be able to opt in to access recommendations such as for bathing suits, based on their body shape and size, virtually try them on and then walk to the counter where a sales associate will be waiting with them. Virtual mirrors allow shoppers to visualize what

an item or garment might look like on them. Colao (2014) cites some examples of entrepreneurial companies that have developed products in this area and within the broad context of in-store interaction and entertainment.

7 **Out-of-store, out-of-home shopping and flexible fulfilment**: this aspect of store development is not new. Many retailers already provide home delivery or variations built around concepts such as 'pre-order and pick up', drop to the office, pick up from distribution centre and so on. We looked at the example of the South Korean shoppers who can identify and place and pay for an order from large visual adverts in subway stations and get the items delivered to their homes or offices. We are most likely going to see more extensive and imaginative variations on this approach over the coming years.

8 **Power to the consumer**: the smartphones, tablets and iPads of today will continue to evolve in terms of functionality and size. They will undoubtedly become even more sophisticated and extensive in terms of usage. Shoppers will be equipped increasingly with such tools and this in theory should place them in a far stronger position with retailers in terms of strategic areas such as price comparison, identifying specific locations or stores where there are special offers, linking up with relevant social media groups to share experience and get some advice and so on. Retailers are having to respond to these developments and will certainly have to become increasingly more transparent in terms of their offerings.

9 **The power of tribes**: the concept of tribal marketing and community-based marketing has gained in credence and popularity over the last decade. This will continue to grow despite ongoing issues surrounding privacy and the potential invasion by retailers of a shopper's personal and virtual space (discussed in Chapter 10 on integrated marketing communications). Mehta (2014) notes that:

> ❝ *as overhead costs stay high, retailers will adopt mobile-first approaches – that leverage beacons, augmented reality and cross-channel customer profiling – to bridge shoppers' online and offline worlds. In the age of mobile-dominant consumers – who have expectations of real-time, highly relevant and personalized experiences – omni-channel innovation is no longer a merely something nice to have at a physical store. It's a must-have. Shoppers, then, are poised to be the big winners.* ❞

What can we take away from the observations made by Mehta? First, they are not necessarily meant to reflect the condensed wisdom of retail experts in general. They only represent the views of one individual who has worked extensively in this area. Some of the trends are already happening with a reasonable degree of adoption. Other aspects may require a 'leap of faith' to believe that they will gain widespread currency and uptake. None the less, they are largely representative of the initiatives currently featuring on the agenda of retailers across different sectors of the industry. The rate and extent of adoption will depend to some extent on the relative state and development of retailing in individual countries and regions globally.

13.4 The impact on product inventory

As we consider the emergence of different retail channels and the role of the physical store, we should also assess the impact such developments will have on the management of inventory.

As we noted in Chapter 10, retailers over the coming years will be tasked with the challenge of ensuring product availability across the different channels that they use in order to connect with customers. While the concept of omni channels is an appealing one, one of the biggest dangers is the risk of inconsistency across the channels with regard to availability of inventory. A retailer that can deliver excellent customer service by way of availability and delivery of products in its physical store outlets will suffer if its online channel fulfilment strategy falls down in terms of reliability. Shoppers increasingly interact with a number of channels during the purchasing process. Such inconsistency will inevitably lead to dissatisfaction, complaints and migration to competitors.

In the context of the physical store, retailers in sectors of the industry that address the hedonic shoppers who seek a strong customer experience face an interesting dilemma. How much actual merchandise should they carry and present to the shoppers in the store? The decision has implications for their cost structures: carrying an extensive and full range and assortment of merchandise incurs high inventory-holding costs. The adoption of other channel formats such as online channels, kiosks in the store and tablets held by sales assistants, can reduce the need to carry high levels of inventory in the store. The shopper can access information about specific products via these complementary channels and use the visit to the physical store to take advantage of the opportunity for interaction with the items.

If we take a broader definition of the retail business as one that is not encumbered by space restrictions that exist in a physical store (there are limits to the amount of stock that you can display in a selling space of 500 square metres for example). If we broaden the view to all of the channels that a retailer uses, then a retailer can (virtually) display endless amounts of merchandise.

This brings us back to the challenge that we raised earlier about the ability of the retailer – via its supply chain structure and strategy – to be in a position to fulfil orders, meet specifications and the requirements of shoppers in terms of customer expectations about availability and delivery of items (for example, same day delivery).

13.5 Case in point: House of Fraser

House of Fraser is a UK department store that was established in 1949 in Glasgow, Scotland. It currently has a store portfolio of 63 stores in the UK and Ireland and has been involved in numerous acquisitions over the decades. It has also been the subject of numerous takeover bids. In April 2014 it was reported that the department store would be taken over by a Chinese conglomerate, Sanpower, which would take an 89 per cent stake in the company. In September 2014 the deal went through.

It has been circumspect about internationalizing its operations. It currently operates one store in Abu Dhabi. The new owner plans to open further stores in Abu Dhabi, Russia and China.

It has also exhibited a degree of caution about its use of other channel formats: currently 10 per cent of its sales come from digital and online channels. It plans to double this figure over the next few years.

House of Fraser is the UK's third largest department store chain by sales, after Debenhams and John Lewis, with 63 stores nationwide in 2012. Turnover stood at £1.1 billion in 2011/12. Recent strategy has involved strengthening its status as a fashion-oriented, premium department store group, with online operations receiving major investment.

It positions its business at the premium end of the market and focuses on stocking a wide range of brands to support this image.

In order to develop an omni-channel presence in the market, senior management in 2010 developed the 'buy and collect' concept. This is based around the principle of shoppers ordering items online by 3 pm in the afternoon and then picking up the purchases the next day in the afternoon from any nominated store in the country. This initiative has proved to be very popular with shoppers and 35 per cent of all purchases are now collected in the store.

The retailer has further developed this concept in an attempt to drive further integration between its online and physical store channels. It allows its sales staff in stores to help customers order stock that is available online but not in the store. The shopper can either return to the store to collect their purchase(s) or have the items delivered to their home.

It has worked closely with web design partners to enhance the quality of its website. One initiative, believed to be the first in fashion retailing, was to allow the shopper to browse and search not just by product categories but also by brands, thus reinforcing the message that the department store is about the 'house of brands'.

It has also introduced a cross-channel loyalty system. This benefits the shoppers as they can build up loyalty points irrespective of which channel they use to make a purchase.

House of Fraser has further developed its buy and collect concept by entering into a partnership with Box Technologies to develop a number of 'Concept Stores'. The unique feature of these stores revolves around the lack of any merchandise appearing within the outlets. Instead, and working in a very small retail space of approximately 1,500 square feet, the store contains a series of large format touch screens and computers. Shoppers can avail themselves of these tools to browse and purchase items. The merchandise is subsequently delivered the next day. House of Fraser's website gives customers access to over 1,000 brands ranging from Biba to Polo Ralph Lauren.

Box Technologies has worked closely with House of Fraser to deliver a structure and system that facilitates the smooth running of the operation and builds on the need to develop a framework that addresses the need for a seamless customer experience across the different retail channels.

It also focuses on providing appropriate customer service. A number of sales advisers are available to help shoppers navigate through the website via the screens and computers and advise them about the merchandise.

Sony's 55-inch LED digital signage screens provide customer information throughout the store. In order to ensure security and discretion when making payments, Box Technologies supplied Toshiba PCs with SpacePole mounting solutions from Ergonomic Solutions.

The Concept Stores include a complimentary coffee bar and comfortable seating environment to further enhance the shop environment.

Sources: Material for this case was adapted from the following links: http://www.boxtechnologies.com/case-studies/hof-concept-store/, http://www.figarodigital.co.uk/case-study/house-of-fraser.aspx

Questions

1 In the context of our discussion about future trends and developments, assess the approach adopted by House of Fraser.

2 Identify areas that they are *not* addressing currently and which might add further enhancement to their value proposition.

3 Using the worldwide web, look for other examples of retailers who are engaging in similar initiatives.

4 How has the role of the store changed in the context of the Concept Store initiative introduced by House of Fraser?

13.6   Store portfolio

Deloitte (2011) observe that retailers are reviewing the quantity of stores that they continue to operate within their portfolio of sites and locations. We should note that around the time of Deloitte's report, the economy in the UK was in the middle of a deep recession. This would also have applied to other economies in other parts of Europe and further afield. However, the developments in online channels and resulting sales have forced retailers to review their position with regard to physical stores.

Deloitte suggest that we will witness a decrease in the number of physical stores as retailers adjust to the changes in the retail environment and shopping behaviour and channel preferences. It is also likely that owners of properties that are available for rental or lease will have to adjust their financial terms of rent in order to continue to attract new retailers.

A reappraisal of the physical store portfolio is also linked closely to investment decisions in the context of improving a retailer's omni-channel strategy. It is likely that retailers in the future will reapportion much of their budget to investment in an omni-channel strategy, with a need to invest in technology and the supply chain to provide consistency across the different channel formats. This may involve (as Deloitte suggest) a rationalization of the number of bricks-and-mortar stores and reduction in the need for as much selling space within the stores. Instead of carrying high levels of inventory, the store of the future is likely to resemble a laboratory where shoppers can sit in front of screens, tablets and other devices. They can browse, assess product offerings, engage in comparative pricing, seek advice from sales advisers and either make a purchase or use another retail channel to do so.

As technology increases in terms of sophistication, shoppers can use a range of tools to simulate the product experience. This has particular resonance for products such as cars where the customer wants to experience the various features of the specific model. It is a moot point as to whether such a 'virtual' experience will replace or compare to the experience that can be obtained from a physical experience of driving a particular car model. Technological developments will ultimately answer that question.

13.7 Retailers and social media: future prospects

In Chapter 10 we considered the role and contribution of social media to the development and implementation of an integrated marketing communications strategy. In this section we consider future trends and developments within the context of how retailers are likely to make further use of social media platforms to connect with their target market(s).

Individuals make extensive use of social media tools in their everyday lives. In the early days of social media, people latched on to popular tools such as Facebook and Twitter to share views, opinions and experiences with each other. As such activities began to grow exponentially, companies and organizations quickly realized that such platforms afforded them the opportunity to engage with their target market. We then witnessed exponential growth in the creation of company-designed social media tools. In the case of retailing, retailers developed their own Facebook pages and quickly built up large numbers of followers (Cooper, 2014).

Such developments created apparent positive benefits for retailers and customers. Retailers could connect with their target markets. They could listen to and monitor comments and the views of customers. They could also interact and as we noted in Chapter 10, they could engage in 'two-way' communications as opposed to the 'one-way' messages so redolent of traditional marketing communications tools such as TV, radio and print advertising.

Retailers increasingly created various retail initiatives largely built around various promotional offers and price-driven incentives and found that shoppers responded positively. The concept of customer relationship management took on an even greater significance due to the nature of social media platforms and their ability to allow retailers and customers to interact with each other across a wide range of activities.

As we noted earlier in this chapter and in Chapter 10, companies recognized further possibilities, particularly with regard to integrating social media platforms with online retail channels and mobile technology. This has led us ultimately to where we are at present: the emergence of omni-channel strategies and the challenge for retailers to respond to a major shift in buying behaviour. In case studies outlined in this book, we can see how retailers have incorporated social media developments into the heart of their overall marketing strategy. While the likes of Amazon constantly feature as pioneers of such developments, there are still literally thousands of examples and case studies of retailers of all sizes that have embraced social media as a fulcrum for their value proposition.

What of the future? Are we likely to see continued exponential growth in these areas?

Belk, the well-known US department store chain retailer, provides an interesting example of how retailers have refined and refocused their use of social media in light of recent developments in digital and mobile marketing. Belk worked with HelloWorld, a multichannel, interactive promotions and loyalty solutions provider, to promote its 125th anniversary. The '125 Days of Prizes' campaign included web, mobile and social channels where consumers were encouraged to participate in a sweepstake for a chance to win one of 200,000 prizes during the 125-day event. Belk saw a significant increase in mobile interactions with 13 per cent of registrants opting in to receive exclusive offers via text message. Social engagement also increased, with Pinterest followers doubling from 7,000 pre-launch to 15,000 post-campaign. More than 61,000 posts about the campaign were added to Facebook. Overall, the campaign saw a significant social lift, gathering 220,000 registrations for the sweepstakes – 80 per cent of those opting in to receive additional information on future promotions.

'Mobile has made social media a form of real-time marketing,' said Matt Wise, the chief executive officer (CEO) of HelloWorld. 'Retailers need to have the right message at the right time in order to get shoppers to engage and participate. When done correctly, however, the user-generated content created will make it much easier' (see http://www.retailtouchpoints.com/features/special-reports/retailers-use-social-media-to-build-communities-and-strengthen-consumer-connections).

This is a good example of how a retailer can take advantage of mobile technology, its online channel and social media to develop and implement a focused and relevant initiative for many of its shoppers. The results generated are a testament to its success.

The case also illustrates a trend that is likely to become even more prevalent over the coming years: the partnering of resources, knowledge and capabilities between retailers and third-party experts in areas such as IT, customer relationship management (CRM) and promotions. The harnessing of such organizations will increasingly allow synergies to develop. It also highlights that retailers can also use social media to attract new shoppers and visitors to its stores and online channels.

We are also seeing the emergence of strong online communities that effectively act as digital malls. One such operator is Wanelo. It has built up a membership of over 11 million customers and it offers them the chance to buy from over 300,000 stores (see http://www.retailtouchpoints.com/features/special-reports/retailers-use-social-media-to-build-communities-and-strengthen-consumer-connections). Large retailers such as Nordstrom participate in this community. In one campaign it asked popular bloggers and Wanelo influencers to create stories on Wanelo with their favourite picks from a recently released Kate Moss collection. The stories would then be collated and reposted to spotlight key influencers and boost their credibility.

A report published by Retail Touch Points (Anderson, 2014) cites the example of Soldsie. This is a platform that allows retailers to sell products through Facebook and Instagram to boost social engagement and sales. Using Soldsie, the brand holds weekly flash sales via Facebook offering online shoppers the chance to bid on products and complete transactions. Soldsie claims that it enjoys a 70 per cent conversion rate of shoppers who post comments and claim an item. Over 60 per cent of these claims occur around 30 minutes after they are made. It is likely that we shall witness more and more of these platforms emerging over the coming years in response to their popularity among shoppers.

In 2014 Pinterest emerged as one of the most popular social platforms. By May 2014 it had built up a user base of over 53 million people. In 2013 it entered into collaboration with UK fashion retailer, Topshop. This allowed shoppers to post pictures from the retailer's website on their own Pinterest board. This example highlights an increasingly common activity by retailers in the context of social media: crowdsourcing. It allowed Topshop to monitor and identify popular fashion lines and items from its customers. It used such information to highlight these items on its online and store channels.

Anderson (2014) quotes the eBay Vice-President of its UK operations who stated that:

> **❝** *Crowd-sourced shopping inspiration – such as Topshop's partnership with Pinterest – shows the power of social media in inspiring people to buy, while PayPal's Check-in app allows retailers to build relationships with local customers in store. There's a huge opportunity for brands to capitalise on the sweet spot between utility and engagement.* **❞**

The introduction of 4G technology and networks in the UK in 2013 and its adoption in other countries will in future allow for more sophisticated content-rich applications. More reliable WiFi connectivity will also ensure a smoother passage for interaction and sharing of information. It is reasonably safe to assume that we are in the early stages of development in this area.

13.8 How receptive are consumers to these developments?

We discussed this issue in some detail in Chapter 2 and will not dwell too long on the issues in this section. In the context of US shoppers, a Gallup poll (Jones, 2014) found that nearly 60 per cent of shoppers indicated that online and mobile technology has not affected their shopping at traditional bricks-and-mortar stores. Not surprisingly, the figure varies according to the age of the respondent. People under the age of 30 are more than twice as likely to say that mobile technology has led to an increase in the use of retail stores. This reinforces the feeling among retailers that shoppers are increasingly more likely to avail themselves of different retail channels, thus providing more evidence of the need to address the issue of omni channels as a central part of overall retail marketing strategy.

We have pointed out the potential dangers of retailers using social media to push an agenda that may not necessarily be beneficial for shoppers. There must be some form of benefit and reward for individuals who use social media platforms and in so doing part with a lot of information about themselves and their shopping habits. Armed with such information, it could be argued that retailers are in a position to manipulate shoppers with the entire attendant dangers associated with such a tactic.

Ultimately, it all revolves around trust and confidence. Shoppers will increasingly embrace these tools as long as they see benefits accruing from involvement in platforms such as Pinterest, Facebook and so on. They may reduce their involvement with retailers' Facebook groups and Twitter feeds if they sense that they are being exploited. These specific tools may ebb and flow in terms of popularity over the coming years. We may see some disappearing to be replaced by new concepts and frameworks.

The use of mobile technology and social media is no longer an 'added extra' for many people: they are ingrained in every aspect of people's lives. Observe people anywhere in a public setting; for example, a restaurant, airport, sports event and so on. Smartphones will feature prominently in what they are doing. People check messages, visit websites, text and twitter on a constant and ongoing basis. These practices are not going to change any time soon.

13.9 Implications for retailers and the supply chain

In Chapters 3 and 4 we considered retailing within the overall context of where it fits in with the supply chain. We argued that it is overly simplistic to consider retailing in isolation. Effective retailers cannot operate without a strong, coherent and collaborative supply chain. In projecting ahead, it is difficult not to arrive at the overall conclusion that successful retailing in the future will be even more dependent on adaptive and flexible supply chains.

The surge in growth across mobile and digital channels allied to the developments in social media mean that there will be ever-increasing pressure on retailers to devise and implement strategies that meaningfully provide value to shoppers.

As noted earlier, managing inventory across the channels and ensuring availability will be critical in meeting the challenge of creating a consistent shopping experience.

The integration of information on the shopper, captured from a range of touchpoints such as 'in-store', online web visits, social media platforms and so on, will provide the 'glue' for retailers to connect and interact with shoppers in a more relevant and consistent manner.

Visibility of information across the supply chain will be necessary for suppliers, distribution centres and store outlets in order to allow them to plan their operations in an adaptable way.

13.10 Conclusions

In this chapter we have attempted to project retailing into the future, in terms of where it might be in a decade's time. We have considered the main trends and developments that we examined in some detail in the various chapters in this book. We note a sense of caution in this exercise. Retailing proceeds at varying levels of speed and sophistication across the different regions of the world. Traditionally, North America and Western European countries such as the UK, Germany, France and the Netherlands have been in the forefront of major developments in the area of IT adoption and supply chain development.

This has changed somewhat over the last 10–15 years with the emergence of powerful retailers such as Zara and IKEA from other countries (Spain and Sweden, respectively). As countries such as China, India and Brazil continue to grow their (already) rapidly growing economies, it is likely that we shall see increasing levels of innovation and adaptation emerging from these regions. In 2014 we saw the emergence of Alibaba, the Chinese online retailer, as a major global player. This will be the first of many such emerging global retailers from this region.

Social media and its interface with mobile and digital technology have already reshaped the retail arena. We can anticipate further developments in these interrelated areas. What is more problematic is whether 'old reliables' like Facebook and Twitter will exist in their current format or brand by 2025. We may see a product life-cycle effect where they will be superseded and replaced by reincarnations or innovative developments.

It is also less clear how consumers globally will adapt their behaviour in light of such further developments. We have highlighted concerns about the potential dangers of intrusion and invasion of privacy by companies in general and retailers in particular into people's shared experiences, opinions and purchasing habits.

We have noted that retailers such as Amazon have become masters of the art of shaping and grooming shoppers on their websites. By continuously monitoring, logging and integrating information about customers, it is in a position to direct and steer a person's purchasing patterns to specific products and categories. What is problematic is how consumers respond to such direction and (possible) manipulation. Some find such guidance helpful and insightful. Others may perceive such intervention as an invasion of their 'space', not unlike someone invading your personal space when you are sitting in a cramped seat on a bus or train.

We are also likely to see potential intervention from government bodies and policymakers in this area of privacy. This will vary across different geographic regions and, according to the attitudes of such governments, consumer interest groups and other stakeholders.

In areas such as marketing communications, we are already witnessing a shift in allocation of resources from traditional media such as TV, print and radio, to social media. It will be interesting to monitor future developments in this area in general and how traditional media owners adapt their technology.

We can be sure of one thing: the retail sector will continue to be volatile, dynamic and innovative in terms of its development. Retailers have been prominent in adopting new technology (IT, social media, supply chain planning and so on). In the future they are also likely to continue at the forefront of such innovation.

In many sectors of retailing, shoppers exhibit a desire for excitement, change, alternatives and experiences. The life cycle of a retail concept can be very short. Unless it is refreshed on a regular basis, or adapted to reflect changing market conditions and behaviour, it is likely to enter the decline phase very quickly.

Retail internationalization also (as we noted in Chapter 12) provides both opportunities and threats. The emergence of powerful economies such as China and India provides graphic evidence of this development. Large and successful retailers have struggled to make an impact in these markets and have had to either divest or substantially rethink essential and core elements of their domestic strategies.

Finally, we noted that the in-store shopping environment is changing. As the surge in online retailing took place, some commentators argued that this would lead to the 'death' of the physical store. However they underestimated the importance of the shopping experience and the role that shopping plays in people's leisure and relaxation activities globally.

We have witnessed situations where the physical store acts as a 'showroom' for shoppers: they visit the store to learn about the brands and their benefits and then subsequently purchase the items on online channels. Stores are countering this phenomenon by rethinking the role of the store, its layout and the role of the salespeople. Stores may not necessarily focus on the 'hard sell' but instead address issues such as product interaction, entertainment and knowledge transfer.

In summary, retailing is a dynamic and constantly changing environment. I hope you too were energized when reading this book and undertaking some of the assignments and discussion questions.

Nothing remains constant. Retailers will come and go. However, shoppers will not go away and it is reasonable to assume that over the next 10–15 years retailers will have to constantly adjust, adapt, reinvent and redefine their value proposition. They will also have to further embrace technology and social media developments if they want to remain relevant and continue to connect and interact with their target markets.

Chapter outcomes

- Increasing usage of technology, mobile marketing and social media platforms is inevitable.
- We will experience regular and radical changes and adjustments to existing technologies.
- While physical space is increasing, we will see retailers engaging in regular appraisal of their store portfolios and some rationalization of the portfolio.
- Shoppers are embedded with the various technologies and the young shoppers of today – soon to be the older shoppers – will continue to reflect this trait in their shopping and purchasing patterns of behaviour.
- Retailers will need to achieve a balance between conversing with and listening to shoppers with the tendency to push information to them. In so doing, they run the risk of antagonizing shoppers, intruding on their privacy and, above all, irritating them.

Discussion questions

1 Assess the view that technology will ultimately determine the future success of retailers over the next decade or so. Use a detailed example to support your point of view.
2 Examine how the physical store has had to alter to take account of changes in shopping behaviour.
3 Managing big data is critical to the success of retailers. Evaluate the relevance of this perception.
4 Getting the balance between interacting with shoppers via social media platforms and pushing information to them is a challenge. How would you advise an electronics retailer to address this challenge?
5 Examine the extent to which you would agree with the view that if retailers manage 'real-time' information effectively, the shopper should benefit from lower prices and better deals.
6 To what extent do you agree with the view that personal shopper apps will revolutionize the way we engage with retailers? Use examples to support your line of argument.

References

Anderson, B. (2014) Retailers use social media to build communities and strengthen consumer connections. Available online at: http://www.retailtouchpoints.com/features/special-reports/retailers-use-social-media-to-build-communities-and-strengthen-consumer-connections 17 June (accessed 9 September 2014).

Baird, N. and Kilkourse, B. (2011) *Omni-Channel Fulfillment and the Future of Retail Supply Chain: Benchmark Report*. Retail Systems Research.

Carroll, J. (2014) Available online at: http://www.jimcarroll.com/category/trends/retail-trends/ (accessed 3 September 2014.)

Colao, J.J. (2014) What does the future of retail look like? Four young companies provide a glimpse. Forbes.com. 18 June.

Cooper, B. (2014) Analysis: Social media transforms consumer engagement for retailers. *Retail Week*. 2 May.

Deloitte LLP (2011) The changing face of retail. The store of the future: the new role of the store in a multichannel environment.

Jones, Jeffery M (2014) For many, mobile technology increasing retail shopping. Gallup.

Mehta, P. (2014) Why the future of retail will blow your mind. Available online at: http://www.entrepreneur.com/article/234407 2 June (accessed 8 August 2014).

Milian, M. (2014) Retailers use big data to turn you into a big spender. Available online at: http://www.bloomberg.com/news/2014-06-03/retailers-use-big-data-to-turn-you-into-a-big-spender.html June 4 (accessed 7 September 2014).

Mobile Payments Today (2014) Shoppers wary of location-based mobile apps. Available online at: http://www.mobilepaymentstoday.com/news/shoppers-wary-of-location-based-mobile-apps/ 23 April (accessed 7 September 2014).

Perez, S. (2012) Location-based shopping app shopkick partners with mastercard on rewards program. Available online at: http://techcrunch.com/2012/06/27/location-based-shopping-app-shopkick-partners-with-mastercard-on-rewards-program/ 27 Jun (accessed March 2015).

PWC (2012) The future of retail: consumer adaptive retailing. Available online at: pwc.com.au/onlineshopping (accessed 7 September 2014).

Savitz, E. (2012) Why big data is all retailers want for Christmas. Forbes.com. 12 December.

Tuk, Y. and Golovanova, M. (2014) Who needs coffee while they're sleeping? Why companies need to embrace location-based marketing. Available online at: http://thenextweb.com/entrepreneur/2014/05/04/needs-coffee-theyre-sleeping-companies-need-embrace-location-based-marketing/ 4 May (accessed 7 September 2014).

Author Index

Brand Index

Company Index

Subject Index